WORKING
WITH
WOMEN OFFENDERS
In Correctional Institutions

Joann Brown Morton, D.P.A.

HV
9471
M68
2004

Mission of the American Correctional Association
The American Correctional Association provides a professional organization for all individuals and groups, both public and private, that share a common goal of improving the justice system.

Printed in the United States of America by Versa Press, East Peoria, Illinois
ISBN: 1-56991-211-4

This publication may be ordered from:
American Correctional Association
4380 Forbes Boulevard
Lanham, Maryland 20706-4322
1-800-222-5646

For information on publications and videos available from ACA, contact our worldwide web home page at: www.aca.org

Library of Congress Cataloging in Publication Data
Morton, Joann, B.
  Working with women offenders in correctional institutions /
    Joann Brown Morton.
    p. cm.
  Includes bibliographical references and index.
    ISBN 1-56991-211-4 (pbk.)
Women prisoners—United States. 2. Female offenders—United States. 3. Female
    offenders—Rehabilitation—United States. I. Title.
  HV9471.M68 2003
  365'.6'0820973—dc22   2003062832

Contents

Foreword

By James A. Gondles, Jr., CAE

Dr. Joann Morton is a long-time member of the American Correctional Association and strong advocate for the specialized treatment of women offenders. Currently, president of the Association on Programs for Female Offenders, she is in a position to know about the characteristics and treatment of women in the justice system. She shares her years of experience and research in this must-read book with those who are charged with supervising incarcerated women and students who are interested in this special population.

Dr. Morton analyzes the issues and presents a comprehensive look at the treatment of women offenders in the criminal justice system. She first interprets the historical realities of women in prison and then provides information on the legal issues prisoners face and how these differ between men and women. Her chapter on "Perspectives on Sex and Gender" offers some insights on society's treatment of women and how women offenders are impacted by this. Based on her first-hand research and extensive contacts throughout the corrections field, she looks at the way a women's facility operates and how it should be different from a men's facility.

Taking a look at the women who are imprisoned, she examines the characteristics of these women—abused, abusers, and mothers. She describes women's physical and mental health issues, again pointing out how their needs differ from those of men. Finally, she turns her attention to security and supervision for women offenders and makes the point, once again, that women's needs are different from men's even in the area of security. Paying attention to these differences can lead to more meaningful treatment for incarcerated women. With proper treatment, these women can be reunited with their families, reintegrated into their communities, and lead productive lives upon release.

James A. Gondles, Jr., CAE
Executive Director

Preface

By Joann Brown Morton, D.P.A.

In 2000, there were more than seven times the number of women incarcerated in local, state, and federal correctional institutions as there were in 1980 (Camp and Camp, 2000; American Correctional Association, 2000). Over this twenty-year period, research and knowledge about women offenders also increased. Early studies focused on demographic characteristics (Crawford, 1990), legal issues (Gabel, 1982), and history and treatment of incarcerated women (Rafter, 1985). Later, scholars such as Pollock (1990) and Belknap (2001) compiled comprehensive overviews of the evolution of prisons for women in the United States and cited the problems women in the system faced. Also, Pollock (2002) and others conducted extensive research on the impact of incarceration on mothers and children and Chesney-Lind and Sheldon (1998) expanded our understanding of girls in the criminal justice system. In 2003, the National Institute of Corrections published a landmark work by Bloom, Owen, and Covington, which consolidated the evolution of gender-responsive theories to enable a better understanding of criminality among women and recommended changing policies and practices to better serve incarcerated women. All these scholars highlighted a number of problems in the criminal justice system's management of women offenders. While there were issues in every segment of the system, policymakers and correctional agency administrators in general were found to have neglected women in the system and to lack comprehensive strategies for working with incarcerated women.

Some correctional agencies, including the Federal Bureau of Prisons, the Florida Department of Corrections, the Idaho Department of Corrections, and the Michigan Department of Corrections developed gender-responsive training programs to improve staff's ability to work with women in prison. The National Institute of Corrections designed a training program on working with women offenders that was given by the National Academy of Corrections.

Building on the work that has gone before, this book is designed to address the management of women in correctional facilities. It is based on the scholarship and knowledge about women in prison that has evolved over time and which becomes the basis for understanding the institutional policies and practices that are necessary to work successfully with female offenders. The book is primarily aimed at staff working in facilities housing women, but should be of interest to policymakers, administrators, or anyone wishing to learn more about women offenders.

It is assumed that those reading this text will hold differing opinions regarding women offenders but will be interested in expanding their views and their expertise in working with incarcerated women. This book is designed to provide a research-based body of knowledge relative to women offenders, an understanding and sensitivity to current issues in the management of female offenders, and a set of specific strategies needed for working with this population.

In writing this book, assumptions were made about women offenders and the correctional system. Women offenders are a reflection of women in the community and represent a microcosm of all the challenges facing women in today's society. While they have many things in common with male offenders, they have a number of needs and issues that are different from their male counterparts. Addressing the gender-responsive aspect of programs and services for women inmates will strengthen the management and security of correctional facilities. It also should improve the women's chances of leading successful, crime-free lives upon release. Prisons for women are different in form and substance from those housing males, and should be operated in compliance with the American Correctional Association's standards and other national standards.

This book is divided into two sections. The first section contains four chapters and provides the historical, legal, and theoretical background information necessary to understand women offenders in the context of American society. It also includes information on the nature of women's involvement in crime and the demographics of incarcerated women. Comparisons are made between men and women in terms of arrest, conviction, and incarceration.

The second section consists of five chapters that focus on the management of women in correctional facilities. These chapters explore the purposes for functional areas in a facility and the issues of dealing with female offenders in each sector. The effects of abuse on women and the impact of incarceration on mothers and their children are examined. Physical and mental health issues are addressed both in terms of specific problems that can occur and interventions that may be necessary. Finally, security and supervision issues are explored including what similarities and differences these two functions have when applied to men and women.

Each chapter contains a set of measurable objectives emphasizing the important points in the section, an introduction providing background about the subject, and a summary highlighting the main points covered. References used in the development of the text are listed at the end of the book.

If the book increases the dialog on what approach society should take toward dealing with women and girls in the corrections system and aids policymakers, administrators, and correctional staff to provide more effective programs and services for female offenders, it will have accomplished its goals.

Joann Brown Morton, D.P.A.

Historical Perspectives on Women Offenders

Objectives

❖ To identify seven phases in the development of facilities and programs for women offenders.

❖ To describe how women offenders have been viewed over time and how they have been treated in the corrections system.

Introduction

As the number of incarcerated women has grown and as correctional systems have become more punitive, some correctional agencies have begun to treat women offenders more like male inmates (Kruttschnitt, Gartner, and Miller, 2000). However, in most correctional systems there are differences in the way women and men are treated.

One major difference is that most jurisdictions have several facilities to house male offenders and only one or two dedicated to female offenders. There are fewer women's facilities because more men than women are incarcerated.

Some differences are easy to identify. For example, the physical plants of male and female facilities are usually not the same. Male facilities housing maximum- and medium-security inmates typically will be large sprawling prisons surrounded with highly visible security such as two or more fences and multiple rows of razor ribbon. Those housing similarly classified women normally will be smaller and have less visible external security. Other differences, such as the provision of more privacy for women inmates, are more difficult to see.

Society's beliefs about people's worth will determine how they are dealt with by the criminal justice system. Children, for example, in the early 1800s were seen as little adults and were treated like them in the criminal justice system (Chesney-Lind and Shelden, 1994).

In the same manner, how society views women helps to determine how they will be treated in the criminal justice system. For example, throughout history, women in much of the world were considered the property of their fathers or husbands with few rights or privileges (Gosselin, 2000). When they committed offenses, they were treated very harshly under the law (Clear and Cole, 2000). In Colonial America, women were tied on dunking stools and submerged in water for minor offenses such as gossiping. Some almost drowned during this punishment. As society and the legal system began to accept women as contributing members of the community with the same civil rights as men, their treatment changed.

Because corrections is a reflection of the values of the community as a whole, whether women are placed in prison and how they are managed while incarcerated also will be influenced by what is happening in the larger society (Keve, 1986; Muraskin, 2000). In the 1980s and 1990s, for example, many jurisdictions began to crack down on crime by passing legislation mandating longer sentences for a number of offenses and making incarceration mandatory for certain crimes. One example of this trend was the passage of federal and state laws making prison sentences mandatory for persons convicted of possession and/or sale of illegal drugs. The implementation of this legislation caused a dramatic increase in the number of women in prison as their arrest and conviction for drug offenses climbed. As Chesney-Lind (2000) notes "in 1979 one in ten women in U.S. prisons (10 percent) was doing time for drugs. Now the population is over one in three (38 percent)" (p. 8). This, in turn, has implications both for the number of women in prison and the programming provided for them during incarceration and after release.

Phases in the Treatment of Women Offenders

A review of the literature suggests that how women offenders are viewed and treated in the correctional system has evolved over time and can be divided into seven general phases. In most cases, the periods are tied to milestones in U.S. history that are commonly used to indicate significant societal changes. The dates are approximations because change does not happen overnight. Also, many beliefs and practices carry over from one period to the next. For example, the idea that evolved during the period of 1870s to 1930s— that women were more treacherous than men—still influences some beliefs about female offenders (Rafter, 1990).

The seven phases in the treatment of female offenders are as follows:

Phase 1. The 1600s to 1760s: The Colonial Years—The Age of Abuse and Neglect

Phase 2. The 1770s to 1860s: Building a Model for Women's Reformatories

Phase 3. The 1870s to 1930s: Implementing the Dream

Phase 4. The 1940s to 1950s: The Forgotten Female Offender

Phase 5. The 1960s to 1970s: Challenge and Change

Phase 6. The 1980s to 1990s: Sameness but Not Equality

Phase 7. 2000 to Present: The New Millennium: Gender Responsive Policies and Practices—A New Model

Exploring each of these phases will aid readers in identifying policies and practices that have changed over time and in understanding those programs and procedures that have their roots in the past. Understanding these ties with the past will better prepare correctional personnel and policymakers to appreciate today's challenges of working with women offenders. As history tends to repeat itself, knowing how the management of female offenders has evolved provides opportunities to glean the best from the past and avoid the worst.

Phase 1. The 1600s to 1760s: The Colonial Years— Age of Neglect and Abuse

Prior to the American Revolution, crime, for the most part, was not considered a major social problem (Clear and Cole, 2000). Institutionalization of offenders, male or female, usually was limited to housing them for a brief period prior to trial. Punishment for those convicted of a crime was swift, harsh, and frequently involved corporal punishments—such as whipping, branding, or executing—even for those offenses that we would now regard as relatively minor (Reichel, 1997).

One of the best-known examples of extreme punishment, in the early colonial period occurred in Salem, Massachuetts, where women who were considered witches were burned at the stake. In 1692, some 200 people, most of whom were middle-aged women, were arrested and charged with witchcraft. Several were tortured and twenty people, three-fourths of whom were women, were burned at the stake or killed by other means (Karlsen, 1995).

The witch trials in New England in the 1600s played on peoples' superstitions and their general distrust of women. Men were seen as the head of the household and protectors of their family. Women were to be subservient to fathers, husbands, brothers, and even adult male children. Most of the women who were accused of witchcraft lacked male supervision and had property or some standing in the community that engendered hatred or envy (Karlsen, 1995).

Some were charged shortly after the deaths of their fathers, husbands, or other male relatives while others were accused of witchcraft long after the death of a key male family member. In most cases, however, there was a tie between the accusations and the inheritance received by the women. Women made good targets because of the accepted view that they should not participate in affairs outside their homes and that they should defer to male authority (Karlsen, 1995). If they did not follow these prescriptions for how to live, they risked severe punishments including being treated as social outcasts or being killed.

Another severe punishment used during the formation of the colonies was banishment. Banishment meant that the offender was driven from the community (Clear and Cole, 2000). Since much of the country was unpopulated, the individual often died in the wilderness. One of the most celebrated incidents of banishment that involved a woman was the case of Anne Hutchinson. Hutchinson came to the Massachusetts Bay Colony in 1634, four years after its founding (Hall, 1968). As a midwife, she was held in high esteem in the community. She also held very popular meetings in her home after Sunday church services. At these gatherings, which were attended by both men and women, she analyzed and criticized sermons of the Puritan ministers. This was considered an attack on established authority. When it was rumored that the colonial governor and other officials were also being criticized at these meetings, Hutchinson was brought to trial both by the colonial government and the board of ministers. After a fiery trial in 1637, she was excommunicated from the church and driven out of Massachusetts because of her outspoken opposition to the religious doctrines of the Puritans and her challenges to the gender roles of the day (Hall, 1968).

Mrs. Hutchinson and her children joined her husband in a newly established community in what later would become Portsmouth, Rhode Island. Following her husband's death in 1642, she and the six youngest of her surviving twelve children moved to the Dutch colony of New Netherlands in what is now known as Pelham Bay Park in the Bronx, New York (Hall, 1968). In 1643, she and five of her children were killed in an Indian raid on the colony. When word of her death reached Puritan church leaders in Boston, they hailed her death and that of her children as a sign from God that they had been correct in their judgment against her (Forbes, 1990). It also sent a message to other women who might challenge the status quo that they should practice obedience and piety.

Two other classes of people who had little standing during this period were indentured servants and slaves. Some 500,000 indentured servants, both male and female, were imported from England to the colonies prior to the Revolutionary War (Morgan, 1993). They usually were convicted of minor offenses in England, deported to the New World, and auctioned off as unpaid servants for a period of years. Their life was difficult and they had no legal standing or protection from the demands of their owners. The plight of one woman is documented in a letter by Elizabeth Sprigs written in 1756 to her father. In it she describes the lack of food, clothing, and bedding and being tied to a post and beaten by her master (Calder, 1935).

Another group of unpaid workers with even less power and little hope that their lives would improve were slaves. The practice of slavery was first established in the Spanish and the Dutch colonies in the Americas and, in 1619, the Virginia colony received its first African slaves (Kerber and De Hart, 1995). Slave owners were in charge of every facet of a slave's life including punishment for disobedience or other offenses. By the 1640s, African-American slaves were increasingly treated as property, which led to the passage of laws that the status of a child (slave or free) would be determined by the status of the mother (Kerber and De Hart, 1995).

The Virginia colony carried the penalties for interracial relationships one step further. According to Kerber and De Hart (1995), if a free white man or woman married a person of another race, whether that person was free or slave, he or she would be banished from the colony forever. If a white woman had a child fathered by a black or mulatto, she had to pay fifteen pounds sterling to the church. If she did not pay the fine, she was to become the property of the church. She would be sold into bondage for five years and any income from her sale was to be split equally among the crown, the church, and the informer. Her child would be bound out as an indentured servant until he or she was thirty-years old. If the woman were a servant, she had to fulfill her obligations to her master; then, she would become the property of the church which would sell her for a five-year indenture. Any money from her sale would be divided as noted above. Her child also would be sold as an indentured servant until his or her thirtieth birthday (Kerber and De Hart, 1995).

Phase 2. The 1770s to 1860s: Building a Model for Women's Reformatories

As a part of the expanding new democracy in the United States after the end of the Revolutionary War, governments explored different approaches to punishment of offenders—other than those that had been adopted from England during colonial rule. While some leaders in the new republic such as Thomas Jefferson urged the abolishment of capitol punishment, it was the Quakers in Pennsylvania who began to implement incarceration as opposed to corporal punishment or death for all crimes except first-degree murder (McKelvey, 1936).

To provide for more humane punishment, the Quakers built the first penitentiary in the United States in 1790 in Philadelphia. At the Walnut Street Jail, men and women were held in separate, individual cells in solitary confinement so they could do penance for their crime. Similar facilities were introduced over the next few years in Newgate, New York; Charlestown, Massachusetts; Baltimore, Maryland; and Windsor, Vermont (McKelvey, 1936). Ultimately, the Pennsylvania system (formerly the Quaker system) and facilities designed on this model became overcrowded, suffered from poor management, and inmates went mad without human contact. These problems and the fact that the innovation was not economically feasible caused it to be abandoned (Teeters, 1955).

While Quakers believed offenders should be housed in individual cells, the prisons that evolved in other parts of the new nation were, for the most part, very primitive for both men and women who often were crowded together in the same rooms. This frequently resulted in women being victimized and suffering other indignities (Pollock-Byrne, 1990). Society at the time did not see this as a problem since women who violated society's rules were considered "fallen women" who were beyond any hope of redemption. Mary Carpenter, an English authority on women and crime wrote in the early 1800s, "female convicts are, as a class, even more morally degraded than men" (Rafter, 1990, p. 13).

Early reforms beginning in the 1830s led to housing women in cells separated from male offenders. However, they often were placed in wings or rooms in male institutions without female supervision (Rafter, 1990). This lack of supervision meant they still were subject to abuse by male staff and male inmates. Typically, women were blamed for any sexual abuse they might suffer and sometimes punished by flogging if they became pregnant (Freedman, 1981). Babies born to women in prison where medical care was either very primitive or nonexistent often died of various communicable diseases that were common in the damp, dark, cold institutions. As the number of scandals involving incarcerated women increased around the country, demands grew for separate housing for women (McKelvey, 1936).

Conditions in prisons were wretched for everyone, but women, in particular, consistently received inequitable, inadequate care. They were housed together without regard to health status, offense, age, or other factors. While men had work and other diversions, women had little to do to pass the time and no opportunity to develop skills that would help them earn a living when they were released (Rafter, 1990). As Chaplain B. C. Smith of Auburn Penitentiary in New York State declared in 1832, to be a man in prison would be difficult but to be a woman in prison "would be worse than death" (Lewis, 1965, p.164). Rafter (1990) summarizes the plight of women in prison between 1830 and 1870 as follows:

> *Probably lonelier, and certainly more vulnerable to sexual exploitation, easier to ignore because so few in number, and viewed with distaste by prison officials, women in custodial units were treated as the dregs of the state prison population (p.21).*

Forces for Change

In the years before the American Civil War, waves of social change swept the United States. There was a general awakening to the plight of the less fortunate, including those in prison. Leading the movement were women, including Dorothea Dix, who toured the country and described in detail conditions in prisons and mental hospitals; Abigail Hopper Gibbons, leader of the Female Department of the Prison Association of New York; Eliza Farnham, chief matron at Mt. Pleasant Female Prison in New York from 1844 to 1848; and others. They believed that women operated in a "separate sphere" or in a different world than did men (Rafter, 1990). They wrote that women were inferior to men in some ways but were morally superior because of their role as homemaker and mother (Freedman, 1981). Believing that many of the problems incarcerated women faced were linked to being housed in male facilities, they advocated that female offenders be placed in separate institutions under the supervision of women (Freedman, 1981). As they searched for ways to improve conditions for female offenders, they discovered Elizabeth Fry's innovative work in English prisons.

In the 1813, an English Quaker, Elizabeth Gurney Fry entered London's Newgate Prison (Whitney, 1937). She found nearly 300 women confined for all types of crimes crowded into two long rooms where they cooked, washed, ate, slept, and kept their children. Most were sleeping almost naked on the stone floor. What devastated "her most was seeing two women stripping the dead body of a child to get the clothes for the living" (Smillie, 1981, p. 18). Appalled by the terrible conditions in which women and their children lived, Fry developed the key concepts for the reforms that were the basis for change in England, most of Europe, and the United States (Smillie, 1981). Among her most far-reaching recommendations were that women should be provided programs in separate, female-only, facilities and that these facilities should be operated exclusively by women (Whitney, 1937).

Building on Fry's principles for the treatment of women in prison and the work of the social feminists concerning the nature of women in society, reformers in the United States believed they had a moral duty to save their fallen sisters and convert them into "true women" (Rafter, 1990, p. 48). The goal was to transform female offenders into pious, virtuous, and submissive women. To reach this objective required the implementation of five basic tenets or principles in prison operations. The recommendations, examined by Freedman (1981) in *Their Sisters' Keepers*, are summarized as follows:

1. Women must be completely separated from male offenders in facilities designed and built for them. These institutions should be in rural areas away from the corrupting influences of the city.

2. Women's facilities must be administered and staffed by women. Men were considered a disruptive influence who should not be allowed to intrude into the separate world being created for women offenders.

3. Sentences should be indeterminate, that is, they should be flexible in length and allow the administrator to decide when the woman was "reformed" and should be released.

4. Women should be treated differently than men were treated. Dr. Ellen Cheney Johnson, a leader in the Massachusetts reformatory movement in

the early 1870s and first Superintendent of the Massachusetts Reformatory for Women, observed that women had "different physical organization and consequently greater nervous sensitiveness" that made them "more difficult to deal with" and they were less responsive to the harsh treatment prevalent in male facilitates (Freedman, 1981, p. 53). Johnson prescribed that women offenders needed "the softening influences of flowers, farm animals, music, and visits to infant nurseries" (Freedman, 1981, p. 54).

5. Facilities should have training programs designed for women. These would help reinforce the ideals of feminine virtue and "true womanhood." Josephine Shaw Lowell, another early advocate of separate facilities for women, wrote in 1879 that:

The unhappy beings we are speaking of need first of all, to be taught to be women; they must be induced to love that which is good and pure, and to wish to resemble it; they must learn all household duties... (Stewart, 1911, p. 99).

The 1870 National Congress of Penitentiary and Reformatory Discipline

Following the Civil War, women activists began to make the public aware of the growing number of female offenders and the terrible conditions in which they lived (Belknap, 1996). The reformers were middle- and upper-class women, primarily in the Northeast, who organized to win the right for women to vote and who established philanthropic programs for women, children, and the poor. They were articulate and had political contacts and organizational skills that they began to apply to a reform movement to save their "sisters" in prison who they had decided were redeemable (Freedman, 1981).

The efforts of the reformers came to fruition at the National Congress on Penitentiary and Reformatory Discipline (later to become the American Correctional Association) held in Cincinnati in 1870. Prior to and during the Congress, an extensive lobbying campaign was undertaken to insure that the delegates incorporated the reformers' new treatment approaches for women offenders in any guidelines developed for prisons (Hawkes, 1994). The Congress proved to be a significant milestone in the development of female offender facilities and programs through the adoption of the following resolution in the Declaration of Principles:

> *Resolved, that this Congress is of the opinion that separate prisons should be established for women, and that neither city, county, nor state prisons should have women incarcerated with men; and further, that women should have charge of the female department in all cases where the sexes are imprisoned in the same enclosure* (Wines, 1871, p. 569).

Phase 3. The 1870s to 1930s: Implementing the Dream

Women's Reformatory Model

To implement the concepts contained in the reformers' model, a new prison design called the "cottage plan" or "cottage system," evolved to house women and to emphasize a home-like or domestic atmosphere (Rafter, 1990). This design usually consisted of a central administration building surrounded by housing units referred to as "cottages" where inmates lived and, in some cases, worked. The reformatory model, since it was designed for misdemeanants and minor felony offenders, often had no fence and limited emphasis on security. In contrast to the earlier custodial model of prison design and operation, the new reformatories were developed for reform not punishment (Rafter, 1990).

The changes for women inmates in these new facilities were dramatic. Sarah Smith, the superintendent of the Indiana Women's Prison, is described as greeting her first prisoner by ordering the officers transporting her from the men's prison to take off her shackles. After this was done, she put her arms around her and said a prayer for her. She then took her to her "room decorated with bedspread, clothed table, curtains, a pot of flowers, a Bible, and a hymn book" (Freedman, 1981, p. 89). This was certainly a contrast from the environment in male facilities and it reflected the principles of the women's reformatory movement to create a home-like atmosphere for female offenders.

The creation of separate facilities for women was not undertaken uniformly across the nation. In 1873, the first separate state prison that was operated for and administered by women opened in Indiana (Freedman, 1981). With the opening of the Reformatory Prison for Women at Framingham in 1877, Massachusetts became the second state with a separate women's facility (Freedman, 1981). The third state to open separate women's facilities was New York. Its most famous women's facility was the New York Reformatory for Women at Bedford Hills that opened in 1901 with Dr. Katherine Bement Davis as its first superintendent (Harris, 1988). All three of these early facilities still held women offenders in 2003.

By 1933, seventeen states had separate facilities for female misdemeanants and minor felons using, for the most part, the women's reformatory model for the basic design (Hawkes, 1994). Some of these states, however, still kept more serious female offenders in their male facilities while other states kept all women offenders in wings of male facilities (Rafter, 1990). Haynes (1939) described the conditions for women still incarcerated in male facilities in the 1930s as follows:

> *Their number is small in comparison with male prisoners, and they are generally provided for inadequately. Their quarters are restricted, and their opportunities for work or exercise outdoors are more limited than those of the men. Their presence in institutions designed and operated primarily for men, where control is largely in the hands of male officials, is regarded as a constant source of trouble and danger (p. 88).*

Haynes (1939) recommended that states that had small populations of women inmates place them in separate wings in juvenile girls' facilities or house them in state mental hospitals to work as domestics.

The new separate facilities for women were seen as more advanced than male facilities because they provided better programming. The physical plants also were considered a plus because they were "attractively furnished" and inmates had "individual bedrooms instead of cells" (Haynes, 1939, p. 89).

However, while considered the best institutions available, there were serious problems in their administration and funding. Haynes (1939) concluded:

> *They often have too small staffs and too many poorly paid and trained minor officials. Their appropriations are insufficient. They deal with a type of offender difficult to reclaim. Their paroled prisoners have a harder fight to make good than men. On the whole, however, they are the most helpful of our penal institutions....They furnish a model after which the institutions for men should pattern (p. 89).*

By 1957, twenty-six states had separate facilities for women and eighteen states still kept women in sections of state prisons for men (American Correctional Association, 1959). That year, the number of female prisoners ranged from 4 in North Dakota to 673 in New York (American Correctional Association, 1959). According to the American Correctional Association data from 2002, all the states reporting had at least one separate facility for women except Maine, Mississippi, and North Dakota, which were listed as having only co-correctional prisons in which to house women. As always, there was a wide range in the number of women incarcerated from state to state—from a low of 58 incarcerated women in Rhode Island to a high of 11,157 in Texas (American Correctional Association, 2003a).

Women Offenders on the Federal Level

The federal government established its first women's facility in 1927. Until that point, women sentenced to prison in federal court were housed in state and county facilities where conditions varied from "good to intolerable" (Brown, 1984, p. 83).

Several forces led to the establishment of the first federal women's facility. World War I marked the end of the old order of the nineteenth century and the beginning of new views on almost everything. Lynd and Lynd described the 1890s to the mid-1920s as "one of the eras of greatest rapidity of change in the history of human institutions" (1956, p. 498). The vision of a "new woman" who demanded freedom from social constraints replaced the genteel "true woman" (Brown, 1987). Women built on the struggles of the suffragettes to expand their educational and career options, stake out new ground in a rapidly changing environment, and seek new meaning in home, marriage, career, and themselves (Brown, 1987). The public's attitude toward women offenders had changed from the earlier "fallen women" to the late nineteenth and early twentieth century view of female offenders as victims of poor homes, economic discrimination, and other debilitating social factors (Brown, 1984).

One of the new women of this generation was Mabel Walker Willebrandt who, at thirty-two, was appointed in 1921 as the first female assistant attorney general of the United States (Brown, 1984). One of the first crises she faced was what to do with the 250 women, most of whom were convicted of drug and liquor violations, who were boarded by the federal government in state and county prisons.

Kate O'Hare, "the most renowned woman in the Socialist party of America" in the 1910s and 1920s highlighted the poor conditions in some of these facilities (Foner and Miller, 1982, p. 1). As a spokesperson for the Socialist party, she decried the working conditions for the masses of men and women laborers in the United States and the exploitation of women and children in a capitalist society. As an outspoken opponent to World War I, she said that "women in the United States were no more than brood cows, to raise children to get into the army and be made [into] fertilizer" (Foner and Miller, 1982, p 19). Although she denied making the remark at her trial, she was arrested, convicted of interfering with the national war effort under the federal Espionage Act, and, in 1917, was sentenced to five years in prison (Foner and Miller, 1982).

While housed in the Missouri State Prison with other federal women inmates, she wrote numerous letters describing the dismal conditions there. Compiled by her husband and published as *Kate O'Hare's Prison Letters*, they were widely circulated. After several illnesses and considerable political pressure, President Wilson commuted her sentence in 1920. Following her release from prison, she published *In Prison* outlining her views on the American prison system (Foner and Miller, 1982).

At this point, the federal government faced widely publicized criticism of its practice of contracting incarceration of women prisoners to state and local facilities. Also, problematical was the growing number of women convicted of federal crimes and the rising costs of housing them. This is when Mabel Walker Willebrandt intervened. She organized a coalition of women's groups including the League of Women Voters, the Women's Christian Temperance Union, the General Federation of Women's Clubs, the National Federation of Business and Professional Women, and others to lobby Congress to establish a federal facility for woman (Brown, 1984). Defeated the first time, she regrouped and with national support of the women's organizations and labor unions, she was successful in having Congress appropriate funds in 1925 to construct a facility for federally convicted women.

Opened in April 1927, the U.S. Industrial Reformatory for Women was located at Alderson, West Virginia and became a model institution incorporating the principles of the reformatory movement (Heffernan, 1994). Symbolically, administration buildings and cottages were named for Elizabeth Fry, Katherine B. Davis, and Mabel Walker Willebrandt among others (Harris, 1936).

Leadership and Staff in Women's Facilities

The women who managed the first women's facilities at the beginning of the twentieth century were well-educated, intelligent, and articulate (Hawkes, 1994). Compared to the women reformers of the nineteenth century, superintendents of women's facilities were "more likely to have their sights on paid professional careers" (Rafter, 1990, p. 65). A number of them had advanced degrees. Katharine Bement Davis, Ph.D., superintendent of Bedford Hills in New York from 1901-1914, received her doctoral degree from the University of Chicago (Freedman, 1981). She recruited Mary Belle Harris, Ph.D., who she met at the University of Chicago while Harris was working on her doctorate (Harris, 1936). Dr. Harris later became the first superintendent of the U.S.

Industrial Reformatory for Women at Alderson, West Virginia, after heading the Women's Workhouse in New York City, and Clinton Farms, the State Reformatory for Women in New Jersey (Harris, 1936).

Many of these leaders experimented with new approaches and conducted groundbreaking research on female offenders (Freedman, 1981). They implemented positive treatment programs including education and vocational training at a time when most male facilities were still entrenched in the custodial model (Haynes, 1939).

Through their character and behavior, female staff in women's facilities were to serve as role models for their charges and to help insure that they, in fact, were reformed. Edna Mahan, superintendent of Clinton Farms from 1928 to 1968, wrote "The success or failure of a women's institution depends primarily on the personnel.... It should be recognized that working with women offenders is a profession calling for high qualities of mind and spirit" (American Correctional Association, 1954, p. 80).

Line staff usually lived twenty-four hours a day in cottage-style buildings with the inmates. They worked twelve-hour shifts, had little time off, and were paid less than their male counterparts who worked in male facilities. Hawkes (1994) quotes a 1940 report of the Board of Managers of the New Jersey Reformatory for Women that described the conditions for staff as follows:

> *Our matrons and relief officers work practically twenty-four hours a day and receive from $50 to $70 a month plus maintenance. Male guards in the reformatories for men work 8 hours and receive a minimum of $150 per month (p.153).*

Inmate Programs

Opportunities for all women during this period were limited. Women could not vote until 1920. In some cases, they could not own property and were not expected to work outside the home if they were married (Kanowitz, 1969). Yet, in 1900, nearly five million women and girls, 23 percent of all females in the United States, were employed with three-fifths clustered in six occupations:

domestic service, farm labor, dressmaking, laundry, teaching, and farming in that order (Richardson, 1909). The majority of these jobs were in what is now referred to as "traditional women's work." They were poorly paid and their work typically related to a woman's role as caretaker and mother.

By 1920, the number of women in the workplace was estimated to be more than eleven million, eight million of whom were between the ages of fourteen and twenty-one (Adams, 1930). Jobs in the professional category were beginning to open up in some areas of the United States for women who managed to earn advanced degrees. Their numbers were small and their roles in both the public and private sector were much more limited than could be found in the 1940s during World War II and later in the 1970s following the passage of Title VII of the Civil Rights Act of 1964 (Cobble, 1993).

Programs in women's facilities reflected women's role in the world of work in the community. Many vocational training programs and other activities in women's reformatories were designed to prepare women for traditional roles as housekeepers and domestic workers (Belknap, 1996). Some have criticized the reformatory movement for perpetuating the training of female offenders in traditional women's work (Belknap, 1996; Feinman,1983; Rafter 1990). In defense of the policy, domestic and other traditional women's work were the primary legal occupations available to poor women who had limited education and a criminal record. Since there were no affirmative action laws or requirements to hire women in the workforce, women offenders who were trained in nontraditional women's jobs probably would not have been employed.

Since many women's facilities were located in rural areas, farming and related skills such as canning were emphasized (American Correctional Association, 1954). As some legislation establishing correctional facilities contained the provision that prisons should strive to be self-sufficient, products produced on prison farms helped support the institution.

Religious programs were an important component in many women's facilities. In addition to a chaplain's regular services, community volunteers were allowed to hold programs for the women's moral salvation (Haynes, 1939). Social work services and counseling began to be available at some women's reformatories early in the twentieth century (Hawkes, 1994).

Recreation programs and other diversions including inmate-produced plays, reading aloud to groups of inmates, arts and crafts, and sewing were available at the more progressive facilities (Harris, 1936). Lekkerkerker, a Dutch lawyer, who came to the United States to observe women's facilities in the early 1900s, described leisure-time activities in some facilities as including "sports, gymnastics, cottage or community entertainment, singing, bible classes, lectures, self-government meetings, etc." (Pollock-Byrne, 1990, p. 53).

A number of women's facilities during this period including Bedford Hills in New York; Clinton Farms in New Jersey; and the Massachusetts Reformatory for Women at Framingham, had nurseries where children were kept during their early years (Freedman, 1981; Hawkes, 1994). When the children grew too old to stay with their mothers, and the women were not eligible for release, the children were sent to a grandmother, some other relative, or placed in an orphanage. Some facilities also had parenting and childcare programs in which inmates could learn how to take care of their children and how to raise them more effectively (Morton, 1994).

Changes in the Reformatory Model

Not all women were housed in reformatories. Some women, including felony offenders and women of color, continued to be housed in male facilities (Rafter, 1990). By 1910, when these women's units became crowded or when space was needed to house male offenders, the more serious female offenders were moved to women's reformatories (Haynes, 1939).

This new type of inmate who needed more secure custody and supervision meant that the reformatory model which had been designed for less serious offenders changed and became more custody oriented (Rafter, 1990). As the reformatories adjusted to meet the needs of their new charges and became seriously crowded, the reformatory movement began to decline (Belknap,

1996). Some states began to call their women's institutions "state industrial institutions, state industrial farms or homes" (Haynes, 1939, p. 88) indicating a change to a more custodial model of incarceration.

For many years, legislative bodies had failed to appropriate adequate funding for women's facilities. As the nation moved into the Great Depression of the 1930s and the winds of war began sweeping around the world, interest in and concern for women offenders waned. Women's prisons were small and female inmates were seen as a limited threat. Since women offenders made few headlines, they generally were ignored. Women offenders and those who managed them became more and more isolated from society and the emerging corrections profession (Belknap, 1996).

Phase 4. The 1940s to 1950s: The Forgotten Female Offender

As the country became involved in World War II in the early 1940s, interest in women offenders rose briefly. Women camp followers and prostitutes were considered a threat to national security because they were seen as carriers of venereal disease and a danger to the morals of the young men training to fight abroad (Heffernan, 1994). For the most part, however, "out of sight and out of mind" was the rule of the day. While some aspects of the reformatory movement remained in women's facilities, it ceased to be a driving force in the day-to-day operations of many women's prisons. Women offenders and their facilities once again slipped into the background and basically were ignored by correctional agencies, administrators, legislators, and the general public.

Similar to previous years, women's facilities during this period were generally small, housing fewer than two-hundred, and were designed in the cottage style (American Correctional Association, 1954). Standards issued in the 1950s as guidelines for the professional organization and operation of correctional programs by the American Correctional Association stressed that, since they were smaller, women's facilities could be creative and have more advanced treatment programs than could male facilities.

The standards noted that women's facilities had developed a number of innovations that were different from male institutions through such things as "getting away from mass treatment and prison-like living situations" and permitting women to develop a "home-like atmosphere" in prison (American Correctional Association, 1959, p. 464). The implication was that by being small, separate, and operated by well-educated women with a minimum of political interference, women's facilities were superior to the larger male prisons. To some extent this was true.

The women who administered these facilities continued to be better educated than their counterparts in male facilities (Rafter, 1990). Also, since women were viewed as less violent and less of a threat to the public than were males, women administrators were able to operate innovative and more community-oriented programs, which were not available in male facilities (American Correctional Association, 1954). The creativity of women administrators in developing new programs to some extent grew from the necessity to improvise as women's facilities received limited funding and other resources (American Correctional Association, 1954, and 1959). As late as the 1960s many still believed that women's facilities were superior in programming and services to male prisons (Morton, 1994).

Remnants of the Reformatory Movement

The 1959 American Correctional Association's *Manual of Correctional Standards* included two programs unique to women's facilities that reflected the tenets of the earlier reformatory movement and which were described as essential to the successful operation of women's facilities. The first, social education, was described as a program:

> *that seeks to accomplish positive changes in social attitudes (and) acceptance of one's social responsibilities . . . to live in accordance with acceptable standards of group and community relationships* (American Correctional Association, 1959, p. 467).

The second was student government. This was described as a system:

by which women can participate in the program in the institution and in discussions on matters of general welfare, thus increasing their sense of social responsibility, self-respect and understanding of democratic group living (American Correctional Association, 1959, p. 467).

The standards also reflected the reformatory-movement management style for women with the recommendation that forms of discipline for them be implemented that "minimized regimentation" and encouraged self-discipline and self-control (American Correctional Association, 1959, p. 468). Corporal punishment of the "humiliating type," including flogging or spanking, and coercive systems of threats and rewards for punishment were discouraged. The standards proposed counseling as the best approach to maintaining order (American Correctional Association, 1959, p. 468).

Women's facilities appeared on the surface to be more relaxed and less structured than male facilities. Most were in rural areas, and they looked like small community colleges (Haynes, 1939). In reality, many had very strict rules governing every aspect of inmates' lives. Increasing populations of more serious offenders and neglect eroded what had begun as a positive approach to the treatment of women offenders under the reformatory movement (Pollock-Byrne, 1990; Belknap, 1996). Women's facilities and those who operated them continued to be isolated from changes taking place in the corrections system as a whole.

Motherhood and Apple Pie

Following World War II, women in the community were encouraged to leave their jobs and return to more traditional roles at home. Women choosing careers were reminded that their first obligation was to be a wife and mother. The U.S. Secretary of Labor in 1958 reminded those at a conference on women and work that:

. . . We must recognize the fact that women's motivations and their orientation in so far as the workforce is concerned are different from those of men. If we fail

to recognize that women who are homemakers will not work when their homes take priority... if we do not recognize that for most women work is a secondary activity, in the main, we may be doing a great disservice to the development of our total resources for work (Zapoleon, 1961, p. 18).

As one occupational planning guide noted when compared to a man:

A girl...usually looks forward to marriage and plans on homemaking as her principal occupation for some years, but approaches it with less certainty and is especially unsure of the timing. If she married, she may continue the occupation she entered before marriage. Her husband's approval and co-operation are necessary if she is to do so. And such approval is not taken for granted, as is a wife's expectation of her husband's employment (Zapoleon, 1961, p. 10).

The attitude that a woman was a dependent extension of a man's world appeared to carry over to women's prisons where there was a strong tendency to treat women offenders as children and rob them of the opportunity to make even the most basic decisions for themselves (Harris, 1988). They were seen as weak, dependent, child-like creatures. Just as women in the community were called "girls," female offenders were called "girls" in many women's facilities. In fact, the practice of calling women "girls" carried into the twenty-first century in some areas of the country. According to Belknap (1996):

The 1940s and 1950s have been characterized as a time in which the reformatories switched from turning women prisoners into good housemaids to making them good housewives (p. 96).

Phase 5. The 1960s to 1970s: Challenge and Change

By the middle of the 1960s, the concepts of social education and student government had been abandoned by most women's facilities. The 1966 version of the American Correctional Association's standards reflected the view that while there were some unique "differing characteristics which should be recognized" in the operation of women's facilities, "the principles established for the operation of male facilities also applied to them" (American Correctional Association, 1966, p. 556).

Men increasingly were assigned to administrator women's facilities. While this was a steppingstone for young male managers, there were few, if any, advancement opportunities for women employed in women's facilities to work elsewhere in the system. Also, women were not paid the same wages as their male counterparts. To address this fact, the American Correctional Association standards called for women to be paid on "an equal basis with men in like positions" (American Correctional Association, 1966, p. 564). According to one female correctional administrator, "Running a women's facility was generally not considered to be a 'like position' to running a male facility unless a man was running the women's facility" (Judy C. Anderson, Personal Communication, October, 2001).

Impact of the Civil Rights Movement

The civil rights movement of the 1960s had a profound influence on society in the United States. Demonstrations for equal rights for minorities were followed by demands that women also receive equitable treatment. The civil rights movement rekindled concepts of equality that had been buried after women achieved the right to vote in 1920 and there was a renewed interest in the status of women throughout the country. Once again, the limited roles and opportunities open to women in employment and in society at large were challenged, and again the idea grew that women were equal to men and should have the same opportunities in society as men.

The women's movement also drew attention to the issues of female criminality (Flynn, 1998). One of the problems of establishing a direction for the treatment of women in the 1960 and 1970s was the lack of information about them and their involvement in crime. In the late 1960s, Freda Adler, who would become one of America's best-known scholars on the subject of female offenders, could find only twenty references to publications on women (Flynn, 1998). Criminologists had all but ignored the existence of women offenders or had marginalized the research that was conducted on them.

Dr. Adler, however, changed that to a large degree with the publication of *Sisters in Crime: The Rise of the New Female Criminal* in 1975. As Flynn (1998) noted:

> *The controversial reception of the book, combined with the unprecedented publicity surrounding it, served an important function. It moved the subject of female crime from the remotest recesses of the academic enterprise to the center of public and academic attention, (p. 8)*

Adler argued that female crime had been trivialized and female behavior should not be based on theories of male behavior (Faith, 1993). She challenged the stereotype that women and girls were passive and pointed out that based on her research, women were "indeed committing more crimes than ever before" and that "those crimes involve a greater degree of violence and even in prison this new breed exhibits a hitherto unmatched pugnacity" much greater than before (Adler, 1975, p. 3). She went on to describe a female bank robber as an example of the "new female criminal" who would "cross the line which once separated crimes into "masculine" and "feminine" categories (Adler, 1975, p. 7).

She would later say she was only pointing out that the changing roles of women in the United States created stress on them which should be taken into account when studying women and crime (Flynn, 1998). However, her critics and the media interpreted her writings as predicting that women would begin to exhibit the same criminal behavior as men if they were given equal rights. This also contributed to the idea that female criminality was becoming the same as male criminality.

One of the more bizarre manifestations of interest in linking the women's rights movement with female crime was the attention given to the Patty Hearst story. Patty Hearst, the daughter of publishing magnate Randolph Hearst, was kidnapped in 1974 by terrorists known as the Symbionese Liberation Army (Cooper, 1979). After being tied up and terrorized in a small closet for fifty-seven days, she was forced to participate in the gang's activities (Hearst, 1982). When pictures of her holding a gun during a bank robbery were flashed around the world. The U.S. Attorney General, ignoring what was known about brainwashing, declared her a "common criminal." She became the poster picture of the "new female criminal."

After a nationwide search, she was captured, tried, and found guilty in spite of extensive testimony from psychiatrists declaring her innocence. She was sentenced to seven years in prison and incarcerated in the Federal Correctional Institution at Pleasanton, California. Two years later, President Jimmy Carter responded to public pressure and commuted her sentence (Hearst, 1982). President Bill Clinton later pardoned her.

In spite of the media hype, the predictions of a different type of female offender did not come to pass. However, a side benefit of this controversy was that women's groups in the community once more began to take an interest in what was happening to women in prison (Heffernan, 1994). Correctional systems were encouraged to provide more parity for women's institutions to include nontraditional job training to enable women to be more self-sufficient when they were released. The Association on Programs for Female Offenders (APFO), an affiliate of the American Correctional Association that represents those working with adult and juvenile female offenders, sponsored a 1975 resolution, which was passed by the American Correctional Association governing body, that called for the following:

Creation of programs to expand economic and social roles of women offenders and eliminate employment barriers for them

Provision of complete health program for women in institutions

Utilization of community resources, development of community corrections, and implementation of diversion programs for women offenders

Examination of laws governing prostitution

Repeal of victimless crime legislation

Creation of services for juvenile status offenders, the majority of which were girls (American Correctional Association, 1975).

Conditions Deteriorate

Unfortunately, actual positive change in women's institutions did not take place to any great extent. In fact, they were beginning to look more like male facilities as fences were built and security tightened. Programming was also affected. From a survey of women's facilities conducted in the 1960s, it would seem that if they ever had been treatment oriented, they no longer were emphasizing programs. Strickland (1976) found that administrators in almost 50 percent of women's facilities described their institutions as custodial or custody-oriented. Less than 30 percent saw their facilities as treatment-oriented or treatment institutions (Strickland, 1976).

The Law Enforcement Assistance Administration (LEAA), a federal program to fund innovations in criminal justice, did provide some money for new programs for women offenders. A number of treatment programs and several halfway houses or community residential centers had their beginnings under LEAA sponsorship (Gowdy, 1998). In spite of these efforts, conditions in many women's institutions did not improve and crowding grew. One study, for example, noted that the Washington D.C. Women's Detention Center built to house 30 women routinely held 171 (Loving and Olson, 1976).

A 1979 U.S. General Accounting Office (GAO) study described conditions in one local detention facility that consisted of a "large cage" holding some twenty-to-thirty women who were awaiting trial as follows:

Furnishings consisted of a few benches, and tables with no television, radio, books, magazines, games, or hobbies for inmates to pass the time. Nor did the jail have any programs for these women.

Each cell holds six to eight inmates. In full view of cellmates and adjoining cellmates each cell has a single washbasin and toilet stand. Bunks are bare mattresses, without sheets or pillowcases; blankets are issued each night and collected every morning.

The isolation cells for violent detainees and those undergoing drug withdrawal contain only a bunk and a hole in the floor to serve as a toilet with no toilet paper, no sink or light (p. 22).

Concerning both local jails and state prisons housing women, the U.S. General Accounting Office reported:

> *With few exceptions neither type of correctional facility today does more than warehouse its female inmates; physical plant, staffing, services, and programs are needed to create an atmosphere promoting positive behavioral change, but these are sadly inadequate. This situation arises from the lack of money, planning, and direction afflicting most penal institutions* (U.S. General Accounting Office, 1979, p. 31).

A 1980 report to the U.S. Congress by the U.S. Comptroller General's Office described similar conditions. It found that women did not have access to job training and other services that men routinely received. The reasons cited for these inequities, found at both the state and federal levels, were the small number of women prisoners and "because many officials feel that women do not need the same type of training and vocational skills as men" (U.S. Comptroller General, 1980, p. 1).

Morton (1998) reported observations in the 1970s of conditions in women's facilities, particularly in the South, that included the following:

> *Women whose heads were shaved for disciplinary infractions and/or who were confined for punishment alone in an out-building the size of an outhouse in winter without heat, water (except for a toilet), bedding, or other basic amenities. They drank from the holding tank of the toilet.*

> *Women detained in local jails without female supervision and with keys to the women's cells in the hands of male inmate trustees.*

> *Women locked in cells alone in an abandoned building for disciplinary purposes whose status was checked every hour by a male staff member.*

> *Punitive confinement cages in a dark airless room that were so small women could not stand up in them.*

> *Open bays for cells with open toilets and showers so that women were in full view of male staff at all times.*

Phase 6. The 1980s to 1990s: Sameness but Not Equality

As a result of intolerable conditions in a number of facilities for women, several major lawsuits were filed on behalf of women prisoners. While these cases will be examined in-depth in a later chapter, the threat of sanctions by the federal court forced a number of changes in the treatment of women offenders at all levels of government (Collins, 1998).

Impact of Legal Action

Many of the early suits dealing with equal protection for women were successful and some thought the courts would be an effective means of ensuring women received equitable treatment (Rafter, 1987). Unfortunately, this approach had a number of drawbacks. Since the judges were not always knowledgeable about the needs of women offenders, there was a tendency to order the same treatment for women that males had, rather than programs that were comparable to the programs for males. By the late 1990s, courts stopped supporting parity cases and litigation was limited to direct constitutional issues such as medical care (Collins, 1998). Also, changes ordered by the court were frozen in time and could not be altered to meet new conditions. Finally, changing the system through the court was a time-consuming, expensive, and slow process.

Agency administrators soon responded to the threat of federal intervention and the tendency to treat women as though they were men increased (Morton, 1998). Sharp (2003) refers to treating women as men as "vengeful equity" that is the "dark side of the equity or parity model of justice particularly when the outcome is punitive, in the name of equal justice" (p. 10). Thus, some facilities for women were supplied with weight rooms, fences with multiple rows of razor ribbon, and other symbols of male prisons. Some new or renovated facilities for women were built using plans designed for males. The hardware, size, and security provisions of male facilities were replicated, even though the majority of women did not need them. Facilities built on the male model were sometimes sarcastically referred to as "male facilities without urinals." Some were actually built with urinals. This author once observed large pots of ferns sitting in the urinals in a juvenile girls' facility. Unfortunately, no camera was available to document this creative camouflage.

To provide the same treatment for women that men received, system administrators and institutional staff sometimes abolished positive programs and services that women had had for many years. One state, for example, had allowed long-term women inmates to prepare meals in their unit's kitchen. This was abolished because male facilities did not have provisions for cooking in units. Community access in this state became more limited for women in part because it traditionally was restricted for men. Visiting policies, security provisions, and other practices from male facilities were imposed on women's facilities. An extreme example of this phenomenon was exhibited by an Arizona sheriff who declared he was an "equal opportunity incarcerator" and established a "volunteer" chain gang for women (Sharp, 2003, p. 10).

Many of these changes were made without regard to their negative effects on female inmates. For example, the requirement that all inmates leaving a medium-security facility be in leg irons and belly chains provided no exception for women in advanced stages of pregnancy. Also, some systems developed property allowances for inmates that did not include provisions for the clothing needs of women.

Early research on the impact of the "get tough" approach on women indicated that harsh treatment in prison environments made women more hostile and fearful and contributed to negative attitudes toward staff (Kruttschnitt, Gartner, and Miller, 2000). In response to the excesses of the equality phase in the treatment of women, issues concerning the differences between men and women began to be raised in the late twentieth and early twenty-first centuries.

In an attempt to address some of the negative things that were evolving around the country, the American Correctional Association developed a National Public Policy for Corrections on programming for female offenders. In 1986, the American Correctional Association endorsed the Public

Correctional Policy on Female Offender Services (Morton, 1991) and reaffirmed its position in subsequent reviews. The complete policy is included in Appendix A but the key points of the recommendation are that:

> *Correctional systems must develop service delivery systems for accused and adjudicated female offenders that are comparable to those provided to males. Additional services must also be provided to meet the unique needs of the female population.*
>
> *Correctional systems must be guided by the principle of parity.*
>
> *Female offenders must receive the equivalent range of services available to other offenders, including opportunities for individualized programming and services that recognize the unique need of this population* (Morton, 1991, p 35).

The tendency throughout the history of the treatment of women offenders in this country has been to have a period of reform followed by a period of neglect. Helping to ensure women would not be forgotten as the new century approached, the leadership of the National Institute of Corrections including the late head of the Prisons Division, Dr. Susan Hunter, developed grant opportunities to fund innovative new policy and program initiatives. Much of the work discussed in the next period was a direct result of these activities.

Phase 7. The New Millennium—2000 to the Present: Gender Responsive Policies and Practicies—A New Model

The concept of gender-responsive services for women developed as a way for correctional systems to base programs and services on women's needs rather than simply transpose what was being done for men to women. Gender-responsive programming begins where women are and addresses "human needs rather than focusing solely on punitive sanctions" (Bloom and Chesney-Lind, 2000, p. 201).

Morton (1998) listed several components that should be contained in gender-responsive programming that are summarized below:

Incarceration should be used only as a last option in sentencing women offenders.

Programs should provide parity with those available for males but they must be women-centered.

Programs should be individualized to maximize the strengths and address the needs of women offenders.

Programs and services should be humane and minimize unnecessary intrusion in to women's lives.

The biological- and gender-induced characteristics of women offenders must be addressed in programs and services.

All agency and institutional policies and practices should be reviewed to ensure gender responsiveness.

Staff and others who work with women must be carefully selected and provided gender-specific training to make them more effective in working with female offenders.

All programs and services for women should be monitored on an on-going basis to ensure that they are meeting their established goals.

For example, security and supervision should be designed to meet the risks and needs of women and not be superimposed from male facilities. Given many women's backgrounds of having been abused, the institutional environment should be supportive and safe so women are not further harmed physically, mentally, emotionally, or sexually (Morton, 1998).

Bloom, Owen, and Covington (2003) developed a very comprehensive guide for gender-responsive services based on an extensive review of what the research on female offenders over the last twenty years has shown. As noted in the reference section, their full report is available from the National Institute of Corrections, and it should be read by anyone interested in service delivery for women offenders in the correctional system. While policymakers and those working with women offenders would benefit from reading the entire report, the following summary will provide some of the highlights of this important study. The authors identified five key findings from their review of the research on women offenders. These are summarized below:

To be effective, programs and services for women and girls must be structured differently than they are for males.

To be gender responsive, policies and practices must be culturally sensitive and provide for interventions to address

— substance abuse issues

— physical, sexual, and emotional trauma experienced by the majority of women in the system

— mental health issues

— issues of economic self-sufficiency (ability to support themselves and their family)

— race and culture issues

Sanctions and interventions should fit the offense patterns of women.

Programs and services should acknowledge women's relationships with family, friends, and community.

Community integration and service should be addressed in all programming.

Based on the findings listed above, Bloom, Owen, and Covington (2003) developed the following six basic principles for successful gender-responsive program implementation.

1. Those developing gender-responsive policies or program must understand that gender does make a difference. Since women-centered issues are normally absent from typical agency policy and practices, implementation of gender-responsive services requires that women's issues become a priority. Someone at the policymaking level in the organization should be given the responsibility for overseeing program implementation and management.

2. Correctional staff should create an environment, supported by written policies and practices, where women can feel safe, physically and

emotionally, and where they are treated with respect and dignity. Those working with women should understand the impact that trauma both as children and adults has on women. The issues of trauma should be addressed in order for women to heal and move on with their lives.

Staff misconduct should be addressed in policy and training. Allegations of misconduct should be investigated and dealt with expeditiously.

Classification and assessment systems should be based on women's needs and risks. The systems and the environment should be monitored on an ongoing basis.

3. Administrators and policymakers should acknowledge the role relationships play in women's lives and make relationship issues a core theme in gender-responsive programming. Maintaining and, if necessary, building positive relationships between women and their children are key factors in improving relationships. Promoting healthy relationships and choices among women and between them and others in their lives as well as helping them build peer-support networks will strengthen gender-responsive programming.

4. Comprehensive services and supervision should address the issues of the interaction of substance abuse, trauma, and mental health. Training in these issues should be provided to all including security staff, and multidisciplinary teams should be used in program implementation.

5. Economic and social cohesiveness and integration must be addressed. This includes providing both traditional and nontraditional academic and vocational training so that women can become self-sufficient. Such programs should link women with jobs in the community in which they can earn a living wage and include transition services to ensure follow through with gains made in the institution.

6. Comprehensive, individualized, collaborative, wrap-around services should be provided to female offenders to insure their successful community integration. Coordination with service providers in the community is essential for program success.

Implementing the concept of gender-responsive programs is not easy because of the degree of heterogeneity among women offenders and the different interpretations of what is meant by gender-responsive services. Some administrators are so used to trying to insure sameness in men's and women's programs that it is hard to convince them that it is acceptable to treat men and women differently.

However, gender-responsive programming is beginning to receive support. For example, at least ten states allow female offenders extended overnight visits with their children (Kauffman, 2001). The National Association of Women Judges in 2000 published a *Curriculum on Sentencing Women Offenders* that it hopes will call nationwide attention to the gender-responsive problems of women offenders, particularly those who are pregnant or have children (Temin, 2001). Both the National Institute of Corrections and the National Institute of Justice are funding programs and research on gender-responsive programming.

It was clear from the Tenth National Workshop on Adult and Juvenile Female Offenders sponsored by the Maine Department of Corrections and co-sponsored by the Association on Programs for Female Offenders in September 2003, that a number of states and local correctional systems are beginning to implement gender-responsive programming. The American Correctional Association has agreed to publish proceedings from the conference that will provide in-depth descriptions of a variety of gender-responsive issues and programs.

Future Prospects

The punitive climate of the 1990s—in which the concern for the less fortunate evidenced in the 1960s and 1970s was swept away and replaced with a strong conservative position—appears to be changing as the twenty-first century begins.

However, the number of women offenders has tripled since the 1970s, which complicates the task of meeting their needs. Since many women offenders are incarcerated for drug or drug-related offenses and appear to pose a limited threat to the community, some recommended that new community approaches to sanctioning them should be implemented. In light of shrinking correctional budgets around the country, this idea might receive more support in the future.

Even with the dramatic increases in the number of women offenders, they make up less than 7 percent of the total number of offenders incarcerated at the state level in the United States (Camp and Camp, 2000). This means there is still an opportunity for implementing new programs and strategies to keep women in the community or if they are removed to provide gender-responsive programs so they can return them to society to live law-abiding and productive lives.

Equality and gender-responsive programming will be an ongoing challenge for administrators and staff. Educating policymakers and the public to the needs of the women in institutions will make the task easier.

There are two caveats or pitfalls to be avoided regarding gender-responsive programming for women offenders. If we learn anything from history, it is to not make the same mistakes again. Looking back at earlier reform periods, we must not attribute unrealistic characteristics to women as was done in the 1870s and attempt to mold them into "true women." Care also must be taken to ensure that women's differences from men do not become synonymous with "difficult" or "inferior" as has occurred in the past.

Summary

In this chapter, we have explored key concepts relative to the treatment of women offenders throughout the history of the United States. We examined several treatment theories to help readers better understand women's facilities and why they operate the way that they do. Hopefully, this discussion will assist those interested in this field to begin to explore their own feelings and beliefs about women offenders, so they can be more successful in working with them.

Points to remember are the following:

The treatment of women offenders has evolved over time and continues to change today.

The way women offenders are treated is dependent on how the public views women in general and what else is happening in the world.

Period 1. The Colonial Years: Age of Abuse and Neglect

Women offenders in the colonial period were considered "fallen women" and, therefore, thought to be beyond help.

Period 2. The 1770s to 1860s: Building a Model for Women's Reformatories

From the end of the Revolutionary War until 1870, a number of changes in the way women were viewed and treated took place. Women offenders who had been confined with male offenders were housed separately from men, but were still under male supervision. This meant they were still subject to abuse from male staff and inmates. The Women's Reformatory Movement was formed based on the work of Elizabeth Gurney Fry with the objectives to reform women not punish them.

Period 3. The 1870s to 1930s: Implementing the Dream

The National Congress on Penitentiary and Reformatory Discipline (later to become the American Correctional Association) in 1870 endorsed the concept of separate facilities for women operated by women.

The implementation of separate women's facilities was not uniform across the nation. (Even by 2002, three states reported not having a separate facility for women [American Correctional Association, 2002a]).

Facilities for women under the reformatory movement became more humane and treatment oriented. Facilities for women looked like small college campuses, but most had strict rules governing all aspects of inmates' lives. Not all women were in separate facilities for women. Felons and women of color remained in separate wings of male prisons.

Period 4. The 1940s to 1950s: The Forgotten Female Offender

The innovations established under the reformatory movement did not last and by the 1940s, women offenders were forgotten by the criminal justice system and the public.

Period 5. The 1960s to 1970s: Challenge and Change

By the 1960s, most of the concepts from the reformatory movement were abandoned and the treatment of women in many local jails and state prisons became more custody oriented. Conditions for women in many facilities in the 1960s and 1970s continued to be inadequate.

The civil rights movement helped heighten awareness about the plight of women offenders, but expanded opportunities for women in the community did not produce a "new female criminal" as some had believed it would.

Period 6. The 1980s to 1990s: Sameness but Not Equality

Federal lawsuits and the threat of court intervention spurred a number of changes in women's institutions, but women still were not provided comparable services or parity with men. The number of women offenders increased dramatically during this period primarily as a result of the war on drugs; however, women still made up less than 7 percent of the total number of inmates incarcerated at the state level in the United States.

The American Correctional Association's Public Correctional Policy on Female Offender Services called for women's programs to be comparable to those available to males and to provide for the unique needs of female offenders.

Period 7. The New Millennium— 2000 to Present: Gender Responsive Policies and Practices—A New Model

Correctional scholars and practitioners began to define and initiate a new direction in the treatment of female offenders. Gender-responsive policies and programs began to be implemented for women offenders in the corrections system.

Legal Issues for Staff and Women Offenders

Objectives

- ❖ Describe how the views of state and federal courts toward inmate rights have changed over time.

- ❖ Identify the four basic constitutional issues most often cited in inmate lawsuits and note the one most commonly used by female offenders.

- ❖ Identify problems that could lead to litigation in women's institutions.

- ❖ Explain the reasons why women are less likely than men to pursue legal remedies.

- ❖ Identify issues that have been litigated by women offenders.

- ❖ Discuss actions facility personnel can take to help reduce potential areas of litigation when working with female offenders.

Introduction

In this chapter, we review the basic tenets underlying the role of courts in the oversight of correctional operations and the courts' impact on the treatment of women offenders. We also review strategies to aid staff who work in women's institutions avoid legal problems.

Federal and state courts have been powerful forces for change during the periods in which they were active in reviewing correctional practices. But, the courts are limited in how far they can go to enforce implementation of more humane practices in correctional facilities. In the long run, it is the responsibility of those who work with female offenders to ensure women's legal rights are maintained.

General Legal Principles

A brief overview of general principles will help put the discussion of legal issues relative to women offenders in perspective. Court oversight of corrections is part of the balance of power among the legislative, executive, and judicial branches of government. The findings of the courts are evolving and changing continuously, so correctional practitioners need to be vigilant to ensure that policy and practice keep pace with legal mandates.

Nonintervention or the "Hands Off" Doctrine

Historically, when convicted offenders were sent to prison they forfeited all of the rights they had in the community and the right to be heard concerning the conditions of their confinement. The courts deferred questions of inmate management to prison administrators in what was known as the "hands off" doctrine (Latessa, Holsinger, Marquart, and Sorensen, 2001).

The "hands off" doctrine meant courts refused to consider inmates' complaints or when judges did hear them, they usually found in favor of prison administrators. According to Wallace (2001), federal courts were reluctant to intervene in what were considered matters for states to resolve. They did not want to violate the principle of separation of powers by interfering in what was an executive branch area, and they felt the need to defer to the expertise of prison administrations.

The "hands off" doctrine also meant inmates had little legal standing or right to be treated as citizens under the Constitution. In an 1871 case, the Virginia Supreme Court issued a ruling that reflected the national consensus and which, with some exceptions, was upheld for the next 100 years. It stated that an inmate "as a consequence of his own crime, not only forfeited his liberty, but all his personal rights... [and] is for the time being a slave of the state" (*Ruffin v. Commonwealth*, 1871, p. 796). In effect, inmates were civilly dead and forfeited many of their rights as citizens under the U.S. Constitution and their rights under state and federal laws (Harris and Spiller, 1977).

Unfortunately, the "hands off" doctrine meant there was limited oversight or checks and balances on prison administrators' actions (DiIulio, 1987). It also gave legislators few incentives to fund programs and services for offenders. Unlimited power in the hands of a few people, crowding, and lack of support from outside the institution created serious problems in many prisons and led to abuse of power and brutalizing conditions in a number of states. Placing inmates in solitary confinement on limited bread and water diets for excessive periods of time, crowding three or more people into single occupancy cells, and failing to maintain adequate sanitation, food, and medical care became commonplace (Parenti, 2000). Since most institutionalized women usually had fewer programs and services than did men to start with, their situation in many facilities was even worse than it was for men.

Abandoning the "Hand Off" Doctrine

In the late nineteenth and early twentieth centuries, there were indications that the slave of the state concept was not supported by some courts. However, judges lacked the "procedural rights or methods" that later became available "to enforce these substantive rights" (Wallace, 2001 p. 232).

In the mid-1960s, the prison rights movement evolved and led to the abandonment of the "hands off" doctrine by the courts (Jacobs, 2001). Well publicized abuse of inmates in the system, prison disturbances, a more activist Supreme Court, and a growing concern on the part of the public for civil rights in general resulted in closer scrutiny of the treatment of inmates.

Inmates brought issues to the attention of the court in three ways. The first was through tort claims. In this type of action, the inmate filed suit, usually in state court, against an individual or the system, for negligence (Collins, 2001). The second type of challenge was through habeas corpus appeals in which inmates challenged the legality of their incarcerations (Wallace, 2001; Collins, 2001). The third way inmates sought relief from the court was by filing a claim in federal court stating that their rights under the U.S. Constitution had been violated. Constitutional cases had a more far-reaching effect on correctional practices than did tort cases or habeas corpus' appeals and could be filed on behalf of one individual or by a group of inmates as class action suits.

The success of actions for violation of Constitutional rights was greatly enhanced by, "the courts first modern prisoner's rights case," *Cooper v. Pate*, ruled on by the U.S. Supreme Court in 1964 (Jacobs, 2001, p. 213). In its decision, the Supreme Court for the first time determined that inmates were entitled to bring suit against departments of corrections for alleged violations under Section 1983 of the Civil Rights Act of 1871.

The Civil Rights Act of 1871 was originally intended to protect citizens, particularly slaves freed after the Civil War, and to guarantee that everyone could exercise his or her constitutional rights. The law stated that anyone in the United States who was acting in an official capacity for a state or local government could be held personally liable for damages if it was found that the individual deprived someone of a constitutional right. The application of this statute to prison employees meant that for the first time, they could be made to pay damages to inmates if the courts found they had violated a prisoner's rights and/or could be enjoined or prohibited from doing what the courts ruled to be wrong (Reichel, 2001).

According to Collins (2001), the most important component in Section 1983 actions, especially in the early years, was the ability of the court to issue remedial injunctions for monetary damages. Monetary awards—particularly punitive damages—had a tremendous impact on correctional administrators and made them begin to lobby governors and legislators for the resources to make needed changes.

The *Cooper v. Pate* ruling opened the floodgates for inmate lawsuits. Inmates in state and local facilities began to file thousands of lawsuits each year. Only 218 lawsuits were filed using the Civil Rights Act of 1871 in 1966, but by 1992 the number had increased to some 27,000 (Hanson and Daley, 1995). Male inmates brought almost all of these suits. Women offenders, for a variety of reasons that will be explored later in this chapter, were much less litigious than men (Rafter, 1987).

Although many suits were filed, very few were actually heard. Even in their most "liberal" phase during the 1960s and 1970s, the federal courts carefully scrutinized inmates' suits and dismissed the vast majority of them. Hanson and Daley (1995) found that 74 percent of the cases filed under Section 1983 were dismissed and prisoners were successful in less than half of the 2 percent of cases that actually went to trial.

Prisoners' Rights Addressed

There were, however, a number of serious violations of inmates' rights that were addressed. Much of the positive change in the management and administration of prisons that occurred during the next several years came as a direct result of court orders or the threat of costly court actions (Collins, 2001; Jacobs, 2001). Arkansas was one of the first states to have its entire prison system reviewed under a class action suit. The Arkansas prisons were dramatized in the film *Brubaker*, in which Robert Redford played a crusading director of corrections who tried to reform the system. While the film focused on brutality and violence among male inmates, the suit on which it was based also addressed the plight of women who were kept in a separate building on the

grounds of the Cummins Prison Farm. The women incarcerated there suffered sexual and other abuses under an armed trustee system and had limited
programs or other opportunities to improve themselves. The case resulted in
the Arkansas prison system becoming the first prison system in the nation to
be declared unconstitutional by the federal judiciary. The court held in *Holt v.
Sarver* (1970) that:

> *Imprisonment in Arkansas State Prison System constituted 'cruel and unusual
> punishment' and gave the state two years to correct the situation or release all
> prisoners then incarcerated in the state facilities (*Task Force on Corrections,
> 1973, p. 356*).*

As a result of this court case, many positive changes were made in the
Arkansas system. The ruling resulted in reforms that included building a modern women's institution in Little Rock, hiring a female superintendent, and
staffing it with trained employees, most of whom were women. Under the
able leadership of then Warden Helen Corrothers, it became the first women's
facility in the United States to be accredited by the Commission on Accreditation for Corrections and the American Correctional Association.

By the end of the 1970s, federal courts had addressed problems and ordered
changes in prisons and jails in almost every state in the nation (Clear and Cole,
2000). Beginning in the 1980s, a variety of forces combined to limit the number of cases coming before the courts and the prisoners' rights movement
began to fade (Reichel, 2001).

Constitutional Rights of Prisoners

The rights of inmates are concentrated in four amendments to the U.S.
Constitution. They are the First, Fourth, Eighth, and Fourteenth Amendments. In reviewing these amendments, remember that cases proceeded from
lower courts to higher courts and conflicting decisions can result as cases move
forward. Also, the concept of what constitutes a constitutional right is not
absolute and changes depending on the composition of the courts involved
and the perceived needs of society at large (Clear and Cole, 2000).

The First Amendment

The First Amendment deals with freedom of speech, correspondence, press, assembly, petition, and religion. The courts ruled that inmates had very limited rights to freedom of speech. For example, inmates had no right to receive mail from each other, (*Turner v. Safley*, 1987), but did have the right to receive mail and visits from their attorneys (*Procunier v. Martinez*, 1974). In a series of early rulings, the court specified prison administrators must have a compelling state interest involving a clear and present danger to the safety and security of the institution in order to limit mail and speech (Clear and Cole, 2000). This criterion was used infrequently and was substantially relaxed by the Supreme Court in *Turner v Safley* (Collins, 2001).

Initially, the courts ruled that administrators must use the least-restrictive means possible when they limited inmates' First Amendment rights. However, increasingly in the late 1980s and the 1990s, the courts began to rely on the judgment of prison administrators. In the 1987 *Turner v. Safley* case, for example, Justice O'Connor, writing for the majority, upheld the Missouri ban on correspondence among inmates as "reasonably related to legitimate penological interests." According to Collins (2001), the *Turner* ruling rejected various legal tests that lower courts had been using to evaluate the restriction on constitutionally protected areas such as the freedom of speech and religion. In saying that restrictions in such areas are valid if they are reasonably related to legitimate penological interests such as security and order, the Court adopted an approach that is much easier for prisons to meet than the standards applied by lower courts. The Court also strongly emphasized that in applying the test from the *Turner* case, courts should give substantial deference to the judgment of correctional administrators regarding matters such as security.

Cases involving religious belief were among the first and most vigorously litigated ones under the First Amendment (Collins, 2001). Some of the cases involved religions that are not among the more common ones practiced in the United States. In other instances, inmates formed new "religions" such as the "Church of the New Song" (CONS) that insisted that steak and wine were a part of its religious sacraments. CONS was the subject of much litigation in the 1970s and was eventually refused First Amendment protection.

The Church of Wicca, in which witchcraft is practiced, was found to be a religion by one court and prison officials had to justify any restriction placed on its practice. While administrators were successful in defending the various restrictions they had placed on inmates' worship of the Church of Wicca, this and other cases do point out the difficulties in defining a religion. As Collins (2001) points out, prison staff should not base their judgment about what constitutes a religion based on their own values.

The Fourth Amendment

The Fourth Amendment addresses freedom from unreasonable search and seizure. Here the courts prohibited only unreasonable searches and seizures for civilians, but have been less willing to expand coverage to inmates (Clear and Cole, 2000). Warrantless searches of cells and other areas in the institution were permitted (*Hudson v. Palmer*, 1984). The searching of prisoners, however, particularly if the search was as invasive as a body cavity search, was limited by what was reasonable to maintain security, order, and other activities in the facility (Palmer and Palmer, 1999). Cross-gender supervision of male inmates in restrooms and showers was permissible if it were financially unreasonably to do otherwise or if it reduced the prison's use of sex as an employment criteria which would violate Title VII of the Civil Rights Act as amended in 1973 (*Johnson v. Phelan*, 1995).

Strip searching of all inmates returning from contact visits and by implication, from any activity outside the secure perimeter of the institution was approved in 1979 in *Bell v. Wolfish*. While most inmates find that strip searches are a humiliating experience, female inmates may react more negatively to them than male inmates. Part of the reluctance to be strip searched may be the expectations of privacy that women are taught from childhood. Also, women with histories of abuse may associate strip searches with their abuse experience.

The Eighth Amendment

The Eighth Amendment provides protection against cruel and unusual punishment. The courts based their rulings in this area on whether they thought the treatment of the offender would shock the general public, was unnecessarily cruel, or went beyond legitimate penological goals (Clear and Cole, 2000). If these conditions were found, the practices could be determined to be unconstitutional (*Estelle v Gamble*, 1976). More recently in *Farmer v. Brennan* (1994) the "deliberate indifference" test established in *Estelle* was made more stringent by requiring the offender to show that prison officials knew of the problem and ignored it even when they knew there was a serious risk to an inmate's health or safety. Pollock (2002) suggests that offenders may have to turn to state courts in the future to address challenges in this area.

In some cases, the courts looked at the "totality of conditions" or how the institution as a whole was operated in making their final decision (*Pugh v. Locke*, 1976; *Rhodes v. Chapman*, 1981). As with other areas, the Supreme Court has tightened the legal tests for reviewing both conditions of confinement and use of force under the Eighth Amendment. The "totality of conditions" approach has been largely rejected (*Wilson v. Seiter*, 1991). To violate the Eighth Amendment, excessive force must be malicious and sadistic (*Hudson v. McMillian*, 1992)

The Fourteenth Amendment

The Fourteenth Amendment grants equal protection under the law and due process. The Fourteenth Amendment has been used to ensure institutional disciplinary procedures were applied fairly (*Wolff v. McDonnell*, 1974) and to prohibit racial discrimination in institutional polices and procedures (*Lee v. Washington*, 1968).

The Fourteenth Amendment has been used extensively in suits involving women offenders. According to Rafter (1989), "Equal protection suits of the last fifteen years have used a comparative approach that has enabled women to raise questions about a wide range of conditions they could not have successfully challenged by focusing on women's units alone" (p. 96). By the mid-1990s, however, federal courts became more conservative and began to reject the comparison of women's and men's facilities and the issues of parity became more difficult to pursue (Collins, 1998). A major factor in the declining impact of the courts has been the conservative U.S. Supreme Court, which has been holding the growth of inmate rights in check, if not actually reducing them for close to twenty years (Collins, 1998).

Another factor in the decline in litigation concerning inmates' rights in all areas was the passage of the Prison Litigation Reform Act (PLRA) in 1996. This statute requires inmates to exhaust all administrative remedies before seeking relief in federal courts (Parenti, 2000). According to Collins (1998), the PLRA requires that inmate lawsuits be limited in scope and accepted by the court only after a determination is made that there is not another way to correct the violation. It further stipulates that correctional agencies can appeal court-orders on the grounds that they are too demanding, it narrows the scope of court ordered consent decrees, requiring them to address only specific federal rights violations, and it limits orders of relief to a period of two years (Collins, 1998).

Finally, the PLRA requires that inmates pay the full filing fee, if not when the suit is filed, then through time payments. It appears that attaching a bill of $150 to filing a civil rights lawsuit deters a number of inmates. Filings of Section 1983 cases since the passage of the PLRA have dropped from more than 41,000 per year to less than 26,000. Collins (2004) attributes this unprecedented drop largely to the filing fee.

As the nation entered the twenty-first century, the federal courts appeared to be returning to a modification of the "hands off" doctrine. They once again placed their confidence in the professionalism of correctional administrators and tried to balance "law and administrative discretion" in such a way as to ensure "they may complement each other in providing punishment in the form of safe, secure, humane confinement" (Samaha, 1994, p. 530).

Legal Concerns of Female Offenders

Research has shown that male and female inmates have many of the same legal concerns. However, women also have legal concerns that are specific to their sex and gender. The specific legal issues that women offenders noted were important (Gabel, 1982) included the following:

Good time/credit for time served and child custody and family matters were of most concern to the women in the study. Among women with minor children, child custody and family matters ranked first. Prison programs and services were second. Appeals and disciplinary matters ranked third.

These issues were followed by concerns over warrants and detainers (Gabel, 1982). In a later study, women's concerns about children and family matters transcended all other issues (Kruttschnitt, Gartner, and Miller, 2000).

In the Gabel study, administrators and others responsible for women's prisons were asked to select the legal issues they believed were important to women in prison. With the exception of recognizing that women offenders were concerned with child custody and family matters, the majority of those in charge of women's prisons felt the rest of the legal issues would not be as important to female offenders as they were to males (Gabel, 1982).

The lack of understanding of the legal concerns of women may result from the fact that male inmates traditionally have been the ones filing lawsuits. Aylward and Thomas (1984) compared the suits filed in a male and a female prison of comparable size and found men filed more than three times as many suits as women. When they did file suit, women were successful 77 percent of the time while men were successful only 56 percent of the time (Aylward and Thomas, 1984)

In those instances where women were included in class action suits, their concerns often received little if any attention. For example, a several hundred-page court settlement of a systemwide federal class action suit in the State of South Carolina had less than one half-page devoted to women inmates. The section only noted that women should have a classification system and programs comparable to those provided for men (*Nelson v. Leeke*, 1982).

Given the history of poor treatment, one might expect that women offenders would file more suits than would men. Concerns about crowding, lack of programs and services, limited medical care, disciplinary procedures, and other conditions of confinement, common in women's institutions, have been the flash points for lawsuits in many men's suits (Reichel, 2001). Additionally, women traditionally have more concerns than men about child custody and are subject to more discrimination and harassment based on their sex than are males (Belknap, 2001). Why then have women sought help from the court less often than men have?

Rationale for Less Litigation

Those studying or working with offenders have suggested a number of reasons why women have been less litigious than men (Collins, 1998). Some of the theories relate to women's perception of themselves and how they were socialized or taught to view authority. Still other reasons for the lack of lawsuits by women involve system issues, such as the availability of law libraries and other support. Several of these rationales are discussed below; however, it should be understood that women have wide variations in their behavior, so comments regarding the socialization of women are generalized (Renzetti and Curran, 1989). Also, correctional agencies and facilities within agencies vary greatly, so again, the systems comments are generalized.

Socialization Issues

1. Women are more accepting of authority and question it less often than men. A study by Figgie International (1988) found that, in general, women property offenders had more belief in the legal system and punishment than did men. This may carry over to an acceptance of punishment as a legitimate consequence of their actions, or women may see punishment as a legitimate consequence of the crime they committed. Many women were taught to accept guilt for what goes wrong in their lives and to feel

responsible for insuring harmonious relationships with others (Kerber and De Hart, 1995). For instance, if a little brother gets in trouble, then an older sister might be blamed and punished for failing to supervise her younger sibling. This socialization to accept guilt (Urquhardt and Cullen, 2003) and punishment may make grown women less willing to fight against the system.

2. Historically, women take fewer risks than men and are less willing to take actions that could be seen as going beyond the traditional roles for females. Studies have shown women and girls, in general, were less willing to take risks and engage in crime than were men. Women also have been trained to be less forceful and less physically aggressive than men (Giordano, et al., 1999; Rafter, 1987). Social pressures to conform to society's expectations are ingrained very early in girls' lives. Studies in elementary school found girls were quite outspoken about their aspirations and needs. However, by the time they reached high school, these same girls were much less willing to express their concerns for fear of appearing unfeminine or of being seen as different from their peers (American Association of University Women, 1993). This socialization, to be less outspoken and less aggressive than men, may affect women's willingness to file lawsuits against the system for fear of being singled out as troublemakers.

3. Women inmates have limited education and experience in the world of work and, therefore, do not have the sophistication to seek legal redress for their situation. Women inmates traditionally have had more years in school than male inmates but they typically have low achievement scores and have limited job experience. Gabel (1982) found more educated women and those who held full-time jobs prior to their convictions were more likely to file suit than were those who had limited education and did not hold jobs outside the home.

4. The nature of women's crimes makes them less interested in seeking legal action to resolve their problems. Women who had committed violent offenses, received long sentences, and had limited previous contact with the criminal justice system were the most likely to be legal activists (Gabel, 1982). In reality, the majority of women in prison have committed either a

property crime or a drug offense (Greenfeld and Snell, 1999). Many have had previous brushes with the law or received a short sentence; therefore, they do not fit the profile of those likely to file lawsuits.

System Issues

1. Some in authority do not see women as having legal issues that need redress. As noted earlier, many prison administrators did not view legal issues, except family matters, as important to women offenders. Women in institutions often were viewed paternalistically by the system. As the courts phrased it in *Canterino v. Wilson*, (1983) "restrictions are imposed solely because of gender with the objective of controlling the lives of women in a way unnecessary for male prisoners." These factors may result in overlooking the legal needs of women offenders or providing fewer legal resources for them.

2. Women's facilities are usually smaller and appear to be less restrictive than male institutions, so women may not feel the need to litigate prison conditions. On the surface, women's institutions often appeared to be similar to college campuses and female inmates seemed to be allowed a greater degree of freedom than that afforded in men's facilities (Belknap, 2001). By being smaller than most male institutions, staff and inmates tended to know each other and have more interactions than in a typical male prison. Also, women's institutions traditionally have had less violence than male facilities (Rafter, 1987). These conditions could foster a more caring environment in which women seek to resolve problems without going to the extreme of filing lawsuits.

In reality, researchers and administrators have cited many deficiencies in women's institutions (Morris, 1987; Pollock-Byrne, 1990; Rafter, 1990; Belknap, 1995; Owen and Bloom, 1995; Morton, 1998; U.S. General Accounting Office, 1999). The problems noted have included fewer programs and services, limited jobs, restrictive classification systems, more rules, less freedom of movement, and more stringent discipline than in male facilities. Also, since there was usually only one institution for women in a state, it had a very heterogeneous population that made it difficult to incorporate the full spectrum of services available at a series of male facilities of varying security levels (Rafter, 1987).

Some states, such as Alaska and West Virginia, contracted for women offenders to be housed in other jurisdictions. Others, including the federal government, housed female offenders in remote locations with limited access to public transportation, which gave women the additional burden of being separated from their families, legal counsel, and other support systems (Rafter, 1987). These conditions provided even more legal problems for female offenders and made it difficult for the correctional system to provide equitable services for them.

3. Women have less access to legal assistance and support for legal action than do men. Access to legal assistance and support is critical to successful court action. Studies have found, starting at the beginning of the criminal justice system with arrest, women traditionally have had fewer resources to hire attorneys and, therefore, have less representation in the court process than men have (Rafter, 1987).

Other systemic problems that have prevented women from having effective access to legal resources and personnel include lack of complete law libraries, limited hours that law libraries were open, and few individuals trained to support the process and provide assistance to women seeking legal redress (Gabel, 1982). To pursue legal action, in either state or federal court, is a long and complex process. Even those with some knowledge of the law need access to complete law libraries and assistance to navigate the myriad problems encountered in filing the necessary papers and taking the other steps necessary to be heard (Parenti, 2000). The lack of access and support might well be the primary reason women traditionally have filed so few lawsuits.

Legal Issues and Women Inmates

In recent years, more suits have been filed on behalf of women as they have become more vocal about their conditions of confinement. The following discussion of some of this litigation is designed to provide an overview of the major sources of lawsuits involving women offenders. Unfortunately, as Muraskin (2000) notes that "even when legal action has been deemed successful, there has been no guarantee that compliance as well as implementation has occurred" (p. 225).

Mother/Child Relationships

Until the 1930s, it was common for women's institutions to have nurseries and to permit women inmates, under certain conditions, to keep their babies with them (Hawkes, 1994). In 2002, only a few state correctional systems— including Nebraska, New York, and Washington State—permitted babies to be kept in prison with their mothers. This creates problems for both mothers and children. Since approximately 80 percent of women and girls in prison have on average two to three children each, there are "nearly one-quarter million minor children with mothers in jail or prison" (Kauffman, 2001, p. 62).

As will be discussed later, a number of systems have provided programs for mothers and their children. For example, the Federal Bureau of Prisons contracts for mother-child centers with community organizations. This program allows the transfer of pregnant women who meet the Bureau's security and other criteria to go to community centers until after the birth of their babies. It also provides for women to stay in the centers for a period of time following the birth to enable the new mothers to bond with their babies. However, the court has not mandated this program. In 2003, U.S. Attorney General Ashcroft in a highly publicized crackdown on white collar criminals issued orders that the Bureau of Prison's policy of sending minor offenders directly to community correctional centers would be abolished. Offenders who had more than 150 days to serve were ordered removed from the program (Isikoff, 2003). The impact of this action on female offenders under Bureau supervision has not been determined but the potential for mothers to maintain relationships with their children given the requirement for mandatory prison time for all offenders could be significant. The then-incoming president of the International Community Corrections Association reported that a number of community centers housing federal women offenders and their children were closing because of the ruling (Denise Robinson, Personal Communication, March, 2003).

Courts have not mandated any programs for mothers to maintain contact with their children and legislators have repealed laws in Florida and California that permitted women to keep their babies in prison (Pollock, 2002). In general, courts have held that women inmates have no constitutional right to have their children visit or have their children stay with them in prison. In such cases, the courts weighed what they believed were in the best interests of the child, the legitimate concerns for facility security, and the safe operation of the institution against any interests the mother might have.

The question of a woman's right to breastfeed her baby while incarcerated was examined in two federal court cases. In *Southerland v. Thigpen* (1986), a Mississippi woman, who had been sentenced to five years for the embezzlement of $388.21, brought suit. She asked the court to force the prison system to allow her to continue to breastfeed her child as she had done in the hospital where she had given birth. She sought to keep the baby with her at Parchman Penitentiary or be transferred to a minimum-security institution where she could keep and breastfeed her child. Her desire to breastfeed the baby was reinforced by evidence presented in court that breastfeeding would be in the best interests of the baby because there was an extensive family history of allergies and diabetes which breast-feeding could aid in preventing. The Fifth Circuit denied her request, finding that the state's interest in punishing the woman and concerns for the safety and security of the institution outweighed any interests or rights of the baby to be breastfed.

In *Berrios-Berrios v. Thornburg* (1989) a woman confined in a federal facility sought to breastfeed her child during regular visiting hours and to require the institution to store and deliver her milk to the child's caretaker during nonvisiting hours. The court, in this instance, said the woman did have a right to breastfeed her baby during regular visiting hours and that breastfeeding would be less of a threat to institutional security than allowing women to bottle feed their babies with formula brought in by visitors. The court also ruled that the burden to the institution of storing and delivering the milk outweighed the woman's interest in breastfeeding her baby and that the institution did not have to go beyond letting her breastfeed during visiting hours.

Child Custody and Family Matters

The issues of child custody and related family matters have high priority among women inmates, particularly among those with minor children (Clear and Cole, 2000). Many of the problems in this area constitute civil matters with outside organizations, such as social welfare agencies and family courts (Seymour, 1998), as opposed to constitutional questions involving the facility or its employees.

Unresolved questions of child custody, visitation, and marital status cases can cause women inmates to act out their frustrations in the institution. Lack of meaningful mother-child relationships also can make reentry into the community difficult for the mother and potentially harm the long-term adjustment of her children. Studies have shown that children whose mothers were incarcerated had a greater chance of suffering emotional and physical problems than did children of nonincarcerated women (Johnston, 1995 and 1995a). These problems ranged from fear, guilt, and depression to withdrawal from friends and remaining family, acting out in school, and exhibiting other anti-social behavior (Osborne Association, 1993; Gabel, 1992). As adults, children of incarcerated mothers were five times more likely than their peers to serve time in prison (Women's Prison Association, 1996). However, as noted by Seymour (1998):

> The extent to which these difficulties are tied to factors apart from the incarceration itself—such as poor parenting or the criminal behavior of the parent—has not yet been explained (p. 473).

Specific programs that can help alleviate some of the mother's anxiety and frustration in this area will be discussed in later chapters. However, it is important to note that the presence of legal aid programs in the institution can improve inmate management and give inmates a sense of control over their own lives that is beneficial to their success on release (Alpert and Wiorkowski, 1979; Thomas, 1984). Having such programs may not necessarily result in fewer lawsuits against the system, but they can reduce complaints. In one study, for example, it was found that the presence of a legal aid program or someone in the institution who could provide legal advice and counseling to women inmates resulted in only 13 percent of the issues in this area progressing to the level of a formal legal complaint (Wheeler, Trammel, Thomas, and Findlay, 1989).

In *Lewis v. Casey* (1996), the Supreme Court held that inmates' constitutionally protected right-of-access to the courts extended to challenges to their criminal conviction and to conditions and practices of their confinement (the traditional inmate-rights type of cases). However, the right that creates a duty for institutions to provide some level of assistance did not extend to other areas such as family law. Therefore, while *Lewis* made it easier for institutions generally to restructure their inmate assistance programs (some facilities eliminated their law libraries), *Lewis* clearly ended any constitutional obligation for the institutions to provide any form of assistance for the issues that are of greatest importance to many female offenders (Collins, 2001).

Medical Care

Failure to provide adequate medical care to inmates is a serious matter and can result in two different types of liability. The first type of liability is known as negligence or medical malpractice in which someone fails to give reasonably appropriate medical care to an inmate. In these cases, the governmental unit can be subject to a tort or civil damages claim. In the second type of liability, the inmate alleges a violation of his or her constitutional rights under 42 USC Section 1983. In civil rights cases, the individual employee can be personally liable if it is found that he or she acted with deliberate indifference to an inmate's serious medical need (Federal Bureau of Prisons, 1993). The court also has the power to issue a remedial injunction, requiring various improvements in the medical delivery system.

According to Collins (2001), although the legal burden in malpractice cases is easier for the plaintiff to meet, in general, inmates tend to litigate medical issues more often as civil rights cases for various reasons. Historically, federal courts (where a civil rights action is typically brought) have been seen as more receptive to inmate claims than state courts, where a malpractice claim would be brought. State laws may impose limits on the damages inmates can obtain from a state court or provide immunity protections for correctional employees and agencies that do not exist in federal court. The availability of injunctive relief in a Section 1983 action, which is not available in a malpractice case, also makes the civil rights route more appealing in that the plaintiff is seeking a reform-oriented remedy (Collins, 2001).

Cases can be brought by an individual and can include such things as failing to treat a specific illness or injury or delaying treatment through a conflict between medical and security personnel. For example, deliberate indifference might occur if an inmate dies because a staff member ignores her complaints of an allergic reaction to fire ant bites and does not take her to receive medical treatment. Another example might be if an inmate has a miscarriage because medical personnel did not see her when notified that she was complaining of abdominal cramps in the middle of the night. In addition to individual actions, the entire medical system can be found to be inadequate by the court. These types of cases are common in situations where intake screening is not properly done, when the medical program lacks the needed number of properly trained and licensed staff for the workload, and when medical records are not properly maintained (Collins, 2001). Additional information on medical care for women is contained in later chapters.

The standards for what constitutes deliberate indifference and serious medical need were established in *Estelle v. Gamble*, (1976) and were based on the Eighth Amendment's guarantee that individuals, including inmates, should not be subject to cruel and unusual punishment. To meet the deliberate indifference test, the staff members had to know or should have known there was a problem and refused to treat it (Krantz and Branham, 1991). The "should have known" liability theories were rejected by the Supreme Court in *Farmer v.*

Brennan (1994). Now, "actual knowledge" of a substantial threat of serious harm is required (Collins, 2001). Deliberate indifference also may refer to placing complex barriers or multiple layers of decision-makers between the inmate and medical care (Krantz and Branham, 1991). The medical problem becomes a serious medical need when a physician diagnoses an illness or injury as serious or when it is so obvious even a layperson could recognize that help was needed (*Estelle v. Gamble*, 1976). The issue of adequate medical care for female offenders has received particular attention in relationship to pregnancy and reproductive rights.

Pregnancy

While most women have a normal pregnancy, female offenders can have high-risk pregnancies because of socioeconomic conditions, drugs and other substance abuse, or other problems, such as being HIV positive. Correctional personnel are particularly vulnerable to claims of negligence or gross indifference to medical needs in this sensitive area.

A local jail case illustrates some of the concerns in failing to treat pregnant women or treating them in such a manner as to jeopardize their pregnancy. A woman who was six months pregnant complained of abdominal cramps and bleeding when she was booked into the City of New Orleans jail. She was placed in a holding cell where she continued to ask for help. Five hours later she was given a brief examination during which a staff person, with very limited medical training, looked at her underclothes, found no blood, and returned her to a cell. Twelve hours after her arrest, a nurse saw her and had her transferred to a hospital immediately. The baby was spontaneously aborted minutes after she arrived at the hospital. As she was in shackles, she could not prevent the baby from falling on the floor. The baby died and the sheriff was held liable for failing to transport her in a timely manner. He also was found to have not followed his own written policies that required pregnant women not be admitted to the jail if they were complaining of abdominal cramps (*Calloway v. City of New Orleans*, et al., 1988).

Care must be taken in subjecting pregnant women to routine searches and following other standard security procedures because they might be construed as cruel and unusual punishment when done to a pregnant woman. The federal courts found in the plaintiff's favor after officers conducted two strip searches of a woman suspected of being a drug addict who they thought might be carrying drugs in her vagina. Two female police officers, who were not trained medical personnel, conducted the strip searches an hour apart in a bathroom, forcing the seven-month pregnant woman to bend over and have her vaginal area examined. On the one hand, the court found the officers did have the right to search her because they had made a valid arrest. On the other hand, the court found that the officers had violated the plaintiff's rights in that they caused her unnecessary pain when they forced her to bend over, they were not trained medical personnel, and did not conduct the search in a medical facility (*Guy v. McCauley*, 1974). This is a classic example of a generally valid search being invalidated because of the manner in which the search was conducted (Collins, 2001).

Abortion

Abortion is a serious medical and emotional issue and for some has grave religious connotations (Muraskin, 1993). The U.S. Supreme Court ruled in *Roe v Wade* (1972) that during the first trimester, the state could not limit a woman's decision to terminate her pregnancy. From that period until the fetus became viable, usually twenty-four to twenty-eight weeks, the state could regulate abortions to protect the mother's health. After that point, states could prohibit abortion, except when necessary to protect the mother's life (Muraskin, 1993).

Complicating the issue for corrections is that some state's restrictions on the right to an abortion in certain circumstances have been upheld in court. For example, the federal government and some states prohibit spending public funds to provide abortions (*Harris v. McRae*, 1980; *Webster v. Reproductive Health Services*, 1989). Additionally, while women do have a right to an abortion, personnel cannot force or coerce an inmate into taking this action.

Court cases on women's right to an abortion while incarcerated are limited. One case, *Monmouth County Correctional Institution Inmates v. Lanzaro* (1987) addressed a woman's right to have an abortion and who was responsible to pay for it (Collins and Collins, 1996). In this case, the Monmouth County jail policy denied women access to an abortion unless the jail physician deemed the procedure was medically necessary. If a woman chose to have an abortion, she was required to obtain a court order for her release and have her own funding for the procedure. The court found that the jail policy did violate a women's right to medical care for the reasons summarized below:

> The jail did not have a legitimate penological interest that would justify denying access to abortion under the Fourteenth Amendment.

> The jail's policy did constitute "deliberate indifference to a serious medical need" because if the woman did not have the abortion in a timely manner she would be subject to "tangible harm" (Collins and Collins, 1996, p. 25).

> The jail had a duty to help the plaintiff find funding for the abortion and implied that if none could be found "the jail would have to pay the costs" (Collins and Collins, p. 26).

While other cases have not been as clear on this issue as *Lanzaro*, Collins and Collins (1996) recommend that correctional agencies develop policies that provide access to abortion services. Policies also will need to address diversity issues including the question of personnel whose religious beliefs would make it difficult for them to be involved in any way with the woman's decision to have an abortion. However, to flatly deny incarcerated women access to an abortion "may be difficult to defend" (Collins and Collins, 1996, p 26).

Privacy

Traditionally, correctional administrators have been sensitive to the fact that women are typically acculturated to expect a greater degree of privacy than men and have implemented procedures to aid privacy while not violating security or employment concerns. However, Human Rights Watch staff noted that some states they visited lacked guidelines for men working in women's facilities and in other states guidelines were "routinely violated" (Human Rights Watch, 1996, pp. 30).

While the U.S. Supreme Court has not ruled on the issue of a right to bodily privacy, "many lower courts have recognized this limited right to bodily privacy" (Human Rights Watch, 1996, p. 29). Cross-gender supervision of women inmates is permitted with some limitations. The courts have weighed the privacy interests of women against the security needs of the facility and the equal employment rights of the staff. In some cases, the courts have required that institutional administrators make what are known as reasonable accommodations to provide privacy while at the same time guaranteeing that security needs and employee rights in the institution are met. These accommodations include such things as:

allowing inmates to place screens around toilets

issuing pajamas

permitting inmates to have a curtain closed on their windows during certain periods of the day.

The courts have been more stringent in weighing the privacy needs of women when it comes to searches, particularly of those women who are in arrest status before they are admitted to jail. At issue is not the sex of the individual but the need for the existence of "reasonable suspicion" to justify such searches. This need decreases, or evaporates, when the woman moves from "arrestee" to "inmate" status (*Mary Beth G. v. City of Chicago*, 1983).

In general, the courts have acknowledged the need for searches, but have specified that the facility staff must balance the following:

1. The seriousness of the intrusion. A body cavity search, for example, is more intrusive than a pat-down search.

2. The manner in which the search is conducted. Only a medically trained individual should conduct a body-cavity search. Staff also should consider

whether there are alternative ways the same objective can be accomplished. This might include placing a woman suspected of concealing contraband in her rectum in a dry cell, without a flushing toilet, rather than conducting a body cavity search.

3. The reasons why the search is being conducted. Strip searches following visiting are more justified by security needs than are strip searches when no outside contact has been made. Searches, in the case of an institutional emergency, may be conducted with more latitude than searches done under routine operations.

4. Where the search is conducted. A search in a public place or with members of the opposite sex present is scrutinized more than one conducted in private. Body-cavity searches should be conducted by medical-trained personnel in an examining room, rather than in other areas of the facility.

Searches by male officers, however, have raised questions. The courts almost always have prohibited strip searches of female inmates by male officers (Human Rights Watch, 1996). Even pat-down searches of female inmates were held to be unconstitutional by the Ninth Circuit in *Jordan v. Gardner* in 1993 (Collins, 1998). This decision was based on testimony "that some women who had been physically and emotionally and sexually abused would suffer severe psychological and emotional harm [when] subject to intimate touching by males" (Collins, 1998, p. 82). Given the problems correctional agencies have with allegations of sexual abuse in women's facilities, policies should be in place to limit physical contact between male officers and female inmates (Human Rights Watch, 1996).

More recently, the federal court ruled that male employees' right to work overrode women's need for privacy. However, men's right to work does not mean that the court has abandoned women's right to privacy. In *Galvan v. Carothers* (1997), which involved among other things officers masturbating outside a woman's cell, the court found "that minimal standards of privacy and decency include the right not to be subject to sexual advances, to use the toilet without being observed by members of the opposite sex and to shower without being viewed by members of the opposite sex" (Pollock, 2002, p. 166).

Equity—Parity

Under the Fourteenth Amendment to the U.S. Constitution, equal protection is guaranteed. While not requiring everyone to be treated alike, it does ban the government from discriminating against people if it is "unjustified or malicious" (Reichel, 2001 p. 524). As noted earlier, historically, women in prison have had less opportunity for education, recreation, medical care, and other programs and services than have men. These conditions have led to a number of suits claiming jail and prison administrators were discriminating against women by failing to provide them with equitable treatment (Muraskin, 2000).

The whole issue of parity is complex and reflects the debate about the treatment of women centering on whether there can or should be differences in male and female programs based on sex and gender. In some instances, strict interpretation of what is meant by equality can mean curtailing women's programs. For example, agencies that allow liberal child visitation programs for mothers, such as overnight stays in prison, but do not provide this same benefit for fathers, could be found to have discriminated against males.

Early parity cases gave some hope that equal protection issues would be applied by the courts to women's institutions to help alleviate disparities that existed (Rafter, 1989). In *Barefield v. Leach*, (1974), women in the New Mexico State Penitentiary successfully questioned, among other things, the lack of educational and vocational programs. In its decision the court ruled that what was required was "parity of treatment" (Collins, 1998, p. 45). Five years later, in *Glover v. Johnson* (1979), the courts expanded the concept in a Michigan case to say the Department of Corrections was required "to provide women inmates with treatment and facilities that are substantially equivalent to those provided the men" (Collins, 1998, p. 45).

In 1983, the courts in *Canterino v. Wilson* dismissed the state's argument that facility size and security considerations justified the disparate treatment of women. The Kentucky Department of Corrections was ordered to eliminate the level systems at the women's facility. Under the level system, women were given an increasing number of privileges including phone calls and other program options depending on the time they had served and their behavior. A similar system did not exist at the male prisons. The Department also was required to provide comparable programs for female offenders (Collins, 1998). Where differences did exist, they had to be justified by critical governmental interests and cost was not considered an excuse for limiting services to women inmates (Collins, 1998; Reichel, 2001).

In three more recent cases, Collins (1998) points out that the courts have taken a more conservative stance. In *Klinger v. Department of Corrections* (1994), women inmates alleged that they were receiving fewer programs than men at the Nebraska men's penitentiary. The U.S. Court of Appeals for the Eighth Circuit ruled the women were not similarly situated in regard to the male maximum-security facility, so there was no issue of parity. In a similar case in Iowa, programs for women inmates were compared to those available in several male facilities. The Eighth Circuit still found that the parity issue did not apply. (*Pargo v. Elliot*, 1995)

Finally, in *Women Prisoners of the District of Columbia Department of Corrections v. District of Columbia* (1996), the Court of Appeals reversed the ruling of the lower court saying that women inmates were not similarly situated to men in types of crimes or size of population. Collins (1998) concludes that:

> *The more recent cases, cases of greater impact and power because they come from courts of appeals, check and may stop this momentum [toward successful parity cases]. It is hard to mount successful reform litigation if the court will not support your efforts. This waning strength of the parity concept may return litigation efforts to improve women's prisons to direct attacks on conditions or practices, for example, if medical care is constitutionally deficient, and so forth (p. 59).*

In a case involving federal prisoners, the U.S. District Court for the District of Columbia agreed in *Butler v. Reno* that the Federal Bureau of Prisons was not providing comparable programs for women as it did for similarly situated male inmates. In 1995, the parties agreed in a negotiated settlement "that the Federal Bureau of Prisons would provide comparable, programs, services, and facilities to both female and male inmates who are eligible for placement in minimum security prisons" (Seiter, 2002, p. 420). The order covered staff-to-inmate ratios, work, educational programs, visitation and recreational opportunities, medical care, and space for placement of women in minimum custody facilities. The Federal Bureau of Prisons and some state systems are addressing problems of equity and finding that by applying what is known about female offenders, positive changes can be made in meeting their needs (Seiter, 2002).

Sexual Misconduct

Sexual misconduct is the overall term used to describe: any behavior or act of a sexual nature directed toward an inmate by an employee, volunteer, visitor, or agency representative. This includes acts or attempts to commit such acts including, but not limited to sexual assault, sexual abuse, sexual harassment, sexual contact, conduct of a sexual nature or implication, obscenity and unreasonable invasion of privacy. Sexual misconduct also includes, but is not limited to conversations or correspondence which suggest a romantic or sexual relationship between any inmate and any party mentioned above (National Institute of Corrections, American University, 2000, Section III).

Sexual misconduct with women inmates is illegal in federal institutions and in at least forty-two state facilities (Human Rights Watch, 1996; National Institute of Corrections, 2000). Employees, volunteers, or others authorized to work in the institution, whether male or female, who engage in improper relationships can be dismissed. Those who engage in improper relationships with women under their supervision also can be subject to criminal charges resulting in heavy fines and/or imprisonment. If convicted, the person may be forced to register as a sex offender under Meagan's Law. Civil charges also can be brought and, if found guilty, a staff member can be required to personally pay damages. Agencies also can be found liable for failing to train and properly supervise staff and for not conducting comprehensive background checks prior to hiring.

Several court cases and a scathing report by the Human Rights Watch Women's Rights Project (1996) brought renewed attention to the issue of sexual misconduct in the mid to late 1900s. One of the earliest suits to receive national attention was *Cason v. Seckinger*, originally filed in 1984 and amended in 1985 to include allegations of widespread sexual abuse of inmates at the Georgia Women's Correctional Institution. The courts found that "prior to 1992, officers raped, sexually assaulted, and sexually harassed female prisoners with little regard for legal or institutional constraints" (Human Rights, 1996, p. 127). Based on a federal court order, the Georgia Department of Corrections instituted new policies and procedures, provided staff and inmate training, and took other steps to reduce sexual misconduct. Additionally, several staff members were terminated and/or tried for sexual misconduct. In spite of these actions, the Human Rights Watch group reported in 1996 that problems still existed in Georgia, four other states included in the study, and the District of Columbia.

Two other cases illustrate the pervasive nature of the problem of sexual misconduct in jails and prisons. The U.S. Court of Appeals upheld a $350,000 compensatory damages judgment against the District of Columbia in a sexual misconduct case (*Daskalea v. District of Columbia*, 2000) that involved staff and inmates engaging in nude dancing and sexual abuse (Collins, 2001a). In a 1998 case, a federal judge found that three women who had been housed in a male wing of the federal prison in Dublin, California had been sold to male inmates by correctional staff. The women who were raped and then were beaten when they complained were awarded $500,000 and several staff members were terminated (Parenti, 2000).

There is every indication that sexual misconduct will continue to be a problem in the future. While effective relationships with women inmates will be discussed in later chapters, it should be understood that sexual relationships of any kind with inmates are serious matters and have grave legal and other consequences for those found guilty of participating in them.

Prevention of Legal Problems

Unfortunately, there are no foolproof ways of ensuring that staff will not be sued while working with women offenders (or male offenders for that matter).

However, there are some actions which correctional personnel can take to minimize the likelihood of suits being brought. In the event they are sued, following these guidelines will help them to be in a better position to defend themselves. A number of techniques can be implemented in correctional facilities that will help resolve disputes among inmates and staff without having to resort to legal action.

Inmate-Grievance Procedures

The passage of the Civil Rights of Institutionalized Persons Act (CRIPA) in 1980 encouraged the establishment of inmate grievance procedures. To comply with the Act, facilities had to establish administrative mechanisms to solve inmates' grievances and to have the procedures certified by the U.S. Attorney General. Increasing the need for grievance mechanisms was the passage of the Prisoner Litigation Reform Act of 1996 (PLRA), which requires inmates to exhaust administrative remedies before bringing a case to federal court. PLRA also repealed the portions of CRIPA that required grievance processes met the U.S. Department of Justice standards to be certified to allow the application of an exhaustion rule. The exhaustion rule means, generally speaking, that inmates will have to pursue all administrative remedies or appeals processes available elsewhere before going to federal court (Collins, 2001).

Having a grievance mechanism in place is helpful in the following ways:

1. It can allow correctional administrators and staff to examine a greater variety of complaints and more complex problems than can be addressed in court.

2. It provides for a more thorough exploration of systemic problems that may underlie the case and provide a more creative approach to problem solving than does a formal hearing.

3. It can be far less time-consuming and less expensive than litigation.

4. It can provide for a solution to be developed before the sides have an opportunity to solidify their positions and participate in a divisive court process.

5. The solution found by local parties can be much more flexible and meet everyone's needs better than a resolution imposed by a judge who has less familiarity with the situation.

Inmate-grievance procedures should provide for inmate participation in the process, informal resolution in the early stages of the complaint, and should require specific time frames that must be complied with by all parties. There also should be limits on the types of actions that may be grieved and a given method or level of appeal (Clear and Cole, 2000).

Ombudsman

An ombudsman program provides for an individual not affiliated with the institution to receive and investigate complaints. Once the findings are made, they are reported to the proper authorities and, if necessary, made public. Much of the success of an ombudsman program lies in the way staff and inmates view the investigator. In the most successful cases, the staff and the inmates have respect for the integrity, independence, and skills of the ombudsman and will listen and respond positively to that person's findings, without having to take the case to higher authorities (Clear and Cole, 2000).

Mediation

Mediation involves having a third party serve as a sounding board to hear and resolve disputes. Since mediators are not bound by the same rules as the court, they can ask more in-depth questions and suggest more creative solutions to the problems brought before them. This approach has only been tried in a few states (Clear and Cole, 1990). In South Carolina, where an outside, nonprofit group heard grievances before they went to the commissioner of corrections for final resolution, the process was very positive. The knowledge that an external group would hear a case often was enough to help the parties agree to a solution before involving those outside the system.

Legal Assistance

One of the ongoing problems women offenders have is securing adequate legal assistance. If a woman can obtain legal assistance to resolve her child custody case, for example, she will be less likely to take her frustration out on correctional staff or other inmates. Provisions for legal staff funded by the corrections system is more effective than inmates who serve as jailhouse lawyers (*Johnson v. Avery*, 1969). However, pro bono or voluntary legal assistance often can be found though local bar associations or law schools. Traditionally, women have had less experience with jailhouse lawyers and other legal support groups than have male inmates. Women inmates, however, can be trained to assist other inmates as another way to provide assistance with legal problems.

Accreditation and Standards Compliance

Complying with national standards can help correctional agencies and staff prevent or mitigate inmate lawsuits. Institutional participation in the American Correctional Association standards and accreditation can help to ensure that the facility is complying with the "best" practices (Reichel, 2001).

In the late 1990s, the American Correctional Association began to develop specific gender-responsive standards. Compliance with these standards and the generic accreditation standards, at a minimum, should help ensure that legal issues related to incarcerated women are addressed. In addition to helping check whether facilities are in fact complying with national standards, participation in the American Correctional Association standards implementation and accreditation process will help ensure that the facility can document what has been done to resolve problems.

By participating in accreditation of health services programs, for example, staff not only can be assured that the facility is providing the services that are needed but also can use the documentation to address any complaints that are false or frivolous. This often can lead to the dismissal of suits by the courts. Agencies also can avoid problems by complying with state and federal laws governing health, safety, and matters such as those concerning sexual discrimination and services for individuals with disabilities.

Staff and Litigation

Correctional staff are frequently the focus of inmate lawsuits. They can best avoid personal liability from inmates' complaints by being cognizant of the following issues.

Training

Correctional employees should take advantage of all the educational and training opportunities offered by the facility (Cripe, 1997). Education and training help staff to better understand the environment and know what actions should be taken. For example, if an inmate is injured on the job and the staff members on duty have been trained in the proper procedures and follow them, then they are less likely to be held liable for failing to provide adequate first aid treatment. It is important for all those working in an institution to become familiar with the laws affecting correctional work and it is also helpful for them to find a good mentor to learn how things should be done (Cripe, 1997).

In addition to taking advantage of all training opportunities provided locally and finding others to assist them, staff should become active with state and national associations and organizations concerned with female offender issues. Some state correctional associations sponsor activities related to female offenders. For example, the South Carolina Correctional Association has a multidisciplinary task force on adult and juvenile female offenders that is open to all members of the organization and which provides information, training, and advocacy for girls and women in contact with the justice system. The American Correctional Association and its affiliate, the Association on Programs for

Female Offenders, provide training and information concerning women offenders. The National Institute of Corrections, the Office Juvenile Justice and Delinquency Prevention, and other federal agencies also provide training and have initiatives directed toward improving conditions for female offenders.

Policies

Staff members must know and follow the institution's policies and procedures (Cripe, 1997). For example, suppose the institution has a policy specifying pregnant women will be seen by medical personnel if they complain of feeling ill. If personnel ensure all pregnant women who are complaining of not feeling well are taken to the medical area immediately, then they are less likely to be found liable if something should go wrong with the pregnancy. If the agency has a policy that staff must report possible cases of sexual misconduct and a staff member sees another staff member taking advantage of an inmate and does not report it, she puts her own career as well as the security of the institution in jeopardy.

It is also important to document actions and steps taken to resolve a problem (Cripe, 1997). If an inmate reports that another inmate has abused her, staff immediately should take the steps required in the facility policy to see that her injuries are treated and that appropriate disciplinary action is taken if the assault is substantiated. A supervisor who insures female inmates are strip searched only by female staff in compliance with the facility's policy and documents her actions is protecting herself and the facility. Such documentation will be invaluable if questions are asked or a lawsuit is filed.

Professionalism

Staff always should act professionally and make a "good faith" effort to do what is right. All women inmates should be treated with courtesy, concern, and fairness. Staff should avoid inappropriate liaisons or inappropriate personal relationships with those under their supervision. Acting in "good faith" means thinking through actions and taking those steps necessary to do the job in a manner that would be seen as "reasonable" to someone outside of corrections. Professionalism also involves not allowing personal views and values to govern behavior especially when there is conflict about policies and procedures. Just because someone does not personally believe in or agree with a policy does not mean that he or she necessarily can refuse to follow it.

Summary

Initially, courts practiced the "hands off" doctrine, meaning inmates had limited legal standing or rights in federal courts. Well-publicized abuses in the system, prison disturbances, a more activist Supreme Court, and public concern for civil rights led to the doctrine's abandonment by the courts in the 1960s. While the court in the 1990s took a more conservative view of correctional administrative reviews and the passage of the Prison Litigation Reform Act (PLRA) made it more difficult for inmates to file suit, the courts still remain a force to be acknowledged when dealing with women inmates.

Inmates can bring issues to the court in a variety of ways. Following the ruling that prison employees could be held personally liable if inmates were deprived of their constitutional rights, the courts were flooded with cases primarily from male inmates. Few cases were ever actually heard and most of those that were heard were dismissed.

However, numerous serious violations of inmates' rights were addressed and positive changes occurred as a direct result of court orders or the threat of costly court actions. The most commonly addressed constitutional issues involved the First, Fourth, Eighth, and Fourteenth Amendments. The Fourteenth Amendment has been used extensively in suits involving parity or equality of treatment for female offenders; however, by the mid to late 1990s the federal courts seemed less willing to examine questions of parity.

Research has shown that there is a general misunderstanding on the part of prison officials about what legal concerns female offenders think are important. Women in prison have many of the same legal concerns as men have plus ones that are specifically sex- and gender-related. Crowding, lack of programs and services, limited medical care, capricious disciplinary procedures, stricter rules, child custody issues, discrimination, harassment, and conditions of confinement are some of the issues that could lead women inmates to seek court intervention.

Traditionally, women inmates have been less willing to file suit than their male counterparts. Socialization issues, the unwillingness to take risks or to act outside the traditional roles for women, limited education and experience in the workforce, and the very nature of the crimes women commit make them less interested than men in seeking legal action to resolve their problems.

Strategies such as inmate grievance procedures, ombudsman programs, mediation, legal assistance, standards implementation, and accreditation of the institution can be used to help minimize the likelihood of suits being brought. These actions also can put staff in a better position to defend their actions if they do have to go to court.

The best ways to avoid personal liability are to: (1) take advantage of all educational and training opportunities offered (2) know and follow institutional policies and procedures, and (3) act professionally and in "good faith."

Women and Society:
Perspectives on Sex and Gender

❖ Describe the difference between sex and gender.

❖ Define what stereotyping means.

❖ List characteristics of gender stereotyping.

❖ Discuss the effects stereotyping has on how people are evaluated.

❖ Explain how the concept of one's gender is established.

❖ List the ways concepts of gender influence how society views individuals.

❖ Discuss the interaction of gender on public policy.

❖ Explain the impact of sex and gender on criminality.

❖ Describe how women offenders have been viewed over time and how they have been treated in the corrections system.

Introduction

Working successfully with female offenders requires an understanding of the forces that have an impact on women's lives. There are a number of critical factors including race, age, and social class that shape women's lives. As corrections enters the twenty-first century, however, the role that gender plays in the growth and development of girls and women has received increased emphasis (Bloom and Covington, 1999; Muraskin, 2000, Belknap, 2001).

To develop gender-responsive services for female offenders, it is essential to understand the concept of gender, its impact on society's views of masculinity and femininity, and to view how it governs what is seen as appropriate roles for men and women in today's world. As Zager (2000) notes:

> *Beliefs about gender lie at the heart of conceptualization of female crime. Deeply rooted in culture, preconceptions about the nature of men and women affect all aspects of understanding of female criminality. (p. 88)*

Women in societies around the world are expected to conform to standards and expectations traditionally based on male norms. When women deviate from these norms, then "the conclusion has generally been that something is wrong with the woman" (Gilligan, 1982, p.14).

In reading this chapter, remember the role men and women play in society has evolved over a long period of time and continues to change. Young women in the twenty-first century do not necessarily have the same beliefs and values as their mothers and grandmothers. But public policy, laws, and governmental programs usually change very slowly and may reflect the beliefs and norms of an earlier generation.

Gender roles and expectations are not the same for all women. Women can be viewed in terms of age, class, race, ethnicity, and kinship or family relationships (Lamphere, 2001). While a discussion of all these variables is beyond the scope of this work, some examples of these differences are included and need to be closely analyzed in the development of truly effective gender-responsive programs. To ignore cultural differences will place today's correctional professionals in a similar position as the women reformers at the turn of the last century who wanted to mold female offenders in their own image. Programming for female offenders must start where the individual women are remembering "they are adults who must be active partners in determining their destiny" (Morton, 1998, p.12).

Sex and Gender

Two powerful forces shape men and women. The first of these is sex, which consists of the biological characteristics inherited from one's parents. Examples of biological heritage or characteristics determined by sex include such things as eye color, whether one's hair is straight or curly, the color of one's skin, and the type of reproductive organs the individual has.

The second main force is gender, which is derived from the beliefs and values about masculinity and femininity that are drawn from society. Examples of cultural heritage are dress, behavioral expectations of others, and perceptions of feminine or masculine characteristics. "Thus, gender is not simply a category, attribution, or a role, it is a dynamic process of constructing particular ways of being masculine or feminine (Zatz, 2000, p. 511).

Biological characteristics are often referred to as nature while culturally derived characteristics are considered nurture (Brettell and Sargent, 2001). Do we become who we are because of nature, our genetic, biological, or inherited factors? Or, is our development controlled by what we learn from our environment or culture? In fact, how we develop is a complex interaction of both nature and nurture.

Unger and Cranford (1992) define sex as the "biological differences in genetic composition and reproductive anatomy and function" (p. 17). More simply stated, sex is the combination of physical characteristics that make an individual biologically male or female and is normally determined at conception (Rhode, 1997). Sex-related functions include carrying a fetus to term or producing the sperm necessary to fertilize the egg.

Gender is defined as the attitudes and behaviors society or culture teaches are masculine or feminine. Unger and Cranford (1992) further clarify gender as being "the ways by which societies differentiate between individuals on the basis of sex" (p. 615). Gender is a very important factor in our beliefs about human development, and until recently most preconceptions about women physically, medically, historically, and psychologically were untested, unproven, or untrue (Hales, 1999). Early criminologists and the public, for example, traditionally "pictured female criminals not merely as bad people—equivalent to male criminals, but also as bad women, violators of male-gender prescriptions" (Zager, 2000, p. 88).

While progress has been made in seeing women as individuals, gender inequity remains a serious problem in the United Sates and gender stereotyping crosses all cultures (Rhode, 1997; Hales, 1999). Gender stereotypes are beliefs that classify behavior or other attributes as male or female based on whether individuals are members of a particular group or category. Unger and Cranford (1992) identify seven characteristics of gender stereotyping that are summarized as follows:

Targets of stereotyping are easily identified and are relatively powerless.

What is believed about a group bears little resemblance to the actual characteristic of the group.

Stereotyping ignores information that does not fit preconceptions.

There is a tendency to continue to believe original stereotypical ideas even when there are many examples to the contrary.

The stereotyped group is often compared negatively to the dominant group.

People often do not know they are stereotyping others and will deny their biases.

The tendency is to judge people in stereotyped groups as being alike and to notice very little difference among them (pp. 107-108).

Gender stereotypes impact beliefs about what appropriate roles are for women and men and can lead to gender bias in the criminal justice system. For example, traditionally, men who broke the law were seen as individuals who were acting out natural aggressive tendencies that had gone too far while women committed crime because of unnatural "lust and greed" (Zager, 2000, p. 89).

Beliefs about women's roles in caring for their children and nurturing those around them may result in women who do not conform to this ideal being treated more harshly by the criminal justice system. A woman who abuses her children may be seen as a more serious criminal than a father committing the same offense. Such beliefs become ingrained in the way individuals explain their world and are very difficult to change (Grana, 2002).

Gender stereotypes change over time and may vary among different cultures. For example, in the United States, men traditionally were considered the breadwinners, and women were to stay home and take care of the children. This belief was particularly strong during the Great Depression and following World War II. Now, it is expected that even mothers of young children will work outside the home. Among families who were poor, however, women always have worked outside the home to make ends meet. For example, historically, employment rates of married African-American women were typically higher than the employment rates of married white women (Landry, 2000).

Some beliefs about gender are obvious. Traditionally, baby girls are dressed in pink and baby boys are dressed in blue. Other examples of how gender is important in structuring human identity and social relationships are less obvious. Many people believe that it is acceptable for a woman to cry but that a man should not show his emotions. A man who is incensed is "angry" or "mad," but a woman is "upset" or "hysterical." The latter carries negative overtones of being "out of control," a common stereotype of how women cope with their emotions.

A man who works to get ahead in the business world may be referred to as a go-getter or an assertive goal-oriented man. Because of the influence of gender stereotyping, these references are seen as positive and are considered a legitimate part of masculine behavior. If a woman is equally assertive, she may find herself at odds with traditional views of appropriate feminine behavior and be classified as aggressive, pushy, or bitchy, all of which have negative connotations when applied to women in our society (Rhode, 1997).

Establishing Gender

A number of factors influence how gender concepts are developed and transmitted. Experiences at home and school have a strong impact on beliefs about gender. Other factors include the impact of race, class or socioeconomic status, media, and language. Each of these factors and its influence on gender is discussed below.

Family Influences

Transmission of gender begins at birth with parents and other family members playing an important role in how girls and boys develop and how they see themselves in relationship to their environment (Bernards and O'Neill, 1989). Gender roles in early childhood encompass learning to (1) distinguish between men and women and understand the characteristics of each, (2) develop one's own gender preferences, and (3) comply with society's prescribed gender roles (Weitzman, 1979).

In addition to handling, dressing, and talking to them differently, parents often give children toys based on whether they are girls or boys. Traditionally, girls are given toy stoves, irons, and doll babies; boys are given action toys such as footballs, erector sets, miniature cars, and other toys that are considered masculine. Based on these reinforcements, girls and boys begin to develop gender-based roles or norms for what is considered appropriate behavior and evaluate themselves on how well they match perceived gender norms (Karsten, 1994). While many parents today may not follow these traditional paths, toy manufacturers still gear many of their advertisements toward boys or girls.

Experiments with young babies show they are treated differently depending on whether the people handling them believe them to be male or female (Doyle, 1985). Using the same six-month old child, Will, Self, and Datan (1976) dressed it first as a boy and then as a girl and observed how eleven mothers reacted to it. When the baby was dressed as a girl, the women held it closer, more securely, and smiled at it more often. The "boy" baby was offered a train to play with and the "girl" baby was given a doll. After the observations, all the mothers stated they believed boys and girls should be treated the same. So, in spite of their stated beliefs, the way the child was treated was based on how it was dressed not what sex it actually was.

Many parents still believe boys should be rough and tough and girls should be neat and willing to express their feelings (Karsten, 1994). Similar gender-based treatment occurs over and over in the home as children grow older. It strongly influences how they see the world around them and what they believe is expected of them.

The Role of School

School experiences and teachers are important sources of gender-based expectations, and school is where much of the learning of gender-based roles occurs (Doyle, 1985; American Association of University Women, 1992). Studies of schoolteachers indicate that they do not treat boys and girls the same even when they think they do (Rhode, 1997). Observations of elementary school classes show that boys receive more attention, both positive and negative, than do girls. Boys are called on for answers more often than girls and disciplined more frequently for disruptive behavior than are girls (Hales, 1999). Thus, gender-based expectations are reinforced in the classroom (Doyle, 1985).

Studies in which girls were tracked through elementary and high school showed that they changed dramatically during that period of time (Hales, 1999). In elementary school, girls were self-confident and saw themselves as having unlimited futures with many career options. By high school, the girls were much more reluctant to speak out in class and many had narrowed their career choices to those traditionally thought appropriate for women (American Association of University Women, 1993).

Others found that as girls progress in school, they begin to accept a sub-servient or subordinate position "even when they may possess superior knowledge and expertise." (Reid and Paludi, 1993, p. 196). According to Hales (1999) in a study of more than 3,500 girls and more than 3,100 boys from grades five through twelve, girls were uniformly more likely than boys to be self-critical and self-doubting. Gilligan (1982) calls this sudden change "hitting the wall" and Maniglia (1998) says it means girls realize "that what once was respected and adored no longer is tolerated or accepted" (p.22).

She also points out that some delinquent girls maintain a belief in their own abilities to change their situations that can have both positive and negative con-sequences for them in the criminal justice system. Young girls coming into the justice system will tend to be outspoken and self-confident. If these character-istics persist as the delinquent girl grows older, she is often seen as rude, mouthy, and ungovernable. Intervention programs that build on this self-con-fidence and focus on girls' strengths can help young women channel their behavior toward becoming successful adults.

There is very strong peer pressure in school for girls to conform to gender norms at a time when the influence of friends and others their own age is at its peak. Much of the pressure adolescent girls experience in school has to do with relationships, particularly with young males (Maniglia, 1998). Interac-tions with young males often lead to sexual harassment so severe it interferes with the girls' lives. A 1993 study by the American Association of University Women found that 65 percent of girls surveyed reported being touched, grabbed, or pinched in a sexual way (Maniglia, 1998). Pressure to become sexually active and to have sex can have life-altering consequences. For exam-ple, more than 80 percent of teenage mothers do not finish high school, which increases the "likelihood of involvement in violent crime for teenage girls" (Jarjoura, 2000, p. 129).

Even the way girls feel about school can have an impact on their delinquency. Graham and Bowling (1995) found that girls who disliked school and thought their performance was below average were more likely to commit crimes. These girls do not see themselves as valuable or fitting in with their peer group at school. This can lead to acting out to gain acceptance and behaviors such as fighting, using drugs, having unprotected sexual activity, running away from home, or even minor activities such as skipping school. These activities are apt to bring them into contact with the criminal justice system. Correctional agencies dealing with delinquent girls should maintain close contact with school personnel and work to help the girls resolve their problems with school so they do not become further involved with the justice system.

The Impact of Race and Class

Race and class also can determine views of gender-appropriate roles and behavior. While limited research has been done on the interactions of race, class, and gender in the criminal justice arena, social scientists have studied the interactions of these factors in the community.

Some researchers did not find any differences in gender roles based on race, particularly when the minorities and whites were from the same economic class. Landry (2000), for example, found many similarities between middle class African-American women and white women of the same class. Working class women of all races with minimum wage jobs had similar struggles to survive (Ehrenreich, 2001). Middle class families regardless of race seemed to encourage more flexibility in vocational choice for girls than did working class families. Some researchers, however, found that Asian-American and Hispanic-American families expected girls to be more passive than white families (Reid and Paludi, 1993).

Sociologists point out that minority groups in the United States such as Hispanic Americans, Asian Americans, and African Americans emphasize the value of the extended family and a sense of personal honor. For example, "machismo" or sense of honor has special significance in many

Hispanic-American families. Under this concept, boys and men are given much more freedom than girls and women and are responsible for defending family honor. In return, in the framework of a patriarchal family, girls and women are expected to bow to the wills of their fathers, husbands, or brothers and sacrifice their own desires and aspirations. Women under this system are seen as having limited status and power and are at a "disadvantage in dealing with coercion by men" (Mahay, Laumann, and Michaels, 2001, p. 202).

Increasing evidence shows that African-American girls are encouraged to be more self-sufficient and ambitious than are girls of other races. Studies of African-American families found that girls from working class homes were less constrained in their choice of occupations than girls from other families (Casenave, 1979; Romer and Cherry, 1980). However, their access to a wide range of jobs was limited until the passage of the Civil Rights Act of 1964 (Landry, 2000). As African Americans relocated to cities following World War I and World War II, working class black men expected their wives to find employment outside the home and as middle class African-American women expanded their "rights in society," they fought for a more egalitarian position at home (Landry, 2000. P. 81).

Poor African-American teenage girls in urban ghettos often find themselves pressured to have sex by males seeking to prove their manhood (Mahay, et al., 2001). In spite of this and a number of serious socioeconomic disadvantages, many African-American girls (70 percent) have positive self-images (Hales, 1999). Building on this strength may be one key to working successfully with African-American women in institutions.

Differences that exist among girls based on race and socioeconomic status or class make girls a very heterogeneous group. However, regardless of their differences and socialization, all girls are expected to incorporate certain gender-based norms, values, and behaviors into their lives. In American society, this traditionally has meant that girls are expected to be nurturant, interested in children, have strong verbal skills, be quieter, and be better disciplined than boys (Reid and Paluid, 1993; Rhode, 1997).

The Influence of the Media

Almost all young people and adults are exposed to advertisements, newspapers, magazines, books, radio, and television. The media plays an important part in what Americans expect others to do and provides examples of gender-role models for how people should act (Taylor, 1989; Creidon, 1993). While there has been some movement in the last several years in how girls and women are portrayed in the media, only limited progress has been made. Rhode (1997) found that almost all images received from the media reinforce traditional, often negative or confining, stereotypes about women and girls. She reviewed a sample of popular books, magazines, television shows, particularly soap operas, movies, and advertisements to determine how women and girls were portrayed. If girls were included at all in the media, they frequently were portrayed as cautious, flighty, passive, afraid, and/or victims or sex objects. Even women in the Olympics often were referred to as "girls" or trivialized as sex objects (Rhode, 1997).

Television is one of the most powerful influences in many people's lives. Many children watch television for hours every day and adopt most of the gender stereotypes they see. These roles often portray girls in subjective, passive roles, or present unrealistic female physical attributes that young girls then believe they should possess (Rhode, 1997).

Of equal importance in television and the media in general are the types of girls and women who rarely are seen (Rhode, 1997). Girls and women are almost never portrayed as overweight, poor, disabled, or old unless they are accompanied by a negative stereotype. With noticeable exceptions such as Oprah Winfrey, strong positive role models for African-American and other minority women also are limited. Again, if they are available, too often they are portrayed negatively (Reid, 1979). For example, poor Hispanic and African-American women who committed welfare fraud were much more prevalent in the welfare reform debate than were the mothers of all races who struggle to stretch inadequate benefits and balance part-time, minimum wage jobs with care of their children (Rhode, 1997).

The messages women and girls receive from movies also can reinforce gender stereotypes. The movie Pocahontas and the subsequent plethora of toys based on the movie portrayed *Pocahontas* as a Native-American Barbie instead of a realistic young teenager. Ariel, in The *Little Mermaid*, gives up her voice and talents to walk on land with her prince (Maniglia, 1998). "Sadly enough, this is the very loss of voice which so many young women experience when they realize that outspokenness, a sharp intellect and sensitivity are not things which make them accepted in society, either by men or other women" (Maniglia, 1998, p.25).

Music is another powerful conveyer of gender roles and stereotypes. Much of the music that is popular with young people today negatively portrays women. Rock and rap videos often contain excessive violence, much of which is directed toward young women. Young women are referred to as "bitches" and "whores" and are depicted as deceitful, hedonistic, subservient, dependent, and passive, while young men are viewed as sexually and physically aggressive, adventurous, and betrayed by women (Reid and Paludi, 1993). Bombarded with these images, young children as well as adults begin to believe them and try to live out these fantasies. Just observe the wide variety of clothing that is preferred by even very young girls which is modeled on the risqué outfits worn by stars such as Britany Spears and other teen idols. Even Saturday morning children's television shows feature young girls and boys dancing in sexually suggestive ways that are inappropriate for their age and young watchers then emulate them.

Language, Communication, and Gender

Gender is conveyed through language and the way men and women communicate. Language is composed of symbols that enable individuals to communicate with each other and it "is the vehicle we employ to reach out to one another" (Caroselli, 1990, p. 3). There have been many arguments about language, such as, whether a person who is heading a committee is a chairman or chairperson. While some may see these discussions as trite, Unger and Cranford (1992) point out that an examination of language and use of words plays an important part in helping individuals understand how women and men are viewed in society.

They suggest the way language is used devalues women by referring to them in negative ways. For example, consider what images come to mind when someone is referred to as a "bachelor" compared to the image of an individual who is an "old maid." As noted earlier, while men become "angry," women become "upset" or "emotional." The latter comparison tends to trivialize women's ability to manage conflicts (Gilligan, 1982).

Men and women often communicate differently (Gray, 1992). Kreps (1993) found at least three verbal differences between them: self-disclosure, assertiveness, and interruption. Understanding these differences can aid in effective communication with female offenders.

Self-disclosure

Girls and women tend to communicate based on relationships while men base communication on power and perceptions of hierarchy (Tanner, 1990). In building relationships, women reveal more about their thoughts, feelings, personal information, and reactions than do men (Kreps, 1993). Disclosing information about themselves can make them vulnerable and can contribute to misunderstandings. Men may read a woman's willingness to talk about personal matters as sexual interest and quickly can find themselves involved in a sexual misconduct situation (Kreps, 1993). As Tanner puts it "women speak and hear a language of connection and intimacy, while men speak and hear a language of status and independence" (p. 42).

Assertiveness

Women are taught from childhood to be tactful and verbally nonassertive (Kreps, 1993). Studies indicate that women are more reluctant to speak in a public setting than are men and, when they do, they tend to apologize for their opinion (Tanner, 1990). Phrases such as "this might be wrong but…" and making statements in the form of questions convey weakness and lack of power. Goodwin (1992) in observations of young black children between the ages of six and fourteen found that boys engaged in a project gave each other orders. "Give me that" and "Do it this way." Girls engaged in a similar task made proposals such as "Let's do it this way" or "Let's go over here and try it" instead of giving commands. Others have found this gender difference crosses racial lines and is evident in boys and girls as young as two year of age.

Interruption

Men consistently interrupt women more than women interrupt men (Kreps, 1993). Interrupting another's conversation is a powerful tool of control and dominance. Tolerating interruption puts a person in a less powerful, more submissive position. Tanner (1990) asserts that this happens because men and women have different objectives in conversation. Men strive to take control and expect resistance in doing so. Women show more interest and caring in their conversations but are seen as weak by allowing men to "grab the conversational wheel" (Tanner, 1990, p. 215).

Some men may claim they have to interrupt because women talk too much. In fact, studies comparing women and men with similar educational backgrounds and in the same type of employment show that, particularly in a public setting, men talked more often and longer than did women (Tanner, 1990). Old stereotypes persist however, in spite of evidence to the contrary.

Much of the English language is, in theory, gender neutral. If the sex is not mentioned, however, many assume that both men and women are included. This is often not the case. Much of the social science and medical research that is conducted, for example, is reported without reference to the sex of the persons involved in the experiments (Hales, 1999). In reality, until recently, most research and scientific findings were based on male subjects (Travis, 1992). If the dosage for a particular type of medicine is decided based on what works for an average man, the dosage for the average women may be quite different. In spite of federal guidelines designed to correct underrepresentation of women in medical studies, an analysis of medical journals after the guidelines had been in effect for three years found that only one study contained gender-specific treatment recommendations (*Harvard*, 1997c).

In the criminal justice setting, there is the tendency to assume research on crime and offenders includes both men and women. Belknap (2001) notes that some positive changes are occurring in this area. More college and university curricula include courses on women and crime. Also, significant research has been done in recent years on the treatment of women offenders in the criminal justice system and the differences in management of men and women in corrections. However, much remains to be done. As Carlen (2001) points out "despite the increase in public rhetoric about women's difference, a need still exists for vigorous campaigning about the complexity of the relationship between social and criminal justice for women" (p.64).

It is important to note that when studies focus only on men, the findings cannot be generalized to women. Theories and programs to address criminal behavior among women must be designed and evaluated with gender differences in mind (Morton, 1998; Bloom and Covington, 1999; Belknap, 2001).

Gender and Employment

With the advent of the Industrial Revolution in the United States, women moved into the workforce in ever-increasing numbers (Goldin, 1990). While women made up more than half of the labor force in 2000, a gap between men and women's wages has remained. In recent years, there has been some narrowing of the wage gap primarily tied to declining wages for men as the shift from a manufacturing economy to a service one grew (Grana, 2002). According to the U.S. Census Bureau (1999), the wage gap decreased until 1996 when women made 74 cents for every dollar men made. By 1999, the gap had increased until women made 72 cents for every dollar men made. Pay equity remains an issue in spite of the Fair Labor Standards Act of 1938, The Equal Pay Act of 1963, and the Civil Rights Act of 1964 all of which prohibited discrimination in employment and pay on the basis of sex.

Since the passage of the Civil Rights Act of 1964, employment opportunities for women have increased. Also, the careers and types of jobs open to women have expanded. In spite of these changes, gender still influences how men and women think about themselves and their work. Valian (1998) argues that women are still taught to put their work in second or third place behind being a wife and mother. She and others point out that girls tend to see their success as accruing because of luck or hard work while men see their success resulting from their own skills and abilities.

Employment barriers, pay inequity, and societal expectations for the appropriate roles for women in the workplace have contributed to a high rate of poverty among women, particularly those with small children and no man in the house. "In 1999, 50.3 percent of female heads of households with children under six were impoverished" (Grana, 2002, p.121). Families headed by women had a 27.8 percent poverty rate while only 4.8 percent of married couples were classified as poor. More than 22.5 percent of families headed by white women were below the poverty line while 39.5 percent of African-American, 38.8 percent of Hispanic, and 23.1 percent of Asian/Pacific families headed by women lived in poverty (Grana, 2002).

Most female offenders are poor minority women who are single heads of households and have young children. Many have limited work histories or have worked at dead-end minimum wage jobs. As Ehrenreich (2001) found, it is almost impossible for even a single woman to subsist on $6.00-$7.00 per hour much less prosper. In 1998, for example, the National Coalition of the Homeless found it took an average of $8.89 per hour to "afford a one bedroom apartment" (Ehrenreich, 2001, p.3).

These and other factors related to gender provide challenges for women's reintegration into the community following incarceration. They also highlight the need for vocational training and other programs in the institution that will help women overcome economic and other barriers to success.

Gender and Social Control

According to Pollock (1995), social control "refers to the limits and restrictions on behavior and values experienced by each member of society" (p.5).

Everyone is subjected to the forces of social control. The process of assimilating what is or is not correct behavior begins in early childhood. Much of this early social control is informal and is incorporated from parents and others into an individual's personality as she matures. It includes such things as language, style of dress, and associates. Depending on the culture, it even can include whether someone makes eye contact when speaking to another, shakes hands, or hugs as a form of welcome. Values and moral constructs are learned through this socialization process.

Formal social control mechanisms, however, are more rigid and are governed by both civil and criminal laws (Pollock, 1995). While failure to obey informal social controls can result in estrangement from family and friends, not complying with formal social controls can result in official sanctions or punishments. In the United States, for example, a woman who marries someone her parents do not approve of may not be welcome at family gatherings, but she is not considered a criminal. If, however she leaves her baby at home unattended and it is injured, she can be charged with a crime.

Throughout history, informal and formal social control mechanisms have treated women differently from men, with many of the differences based on gender stereotyping (Grana, 2002). For example, until 1970, some states did not allow women to serve on juries. The reasons varied, from such things, as women should not be exposed to the harsh realities of life, to a woman's role should be in the home not in the courtroom. Women often were believed to be too emotional to judge others' behavior. All of these rationales were based on women having a different gender-based role in society.

At the insistence of the National Organization of Women's Judicial Education Program, more than forty states and nine of the thirteen federal circuits established task forces to study whether gender bias continues in the court system (Muraskin, 2000). The task forces found that gender bias was widespread in issues of "domestic violence, divorce, child custody, sexual harassment and discrimination, occupational and pay range segregation, haphazard commitment to affirmative action and benefit packages for women" (Muraskin, 2000, p. 55).

Many other examples of the negative impact of gender-based social control mechanisms on women can be found. The so-called "protective legislation" passed both before and after World War II was based on gender stereotypes that frequently had negative consequences for women. Women were prohibited from working as bartenders, for example, but were allowed to work in lower paying positions as waitresses. This was based on the belief that bartending was not an appropriate occupation for women (Goldin, 1990).

Until the Federal Equal Credit Act was passed in 1976, a woman's right to obtain loans and credit in her own name was restricted by banks and other businesses in many states. This was done in part because women were seen as frivolous spendthrifts who were not capable of being fiscally stable. There was also a concern that a woman might become pregnant, stop working, and not be able to repay her debt.

One of the most promising changes in gender-based social control has been in the area of education (Grana, 2002). In 1972, when Title IX of the Educational Act was passed, women made up 18 percent of those with undergraduate or graduate degrees. By 2000, more than 50 percent of the undergraduates and masters' level students were female and more than 33 percent of doctoral-level candidates were women (U.S. Department of Education, 2001).

While these data are encouraging and many of the inequities in the treatment of women under formal social control mechanisms have been abolished in recent years, some still remain. Many see the cuts in federal funding for traditional programs used by women and children as proof that policy decisions are still made on the basis of gender. The Personal Responsibility and Work Opportunity Reconciliation Act of 1996 that replaced Aid to Families with Dependent Children (AFDC) has received both positive and negative reviews. Under the new act, more restrictions were placed on those (mostly women) who received benefits to care for their children.

Included in these changes is a one-year limit for vocational education when two years are required for degree completion in most community and technical colleges. This reinforces the lack of adequate education which negatively impacts women's ability to break the bonds of poverty and adequately support themselves and their children (Grana, 2002). Other aspects of the legislation that has an impact on preparing female offenders to reenter the community will be discussed later. It is clear, however, that this legislation was developed and implemented with more attention to short-term savings for federal and state governments than to the gender-based realities of poverty-stricken women and children in the community (Grana, 2002).

Gender and Crime

Crime data indicate that although their numbers are growing, women are ar-rested, convicted, and incarcerated at much lower rates than are men (Gowdy, 1998). In 2003, for example, women constituted only 6.9 percent of the U.S. state and federal prison population, but that number had increased from 6.1 percent in 1995 (Harrison and Karberg).

Several theories have evolved in an attempt to explain the differences between the crime rates of women and men. These theories often reflect beliefs about appropriate behavior for women and their role in society. Early Greek and Roman philosophers and religious leaders developed the concept that woman were the center of virtue and morality (Grana, 2002). These beliefs were strengthened by Darwin's theory of evolution that emphasized the survival of the fittest. Defenders of the theory of patriarchy used Darwin to further the belief that males were superior to females. Based on the concept that men were superior, women's role as mothers was used to deny them access to economic and educational opportunities (Lerner, 1986).

At the same time, women were thought by some to be morally purer than men (Rafter, 1990). The saying, "the hand that rocks the cradle rules the world" reinforces this concept. Women were assigned to two categories, Madonna (good girls, virgins, mothers, sisters, wives) or whore (bad girls, sexually promiscuous, evil women, deviant rule breakers, unscrupulous persons, manipulative individuals, threats to social order and stability) (Feinman, 1980; Merlo and Pollock, 1995). As mothers and the moral arbitrators of society, women were to be placed on pedestals and protected from the harsher side of life. If a woman stepped off the pedestal and committed a crime, she was considered a "fallen" woman beyond any hope of redemption. Men would protect and care for women as long as they conformed to their proper role in life and stayed in their place. Those women who fell from grace were to be severely punished because they had sinned against their true nature.

In reality, few women lived on such an exalted plane and the Madonna/whore dichotomy restricted women's freedom and became the basis for blaming women for crimes committed by men. Women were portrayed as leading boys and men astray. *Cherchez la femme* (search for the woman) was a criminological theory taught as late as the 1970s. It postulated that behind every crime that a man committed was a woman who caused his actions. This and other theories furthered the view that women contributed to their own victimization (Facella, 2000). In other words, if a woman were raped or assaulted by her husband, for example, she got what she deserved. Caesare Lombroso (1895), an early criminologist, concluded:

> *We have seen that the normal woman is naturally less sensitive to pain than man. . . . We also saw that women have many traits in common with children; that they are revengeful, jealous, inclined to vengeance's of a refined cruelty (which) are neutralized by piety, maternity, want of passion, sexual coldness, by weakness and an underdeveloped intelligence. But when a morbid activity of the physical centers intensifies the bad qualities of women, and induces them to seek relief in evil deeds. . . the normal woman must be transformed into a born criminal more terrible than any man (p. 150-152).*

The father of modern psychoanalysis, Sigmund Freud, also taught that women were biologically inferior to men. He expanded this theory to encompass the idea that women were also mentally inferior to men. He postulated that women committed crime because they rejected their "proper" roles in society (Young-Bruehl, 1990).

Freud had his critics. Karen Horney, a prominent psychoanalyst, who was originally a disciple of Freud, later argued against him and his supporters stating that while females and males were physiologically different, they were equal in other ways and that women were not inferior to males (Berger, 1994). Horney understood the ramifications and limitations inherent in projecting women as emotional creatures who could function only on the basis of personal relationships. As she wrote in *The Differences Between the Sexes*, limiting women to the areas of emotions and relationships unfortunately made them "incapable of exercising justice and objectivity. . . . (Thus) women may be industrious and useful but are incapable of producing independent work" (Berger, 1994, p.12).

Criminologists continued to use women's physical and emotional makeup to explain their lower crime rates. Moyer (1992) notes that Otto Pollak, as late as 1950, attributed female criminality to women's deviant biology. Pollak claimed that women committed as much crime as men, but had learned to conceal it as they had learned to fake orgasms during sex. He also believed women manipulated men into committing crime for them (Pollock, 1995).

Others believed women's crime was linked to their social and cultural environment. The thought was that women committed less crime because they feared the social stigma involved in being caught and punished more than did men. Also, since they theoretically were more cloistered and protected from working outside the home, they had less opportunity to commit crimes than did males (Vito and Holmes, 1994).

In 1975, Freda Adler published *Sisters of Crime: The Rise of the New Female Criminal*, which was a major milestone in bringing attention to female criminality. She postulated that if women had full access to the workplace, there would be a rise in crime by women. These women would be a "new breed" of more aggressive, violent women. Adler theorized that if women were given the opportunity to fully participate in society, they would develop the same competitiveness and aggressiveness as men have based on the premise that men and women had the same inherent tendencies (Merlo and Pollock, 1995).

Liberating women from traditional social controls and improving women's economic opportunities would result in changes in women's behavior with their criminal behavior becoming more masculine in nature (Adler, 1975).

Another criminologist, Rita Simon, writing at approximately the same time as Adler, developed a similar theory about the impact of social and economic equality on women's criminal behavior. She proposed that as women gained full participation in the world of work and had access to positions of power and influence, they would commit more crimes because they had opportunities that had not been open to them before (Simon, 1975).

As opposed to Adler, Simon believed that as women became more powerful and socially and economically secure, it would not be necessary for them to commit violent crimes (Merlo and Pollock, 1995). They, however, would commit more property and white-collar crimes, and the amount of female criminality would increase (Simon, 1975). Thus, while both theories predicted female crime would increase, Adler predicted female offenders would become more violent and Simon anticipated women would participate in more white-collar crime.

Subsequent research has shown that patterns of crime among female offenders have remained relatively stable for the last forty years or so. Women arrested between 1960 and 1990 were more likely to be charged with minor property crimes, substance abuse offenses, and petty thefts than were males. In the more violent and lucrative crimes, women were most often charged with serving as accomplices to male partners (Steffensmeier and Allan, 1991).

An analysis of the 1968 Philadelphia birth cohort found adult women were three times less likely to become involved with crime than their male counterparts. However, when race and income levels were considered, women from low socioeconomic levels and those who were nonwhite were almost twice as likely to be involved in crime as women who were not in these categories (Tracy, Wolfgang, and Figlio, 1990). This strengthens the theory that economic

---

status and crime are related but the association is more complex than that one causes the other.

More recent research indicates that the increase in the number of incarcerated women is less related to criminality by women than it is to changes in crime policy (Edwards, 2000). The ratio of violent offenses per 100,000 residents remained stable for men and women between 1993 and 1997 with victims reporting about one violent offense committed by a woman for every seven violent offenses committed by a man (Greenfeld and Snell, 1999).

The major rise in the number of women incarcerated from 1980 to the present is related to changes in drug enforcement policies (Belknap, 2001). The percent of women in state prisons for violent crime fell from 49 percent in 1979 to 28 percent in 1997. Incarceration of women for property crime exhibited a similar decline falling from 37 percent in 1979 to 27 percent in 1997. Drug crime incarcerations at the state level for women during the same period rose from 11 percent in 1979 to 34 percent in 1997 (Edwards, 2000). At the federal level, more than 60 percent of incarcerated women were sentenced for drug offenses, and the percentage of women incarcerated for those crimes continues to rise at the local, state, and federal level (Bloom, Owens, and Covington, 2003).

So, although Adler and Simon's theories have been criticized and did not come to fruition exactly as anticipated, they did stimulate interest in the study of female criminality and the relationships of gender, economic standing, and patriarchy to the types of crimes women commit and the way they are handled by the criminal justice system. Current theories about female criminality are much more complex than earlier ones and attempt to integrate the interaction of gender, poverty, race, class, family, legislation and public policy on female crime. Zager (2000) notes that despite recent research on women and crime, "gender roles probably continue to bias our understanding of female criminality" (p. 90).

Summary

Sex and gender are complex and strong forces in society and in the justice system. Both are subject to considerably different interpretations. Both affect views of men and women and how these perceptions have evolved over time.

Gender is a powerful force in the everyday lives of both men and women. Individuals develop an understanding of gender roles from family members, participation in school, and involvement in other social venues. Race, class, and the media also have an impact on gender roles.

Language and communication patterns differ between men and women and these differences provide another way that gender roles are developed and maintained. Employment choices are influenced by gender and many traditional social control mechanisms are gender based.

There is no general agreement on why women do or do not commit crimes. Some criminologists argue that women become criminals because they are biologically inferior to men and commit crime because of inherited weakness not found in men. Others theorize that women's criminal behavior is related to their environment and the way they were raised, plus the strong lifetime influences of culture and society. No one theory will answer all the questions one might have; however, it is important to continue to search for answers since much of the way female offenders are managed in the criminal justice system is based on beliefs about sex and gender.

Clearly, crime is the result of a complex interaction between nature and nurture. Other forces including access to health care, economic pressures, legislation, poverty, and crime policy also complicate the problem. The bottom line is that women, just as men, commit crimes for a wide variety of reasons. Thus, no one theory can be used to explain all crime, nor can any single approach or response to crime among women be totally successful for everyone. It takes a wide variety of options to address the issues of crime among women. For any strategies to be successful, they must take into account the influences of sex and gender.

Profiling Female Criminality and the Characteristics of Incarcerated Women

Objectives

❖ Identify and discuss major sources of national criminal justice statistics.

❖ Describe types of crimes committed by women.

❖ Compare differences in arrest and incarceration data based on gender.

❖ Describe the general demographic characteristics of incarcerated women in the United States.

❖ Identify specific characteristics that might have an impact on programming and supervision strategies for women offenders.

Introduction

When working with female offenders, it is important to understand their traits and characteristics. This knowledge may help staff anticipate problems before they occur or be better equipped to handle any conflicts that arise between individuals and groups in the facility. It also will help ensure that programs, security, and the physical plant can be modified to meet the risks and needs of the changing incarcerated population. For example, the large influx of women incarcerated for drug-related offenses has necessitated the development of drug treatment programs in women's institutions around the country. Age, race, type of crime, and criminal history are important factors to better understand offenders in the institution. The culture and values of different groups in the institution may have an impact on both supervision and programs. "Recognizing such trends in population changes as they are occurring is a useful skill for all correctional staff" (Michigan, 2000, Unit 6, p. 3).

Fairly frequently someone will say, "Women are becoming more involved in crime than ever before," or they may maintain that, "Female inmates are more dangerous than male inmates." They even may state, "The women in our institution are more dangerous than female inmates ever were in the past." Are these statements based on facts or are they the result of selective perception or misinterpretation of the data on women offenders?

This chapter offers the answers to these questions. We will examine the frequency of crime committed by women and the types of crime women commit. Victimization data will help explain the number of women who are reported as the perpetrators of crime. Arrest data and conviction data document how many women are coming into the criminal justice system. Incarceration data will show the number of women being sent to jail or prison and their most serious crimes. A comparison of arrest and incarceration data for men and women provides a picture of the similarities and differences between them. Finally, a review of the demographic characteristics of incarcerated women and a discussion of the changes in this population provides the basis for the level of supervision and programs that are provided in the institution.

Analyzing crime data by sex can result in public policymakers and correctional staff making better decisions about how to address crime prevention and treatment of women who commit crimes. When sex-specific data are available, they can help us understand women's involvement in crime. For example, women make up 52 percent of the general population in the United States and yet account for only 22 percent of persons arrested (Greenfeld and Snell, 1999). While the number of women coming into the corrections system is rising, women represent about 21 percent of those on probation, 11 percent of those in local jails, and around 6 percent of those incarcerated for one year or more (Greenfeld and Snell, 1999).

Types and Sources of Data

There are in general three types of date available for understanding women offenders. The first are summaries of data from large groups of women that describe overall characteristics (Morash and Schram, 2002). These data can be collected from national, regional, or statewide perspective and are useful in understanding the prevalence of crime among women and the general characteristics of those in prison. Reports of this type of data include *Prison and Jail Inmates at Midyear 2003* collected by the Bureau of Justice Statistics or *Women in Prison* that also is published periodically by the same agency.

The second type of data is that collected from comprehensive interviews with small groups of inmates or case studies conducted on particular issues such as the North Carolina and New York studies on abuse among women inmates in those systems. Information from such research is helpful in understanding offenders in the groups being studied but cannot be generalized to all female offenders (Morash and Schram, 2002).

The third type of data is that contained in the individual woman's case file or institutional record. Group data cannot explain the characteristics and circumstances surrounding a particular inmate who may not be like those described in the larger group. This is why correctional personnel collect and maintain data on each inmate because it enables staff to assess individual risks and needs.

There are several sources of data on the extent of crime in the United States. Two of the most widely used databases are the National Crime Victimization Survey (NCVS) and Uniform Crime Report (UCR) (Miller and Whitehead, 1996). The results of analysis from each of these databases are published periodically by the U.S. Department of Justice. These two reporting systems address different aspects of the crime problem and, therefore, should not be compared.

The National Crime Victimization Survey began in 1972 and is administered annually by the Bureau of Justice Statistics. This report contains estimates of personal and household victimization based on the responses to questions about whether individuals were victims of crime in the previous year.

While there are some problems with survey measures of this type, the National Crime Victimization Survey reports provide very useful information to capture a picture of crime in the United States and the households that are touched by it in a given year (Miller and Whitehead, 1996). The reports also provide information on the characteristics of offenders since victims are asked to recall the age and sex of the offender, any details of a weapon, and the relationship of the victim to the offender. This, in turn, gives some ideas about the public's perception of crime committed by women and the level of fear generated by female criminality.

The Uniform Crime Report is published annually by the Federal Bureau of Investigation. It consists of voluntary reports of the numbers and types of crimes that are reported to the police nationwide and is useful in examining changes in the amount and rate of crime in the United States. Local and state law enforcement agencies submit reports to the Federal Bureau of Investigation that contain the volume and rate of crime handled in their jurisdiction during the previous year. While not all agencies report, it is estimated that approximately 95 percent of the nation's population is covered by the reporting system (Flowers, 1995).

The Uniform Crime Report is one of the best ways to view the extent of crimes reported to police and arrest data. For example, it lists how many women were arrested for any given year and also allows for some general comparisons over several years. The Uniform Crime Report contains what is known as the Crime Index. The Crime Index is made up of the eight violent and property crimes considered the most serious ones committed in the United States. These crimes consist of violent crimes (murder and nonnegligent manslaughter, forcible rape, robbery, and aggravated assault) and property crimes (burglary, larceny-theft, motor vehicle theft, and arson). Non-Index offenses, or the majority of crimes for which individuals across the country are arrested, are also reported in the Uniform Crime Report. The non-Index crimes consist of twenty-one offenses including, for example, prostitution, drug abuse violations, driving under the influence (DUI), fraud, and embezzlement.

Many other sources of data are important in understanding women and crime. The U.S. Department of Justice through the National Institute of Corrections, the National Institute of Justice, and the Bureau of Justice Statistics publish scores of reports each year, many of which are available to corrections practitioners at little or no cost. The National Criminal Justice Reference Service (www.ncjrs.org) and the National Institute of Corrections Information Center (www.nicic.org) websites supply a broad range of information about female offenders. The General Accounting Office from time to time publishes reports on the status of women in institutions. Regional organizations such as the Southern Legislative Conference, which is a part of the Council of State Governments, periodically profile female offender issues in reports they publish.

Correctional agencies that have automated inmate recordkeeping systems also can produce reports that provide a comprehensive overview of the women under the agency's jurisdiction. The Florida Department of Corrections, for example, has reports on the status of women under its jurisdiction available online. Such reports are a valuable starting place for developing a better understanding of differences and similarities among state prison populations in the United States. Correctional staff can use their state's report to identify the general characteristics of the inmates they will be supervising and regularly should review the data regularly to identify changes or other factors that might suggest needed programs or security modifications.

Victimization by Women

While women in the community are frequently the victims of crime, less frequently they are identified as the perpetrators of crime. Based on National Crime Victimization Survey, about 14 percent of all offenders committing violent crimes were reported to be women, with the highest percentage of women perpetrators being in the simple-assault category (Greenfeld and Snell, 1999). Three out of four victims of violent female offenders were women and almost two out of three victims had a prior relationship with the female offender (Greenfeld and Snell, 1999).

Arrest and Conviction of Women

Overall serious crime in the United States is at its lowest level since 1978 (U.S. Federal Bureau of Investigation, 2001). Large cities and suburban areas experienced the greatest drop in reported crime while smaller cities and rural areas experienced slight increases. Among geographic areas of the country, only the Western states experienced an increase in crime. In spite of this overall drop in crime, arrests and convictions of women have increased.

Arrest Data

A total of 9,116,967 people were arrested in 2000. Of these, 2,020,780 or 22 percent were girls or women (U.S. Federal Bureau of Investigation, 2001). Of those females arrested for the most serious crimes listed in the Uniform Crime Report, less than one-fifth were charged with violent crimes.

Of the women arrested for the eight Index Crimes, 72,131 or 18 percent were charged with violent crimes and 323,312 or 82 percent were arrested for property crimes (*see* Table 1). Arrests for larceny-theft accounted for 280,976 of the 395,443 women arrested for Index Crimes (U.S. Federal Bureau of Investigation, 2001).

The majority of women were arrested for non-Index Crimes. Almost 80 percent of all the women taken into custody in 2000 were arrested for non-Index Crimes. Of those arrested for non-Index Crimes, 504,401 were charged with "all other offenses (except traffic)" which is a catchall group for those crimes not otherwise listed. The next two largest groups were the 197,175 women arrested for "other assaults" and the 183,701 charged with "drug abuse violations." Combining drug abuse violations, driving under the influence, liquor laws, and drunkenness, more women (489,491) were arrested for substance abuse violations than were charged with Index Crimes (U.S. Federal Bureau of Investigation, 2001). Four out of ten victims of crime committed by a woman reported believing the woman was under the influence of drugs or alcohol when the crime was committed (Greenfeld and Snell, 1999). These data highlight the relationship of substance abuse with many women's entry into the criminal justice system.

Conviction Data

According to Greenfeld and Snell (1999), more women are being convicted of crimes than in the past. Between 1990 and 1996, felony convictions of women in the United States increased 42 percent. The conviction rate for women increased at two and a half times that of men. By category, between 1990 and 1996, violent crime convictions among women increased 30 percent, felony property crime convictions increased 44 percent, and felony drug convictions increased 37 percent (Greenfeld and Snell, 1999).

The impact of these increases on the criminal justice system varies depending on the initial number of women in a category. For example, dramatic change such as the 119 percent increase in women convicted for rape/sexual

Table 1. Female Arrests by Crime and Age, 2000

Offense Charged	Total all ages	Ages under 15	Ages under 18	Ages 18 and over
Percent distribution*	100.0	7.5	21.4	78.6
Murder and nonnegligent manslaughter	926	14	91	835
Forcible rape	202	21	34	168
Robbery	7,294	500	1,696	5,598
Aggravated assault	63,709	3,902	10,246	53,463
Burglary	25,178	3,183	7,279	17,899
Larceny-theft	280,976	35,303	90,342	190,634
Motor vehicle theft	15,548	1,827	5,620	9,928
Arson	1,610	469	670	940
Violent crime**	72,131	4,437	12,067	60,064
Percent distribution*	100.0	6.2	16.7	83.3
Property crime***	323,312	40,782	103,911	219,401
Percent distribution*	100.0	12.6	32.1	67.9
Crime Index total****	395,443	45,219	115,978	279,465
Percent distribution*	100.0	11.4	29.3	70.7
Other assaults	197,175	20,541	47,870	149,305
Forgery and counterfeiting	27,785	192	1,421	26,364
Fraud	95,906	391	2,094	93,812
Embezzlement	6,293	22	614	5,679
Stolen property; buying, receiving and possessing	13,714	962	2,882	10,832
Vandalism	28,628	4,266	9,352	19,276
Weapons; carrying, possessing, and so forth	8,510	1,156	2,570	5,940
Prostitution and commercialized vice	38,146	73	506	37,640
Sex offenses (except forcible rape and prostitution)	4,516	431	818	3,698
Drug abuse violations	183,701	4,439	19,567	164,134
Gambling	789	15	41	748
Offenses against the family and children	20,444	896	2,172	18,272
Driving under the influence	150,251	112	2,242	148,009
Liquor laws	100,054	4,677	31,899	68,155
Drunkenness	55,485	655	2,829	52,656
Disorderly conduct	96,077	12,970	30,823	65,254
Vagrancy	4,586	143	474	4,112
All other offenses (except traffic)	504,401	22,715	69,283	435,118
Suspicion	725	41	174	551
Curfew and loitering law violations	33,116	10,458	33,116	———
Runaways	55,035	21,748	55,035	———
Total	2,020,780	151,122	431,760	1,589,020

*Because of rounding, the percentages may not add up to the total.
**Violent crimes are offenses of murder, forcible rape, robbery, and aggravated assault.
***Property crimes are offenses of burglary, larceny-theft, motor vehicle theft, and arson.
****Includes arson.
Adapted from Table 40—Arrests—Females by Age, 2000. Uniform Crime Report, 2001, p. 230.

assault between 1990 and 1996 only resulted in the actual number of women offenders increasing from 202 to 442 because the initial number was small. However, a small increase in a crime category where there is already a large number of women can make a considerable impact on the number of women coming into the system. For example, a 44 percent increase in women convicted for property felonies during 1990 to 1996 accounted for more than 21,000 additional women coming into the system.

Women under Correctional Supervision

The number of women under correctional supervision has grown in every component of corrections. Since 1990, the number of women on probation has increased 40 percent; the number in jail grew 60 percent; imprisonment increased 88 percent; and the number on parole increased 80 percent (Greenfeld and Snell, 1999).

Incarcerated Female Populations

Of particular concern to institutional personnel is the fact that between 1980 and 1999, the number of women in federal and state prisons grew by 500 percent (U.S. General Accounting Office, 1999). Greenfeld and Snell (1999) estimate that 11 women out of every 1,000 will be incarcerated at the federal or state level at sometime in their life. Approximately five of every white, thirty-six of every African-American, and fifteen of every Hispanic woman for every 1,000 in each group will be subjected to prison during her life. For males, the numbers are much higher. About 90 out of every 1,000 males will be incarcerated at some point during their lifetime. The estimates are that 44 white, 285 African-American, and 160 Hispanic males for every 1,000 in each group will serve prison time (Greenfeld and Snell, 1999).

Jails

According to the Bureau of Justice Statistics, women made up 11.6 percent of the jail population at midyear 2003 (Harrison and Karberg, 2004). The number of females in jails has grown steadily over the last several years increasing from 19, 077 in 1985 (Gilliard and Beck, 1996) to 82,169 in midyear 2003 (Harrison and Karberg, 2004). Jails house both pretrial and convicted women; however, typically more women are being held awaiting trial than are serving a jail sentence (34,600 pretrial versus 24,700 convicted in 1997) (Gilliard and Beck, 1996).

State and Federal Prisons

By June 2003, the number of women held in state and federal prisons in the United States with sentences of more than one year totaled 100,102 or 6.9 percent of the total of all state and federal incarcerated inmates (Harrison and Karberg, 2004). There has been considerable growth in the number of women incarcerated in state and federal prisons. At year-end 2002, there were 97,491 women incarcerated in state and federal prisons (Harrison and Beck, 2003) compared to only 12,331 women incarcerated in 1980 (Camp and Camp, 2000).

Incarceration of women varies by state and region with some areas placing more female offenders in prison than others. To illustrate this point, Table 2 provides an overview of the incarcerated female population showing the region/state, number of female inmates incarcerated in 1995 and 2002, the change in the percentage between these years, and the incarceration rate per 100,000 U.S. residents.

All state facilities combined held more women than did the Federal Bureau of Prisons. According to more recent statistics than shown in Table 2, the Southern region with 41,559 held the largest number of women while the Northeast region with 9,381 held the smallest number. Texas incarcerated more women than any other state and California was next. Smaller states such as Vermont, Maine, Wyoming, and North and South Dakota held the fewest number of women (Harrison and Beck, 2003).

In 1999, the states of Oklahoma and Texas had the highest incarceration rates of women per 100,000 U.S. residents—more than other states in the

Table 2. Women in State and Federal Correctional Facilities, 1990-2002

	Number of Female Inmates 1990	Number of Female Inmates 2002	Percent Change 1990-2002*	Incarceration Rate 1998**
U.S. Total	44,065	84,427	8.5	57
Federal	5,011	9,186	7.9	5
State	39,054	75,241	8.5	51
Northeast	6,293	9,367	5.1	31
Connecticut	683	1,357	9.0	43
Maine	44	63	4.5	9
Massachusetts***	582	750	3.2	13
New Hampshire	44	116	12.9	19
New Jersey	1,041	1,653	6.0	39
New York	2,691	3,631	3.8	38
Pennsylvania	1,006	1,517	5.3	24
Rhode Island	166	235	4.4	18
Vermont	36	45	2.8	9
Midwest	7,521	13,684	7.8	42
Illinois	1,183	2,646	10.6	43
Indiana***	681	1,198	7.3	39
Iowa	212	491	11.1	33
Kansas	284	523	7.9	39
Michigan***	1,688	2,052	2.5	41
Minnesota	159	288	7.7	12
Missouri	777	1,880	11.7	67
Nebraska	145	254	7.3	28
North Dakota	20	69	16.7	19
Ohio	1,947	2,912	5.2	50
South Dakota	77	202	12.8	54
Wisconsin	348	1,169	——	42
South	15,366	33,345	10.2	65
Alabama	955	1,525	6.0	64
Arkansas	435	696	6.1	52
Delaware	226	440	8.7	51
District of Columbia	606	478	-2.9	173
Florida	2,664	3,526	3.6	45
Georgia	1,243	2,474	9.0	61
Kentucky	479	1,046	10.3	51
Louisiana	775	2,126	13.4	94
Maryland	877	1,140	3.3	39
Mississippi	448	1,213	13.3	77
North Carolina***	945	1,932	9.4	35
Oklahoma	1,071	2,091	8.7	122
South Carolina	1,053	1,412	3.7	63
Tennessee	390	886	10.8	31

	Number of Female Inmates 1990	Number of Female Inmates 2002	Percent Change 1990-2002*	Incarceration Rate 1998**
Texas****	2,196	10,343	——	102
Virginia	927	1,806	8.7	47
West Virginia	76	211	13.6	23
West	9,874	18,845	8.4	58
Alaska	128	302	11.3	54
Arizona	835	1,780	9.9	66
California***	6,502	11,694	7.6	67
Colorado	433	1,070	12.0	53
Hawaii	171	430	12.2	60
Idaho	120	321	13.1	52
Montana	76	248	15.9	56
Nevada	406	743	7.8	85
New Mexico	193	315	6.3	32
Oregon	362	523	4.7	29
Utah	125	270	10.1	25
Washington	435	1,018	11.2	35
Wyoming***	88	131	5.1	55

—— Not calculated because of changes in reporting procedures.

*The average annual percentage increase from 1990 to 2002.

**The number of female prisoners with sentences of more than one year per 100,000 U.S. residents.

***Growth from 1990 to 1998 may be slightly overestimated due to a change in reporting from custody to jurisdiction counts.

****Excludes an unknown number of female inmates in 1990 who were "paper ready" state inmates held in local jails.

Adapted from Allen J. Beck and Christopher J. Mumola. August 1999. "Table 7 Women under the Jurisdiction of State and Federal Correctional Authorities, 1990-1998," Prisoners in 1998, *p.6*

"Prisoners in 2002," p. 5, *Bureau of Justice Statistics Bulletin*, July 2003.

country. Maine and Vermont had single-digit incarceration rates per 100,000 making them the lowest incarcerating states in the nation (Beck and Mumola, 1999).

Comparison of Male and Female Crime

Comparing women with men in the criminal justice system helps to put the crimes for which women are arrested and convicted and the prevalence of their incarceration in perspective. This can be accomplished by reviewing the Uniform Crime Report for arrest data and the Bureau of Justice Statistics data for incarceration information by sex.

Arrest Comparisons

Numbers

The number of males arrested in the United States far exceeds the number of women taken into custody. As illustrated by Table 3, in 2002 men accounted for 77.8 percent of all arrests. Among Index Crimes, they made up 82.6 percent of arrests for violent crimes and 70.1 percent of all property crime arrests. Among all other crimes, the only two areas in which the percentage of women arrested exceeded that of men were in "prostitution and commercialized vice," (62.1 percent female to 37.9 percent male) and "runaways," 58.8 percent female to 41.2 percent male. The only other crimes in which women were arrested in similar numbers to males were in property crime areas such as embezzlement, fraud and forgery/counterfeiting.

Incarceration Comparisons

Incarceration Increases

The number of individuals incarcerated in the United States rose to its highest rate in history in the the twenty-first century. In 1980 there were slightly more than 310,000 persons in state and federal prisons (Camp and Camp, 1996). By 2003, there were more than 1,380,776 inmates in federal and state prisons (Harrison and Karberg, 2004). Of the almost one and a half million people incarcerated, women made up only 6.9 percent of the prison population in state and federal facilities (Harrison and Karberg, 2004).

Table 4 (on page 122) includes the most serious offenses for which men and women were incarcerated in state facilities in 1986 and 1991. As noted, the percent of women incarcerated for violent and property crimes actually decreased during this five-year period. The percentage of men incarcerated in these two categories also declined.

Incarceration for drug offenses for both women and men grew dramatically in the 1990s (U.S. General Accounting Office, 1999). The impact of the intensification of the war on drugs resulted in a higher percentage of women being

Table 3. Total Arrest Distribution by Sex, 2000

Offense Charged	Number of persons arrested (Total)	Number of persons arrested (Male)	Number of persons arrested (Female)	Percent (Male)	Percent (Female)
Total	9,116,967	7,096,187	2,020,780	77.8	22.2
Index Crimes					
Murder and nonnegligent manslaughter	8,709	7,783	926	89.4	10.6
Forcible rape	17,914	17,712	202	98.9	1.1
Robbery	72,320	65,026	7,294	89.9	10.1
Aggravated assault	316,630	252,921	63,709	79.9	20.1
Burglary	189,343	164,165	25,178	86.7	13.3
Larceny-theft	782,082	501,106	280,976	64.1	35.9
Motor vehicle theft	98,697	83,149	15,548	84.2	15.8
Arson	10,675	9,065	1,610	84.9	15.1
Violent crime	415,573	343,442	72,131	82.6	17.4
Property crime	1,080,797	757,485	323,312	70.1	29.9
Crime Index Total	1,496,370	1,100,927	395,443	73.6	26.4
Non-Index Crimes					
Other assaults	858,385	661,210	197,175	77.0	23.0
Forgery and counterfeiting	71,268	43,483	27,785	61.0	39.0
Fraud	213,828	117,922	95,906	55.1	44.9
Embezzlement	12,577	6,284	6,293	50.0	50.0
Stolen property; buying, receiving and possessing	78,685	64,971	13,714	82.6	17.4
Vandalism	184,500	155,872	28,628	84.5	15.5
Weapons; carrying, possessing, and so forth	105,341	96,831	8,510	91.9	8.1
Prostitution and commercialized vice	61,183	23,237	38,146	37.9	62.1
Sex offenses (except forcible rape and prostitution)	61,172	56,656	4,516	92.6	7.4
Drug abuse violations	1,042,334	858,633	183,701	82.4	17.6
Gambling	7,197	6,408	789	89.0	11.0
Offenses against the family and children	91,297	70,853	20,444	77.6	22.4
Driving under the influence	915,931	765,680	150,251	83.6	16.4
Liquor laws	435,672	335,618	100,054	77.0	23.0
Drunkenness	423,310	367,825	55,485	86.9	13.1

Continued on next page

Table 3. Total Arrest Distribution by Sex, 2000 (continued)

Offense Charged	Number of persons arrested (Total)	Number of persons arrested (Male)	Number of persons arrested (Female)	Percent (Male)	Percent (Female)
Disorderly conduct	421,542	325,465	96,077	77.2	22.8
Vagrancy	21,988	17,402	4,586	79.1	20.9
All other offenses (except traffic)	2,411,162	1,906,761	504,401	79.1	20.9
Suspicion	3,704	2,979	725	80.4	19.6
Curfew and loitering law violations	105,683	72,567	33,116	68.7	31.3
Runaways	93,638	38,603	55,035	41.2	58.8

Note: Violent crimes are offenses of murder, forcible rape, robbery, and aggravated assault. Property crimes are offenses of burglary, larceny-theft, motor vehicle theft, and arson.
Adapted from "Table 42. Arrests, by Sex, 2000," Uniform Crime Reports for the U.S. 2001, p. 233.

incarcerated for drug-related offenses. In 1986, 40.7 percent of the women in state prisons were incarcerated for violent crimes, 41.2 percent were sentenced for property offenses, and only 12.0 percent were held for drug offenses.

Five years later, crimes for which women were incarcerated were almost evenly split among violent, property, and drug offenses, with drug offenses being the highest by .5 percent. Incarceration for drug offenses accounted for 55 percent of the increase in the female prison population between 1986 and 1991. While the percentage of men incarcerated for drug offenses rose during this period from 8.4 percent to 20.7 percent, men in 1991 were incarcerated at almost twice the rate for violent crimes and property as they were for drug offenses. If Federal inmates were included, the impact of incarceration of women for drug offenses would be even greater (Snell and Morton, 1994).

Demographic and Socioeconomic Characteristics

While some conclusions may be drawn from examining the types of crimes committed by women and comparing their criminality to that of men, it does not provide a comprehensive profile of the demographic characteristics of the women who are incarcerated. In reviewing the following information on the demographic profile of incarcerated women, it is important to note that the characteristics of female offenders may vary by region and state. The impact of other factors including local crime policy, racial makeup of the population, socioeconomic conditions, and the availability of community resources also may vary by jurisdiction so it is important to conduct agency and facility analysis in addition to developing an understanding of national data.

The data examined are demographic and socioeconomic characteristics that provide descriptive information about groups of offenders. Demographic characteristics include information about sex, age, race, marital status, criminal history, physical and mental health status, educational attainment, and family background. Socioeconomic data contains information about the social and economic status of the individuals.

Demographic and socioeconomic characteristics can be obtained by observing the inmate, interviewing her, testing and examining her, analyzing records that accompanied her from court, and reviewing relevant records concerning the offender that might be available in the community. Most information about an offender is a combination of inmate self-reported data and that obtained through more verifiable sources such as tests and record checks. To increase the accuracy of inmate characteristics, it is always better to have at least two independent sources to verify the validity of the information. Unfortunately, some information is difficult and expensive to verify so it is usually not done.

Awareness of demographic and socioeconomic characteristics of offenders is an important starting place in developing an understanding of the individual and her relationship to other offenders. Combining individual characteristics enables staff to obtain a picture of the groups of female offenders and begin to recognize general problem areas, supervision needs, and program considerations for incarcerated women. It is also important to remember that, for the most part, the majority of women in prison will be returning to the community at some time. Information about the characteristics of incarcerated women will help staff implement strategies that will enhance supervision and improve chances of success upon the woman's release.

Most correctional agencies have reports on the characteristics of the populations under their jurisdiction. Comparison of individual state or facility data

Table 4. Most Serious Offense of State Prison Inmates by Sex, 1986 and 1991

Most serious offense	PERCENT OF PRISON INMATES			
	1986 — Female	1986 — Male	1991 — Female	1991 — Male
All offenses	100%	100%	100%	100%
Violent offenses	40.7	55.2	32.2	47.4
Murder*	13.0	11.2	11.7	10.5
Negligent manslaughter	6.8	3.0	3.4	1.7
Kidnapping	.9	1.7	.4	1.2
Rape	.2	4.5	.4	3.7
Other sexual assault	.9	4.7	1.3	6.2
Robbery	10.6	21.3	7.8	15.2
Assault	7.1	8.1	6.2	8.3
Other violent**	1.2	.8	1.1	.5
Property offenses	41.2	30.5	28.7	24.6
Burglary	5.9	17.0	4.5	12.9
Larceny/theft	14.7	5.6	11.1	4.5
Motor vehicle theft	.5	1.4	.7	2.3
Arson	1.2	.7	1.0	.7
Fraud	17.0	3.2	10.2	2.4
Stolen property	1.6	2.0	1.0	1.4
Other property***	.4	.5	.1	.5
Drug offenses	12.0	8.4	32.8	20.7
Possession	4.0	2.9	11.8	7.3
Trafficking	7.3	5.3	19.8	13.0
Other/unspecified	.7	.2	1.3	.4
Public-order offenses	5.1	5.2	5.7	7.0
Weapons	.9	1.5	.5	1.9
Other public-order****	4.3	3.7	5.1	5.1
Other offenses	.9	.7	.6	.4
Number of inmates	19,761	430,151	38,462	665,719

Note: Excludes an estimated 7,462 inmates in 1991 and 505 inmates in 1986 for whom their offense was unknown. Details may not add to total because of rounding.
*Includes nonnegligent manslaughter.
**Includes blackmail, extortion, hit-and-run driving with bodily injury, child abuse, and criminal endangerment.
***Includes destruction of property, vandalism, hit-and-run driving without bodily injury, trespassing, and possession of burglary tools.
****Includes escape from custody, driving while intoxicated, offenses against morals and decency, and commercialized vice.

Adapted from Tracy Snell and Danielle C. Morton. 1994. "Table 2. *Most Serious Offense of State Prison Inmates, by Sex, 1991* and 1986." *Survey of State Prison Inmates, 1991: Women in Prison,* p. 3.

with the information provided here will enable the identification of any major differences that might have an impact on specific agency programming.

Each demographic and socioeconomic characteristic of incarcerated women has implications for institutional programs and management. In several instances in this section, similarities and differences between incarcerated women and men, where available, are described. The differences between men and women offenders should have a significant impact on the operation and management of women's prisons. Unfortunately, most institutional programming and security practices are based on traditional male models.

Early Study

In 1977, Ruth Glick and Virginia Neto conducted one of the earliest national studies that focused on female offenders. From a sample of women held in jails and prisons in fourteen states, they found most were under thirty-five years of age and more than 50 percent were African-American. The majority of the women were single mothers and 75 percent of them had at least one child. More than half of the women had been on welfare before they were incarcerated and those who worked held low skilled, low-paid clerical or service jobs even though more than 50 percent had graduated from high school. Most of the women surveyed had previous contact with the criminal justice system and one-third had been in juvenile facilities (Glick and Neto, 1977). The female offender profile identified by Glick and Neto has remained relatively constant over a number of years.

Criminal History

Women in prison are less likely than men to have long criminal histories. According to Greenfeld and Snell (1999), some 65 percent of women in state prison had previous convictions compared to 77 percent of men who had prior records. Men were twice as likely to have a juvenile record (38 percent versus 19 percent), and about one in six women and one in three men had both juvenile and adult criminal records (Greenfeld and Snell, 1999).

When women commit a violent offense, they are twice as likely as men to hurt someone close to them—often attacking their victims at home or school (Greenfeld and Snell, 1999). Among those women incarcerated for a violent offense, 62 percent victimized a relative, a friend, or an acquaintance. The majority of men carry out their crimes in areas other than the victim's home or school, and their crimes are more likely than women's to result in serious injury to the victim. Some 40 percent of both men and women are reportedly under the influence of drugs, alcohol, or both when they commit their crime (Greenfeld and Snell, 1999).

Males were more likely to have previous convictions than women. Approximately 43 percent of men compared to 30 percent of women had records of at least three prior convictions (Greenfeld and Snell, 1999). However, more women (one in three) were on probation when they committed offenses that led to their incarceration compared to one in five male inmates (Greenfeld and Snell, 1999).

Differences in criminal-offense histories are reflected in the sentences women and men receive. Women are more likely to receive a shorter sentence than are men except for property offense where their sentences are the same (Greenfeld and Snell, 1999). One-half of incarcerated women have sentences of five years or less, while one-half of the men have sentences of ten years or less. On average, excluding death and life sentences, women's sentences are forty-eight months shorter than are men's. Approximately 7 percent of the women receive sentences of life or death compared to 9 percent of the men (Snell and Morton, 1994).

Age

The average woman in the United States is almost two and one-half years older than is the average man (Greenfeld and Snell, 1999). This is reflected in the prison population where women are on average approximately two years older than incarcerated men. In 1998, only one in eight women in state prisons and one in eleven women in the federal system were under twenty-five years of age. Almost a quarter of the women inmates incarcerated by the Federal Bureau of Prisons were forty-five years of age or older (Greenfeld and Snell, 1999).

The average age of women in prison is likely to continue to increase in the foreseeable future as a result of both the aging of the general population in the United States and increasing sentence lengths. Women's prisons will need to gear-up staff and programming particularly in the health area and modify physical plants to manage an increasing number of women fifty years of age and older (Morton, 1992).

Race

Minority women are incarcerated at a much higher rate per 100,000 than are white women. The rate of black women incarcerated between 1990 and 1998 grew from 117 to 212 per 100,000 while the rate for white women increased from 19 to 34 per 100,000 (Beck and Karberg, 2001). African-American women were six times more likely to be in jail or prison than white women and three times more likely than Hispanic women to be incarcerated (Beck and Karberg, 2001). By mid year 2002, the racial gap was even wider. The incarceration rate for black women had increased to 349 per 100,000 while incarceration of white women increased to 68 per 100,000 (Harrison and Karberg, 2003). Among women in the thirty to thirty-four age group, the incarceration rate of African-American women was an astounding 1,024 per 100,000—five times what it is for white women in the same age group (Harrison and Karberg, 2003). For Hispanic women in this age group, the incarceration rate was 366 per 100,000 and for white women the rate was 213 per 100,000 (Harrison and Karberg, 2003).

Whites made up 41 percent of women in federal and state prison and local jails, African-Americans comprised 39 percent of the incarcerated population although they were only about 15 percent of the citizens in the United States, and Hispanics accounted for 15 percent of incarcerated women (Harrison and Karberg, 2003).

This racial data underscores the need for staff in women's facilities to be particularly sensitive to racial and cultural differences in the prison population. Diligence is needed to prevent discrimination against any individuals or even the appearance of unfairness based on race.

In the federal system, the percentage of white female inmates dropped from 58.7 percent in 1992 (Kline, 1993) to 29 percent in 1998 (Greenfeld and Snell, 1999). Hispanics accounted for one in seven women in state prisons, but they were one in three in the federal system (Greenfeld and Snell, 1999).

The differences between federal and state prisons and local jails may be explained by the types of crimes women are incarcerated for in state and local facilities compared to the reasons they are incarcerated at the federal level. Almost 72 percent of women incarcerated at the federal level were held for drug-related offenses. At the same time the crimes for which women were incarcerated at the state and local levels were almost evenly divided among property (27 percent), drug (34 percent), and violent offenses (28 percent) (Greenfeld and Snell, 1999).

Family History

Women in prison are more likely than women in the general population to grow up in a single parent, often dysfunctional, home. Research has shown that during the time today's female offenders were growing up, some 80 percent of children in the United States lived in two-parent households. In contrast, more than 50 percent of incarcerated women grew up in households without both parents present (Snell and Morton, 1994). According to Snell and Morton (1994), 42 percent of the women in prison grew up in homes with one parent present, usually the mother. Another 16 percent lived with other relatives or in foster care. More than 50 percent of white women but less than 30 percent of African-American women in prison lived in two-parent homes. Among Hispanic women inmates, 40 percent lived in two-parent homes. Almost 17 percent of all women incarcerated lived in foster care or in an institution at some point when they were growing up (Snell and Morton, 1994).

Women in prison are more likely than are men to have at least one family member who has been in prison at some point. According to Snell and Morton (1994), some 47 percent of the women and 37 percent of men had family members who were or had been incarcerated. The family life of many men and women was unstable with 33 percent of the women and 24 percent of the men reporting that parents or guardians abused drugs or alcohol while the inmates were growing up (Snell and Morton, 1994). This supports other studies that found female prisoners "tend to come from dysfunctional families" characterized by "alcoholism, drug addiction, mental illness, erratic use of authority, and desertion" (Pollock, 2002, p. 56).

Marital Status

In 1998, nearly 50 percent of incarcerated women reported they had never married (Greenfeld and Snell, 1999). This compared to 46 percent in 1991 who said they had never married (Snell and Morton, 1994). Approximately 17 percent of the women were married compared to about the same number of men (18 percent). However, more women (6 percent) than men (1.6 percent) had been widowed. About 31 percent of women in prison were either separated or divorced (Snell and Morton, 1994).

Children

The majority of women in prison at all levels have children—many of whom lived with them prior to incarceration and may return to their mother's care upon her release (Pollock, 2001). Seventy percent of women in local jails, 65 percent of women in state facilities, and 59 percent of women in federal prisons have minor children (Greenfeld and Snell, 1999). Conservatively, almost 200,000 children under eighteen have mothers who are incarcerated (Greenfeld and Snell, 1999).

Over 78 percent of women in prison reported having children while 64 percent of the men noted they had children. In addition to more women reporting having children, another significant difference between men and women is where their children live while the parent is incarcerated. Some 90 percent of the male inmates with children reported that their children live with the children's mothers. Only 3 percent to 21 percent of women offenders' children live with their own fathers (Pollock, 2001). Grandparents were the most likely caregivers for children of female offenders, and 3 percent to 38 percent reported their children were in foster care or in another institution (Pollock, 2001). This lack of stability in the lives of children of female offenders makes their mothers' time in prison more difficult for them than having their fathers in prison.

Women tend to stay in touch with their children once incarcerated. Nearly 90 percent of the women compared to 80 percent of the men reported having contact with their children while being incarcerated. Personal contact, however, was decreasing. According to Pollock (2001) only 2 percent of mothers in 1978 reported not having personal visits with their children while by the 1990s more than 50 percent reported they had not had a visit from their children. Belknap (2001) attributes the lack of personal visits between female offenders and their children to the isolated locale of many facilities and institutional visiting policies that might not facilitate visiting. Some 46 percent of the women with minor children reported talking with them by phone at least once a week, 45 percent had contact by mail, and 9 percent had visits once a week (Snell and Morton, 1994).

Education and Work History

The majority of women in prison have a high school degree. In 1998, an estimated 55 percent of women in local jails, 56 percent of those in state prisons, and 73 percent of women in federal prisons had a high school degree (Greenfeld and Snell, 1999). This represents a considerable increase from 1991 when an estimated 23 percent of women incarcerated at the state level had completed their high school education compared to 22 percent of males (Snell and Morton, 1994).

Women are less likely than men to have taken any vocational training prior to coming to prison. Those who did receive vocational training in the community tended to take courses that were considered to be traditional women's work. These included cosmetology, clerical work, and food service. This training does not provide for the comparatively lucrative wages that can be earned in male-centered occupations such as auto mechanic, welder, and electrician. A number of correctional facilities are beginning to offer nontraditional vocational training for women to aid them in overcoming the earnings gap between men and women.

While most female offenders worked full or part time during their adult life, they had less earning power than did men. Almost 40 percent of the women in state prisons reported they were employed full time at their arrest. This compares with almost 60 percent of males who reported they were working full time at their arrest (Greenfeld and Snell, 1999). Most of the jobs held by women were entry level, low skilled with low-pay and limited fringe benefits. More than 37 percent of the women and 28 percent of the men who had been working reported they had income of less than $600 per month prior to their arrest. Two-thirds of the women reported they had never held a job that paid more than $6.50 per hour (Crawford, 1990).

"Nearly 30 percent of the women compared to 8 percent of the males, in prison reported receiving welfare assistance at the time just before the arrest that brought them to prison" (Greenfeld and Snell, 1999, p. 8). The dependence on welfare is particularly significant in working with female offenders since recent legislation limits welfare eligibility for many of them.

Abuse

Studies consistently have found high rates of abuse among incarcerated women. In a national survey, 48 percent of women reported that they had been physically or sexually abused during their lifetime (Greenfeld and Snell, 1999). "Sixty-nine percent of incarcerated women reporting an assault said it had occurred before age eighteen" (Greenfeld and Snell, 1999, p. 8).

Other national surveys reported even higher rates of abuse among incarcerated women. More than 50 percent of the women in Crawford's 1990 study reported they had been physically abused and 36 percent reported sexual abuse. Many reported they had been sexually assaulted multiple times, much of it happening when they were children. It is interesting to note that among a significant proportion of the women, reporting the abuse did not resolve the matter and in some cases made it worse (Crawford, 1990).

Levels of abuse are even higher when clinical interviews are conducted with individual inmates. In a clinical study of women incarcerated in North Carolina's state prisons, more than 80 percent reported they had been physically and/or sexually abused (Jordon, Fairbanks, and Caddell, 1996). In comprehensive interviews with general population inmates at the Bedford Hills facility in New York State, Browne, Miller, and Maguin (1999) found that, taking all forms of violence into consideration, "only 6 percent of the respondents did *not* report experiencing at least one physical or sexual attack during her lifetime" (p. 315).

Drug and Alcohol Use

Drug and alcohol use among women offenders is growing and more women than men in state prisons reported they used drugs before their current offense (40 percent for females to 32 percent for males). About half of the women in state prisons reported using alcohol, drugs, or both at the time they committed their crime (Greenfeld and Snell, 1999). Almost one in three women in state prisons said she committed her crime to obtain money for drugs.

More women reported they used needles to inject illegal drugs than did men—33 percent for females compared to 25 percent for males. Almost 18 percent of the women who used needles indicated they had shared them with others (Snell and Morton, 1994). This practice raises the risk they will contract one or more contagious diseases including HIV/AIDS.

The actual involvement of women in drug use is probably much higher than self-reports would indicate. In a survey of twenty-one metropolitan area jails, among women actually tested for drug use at arrest, 64 percent tested positive (Maguire, Pastore, and Flanagan, 1993). Those who tested positive for drug use were more likely to be charged with nonviolent crimes. Of those arrested for larceny/theft, the most likely crime for which women were charged, 58 percent tested positive for drug use. In the second largest category of crime, drug possession and sale, 79 percent tested positive. Among those arrested for prostitution, the third largest category for arrests of women, 85 percent tested positive. The link between female criminality and drug use is very strong, with research showing women are more likely to be involved in crime if they use drugs (Merlo and Pollock, 1995).

Abuse of alcohol was reported to be slightly less of a problem for women than it was for men. According to Greenfeld and Snell (1999) 25 percent of the incarcerated women reported using alcohol daily compared to 29 percent of the incarcerated men. Twenty-nine percent of incarcerated women reported being under the influence of alcohol when they committed their offense compared to 38 percent of incarcerated men (Greenfeld and Snell, 1999). In the community, women were less likely to have participated in alcohol treatment programs, but once in prison, if given the opportunity, they were about as likely as men were to participate in Alcoholics Anonymous or Al-Anon groups. Among frequent users (at least once a week), women were more likely to seek treatment than were men (Snell and Morton, 1994).

Physical and Mental Health Data

In general, women entering prison have more physical and mental health-related problems than men do in similar age groups (Morton, 1992). Since they have more health problems, they use sick call at a higher rate than do men. It has been estimated that between 7 and 10 percent of men go to sick call daily compared to between 20 to 35 percent of women.

Many women come to prison with little knowledge about their bodies and how to maintain good health. Most of the women have not had regular preventive medical care, good eating habits, or proper exercise, and a large number have abused prescription and/or illegal drugs.

While the number of studies on the medical histories of incarcerated women is limited, those that have been conducted indicate women enter jails and prisons with a multitude of medical problems. One study of women entering jail found 72 percent had at least one medical problem upon admission (Novick, Della-Penna, Schwartz, Remlinger, and Lowenstein, 1977). These included drug addiction (23 percent), psychiatric illness (10 percent), hypertension (10 percent), and respiratory disorders (6.7 percent). While all these illnesses can be serious, hypertension is of major concern because it is a major cause of strokes. Among women in the general population, strokes are the second leading cause of death. Among African-American women, as many as one in four will have hypertension (McGaha, 1987).

Studies by Wishart (1984) and others of women entering the New York City Correctional Institution for Women found the following:

38 percent required drug detoxification

12 percent had abnormal pap tests

7 percent were pregnant

20 percent had a history of venereal disease

Almost 17 percent had history of asthma

9 percent had a history of seizures

7.5 percent had a history of hypertension.

Nationally, more than 6 percent of women admitted to local jails and 5 percent who entered prison in 1998 were pregnant (Greenfeld and Snell, 1999).

Most of the pregnancies of incarcerated women are considered high-risk because of their lifestyles and lack of medical care. They also may lack basic knowledge about pregnancy and childbirth (Epp, 1996).

Also, associated with problem pregnancies among women inmates is the abuse they may have been subjected to prior to their incarceration. Among abused women in the community, there is a strong likelihood (40 - 60 percent) the abuse will increase when they are pregnant (Walker, 1979; Walker 1984). Frequently, the blows will be directed to the abdomen, breasts, and genitals. This battering often leads to obstetrical complications, miscarriages, stillbirths, premature delivery, and low birth weight babies (Dobash and Dobash, 1979). Studies have found women who were abused during pregnancy were significantly more likely to abuse alcohol and illegal drugs and to be depressed than women who were not abused (Campbell, Poland, Waller, and Ager, 1992).

Infectious diseases such as HIV/AIDS, hepatitis and tuberculosis are more of a problem among female offenders than they are among male inmates. At the end of 1997, almost 3.5 percent of women incarcerated at the state level tested HIV positive compared to 2.2 percent of all male inmates who were infected (Greenfeld and Snell, 1999). The percentage of women infected with HIV has increased 69 percent since 1991 while the percentage of infected male inmates decreased by 22 percent. According to Greenfeld and Snell (1999), the HIV-positive female population peaked at 4.3 percent in 1993. In New York more than 10 percent of the women admitted to state prisons tested positive for HIV. Texas had 7 percent, Maryland 15 percent, and North Carolina had 6 percent who tested positive for HIV (Ross and Lawrence, 1998).

Acoca (1998) noted that sexually transmitted diseases including hepatitis B and C and tuberculosis were also problem areas. As many as 54 percent of incoming women in California tested positive for hepatitis C (Acoca, 1998.) Ross and Lawrence (1998) note that more women tested positive for tuberculosis than did men in New York.

Another medical problem among women offenders is cancer. Breast cancer is the leading cause of death among women ages twenty-two to twenty-four years of age and lung cancer is not far behind, particularly among women who smoke and use alcohol (McGaha, 1987). Cervical cancer among young women is on the rise. Among African-Americans, a woman's chances of contracting cervical cancer is twice that of a white woman, and she is three times more likely to die of it than is a white woman (McGaha, 1987).

Diabetes mellitus is another serious medical problem, which is twice as prevalent among women as it is among men and is highest among African-American women (McGaha, 1987). Women who are overweight, have a family history of diabetes, who do not eat a balanced diet, or who do not exercise regularly are more likely to contract diabetes than others who do not have these risk factors.

Older female offenders present another series of health problems (Morton, 1992). Medical problems associated with aging are on the rise in prisons across the nation. The percentage of inmates more than fifty years of age grew to 7 percent of the prison population in 1998 up from 4.9 percent in 1990 (Camp and Camp, 1998). While there are fewer women fifty years of age or older in prison than there are men, women on average live longer. In 2002, there were more than 3,000 women between the age of fifty and fifty-five and more than 1,600 older than fifty-five (American Correctional Association, 2003a).

The average woman today can be expected to live until she is eighty years of age. However, she will suffer more chronic illness than do men of a comparable age. After menopause, for example, women become more likely to develop osteoporosis, a crippling bone disease that affects one out of four older women. The bones degenerate causing them to break which is the underlying cause of broken hips among women, a condition that often can be permanently debilitating.

Among another health problems of postmenopausal women are heart attacks that are the leading cause of death among women in this age group. Women who suffer a heart attack are more likely to die than are men. They do not expect to have heart trouble so they do not seek treatment and subsequently are more likely to die with their first attack. Older women are more likely than are men to suffer from arthritis, hypertension, and incontinence. Also breast and cervical cancer become more prevalent with age.

Alzheimer's disease, a degeneration of the central nervous system, usually begins to manifest itself in later life. The symptoms of Alzheimer's disease include the loss of memory and erratic behavior. It is progressive and although the rate of deterioration varies with the individual, it ultimately results in death.

Many women enter prison with mental illness or develop it while in prison. In one national survey, 24 percent of women in state and federal facilities were categorized as mentally ill compared to 16 percent of men (Ditton, 1999). A study of incarcerated women in North Carolina found that about two-thirds of them had over their lifetime at least one specific psychiatric disorder for which they were tested (Jordon, Fairbanks, and Caddell, 1996). More than 40 percent had at least one disorder in the six months preceding their incarceration, with substance abuse disorders and borderline personality disorders among the most prevalent illnesses. When compared to women in the community, women in prison had a higher incidence of most of the mental disorders measured. One of the reasons proposed for the high number of mental problems was the higher rate of exposure to psychological trauma experienced by incarcerated women. This seemed to be true particularly among those who had been the victims of sexual abuse before ten years of age. The authors of the study concluded that:

> *Many of the behaviors that appear to be related to being arrested and sent to prison, e.g., impulsivity and use of illicit substances, are symptoms that are often associated with exposure to trauma and trauma-related disorders such as post traumatic stress disorders, borderline personality disorders and the substance abuse disorders* (Jordon, et al., 1996, p. 519).

Recidivism

In general, women have lower recidivism rates than do men. Note that prior arrest history is "an important predictor of past prison recidivism" (Greenfeld and Snell, 1999, p. 11). Based on a three-year study of recidivism of more than 100,000 people, 6,400 of whom were women, the researchers found that among the offenders who had been released from eleven state prisons in 1983:

> That the more times a woman had been arrested prior to her first incarceration, the more likely she was to be rearrested during the first three years after release.

> For women with one arrest, only 21 percent were rearrested but among those with four to six prior arrests, the recidivism rate was 47 percent.

> Almost 80 percent of the women with eleven or more prior arrests were rearrested (Greenfeld and Snell, 1999).

Summary

As illustrated by arrest and incarceration data, more women than ever before are becoming involved in criminal activity. In spite of the dramatic increase in the number of women coming into the criminal justice system, they still account for only a very small proportion of those arrested and incarcerated in the United States.

Based on criminal arrest and incarceration data, men are far more likely to be involved in violent crime than are women. In fact, the percentage of women incarcerated for both violent and property crimes decreased over the last several years (U.S. General Accounting Office, 1999). The major increase in arrest and incarceration of women was for drug offenses. More than 33 percent of women incarcerated in state prisons and more than 72 percent of the women in federal custody in 1998 were serving a drug-offense sentence (Greenfeld and Snell, 1999).

Since most jurisdictions have limited placement options for incarcerated women, the rise in the number of women prisoners has resulted in severe crowding in many correctional systems (57 percent overcapacity for women's facilities versus 40 percent overcapacity for male facilities) (U.S. General Accounting Office, 1999). Based on the growth in the number of women in the criminal justice system for drug offenses, the increase in female criminality appears to be more closely related to changes in government enforcement and incarceration policies rather than on any modification of behavior among women in our society.

In general, the demographic characteristics of incarcerated women have stayed relatively constant over the last thirty years and can be summarized as follows:

Incarcerated women average thirty years of age and are more likely to be a minority than white.

They have grown up in a dysfunctional family, and they are not likely to have a spouse to return to upon release.

They will have children who have been displaced by their mother's incarceration and who will likely be living with the children's grandmother.

They have a high school degree but limited vocational training and a spotty work history.

They have been victims of physical and/or sexual abuse often as both children and adults.

They have significant substance abuse problems.

They have multiple medical problems and also may suffer from a mental disorder.

They are most likely to have been convicted of a drug or drug-related offense.

The primary change in the population lies in the crime for which the women are incarcerated. During the last ten to fifteen years, the percentage of women incarcerated for drug or drug-related offenses has risen to equal or exceed the percentage incarcerated for violent or property offenses. As noted in a 1999 Florida Department of Corrections' study of women offenders: "crimes committed by women have not gotten more serious: instead the system is now 'tougher' on all offenses, including those traditionally committed by women" (Bartlett, 1999, p. 2).

An understanding of the national trends for arrest and incarceration of women is important for planning facilities, programs, and services that will be relevant to the correctional populations under supervision. These characteristics may vary in some areas from jurisdiction to jurisdiction and from institution to institution. Also, since correctional staff primarily deal with individuals, it is important to look at how "each woman will be similar in some ways to, and very unique in other ways from the profile" (Michigan, 2000, Unit 6, p. 20).

Functional Operations in a Women's Facility

Objectives

❖ Describe the positive and negative factors in having all the functions of a correctional system in one facility.

❖ Identify and describe thirteen general functional areas in a women's institution.

❖ Explain the role that each of the functional areas plays in the supervision and management of incarcerated women.

❖ Identify and discuss at least two issues that may occur in the implementation of each of the functional areas in a women's facility.

❖ Define the "pains of imprisonment" and how women and men differ in this area.

Introduction

Traditionally, most states have had only one or two facilities for women (American Correctional Association, 2003a). The limited number of facilities for women means existing institutions have to provide all the functions of a typical correctional system (Belknap, 2001). In other words, a women's institution normally contains all the operational functional areas that are present in a total correctional agency, from intake to release. This has both positive and negative effects on the operation of women's institutions.

On the positive side, having all women in one facility in a state means it is possible to track an individual woman throughout her incarceration. From a security or risk-management standpoint, staff can monitor her progress, control her environment, and give her more freedom as the situation warrants. She can be observed in a number of situations and any risk she possesses for the security of the institution or any problems that might threaten her own safety can be identified. Does she tend to act out in certain situations? Is she an escape risk? Is it possible that she may try to hurt herself or someone else? Does she try to manipulate staff in some situations? What inmate games does she play or does she not engage in such behavior?

From a program services or treatment standpoint, having a woman complete her institutional stay in one facility allows staff to get to know her as a person, understand her strengths and weaknesses, and better meet her programmatic needs. Planning for release that begins on admission includes her work assignments, education, counseling/treatment services, prerelease, and other components of her stay, which can be coordinated.

On the negative side, having only one or two facilities for women in a system means sending difficult-to-manage inmates to another facility or separating inmates who committed crimes together into two or more facilities, as is often done with male offenders, may be difficult. It also means women may have fewer opportunities to advance to less secure environments than do men. Women frequently complete their sentences in a higher security level facility than men and have fewer opportunities to adjust to the community prior to release.

Another problem is that many of the facilities housing women were designed for men (Belknap, 2001). According to the Crawford (1990), two-out-of-three facilities housing women in 1990 were designed for men. This can reduce the flexibility needed to house women in small groups according to their security and program needs and creates other challenges in adapting the physical plant. It also can be a costly option if women are kept in a more secure facility than their supervision or risk level requires.

Having one or two facilities makes it difficult to locate the inmate closer to her home. Since most women's facilities are located in rural areas that are not accessible by public transportation, family visits that may be critical to women's future success on release are difficult. Job assignments and program opportunities often are limited in number and type making it difficult to get the breadth of experiences that are available to male inmates and that are needed by incarcerated women (Seiter, 2002). These limitations may be mitigated by a well-trained, compassionate staff who can have a very positive influence on women during their stay and may make the difference in their success on release.

In this chapter, we will review standard operational components of women's facilities and the role each plays in providing for the safe, effective, humane operation of the institution. Facilities may have different names for these components and may have some activities that are not included here. Staff may recognize the components in their facility that are referred to as something different, but which have similar functions as the ones described here. Also, they may identify functional areas in their facilities that are not described here and should analyze how they fit into the operation of the institution. This will enable them to have a complete picture of the total facility operation. Even though staff members may work in only one area, it is important for them to see how their jobs fit with those of others in the facility. Several of the topics included in this chapter are discussed in more depth in subsequent chapters. The purpose of the brief discussions included here is to provide an overall picture of the major functional areas in a women's institution.

Functional Areas

Intake

Purpose

Correctional facility personnel have no control over how many women are sent to the facility nor do they control the length of the inmates' sentences. They are responsible, however, to ensure they legally confine the right person for the right amount of time, and this process begins with intake.

Almost every facility has a way to process inmates into the system and a location in which this activity can occur. It may be called "reception and evaluation unit," "intake unit," "initial assessment area," "diagnostic or classification unit," or have some other designation describing the function of this component. The purpose of the intake process is to make certain that women are "not placed in a more restrictive custody setting than necessary to ensure their continued safe . . . confinement" (Henderson, Rauch, and Phillips, 1997, p. 15) and transition the women from free world citizens into inmates. While this may sound harsh to some, any organization—whether hospital, school, or business—has a mechanism to incorporate individuals into the whole. In the process, people lose some of their individuality and freedom. In a prison setting, such a transition can be quite traumatic and sometimes makes it very difficult for the person to adjust to the free world when she is released from the institution.

Several important things must occur in the initial intake process. The staff must make certain they have the right individual and that they have the legal obligation to confine her. The officers who transport the woman will normally have the appropriate paperwork with them, but it must be checked to ensure it is accurate. There should be an official record from the court or other committing official that indicates why the woman is being confined and how long her maximum stay will be. In some instances, the judge may order specific conditions or treatment that must be provided for a particular inmate. Failure to comply with a court order can place correctional system administrators in contempt of court. If the woman has been in a comprehensive local jail, there may be some initial medical records from the jail-intake process and documentation of her behavior while at that facility.

In some instances, a presentence investigation (PSI) report may accompany the woman. This report is normally completed by probation personnel in the community for the judge to use in sentencing, but it can become the basis for beginning the institutional evaluation. The Federal Bureau of Prisons uses a post-sentencing investigation report if a PSI is not available (Seiter, 2002).

For the safety of all in the facility, staff must determine if the incoming inmate has any contagious diseases, is on prescription medicine, or has other mental or physical problem that might cause her to be a threat to herself or to others in the institution. This means there will be an initial interview with the woman, sometimes referred to as "triage" taken from the hospital emergency room procedure to determine who needs care the most and who can wait. Any immediate problems the woman may have at this point should be brought to the attention of the appropriate staff.

The inmate will be strip-searched (this process will be discussed in more detail later), required to take a shower, and be deloused. This ensures that she is clean and does not bring any body lice or other vermin into the facility.

She will be issued institutional clothing and all the clothing she has brought with her will be taken and either returned to her family, usually at her expense, or disposed of in compliance with state law or departmental policy. She may be allowed to keep a few personal possessions such as pictures of her children, but usually belongings are severely limited until staff can have a complete overview of her security and treatment needs.

When this process is completed, she will be given a brief orientation to the facility and assigned a bed usually in a single cell if one is available. Normally, women on intake or reception status are kept separate from the general population. This is done to protect the security of the facility since a thorough evaluation of the new inmate has not been completed. It also protects the new inmates from getting information about the institution from other inmates instead of staff and can help ensure inmates do not get erroneous information about the facility.

Following this initial reception process, the women normally go through an assessment or diagnostic phase. This activity usually includes a complete physical examination by a medical professional. Additionally, an employee specializing in the intake process will conduct an in-depth interview. The specialist will go through a series of questions designed to elicit everything about the woman from her criminal history to her personal background. The list of questions usually covers such things as martial status, number and placement of children (if the instrument is gender responsive), mental health background including suicide attempts, and other data relevant to learning as much about the inmate as possible. Staff will start a permanent record that will allow the inmate to be monitored throughout her stay. If she has been incarcerated in the same system before, her new record may be added to her previous one. She also will undergo a number of individual or group tests for intelligence level, educational functioning, and personality analysis. Given the high level of stress women experience during this period, staff must take care in the interpretation of test results.

Often, the initial assessment will include an appraisal of behavioral and social functioning. Staff may be asked to observe the interaction of the new inmate with others in the unit and then report these observations. The woman should be referred to the appropriate staff person for further testing or treatment if any problems are identified by the medical, psychological, educational, and other tests, or from observation.

Staff analyze the intake information and observation reports so they can make a series of classification decisions and design a security and treatment plan that will affect every aspect of the woman's life in the institution. The woman's custody level and security supervision requirements will be determined based on the type of crime she committed, the length of her sentence, previous criminal history, and other assessments of the risk she represents. Mental health or behavioral counseling, educational or vocational training, or other assignments will be made to meet the treatment or program needs identified in the initial assessment. The woman is then assigned to a housing unit and if she is able to work, she will be given a job. She should be provided an in-depth orientation to the institutional rules and regulations and any available programs or services. She should be provided a copy of the institution's rules and regulations (inmate manual or handbook). Non-English speaking inmates should provided a manual in their own language, and women who are illiterate should have the rules read to them over a period of time starting with the most important ones.

Issues

Research has shown the process of becoming an inmate is more than just losing one's freedom. Both men and women suffer from the loss of freedom and rejection by society, or the "pains of imprisonment," in different ways. While institutionalization is difficult for men, it is particularly painful for women and they respond in different ways (Michigan, 2000). It is important to notice the differences in areas of concern and the different order or priority men and women place on them. These variances will have an impact on the way male and female inmates do their time and the subcultures or internal social structures they build while in prison.

Men report being bothered by:

lack of freedom to make their own decisions and loss of status in their community

loss of material possessions

loss of normal sexual relationships with the opposite sex

having to follow someone else's rules

fears about their personal safety (Ward and Kassenbaum, 1965).

Women, report the most difficult things about prison for them are the following items:

the loss of family, particularly children

being forced to interact with people they do not want to deal with—both other inmates and staff

loss of social life, friends, and normal social interaction

loss of privacy

having to conform to rules made by others that they often see as petty or not warranted (Ward and Kassenbaum, 1965).

Of all these issues, Kruttschnitt, Gartner, and Miller (2000) found that "absence from children and family was uniformly defined by women as the hardest part of doing time" (p. 711).

Institutionalized men tend to concentrate more on issues of power, prestige, dominance, and fear. These concerns often lead to the formation of gangs that hustle goods and services and protect their members from real or imagined enemies.

Women's concerns appear focused on personal relationships. In the facility, these relationships often lead to the formation of "families" and close friendships (Owen, 1998). These relationships may be positive or they may lead to the development of jealousies or one-on-one hostilities.

Their views about rules and regulations may lead women inmates to question staff actions and almost every aspect of their incarceration. While this can become very annoying, it is important for staff to remain calm, objective, and be prepared to respond appropriately. Giving answers to questions can help defuse everyone's frustrations and make managing the inmate population a lot easier.

There may be several women going through initial intake at the same time or there may be only one woman involved. Whether there is one or several, the process is traumatic for incoming women. Even if they have spent a long time in a local facility or have been institutionalized before, women never become used to the invasion of privacy entailed in a strip search, supervised shower, and delousing. If this is a woman's first time in a prison, intake can be particularly distasteful. If she has been a victim of physical or sexual abuse, the strip search process can bring back the feelings of helplessness and anger that the initial assault engendered (Farkas and Rand, 1999).

The saying "clothes make a woman" has some basis in fact. Taking away a woman's clothes and the many items such as creams, sprays, makeup, and other items that she uses to maintain her appearance robs her of her individuality. Goffman (1961) calls this depriving people of their "identity kits." This is why you often will observe, even in a facility with a strict policy on uniforms, that women will manage to make themselves look as different from each other as they can. Her possessions, no matter how few, are her lifeline to the free world, and she will not want to part with them. It is important for staff to understand what the woman may be feeling during this process. The loss of the tools to maintain personal appearance also may result in a loss of self-esteem, confidence, and, in effect, a sense of self (Michigan, 2000).

Whether it is a military organization, a hospital, or prisons, one of the reasons uniforms are introduced in an institutional setting and possessions are taken away is to strip the person of her individuality and to make clear who is in charge. Staff members might remember the way they felt in the hospital, the military, or in other regimented program in which they were stripped of their clothes and other possessions. This will give them some understanding of how the new inmate feels.

Since these feelings are not helpful to women's positive adjustment in the facility, some institutional administrators are reexamining policies that strip women of makeup and other possessions that do not threaten the security of the facility. A number of institutions allow women to keep specific clothing, pictures, or other items as long as they do not jeopardize the safety and security of the facility. Some institutions may allow women to wear their own clothes, particularly in lower security levels. Such policies, particularly when related to clothing, can save taxpayer money by eliminating the need for the state to buy or make the women's clothing. When uniforms are required, they should be designed to fit women's bodies not men's. They also should have pockets so women can carry sanitary pads or other items as needed and incorporate other features such as being in two pieces for ease of use.

Men may be comfortable in jumpsuits, but the one-piece design for women means that they have to almost completely disrobe to use the lavatory. While it may seem a small thing to some, it is just one of the ways women's facilities' policies and practices need to be designed for women and not simply transferred from male institutions. Women also need more changes of clothing, particularly underwear, than do men. Allowing women to do their own laundry gives them more responsibility for their possessions and eliminates the fear of transmission of disease. At a minimum, if there is a central laundry, there needs to be a system by which each woman's underwear is returned to her.

Even if the new inmate has been institutionalized before, she will be anxious about being incarcerated. She may not be as afraid of physical assault as a man would be in his facility, but she may fear being locked in a small place alone. Depending on her situation, she may not have spent very much of her life away from her children and other family members. Therefore, just being locked in a cell alone may cause problems.

The new inmate also may be coming down from being under the influence of drugs, including misused prescription medication, or alcohol and need medical intervention for detoxification. Coming off drugs or alcohol is a serious medical problem and may cause death if not managed properly. It goes without saying, strict control of access to drugs or other such substances is very important not only during the initial processing but also throughout the rest of her stay in prison.

She may be very concerned about her health and most certainly will be worried about her children. Being convicted of a crime does not automatically mean a woman has been a bad mother. Even if she has not been the picture perfect mother while at home, once she is institutionalized, her children tend to dominate her thoughts. It can be helpful if calls home can be arranged as soon as possible to relieve some of her initial anxiety about her children.

The intake period is when the new inmate will form many of her ideas about her stay and how she can "do her time." She will begin to establish the patterns she will follow throughout her incarceration. She also will begin to come to grips with the reality of her situation. As the finality of her circumstances begins to dawn, she will likely be reduced to tears and may be very depressed. She may be very verbal about her concerns, or she may withdraw into herself. Staff must carefully observe her physical and mental health status during this period and take appropriate action, when needed.

Many of the women will have a history of attempted suicide prior to admission and incarcerated women have "a relatively high rate of self-mutilation" (Belknap, 2001 p. 173). While men normally will take out their frustrations and anger by striking out at others, women will internalize their feelings and may try to injure themselves. Some may see self-mutilation, "cutting," or even suicide as a means of escaping their situation. While some may be directing their anger internally, others may be survivors of childhood sexual assault (Faith, 1993; Skinner, 2000). Therefore, special care must be taken, particularly in the early stages of the intake process, to ensure that the new inmate does not harm herself. Providing constructive attention to women's emotional needs can reduce incidents of self-injury (Skinner, 2000). If she strikes out at others, she must be handled judiciously; however, it is to everyone's advantage for staff to treat women coming into prison professionally and with compassion.

Classification

Purpose

While there are many variations in their approaches, most correctional agencies have a system for inmate placement in the appropriate facility, housing, work, and program assignments. Such systems typically consist of intake, initial classification, reclassification, and prerelease classification (Seiter, 2002). While release planning should begin at intake, prerelease classification, according to Seiter (2002), should be initiated the last year of incarceration to help the offender transition to the community.

Usually, two areas are addressed in any classification system. The first is risk. Risk assessment focuses on what security/custody level is required to keep the inmate from escaping or endangering herself or others in the institution. The second element of classification is the offender's treatment needs or rehabilitation concerns. When assessing treatment and program needs, correctional personnel should examine the offender's medical, psychological, educational, substance abuse, vocational, and other levels of functioning, as well as her history of physical, sexual, and emotional trauma/abuse.

Ideally, risk and program assessment components will be balanced so both concerns can be taken into account. Recently, as some system administrators have decreased their emphasis on programs, the needs or habilitation components of offender classification systems have been deemphasized. This is particularly damaging for women inmates since they usually have a number of critical program needs. If these needs are not met, they may be more difficult to manage in the institution and their success on release can be jeopardized.

If the classification system is properly designed and implemented, it can be used to ensure agency resources are properly employed and inmates are treated consistently and fairly based on an objective assessment of their risks and needs. Also, it can be used to identify additional resources the agency may need. For example, if through the initial classification process, there are more inmates identified as needing maximum-security placement than there are beds available, this data can be used to justify building a new maximum-security facility or renovating an existing one. Program needs can be identified in the classification process. If during classification, it is learned that a sizable number of inmates are mentally retarded or have specific medical problems, resources can be sought to meet these needs (Seiter, 2002).

Issues

One of the traditional problems with classification systems is that women inmates are usually left out when policies and instruments determining risk and needs are developed. Some argue that instruments and scoring designed for men such as those developed in Canada and that are becoming increasingly popular in the United States can be used for effectively for both males and females (Dowden and Andrews, 1999; Blanchette, 2002). Others argue that, "Applying any type of prediction instrument to a population other than the one used for its construction and validation is scientifically improper and professionally unethical and can result in inappropriate decisions for the group being (mis)diagnosed" (Van Voorhis et al., 2002, p. 4).

By not designing classification systems for women, correctional systems are not taking into account the differences between male and female inmates including the fact that women pose less of a security risk than do men (Farr, 2000). As a result, critical information may not be collected or the wrong emphasis may be given to certain items.

The first problem in not modifying systems to accommodate women is that important data concerning women are not collected or data are misused. For example, some systems do not collect information on inmates' children and where the children are located. As noted earlier, this is a critical issue for women and has an impact on their institutional adjustment. Without this information, it becomes difficult to implement meaningful parenting and release programs for incarcerated women with children. In other instances, women who have stayed at home with their children are "scored as unemployed, thereby, inflating their custody score" as though parenting meant they lacked stability (Van Voorhis and Presser, 2001, p. vii). Other scores such as equating self-injury and suicide attempts as predictors of future violent crime can result in overclassification of women and delay their release (Shaw and Hannah-Moffat, 2001).

The second problem involves the system overclassifying women or ignoring their treatment needs. If, for example, the system focuses only on the offense and criminal history and minimizes programmatic issues such as parenting, acquiring of job skills, and treating prior victimization, women may be negatively affected. Some correctional systems are reexamining their systems and making adjustments to ensure they do not place women in a more restrictive environment than is required. For example, the Federal Bureau of Prisons found using the same instruments for men and women resulted in women being overclassified or placed in higher security than their crime and behavior warranted (Seiter, 2002). Through a comprehensive review and modification of the system, which had been initially designed for men, the Bureau was able to place more women in less expensive minimum security. Some agencies do not apply their systemwide classification programs to female inmates. Instead, they develop systems that are applicable to the women in their jurisdiction.

According to Burke and Adams (1991), classifications systems based on data from male populations tend to place women in a higher custody classification than is necessary. Morash and Bynum (1995) found that thirty-nine states used the same classification system for men and women, seven made adjustments for women, and only three had systems designed for women. Burke and Adams (1991) assert that gender-neutral systems can be designed if appropriate numbers of males and females are included in its development and instruments used are properly validated.

To be effective, the classification system used in women's institution must be based on women's risks and needs—not men's. It must take into account the experiences of women and how they differ from men's experiences. Further the system must be (1) understood by staff, (2) appropriately and consistently applied to all the incarcerated women, and (3) followed in the day-to-day operations of the facility (Seiter, 2002). If successful, the institutional classification system should help staff effectively and safely manage women in the institution, ensure inmates have an opportunity to change their lives, and enable them to be successful upon release.

Security/Custody

Purpose

Security is the primary component of any correctional institution (Henderson, Rauch, and Phillips, 1997). The purpose of the institution's security program is to provide a safe environment in the facility in which the community at large, staff, visitors, and inmates are protected. It includes maintaining order, preventing disturbances and escapes, stopping importation of contraband, and impeding inmate misbehavior (Seiter, 2002).

Security also entails using physical plant provisions including fences, bars, and other hardware. Because of the nature of the population, if the facility design is gender responsive, signs of physical barriers and hardware associated with male facilities often are minimized in women's institutions. Procedures must be in place to maintain accountability and control of the population in campus-style facilities but the construction costs of the facility are reduced with this type of design.

All staff members in a correctional facility have a security function. While correctional officers have the primary responsibility to provide security, the safety of the institution must be a concern for all employees, volunteers, contract personnel, those delivering supplies, and all others who enter and exit the facility.

Issues

Security procedures should be very obvious even to the casual observer in large institutions housing great numbers of inmates or in facilities with particularly violent inmates. Security concerns tend to dominate all policies, practices, and decisions made in such facilities (Henderson, Rauch, and Phillips, 1997). It is difficult to have any flexibility in these settings and all inmates are subjected to the same rules. This arrangement is the predominant one in male medium- and maximum-security facilities.

Given the profile of women inmates, some might think security is not as much of a problem in a female facility. In fact, it is more complex. As discussed earlier, there are a limited number of institutions for women. Therefore, all security/custody levels may be in one institution whereas a male facility usually will have only one or two custody levels. In most cases, a women's facility will have an intake unit, lock-up area, maximum-security section, medium-security units, minimum-security areas, prerelease, special needs including mental health, and perhaps even a work release unit. Recently, some women's institutions have added a boot camp or other form of short-term punishment unit.

Having a variety of security classifications added to the fact some women's facilities are trying to be more program or rehabilitation oriented than male facilities places greater demands on security. Security in a women's facility requires a great deal of flexibility, both in the physical plant and from staff. Each unit or security level housing area usually will have different floor plans and hardware. Thus, checking the physical plant will require more thought and planning. Each custody level normally will have different rules. What inmates are allowed to possess, for example, may be different for medium- and minimum-security levels while items considered contraband for medium-security inmates, may be allowed for work-release inmates.

Staff who transfer from male facilities or who observe a women's unit without understanding the differences between the two institutions may be confused, contemptuous, or even angry about what they see. In reality, there is a great deal of structure in a well-managed women's institution, even though groups of women will be treated differently. The concept of having different rules and programs for diverse groups of inmates in the same facility makes some correctional professionals uncomfortable. It is important for staff to study the security rules and regulations in the institution and develop an understanding of their relationship to the types of inmates in the institution and the programs being offered. In fact, not all correctional professionals can handle working in such a flexible environment where, multiple rules and programs exist. If staff are not comfortable with a gender-responsive environment, they should consider working in another part of the system.

Additionally, security in a women's institution relies on the communication skills of staff more than on the authority based, or power model, common in male facilities (Seiter, 2002). Interaction with staff tends to be less formal and more relaxed than in male facilities. Pollock-Byrne (1990) notes that women are also more willing to get involved in other women's problems. This can be positive and helpful to the individual needing assistance or women can "spread rumors and gossip about one another's activities as a form of social control or merely as a social pleasure." (p. 131)

As stated earlier, women inmates question rules more than men do. They have difficulty understanding why inmates in other custody levels are allowed to have possessions or participate in activities that are not approved for them. This is a problem not faced by male inmates who are in the same custody status. Some women will adopt an "in-your-face" approach to dealing with their frustrations that is self-defeating for the inmate and annoying to the staff. Staff must keep their professional demeanor particularly when working with inmates who take a confrontational approach. They must try to help the inmates deal with their anger more effectively and learn to resolve conflicts peacefully.

As noted in the discussion of gender differences, women inmates tend to be more verbal and question rules and regulations more than men do. Most women inmates do not willingly march in step. While staff can expect women to question why they should comply with requests, most women will be less likely to use violence than will men. A patient, reasonable approach to women inmates will be more effective than threats or physical intimidation. Women will be observing staff as much as correctional personnel observe them. Inmates may model staff members' approaches to problem solving and can learn effective conflict resolution from well-trained, professional staff. They also need to see that women can manage difficult situations and can work together as a team rather than as individuals competing against each other or waiting for a man to "solve" their problems.

Work/Job Assignments

Purpose

Work programs in prisons play a vital role in institutional life (Seiter, 2002). First, they help offset the cost of incarceration to the taxpayer. Work assignments help maintain the ongoing operation of the facility. There are never enough staff to do all the work required to keep an institution clean, inmates fed, and meet the other day-to-day operational needs. Inmates can help fill these work requirements. The sale and use of prison industry products also contribute to the agency's budget and help reduce the costs of incarceration.

Second, work assignments provide something for inmates to do. The common public perception—that inmates are lazy and simply want to lie around all day—is not accurate. While some women will attempt to avoid the harsh realities of incarceration by sleeping and others will become clinically depressed and not want to participate in daily activities, most inmates want to stay busy. Work makes time go faster, keeps them out of trouble, and, if properly structured, can enhance their feelings of self-worth, help decrease feelings of depression, and improve their mental health.

If designed correctly, job assignments can contribute to reinforcing a positive work ethic, including getting to work on time, maintaining a productive work day, accepting supervision, and assuming appropriate relationships with coworkers and supervisors. Work assignments also provide an opportunity to learn new skills or maintain existing ones. As noted earlier, many women offenders have spotty or nonexistent work histories and need to improve the skills necessary to work full-time. If women are paid for their labor, it can enhance their self-worth, enable them to pay for items they might not be issued, save money for their transition back into the community, send money home for their children, and make restitution or other payments required by the court.

There are two major sources of work/job assignments in a prison. Facility work assignments are those activities necessary to maintain the ongoing operation of the institution. These include such things as kitchen duty, grounds details, and physical plant maintenance. Prison industry is the other major source of work assignments for women inmates. These programs can be operated by the prison system or in some cases provided through contracts with the private sector. Depending on federal and state laws, prison industry programs normally produce goods or services used by the system or sold to other governmental agencies to help offset the cost of the overall correctional system. In some cases, when the prison industry program is contracted to the private sector, goods or services can be sold on the open market.

Issues

Traditionally, work assignments and prison industries in most women's institutions have been limited to those areas considered as "women's work"—cleaning, cooking, institutional housekeeping, and sewing, as a prison industry (Belknap, 1996). While there is nothing wrong with these activities and they certainly have to be conducted, a wider range of work and job assignments will broaden the base of experience for women in the institution. Teaching inmates how to do electrical and heating/air conditioning maintenance, for example, will eliminate the need to have male inmate crews come into the facility and will enable women to learn skills necessary to gain higher paying jobs on release. Since many women will have to support themselves and their children on release, work in women's prisons should be geared to preparing women to earn a living wage not just the minimum wage upon release.

As most women enter the institution with limited job skills, staff working with work crews and inmates in prison industries will have to teach inmates how to do their job assignments. Many, for example, will never have been taught how to use a hammer, drive a nail, use tin shears, or properly do the multitude of other skills experienced skilled craft persons take for granted. Unless the needed skills are taught and learned, the level of frustration for staff and inmates will be intolerable. Becoming proficient in use of common tools can contribute to the women's self-reliance when they return to the community often as single heads of single parent households.

Another important aspect of job assignments and prison industries is that the work should mirror employment in the civilian world as much as possible. Assigning more people to do a job than is necessary is an ongoing problem in some women's institutions, particularly those with more inmates than they were designed to hold or those in which beds were added but work assignments were not expanded. Constant interruptions of work schedules for counts and call-outs for medical or other activities also can cause problems. While some interruptions will be necessary, they should be kept to a minimum. Some states such as South Carolina have collaborated with private industry to establish more realistic work environments. Carefully selected inmates at Leath Correctional Institution in South Carolina worked under contract with a travel agent making reservations until the post 9/11 travel slump forced the cancellation of the contract. While a civilian employee of the company took the client's personal and financial information, in every other way, the program functioned as a normal travel office. Inmates worked eight plus hours a day—even having lunch in the work area.

Education

Purpose

Educational programs are usually divided into two types, academic and vocational (Reichel, 2001). Academic education is provided in a classroom setting and focuses primarily on learning basic skills. Academic programs can include everything from basic literacy to subjects such as writing, math, social studies, and others topics necessary for students to pass the general equivalency exam and receive a General Equivalency Diploma or high school degree. Over the past twenty years, some women's institutions have expanded their academic educational programs to include college courses. However, many of these programs were abandoned in the late 1990s when federal laws prohibited inmates from receiving grant money for higher education (Reichel, 2001).

Vocational education is focused on teaching specific, marketable job skills. It usually includes some classroom work, but the major emphasis is on hands-on learning in simulated or actual work settings. Examples of vocational programs include such subjects as word processing, electrical or other construction skills, cosmetology, and horticulture. Life-skills training reinforces vacational education.

Life Skills

Life-skills programs normally involve teaching women the skills necessary for them to function successfully in the community. However, learning these skills often assists women in making the most of their time in prison and, therefore, they are less of a problem for staff. Topics addressed in life-skills programs include such things as: budgeting, managing time, finding a job, handling conflict in the workplace, and balancing home and work. Programs even may include elements from traditional home economics courses such as understanding nutrition, preparing food, housekeeping, and maintaining a healthy lifestyle.

Issues

Ideally, both academic and vocational educational experiences will be available in a women's facility. For the most impact, they should be closely coordinated both with each other and with other institutional programs such as work assignments, prison industries, and prerelease activities. This is often difficult to accomplish. When contract staff provide programs, interaction with the other personnel in the facility will require additional advanced planning and monitoring. Even when educational programs are provided by in-house staff, cooperation with other programs in the facility should to be encouraged.

A close link between the educational component, work assignments, and prison industry means inmates will have the opportunity to apply what they are learning to real-life situations. This will strengthen their comprehension of what is being taught and improve their performance on the job. Experiential learning is also one of the best way for adults to learn.

Women may need encouragement to start and complete their education. For many, education in the community was not a positive experience (Crawford, 1990). Also, a number of them have come from families in which education was not valued or encouraged. It is not easy to start back to school as an adult under any circumstances and it is particularly difficult in a prison setting. In spite of these obstacles, it is critical for those inmates who are functionally illiterate to learn how to read. Often, people who have difficulty reading develop elaborate schemes to cover up the fact that they are illiterate. If they do not develop skills necessary to be functionally literate, they will have a hard time supporting themselves and their children when they return to the community.

Staff must help women expand their horizons relative to the world of work. As most women's vocational experiences were limited prior to coming to prison, they will need extensive vocational counseling to become aware of the occupations open to them and those that bar ex-offenders. Many women in prison come from backgrounds where women worked in traditional women's jobs including cleaning houses and offices, caring for children or older people, and waiting on tables (Crawford, 1990). These jobs are typically minimum-wage positions with few if any benefits and do not provide women with enough money to support themselves and their families.

Female offenders usually pursued the same types of jobs that they observed people doing when they were growing up. Since most of them grew up in low-income settings, it is often difficult to help women see beyond the culturally and economically imposed barriers to jobs paying a living wage. Surveys of women inmates performed to determine what vocational training programs they would like to see in the facility often show they aspire to what may be unrealistic positions such as surgeons or lawyers or may seek familiar traditional women's work. Helping them look at nontraditional jobs will open doors to occupations that will enable women to support themselves and their families. Entrepreneurial instruction also may be useful. Helping interested women understand the intricacies of starting their own businesses may be a viable employment option for some on release.

Because of limited previous experience, women will need instruction in job-seeking skills including preparing a resume, filling out applications, and interviewing for a position. Life-skills classes also will improve women's chances for success on the job.

Sometimes staff may not understand why inmates are being given the chance to better themselves and some may resent that educational and other programs are being provided for inmates. This is more likely to occur in those cases where individual staff members had to work very hard to overcome obstacles in their own lives. It also occurs when staff members have not had the opportunity to obtain an education or did not take advantage of their chance for advancement when it presented itself. When this happens, staff can sabotage the program in any number of ways. Harassment may include such things as ridiculing the student inmates or failing to provide passes or other assistance necessary to get to class on time. It is difficult, but essential, that all staff in a women's facility understand educating offenders saves money and provides better protection for the public in the long run. If the inmate leaves the institution more adequately equipped to make a living wage than she was when she started her sentence, she will be less likely to reoffend. This is not coddling—it is common sense.

Library Services

Purpose

Most women's institutions offer some library services. Access to reading material and other activities normally associated with community libraries can open new worlds to women inmates. Libraries also can house the legal materials required by the court in the general library or they can be provided in a separate area. While women inmates are traditionally far less litigious than are male inmates, they should be provided with the means to pursue legal actions if they choose to do so. As noted earlier, these actions frequently will involve the custody of their children or other family matters. The best inmate libraries have trained staff, volunteers, or trained legal aides who can assist inmates with legal materials and other library matters.

Issues

Given the small number of inmates in some women's facilities, correctional agencies may find it difficult to provide the full range of materials available in large male facilities. It is very important that the library be stocked with material and books of interest to women inmates. The diversity of cultures among the population also should be reflected in the material available in the library.

Computers and computer services can equalize the opportunities for women and provide inmate access to self-help programs that vary in nature from educational to mental health. Proper security must be in place, but having computers available will help mirror community libraries and will help inmates be able to use this resource upon release.

The library should be open and staffed at times when the majority of inmates can use it. This usually means it needs to be open in the evenings and on weekends, which adds to supervision requirements.

Program Services

Purpose

Program services encompass any number of activities geared toward rehabilitation of the female offender. Such services include counseling, parenting classes, spirtual or religious support, and visitation programs. They may help her both acquire the skills necessary for her to effectively deal with the pains of imprisonment and to succeed in the community on release. For those with long sentences or life sentences without parole, program services can help women learn to cope with life in the institution and to make their time as productive as possible. Program services can help women accept responsibility for what they have done and cope with the consequences. They also can reinforce personal accountability and begin to help women take control of their lives. Maunsell (2000) notes "Programming for women today must acknowledge the differences between men and women, their experiences, as well as the realities of the work beyond the institution" (p. 12).

Many programs have been implemented in women's facilities around the country. The ones discussed here are some of the most common.

Counseling

While only limited psychiatric services are usually provided, most facilities for women have some psychological counseling furnished by clinical specialists with advanced training. This may range from brief one-visit therapy to ongoing extended services lasting several months. Women who need more intensive psychiatric services than are available in the facility may need to be referred or committed to a mental hospital or other appropriate facility. Often, an involuntary commitment is necessary and involves a due process hearing. Correctional staff may be asked to testify at the pre-commitment hearing or provide written documentation of their observations. This can be of concern or even be upsetting for staff, but must be treated as part of their professional obligation. Counseling services in the women's facility also may be provided by social workers or other staff trained in counseling techniques.

Counseling services are given to inmates individually or are provided in a group setting for those inmates who have similar needs and who can benefit by being in a group (Jacobs and Spadaro, 2003). Group counseling is favored by correctional administrators because it is more economical than individual counseling and can be provided to more women at less cost per person. It is also believed to be more effective than individual counseling in treating some problems—so it is not just cost effective—it may be the best level of treatment available.

Counseling, whether individual or group, usually encompasses problems of adjustment to the institution, as well as, the issues women brought with them when they came into the system. The subjects addressed in counseling include such things as coming to grips with a history of physical and/or sexual abuse, anger management, conflict resolution, empowerment, forming positive relationships with family and friends, and other topics to help the women function more effectively in their day-to-day lives.

Trauma/Abuse Counseling

As noted earlier, the majority of women coming into correctional facilities have been the victims of sexual, physical, and/or emotional abuse as children and often as adults. Unless being a survivor of abuse is addressed in correctional programs, it may continue to have an impact on the women's ability to get on with their lives and have the motivation to become involved in other activities that are available in the facility. Programs aimed at helping women understand their situation and move on are vitally important and should be a part of programming in all women's institutions. Domestic abuse and rape crisis programs in the community often can be of assistance in developing programs in institutions and in providing follow-up services once women are released.

It is particularly important that women returning to the community understand the resources that are available to them if they find themselves in a domestic abuse situation. One of the speculations regarding the reduction in the rate of women killing their spouses that is occurring in many parts of the United States is that women are using shelters and other services rather than resorting to violence

Substance Abuse Counseling

Closely related to problems of being a survivor of abuse is the use of alcohol and/or drugs to dull the pain and guilt. Since a high percentage of women inmates have abused alcohol and/or drugs, most women's facilities have some treatment program for substance abusers. These programs may vary from Narcotics Anonymous or Alcoholics Anonymous programs operated by volunteers to a comprehensive residential therapeutic treatment program with a community follow-up component. The latter is preferable since addiction to drugs and or alcohol is very difficult to break and if not resolved may result in the woman returning to prison.

Parenting

Even those women who may be excellent parents in the community will need assistance in maintaining ties with their children while they are in prison. They also will need to develop strategies for smoothing their transition back into the family on release. Many will have had little stability in their own lives when they were growing up and, therefore, may have limited parenting skills. Without intervention, children of an incarcerated parent have a high risk of becoming delinquents themselves. Therefore, it is very important for women to have an opportunity to learn how to be better parents while incarcerated and how to effectively manage their children upon release.

The quality of care children receive while their mothers are incarcerated is of great concern. Some of these children may have suffered abuse and/or neglect prior to their parents' incarceration and are at risk "if placed with caregivers who are unwilling or unable to provide appropriate care" (Seymour, 1998, p. 474). Studies indicate that 97 percent of child welfare agencies do not have polices to guide their staff in working with these children or with correctional agencies (Seymour, 1998). Given the anxiety that women inmates have about their children who are in foster care, it would be useful for women's institutions to forge relationships with welfare service providers to ensure children in foster care are given the opportunity to visit. Welfare agencies also can work with the incarcerated parent in prerelease counseling.

Spiritual/Religious Support

A feeling or sense of being connected with a higher being is important to most women, in general, and those in institutions are no exception. Most facilities have a chaplain or religious leader who will provide guidance and assist in spiritual growth. Chaplain's services may include individual or group counseling in addition to regular religious activities. Institutional chaplains also can render invaluable services when there is illness or death in the inmate's family. Pastoral services can be augmented or broadened by the use of spiritual leaders from the community. Regular religious services and observance of religious holidays will help women maintain or strengthen their spiritual self- and personal development.

Visiting Programs

Maintaining contact with their family, particularly their children, is an important component in the lives of most women inmates. Visiting is frequently more difficult because most women are institutionalized further from their families than are male inmates (Farrell, 1998). Also, family and friends too often place a higher value on the males who are incarcerated than they do on females and visit women less often than they do men (Belknap, 2001).

Visiting policies and practices should encourage visiting. Visiting hours should be at various times, particularly to facilitate visits from children in foster care who may be brought by social workers during regular working hours or to allow visits from families who may have to travel long distances. Visits with children should be contact visits and the woman should be allowed to hold her children unless some very unusual security problem exists.

Processing visitors, particularly children, into and out of the facility should be as relaxed as security allows. Children and other visitors should not feel threatened or demeaned by the visiting procedures. Visiting policies should be developed based on the realities of having children visit. Children, for example, cannot go for long periods without eating, drinking, and going to the bathroom. If families are not allowed to bring in food, healthy snacks and drinks should be readily available.

Space should be provided to allow mothers to play and interact as naturally as possible with their children. Family counseling should be available to aid women and their families cope with her incarceration.

Bonding between the mother and her child and maintaining of an ongoing relationship between them are critical to the emotional, physical, and psychological well being of both mother and child. However, these are often difficult to achieve in a prison setting. Programs allowing children to have extended visits with their mothers can have a positive benefit on both the mother and the child. Visitation and other activities also can provide an opportunity for practicing good parenting skills. Other activities such as taping or video recording messages, writing letters, and liberalizing phone privileges also can help to maintain family ties.

Program Service Issues

A number of issues arise concerning program services in women's institutions. One of the more difficult problems is having enough services to meet the heterogeneous needs of the population. It is also difficult to achieve the optimal mix of programs given the small numbers of inmates (Seiter, 2002).

Since women's institutions often do not receive high priority in the agency planning and budgeting processes, problems frequently arise in finding the funding and other resources for meaningful program services. This often leads to seeking outside funding, which can help with initial start up of specific programs. However, additional problems occur when the agency or the institution is not able to assume the cost of the program when the outside funding is no longer available. This starting and stopping of programs contributes to a lack of stability in services at women's institutions and creates a certain degree of cynicism on the part of both inmates and staff toward the implementation of new activities. Carlen (2001) found that developing programs that lasted "more than a year or two was a problem in the United States, United Kingdom, Scotland, and Israel." While lack of funding was usually given as the reason for the abandonment of the program, additional problems included changing objectives of the funding agency, poor or adverse publicity, lack of support by referring agencies or groups, loss of gender-responsiveness, and unrealistic expectations by the funding agencies.

To address these problems Carlen, (2001) notes that for gender-responsive programming to be successful, the facility has to be creative and flexible in managing and monitoring the program. Program managers noted that the needs of the organization should "come second to the needs of the program participants, thereby ensuring that the form and structure for the organization is appropriate to the delivery of services tailored for whom it was set up to serve "(Carlen, 2001, p. 51).

An example of this type of sensitivity would be in an order issued by the central office when the Florida Department of Corrections was implementing the Girl Scouts Beyond Bars program. It stipulated that movement of women from the institution to other facilities should not be routinely done if it affected women who had children in the program. This allowed women and their children to continue in the program without the mothers summarily being moved.

All staff in the institution and those working with it in the community should have ownership in the program. This is particularly critical in institutional programs where correctional officers and other staff can have a negative impact on its activities.

Programs should consider all the needs a woman has—not just focus on one aspect of her treatment. Women have multiple needs and agencies often focus on only one aspect of their problems. Focusing on the whole woman and providing what is known as wrap-around services can help women gain access to the variety of resources they need.

Treatment programs, particularly in drug rehabilitation, must be realistic. Accountability evaluations must take into account the nature of the program and what is realistic for women to achieve. Women did not develop their treatment needs overnight and staff and others working with offenders in programs and services must recognize that change will come slowly and may involve relapses along the way.

Care must be taken that the gender-responsive nature of the program is not eroded. That is, some jurisdictions will pressure women's programs to admit male offenders. When this happens, the program loses its focus on women and the women can be subjected to abuse by male offenders. The program staff must convince policymakers and the public that they share "a common interest in reducing future re-offending through improvements in the quality of women's lives in the present" (Carlen, 2001, p. 51).

Those referring women to the program, agency personnel, policymakers, and the general public must be educated regarding the program's goals and objectives. Those managing community-based programs should continually educate others about the low risk the women represent to the public and "the very complex, gender-responsive social and health issues that must be addressed in order to reduce the risk of their re-offending" (Carlen, 2001, p 52).

Too often, programs designed for males are imported into women's institutions. Carlen (2001) found concern among administrators of women's services that programs including those imported from other countries, "such as cognitive skills acquisition" (p. 51), were being imposed on women offenders without taking the differences between women and men's offending patterns and needs into account. Such programs must be modified or redesigned to include components that meet the specific needs of women. Additional programs also must be developed which are specifically geared to concerns of women. Program staff who have been trained without any emphasis on providing women-centered services or who have had experience in male facilities will have to learn new approaches and strategies to make programs effective for women inmates.

A final issue, not unique to women's institutions, but which vitally affects inmates' rates of success on release, is the availability of services in the community. Substance abuse programs, for example, in the institution can address a certain number of problems, but if the women do not have community programs to transition into, they may not be able to stay alcohol/drug free once released. The same is true for mental health services. This type of continuity of care from the institution to the community requires coordination by staff. Staff will have to serve as advocates to help women gain access to the programs they need. This also will involve teaching the women about the resources that are available and how to be effective advocates for their own service needs.

Health Services

Purpose

A critical function in any women's institution is the provision of health services. These services include intake and routine physicals, treatment for communicable and other diseases, and evaluation of women's ability to work or participate in the daily activities of living. Treatment of acute and chronic illnesses, mental health services, dental care, health education programs, sick call services, supervision of medications, and referrals to community specialists and hospitals are a few of the other duties incorporated under health services (Faiver, 1998).

Issues

Physical and mental health issues are discussed in Chapters 8 and 9. Because this is such a critical area, a brief overview is included here. Ensuring competent medical services meet prevailing community standards is a critical component of any women's institution. Many women enter the institution with multiple medical problems including limited access to medical care in the community, poor nutrition, substance abuse problems, and limited exposure to information on what constitutes good health (Ross and Fabiano, 1986). Also, women in the community are more likely to seek medical treatment than are men, and this trend does not end when they come to prison. For many women "lack of control of their medical care can be one of the most frightening aspects of prison life" (Michigan, 2000, Unit 11, p. 26).

Unfortunately, several studies of health care in prison show that women's health concerns are often seen as complaints while men's health care issues are viewed as legitimate (Belknap, 2001). All staff, therefore, including medical specialists, must be sensitive to the fact that women use medical services more than male inmates do. It also takes longer to do certain procedures on women than it takes to provide similar services to men. For example, a routine physical for a woman will take longer than one for a man because of the pelvic exam. Women also may manifest more mental health problems than do men. These issues again make it important for programs and services to be designed specifically for women, and staff members should be trained so that they are empathic to the needs of women who may be ill.

Facility health education programs should be built on a wellness model stressing prevention and positive lifestyles. This is particularly true of prenatal programs. Activities to manage high-risk pregnancies are an important part of any health services program and attention needs to be paid to education of inmates as to what is normal during pregnancy and what is not. The goal should be how best to ensure a healthy fetus can develop in a woman who is institutionalized. If medical services are concentrated in one institution, medium or maximum institution, there may be a tendency to hold pregnant women in a higher custody situation so as to maximize the use of limited resources. It is important, however, that women who are pregnant are not denied access to lower levels of security, work release, or other programs they would be eligible for if not pregnant. Such actions may delay release or limit other positive benefits simply because the woman is pregnant.

Postpartum depression is another problem for new mothers, particularly if they do not have an opportunity to care for their child. Staff must be knowledgeable about the manifestation of postpartum depression and know how to deal with it effectively. New mothers who appear depressed should be referred to the appropriate mental health specialist.

Aging in prison or coming into the institution after fifty years of age presents a whole set of issues that medical and other staff often are not equipped to handle. Having appropriate programming, as well as medical care, is essential if this small but growing group is to maintain its health and well-being.

Facility personnel sometimes find it difficult to accept the idea that inmates are receiving free services when staff must work to provide for their medical care. Women who have worked throughout their pregnancies, for example, may find it difficult to accept a prenatal program for inmates if it does not contain a work component. It is important to remember there are legal, moral, ethical, and professional obligations correctional facility staff must meet in providing for those who are under their jurisdiction. Since incarcerated women do not have the choices available to free citizens, the government must provide services for them.

Medical co-pay programs that charge inmates for going to sick call or receiving other medical services can have a differential impact on women and discriminate against them. As noted, women have more medical problems than do male inmates of similar age and use medical services more often than do men. They have more medical conditions that need treating, and they usually have less support from family that would enable them to pay for services. Co-pay can discourage women from seeking medical care until the problem is so serious that it will result in more cost to the system than would have been true by providing free care. Efforts to make inmates financially responsible for their care should be linked to giving women the opportunity to earn wages.

Recreation/Leisure Time Activities

Purpose

The development of strategies for effectively using leisure time is important for women inmates. Such activities can contribute to positive mental and physical health of women who participate in them thus reducing costs of incarceration. Exercise and physical activities, for example, are an integral part of a wellness program. Exercise, like good nutrition, is required for women to be healthy.

Recreation/leisure time activities should include both individual and group activities. Individual programs may include crafts, gardening, and other activities that can be done alone. Group activities can vary from active team sports such as softball and basketball to more sedentary programs such as reading clubs.

Many women in prison have weight problems. Having positive programs for exercise, strength building, and weight control can go a long way to help prevent diabetes, osteoporosis, and other debilitating conditions. Weight control alone fosters a more positive self-image and improves self-esteem which many women inmates lack.

Issues

Leisure time and recreation programs must be women centered and based on the needs of the population in the facility. Simply letting women go out on a concrete pad and hand them a basketball does not constitute a comprehensive recreation program. Activities should be based on needs that women have as well as their interests. Women with skills in particular areas such as sewing, basket making, and drawing or painting can share these with other inmates. Volunteers also can be used to augment leisure time and recreational activities.

It is sometimes difficult to get women to participate in structured recreational programs because typically they have not been involved in such activities in the community. Staff should be proactive in recruiting them to be become involved and provide encouragement for them to become more active.

Often, new staff and the general public have difficulty understanding that while these programs do help inmates make their incarceration more bearable, they also make inmates more manageable and save taxpayers money in the long run by helping prevent illness and encouraging a healthier lifestyle.

Community Involvement

Purpose

Inmates can maintain contacts with the community in several ways. One of the most important ways this occurs is through visits with their family, particularly their children. Another valuable component of community involvement is volunteer services. This involves designing of programs, recruiting and training of citizen volunteers, and careful supervising and monitoring of their activities. A meaningful volunteer program not only increases women's opportunity to have contact with people in the community, but also helps educate the volunteers who then share with others the general needs and issues facing women offenders.

It is also possible to encourage community involvement by having things for women in the facility to do to assist people in the community. A woman who knits, for example, can make booties for newborn babies at the local community hospital. Women who read aloud and have good delivery can read books on tape for those with visual impairments. Selected women who meet security requirements can participate in community activities outside the facility. For example, participation in "speak-outs" with battered women's programs can be helpful to the community and the inmate. The involvement will help those on the outside understand the domestic violence experienced by inmates and will help the offenders understand they are not alone in their battles against it.

A program with numerous benefits for both women and their children, which also involves the community, is Girl Scouts Beyond Bars. This program consists of volunteers and staff from the Girls Scouts of America who develop Girl Scout troops for inmates' children in the community and also bring them to the institution periodically for scout meetings. At the same time, women in the institution meet regularly to learn how to work with their daughters and maintain closer ties with them. Several states and the Federal Bureau of Prisons have implemented this program and in some instances women and girls have continued in Girl Scouting following the mother's release (Moses, 1997).

Issues

Having volunteers enter the facility means institutional staff must process them in, supervise their visits, and see that they leave the facility at the appropriate time. It is necessary to have effective security policies and apply them consistently. A careful balance must be maintained, however, between the application of realistic security procedures and implementation of those that are burdensome and demeaning to visitors. Long lines, rude staff, and invasive or inflexible procedures will discourage and alienate the volunteers needed to help augment staff services. Being unnecessarily invasive or searching inmates and volunteers more than necessary can discourage their participation in community activities.

Discipline

Purpose

All institutions need rules and regulations to be administered consistently and fairly. Most institutions have major and minor classifications for violations of institutional rules. They also have a graduated system of punishments for disobeying the rules. Seiter (2002) notes that inmate disciplinary systems should have:

> a "written policy outlining what behavior is prohibited which is given to all inmates
>
> a fair and equitable set of corresponding sanctions increasing with the severity of the rule violation
>
> a process to appeal the sanctions
>
> a procedure to separate the accused inmate from the rest of the population, when necessary
>
> a capacity for long-term separation or special security housing for those who continuously threaten institutional security or against whom a serious threat of violence exists" (p. 236)

It is also important that staff have positive incentives to encourage good behavior and have privileges that can be taken away if conduct merits it.

Issues

Women rarely commit major infractions of rules such as escaping, attacking staff, or performing other actions that endanger staff and the institution (Seiter, 2002). However, staff never should forget that some women are just as dangerous as any man and the threat that these women pose should not be ignored (Michigan, 2000).

The majority of women inmates typically will be charged with more minor incidents than are men. McClellan (1994), for example, found that women in Texas prisons were much more likely to be charged with minor rule infractions and punished more severely for them than men were. Some of this misbehavior is the result of women's resistance to being told what to do and how to live. Staff attitudes toward what is "proper" behavior for women is another factor contributing to the greater numbers of minor disciplinary charges in a women's facility (Belknap, 2001). Also, since there are multiple security levels in women's facilities, there will be the need for different rules for different groups in the facility. This can raise questions of which rules apply to which groups and questions as to why some can have certain privileges and others cannot. Overly harsh discipline and regimentation can make some women even more rebellious or make them relive their trauma/abuse history (Kruttschnitt, Gartner, and Miller, 2002).

It is important not to have too many rules or rules that are only rarely followed or are selectively applied. In planning discipline programs, it is useful to ask what is really important to maintaining a safe and secure facility and design rules to foster that goal. Those implementing and administering the rules must find a balance between the requirement to maintain order and the need to allow women to learn to make decisions for themselves.

Prerelease and Work Release

Purpose

Planning for release should begin when the inmate enters the institution. As she progress through the program toward her actual release time, prerelease activities should intensify. As many of the transition problems as possible should to be solved before she leaves the facility. These include such things as securing a place to live, beginning the process to regain custody of her children, obtaining a social security number and picture identification, finding employment, linking up with community substance abuse and/or mental and physical health services, and starting the progress of qualifying for social security benefits for those sixty-two years of age or older.

Work release is another important function because it allows women to hold jobs in the community and return to a facility to live. Work release participants pay taxes, court fines, restitution, child support, and other fees that may be levied against their salaries. It gives them an opportunity to work in the community under supervision, live in a structured setting, become accustomed to the world of work, and earn money for use upon their release.

Issues

Correctional facilities are generally better at transitioning women from civilians to inmates than they are at transitioning women back to free world status. "Prisonization," or the process by which inmates learn the rules and regulations and how to cope in a structured institutional environment, is very hard for some inmates to overcome once they are released from prison (Reichel, 2001).

Normally, the longer an inmate has been in the institution and the fewer opportunities she has had to make decisions about her daily life, the more institutionalized she will become. There are incidents in which women will commit serious rule infractions just prior to release so their return to the community is delayed. While they may not be conscious of it, they, in effect, are acting out because they have become so institutionalized that they fear returning to the community and failing again to have a successful life.

Work release and prerelease programs should be located away from the main institution to help the women gradually transition from the prison environment to the free world. This will help overcome some of the problems of adjusting to freedom in the community and provide supervision as women encounter the temptations that can lead to future criminal activities. Again, the purpose is not to "coddle" the women but to make it possible for them to successfully accept their responsibilities as free-world citizens and help them avoid the problems that led them to commit a crime in the first place.

Since the release decision is usually not in the hands of institutional staff, it is sometimes difficult to know exactly when a woman will be released. This means the prerelease program must be flexible and be ready to provide assistance, as needed, to those whose departure was not expected.

Release

Purpose

Almost all facilities have a process or checklist that inmates must complete in order to be released. This includes such things as returning all state-issued clothing and supplies; being cleared for release by medical services, classification, and other departments which certify that the inmate is, in fact, the one who is to be released and the facility has the legal authority to release her.

Issues

Next to concern about their families, women in prison are anxious about how they will manage their lives once they are released from prison (Kruttschnitt, Gartner, and Miller, 2000). Women often will have formed close friendships while in the institution, which are difficult to leave. They may have unrealistic expectations about how their life will be on the outside. Lack of money or the means of supporting themselves and their families can create difficulties in finding housing, work, and medical care. They may have problems regaining custody of their children or adjusting to reassuming their role as caregivers. Having meaningful transition programs that are geared to meet the needs of the women being released can help resolve these problems.

Summary

Women's institutions are complex operations because they have to conduct all the functions incorporated in a traditional prison system in one facility. This has both positive and negative implications but does result in challenges to institutional operations not found in most men's facilities.

The general functions found in most women's institutions cover the gamut from intake to release and require vigilance to make certain they are women-centered and responsive to the needs of incarcerated women.

Women and Abuse

Introduction

Research indicates that a number of men and boys in the corrections system have been victimized, particularly as infants and young children; however, their rate of abuse is considerably lower than that of incarcerated women and girls (Harlow, 1999). Increasingly research is showing that as high as 94 percent of women in trouble with the law have suffered severe sexual or physical abuse as children or adults (Browne, Miller, Maguin, 1999). It should be clear that a history of abuse does not excuse criminal behavior. Many women who have been abused as children or adults do not engage in crime. However, given the high prevalence of abuse in the lives of incarcerated women, it is important to understand the potential impact that violence can have on girls and women. This may aid in understanding the behaviors of female offenders when they are faced with certain situations and help staff manage them more effectively.

Prevalence of Abuse in the Community

Abuse of girls and women is a serious problem in the United States (Gosselin, 2003; The Centers for Disease Control and Prevention, 1990). Tjaden and Thoemmes (2000) noted that: The large number of rape, physical assault, and stalking victimization committed against women each year and the early age at which violence starts for many women strongly suggests that violence against women is endemic (p. v).

Consider the following statistics summarized from Tjaden and Thoemmes (2000): Physical assault is widespread; 51.9 percent of women surveyed reported being physically assaulted as a child by an adult caretaker or as an adult by any type of attacker.

Many women are raped at an early age as evidenced by the fact that of the 17 percent of all women surveyed who reported they had been the victims of rape or attempted rape at some time in their life, more than half were under eighteen and 21.6 percent of that number were under twelve.

More than 8 percent of women surveyed reported being stalked at some time in their life and approximately 1 million women are stalked annually.

There were ethnic/racial differences in reported abuse. American Indian/Alaskan Native women reported more victimization than women in other racial groups particularly for the crimes of rape and stalking. Hispanic women reported significantly less victimization for rape than did non-Hispanic women. Women who reported being victimized as children were twice as likely to report being raped or physically assaulted as adults and seven times more likely to report being stalked as an adult. Twenty two percent of women reported they were physically assaulted by an intimate partner in their lifetime. Intimate partner violence accounted for 64 percent of all violence against women.

Abuse of girls and women is not an isolated occurrence in the United States. Consider the following grim statistics: Twenty-eight percent of American couples experienced an act of partner abuse during their marriage, 16 percent had at least one violent incident per year and 6 percent had severely violent acts per year (Gelles, 1997).

According to the FBI, a woman is battered every twelve seconds in the United States, but only 4 percent of abusers are prosecuted (Jones, 1999). More than 4.7 million women are victims of violent crimes each year and much of it is committed by intimate family members. In 1987, husbands or boyfriends killed 38.7 percent of all women murdered (Reiss and Roth, 1993).

Oliver (2000) points out that race is a factor in domestic violence. Black males "had higher rates of severe violence toward their wives than did white husbands" and "black women are more likely than white or Hispanic women to commit acts of severe violence against their husbands or boyfriends" (p. 534). In one study of eight counties, 47 percent of victims of black spouse abuse were husbands and 53 percent were wives compared to whites in which 38 percent of victims were husbands and 62 percent were wives (Langan and Dawson, 1995). In spite of declines in intimate murder rates over the last several years, black males murder their spouses eight times more often than white males and black women's murder rate was three times higher than that of white women (Oliver, 2000). Since black women are more likely to be victims of severe husband-to-wife violence than are white women, this may account for their overrepresentation "among women who commit acts of victim-precipitated homicide" (Oliver, p. 535).

Prevalence of Abuse among Incarcerated Women

While not all women and children who are abused go on to commit crimes, the prevalence of abuse among female offenders is considerably higher than among women in the general population. The prevalence of abuse varies with whether the study is done through national surveys such as those conducted periodically by the Bureau of Justice Statistics and the one conducted by Jackie Crawford for the American Correctional Association in 1990 or if they are conducted by trained clinicians in one facility.

The American Correctional Association in a national survey of female offenders found that 53 percent reported they had been physically abused in their lifetime and 36 percent reported they had been sexually abused (Crawford, 1990). These figures are similar to those found by Harlow (1999) in a national survey in which 57.2 percent of women in institutions reported they had been physically abused and 39 percent reported they had been sexually abused in their lifetime.

Local studies conducted using clinical interviews tend to find higher rates of abuse. Browne, Miller, and Maguin (1999) conducted one of the most comprehensive of such studies. Using trained clinicians they interviewed 150 general population female inmates admitted to Bedford Hills Maximum Security Correctional Facility in Bedford Hills, New York. They used the Conflict Tactics Scale developed by Straus to obtain data on violence committed against the women during childhood and as adults. The scale is divided into minor (pushed, grabbed, shoved) and severe (kicked, bitten, punched, choked, burned, threatened with knife or gun or used a knife or gun). Only severe incidents were included in the data. According to the authors "when all forms of violence are considered together, only 6 percent of respondents did not report experiencing at least one physical or sexual attack during their lifetime" (Browne, Miller, Maguin, 1999, p. 315). More than 70 percent reported severe physical violence as children; more than half of all respondents reported sexual abuse as children or adolescents, and 75 percent of all respondents reported experiencing severe physical violence by intimate partners in adulthood. Nearly half of those injured by their partners needed medical treatment. Over the course of their lifetime, 77 percent of all respondents had been victimized by nonintimates. This included muggings, assaults with weapons, and one-third reported violent sexual attacks by nonintimates.

Violence and particularly family violence is a challenge for corrections, because facilities receive both the victims and perpetrators of abuse at all levels of the system. Women and girls who enter the corrections system may have been both victims and perpetrators of family violence. An unanticipated consequence of legislation making it mandatory for law enforcement to arrest someone when responding to a domestic violence call is that an increasing number of women and girls are being arrested and convicted of criminal domestic violence or aggravated assault. Between 1990 and 1996 the greatest increase in the number of violent women felons were those charged with aggravated assault. Greenfeld and Snell (1999) attributed this increase to the rise in prosecution of women for domestic violence.

The system and ultimately society cannot afford to ignore any dimensions of the offenders' prior experiences if interventions are to be provided to help them live violence-free lives in the future. Obviously, prevention and early intervention in children's lives to address their trauma would prove more cost effective than incarcerating women in adulthood. However, there are indications that programs and strategies designed for women offenders who have been victimized can aid their adjustment in prison and increase their potential for success once released (Morash, Bynum, and Koons, 1998). A study of a New York Department of Correctional Services comprehensive program to address issues of the women inmates who had suffered family violence found that those who participated in the program had less than half the recidivism rate of women who did not participate in the program (Canestrini, 1994). Browne et al. (1999) noted:

> *[The New York study] illustrates the potential impact on recidivism of focused interventions that deal directly with histories of traumatic victimization... Addressing some of the long-term effects of violent victimization is particularly important in the incarcerated population. If left un-addressed post-trauma effects—potentially part of the pathway leading to incarceration—would be expected to markedly worsen the prognosis for a successful return to life outside correctional facilities upon release (p. 319).*

Overview of Domestic Violence

Much of the violence against women and children takes place in the home. Over the centuries and in almost all cultures, women were beaten by their partners without interference from family, friends, or forces of order (Gosselin, 2003). Early legal codes indicate men were permitted to use corporal punishment to include death to discipline their spouses (Jones, 1994). Women were considered property, first of their fathers and then their spouses. Children were also considered property and neglect and abuse was common (Gosselin, 2003). As chattel, women could not own property in their own right, a situation that still prevails in some societies. Husbands, in the United States, were held legally responsible for their wives' actions and debts until modern times. For example, until the Equal Credit Act passed in the 1975, wives in several states could not obtain credit or loans in their own names without countersignatures from male relatives.

Some attention was given to domestic violence in Colonial American when the Puritans passed laws to prohibit wife beating. However, between 1633 and 1802, only twelve cases of domestic violence were prosecuted in the Plymouth Colony (Pleck, 1989).

During the social enlightenment period at the turn of the twentieth century, the plight of women and children, and domestic violence were addressed both in the United States and in Europe. The whole concept of a woman being a

187

mature responsible person was the subject of many debates during the Women's Rights Movement in the late nineteenth and early twentieth centuries. Unless women were considered mentally and emotionally equal to men, it would be difficult for them to have any legal or other standing in the community. On another front, much of the Women's Temperance Movement's rhetoric from the turn of the twentieth century dealt with the "evil impact of hard spirits" on the tranquility of the family. Graphic descriptions of the brutality of drunken husbands, the neglect of children by drunken mothers, and other perils of drinking on the health of the American family helped ensure the passage of the Eighteenth Amendment outlawing alcohol production and consumption in the United States.

During this same period, the U.S. courts began to limit the legality of physical abuse of women. By the turn of the twentieth century, most courts had begun to hold that wife beating was a criminal offense but laws prohibiting beatings often limited prosecution unless the injured required stitches (Gosselin, 2003). Unfortunately, a man's home was still seen as his castle as was reflected in the famous 1874 North Carolina Supreme Court case in which it was held that corporal punishment was illegal, under any circumstances. However, the court went on to say:

> *If no permanent injury has been inflicted, nor malice, cruelty nor dangerous violence shown by the husband, it is better to draw the curtain, shut out the public gaze and leave the parties to forget and forgive (State v. Oliver, 1874).*

The curtain of privacy in the home remained drawn for the next hundred years. The concept of the sanctity of the home was and continues to be influential in the development of legislation, social policy, court processes, and criminal justice practices.

In 1962, Kempe originated the term "battered child syndrome" to describe physical and sexual abuse of children (Gosselin, 2003). Medical personnel began to develop protocols using x-rays and other diagnostic tools to document child abuse cases and make them easier to prosecute.

Not until the rebirth of the Women's Rights Movement in the early 1970s was attention focused on abuse against women in the home. Various women's groups in the United States and in Great Britain began documenting the extent of abuse and the need for intervention (Straus, Gelles, and Steinmetz, 1980; Renvoize, 1978). The first shelter in the United States was opened in 1974 (Schechter, 1982), and by 1990, shelters were available in most jurisdictions throughout the country. Unfortunately, the supply of beds is frequently outstripped by the thousands of women and children seeking assistance, so as many as half of those women needing help in some communities cannot find shelter. Some estimate at least 50 percent of all homeless women and children are fleeing from an abusive home situation (Jones, 1999).

In the 1970s, researchers, led by Dr. Lenore Walker, began to identify patterns of violence against women perpetrated by their spouses or partners. In Walker's cycle of violence theory, three main stages occur. The first is the tension-building phase during which minor incidents including slaps, verbal abuse, and threats take place.

Phase two is the actual beating, which can last hours or even weeks (Walker 1979; Browne, 1987; Jones, 1994). In the third phase, known as the honeymoon, the batterer tries to convince his victim and others that he is abjectly sorry, will not commit any further violence, and is willing to seek counseling or whatever his victim wants him to do to maintain the relationship. During this phase, some will threaten suicide as a form of control. It is not an idle threat considering the number of men who kill their partners and then commit suicide. The honeymoon phase does not last long and soon the cycle begins again. As the battering continues, the third phase becomes shorter and shorter. Further research by Walker (1994) led to the conclusion only one-third of abusers actually apologized for their behavior. The rest simply went back to stage one.

Dobash and Dobash (1979) proposed the continuum theory to describe the ongoing violence characterizing many relationships. After the initial abuse, women blame themselves and attempt to placate their partners. As the violence continues, they begin to understand their mates are dangerous people who cannot be satisfied or appeased. It is at this point the woman really begins "to change and fear becomes an integral part of daily life" (Dobash and Dobash, 1979, p. 137).

During the early stage in the violence continuum, the victim may seek advice or help from family and friends. If told to "just work it out" or given other platitudes, the woman may begin to question her own judgment. As the battering continues, she may call the police or go to a shelter.

The limited research done on African-American women indicates they sought assistance from medical facilities more often than they did from shelters, police, or other social service agencies (Coley and Beckett, 1988). This means that if hospital personnel do not recognize the symptoms associated with battering or do not follow proper protocols to help black women, the battering will continue often with deadly consequences for one or both of the partners. Ways of successfully intervening and other aspects of violence among different racial and socioeconomic groups need more extensive examination.

When the abuse continues to escalate, and in many cases begins to involve the children, women may seek legal help and try to plan their escape from their batterers. If their efforts are unsuccessful, and the support and legal systems fail to protect them, they may stay in the relationship and cope as best they can or take drastic measures to protect themselves and their families, which may result in their committing a crime and being incarcerated.

Many women who are victims of abuse develop multiple medical problems, including psychiatric illnesses, chronic headaches, abdominal pains, complaints of sexual dysfunction, recurrent vaginal infections, muscle aches, sleep and/or eating disorders, alcohol and substance abuse, and problem pregnancies (Randall, 1990). As noted earlier, pregnancy is a particularly vulnerable period for victims as batterers frequently hit women in their abdomens, which may result in miscarriage, low birth weight babies, pre-term labor, impaired bonding, and delayed postpartum recovery (Helton, 1986).

In a random sample of women at public and private neonatal clinics, 8 percent reported being battered during pregnancy; another 15 percent reported battering prior to pregnancy and of those who were battered prior to becoming pregnant, 29 percent reported battering increased while they were pregnant (McFarlane, 1989). Other studies have identified rates of battering during pregnancy as high as 17 percent with a 50 percent rise in battering during pregnancy of those abused prior to pregnancy (Bacon, 1996).

Newell (2000) notes that battered women normally go through five stages in the progression of violence that are summarized below:

Denial—To declare there is no problem is normal in any traumatic situation.

Blame Herself—Women are often taught that they are responsible for creating a happy home so they blame themselves when they are battered. They hope that if they just do things right it will stop. The abusers also destroy the woman's feelings of self-worth, and she begins to believe she is getting what she deserves. Others may blame her or not believe her.

Seek Help—It is difficult and dangerous for her to seek help. If she does not get a receptive response from friends, family, law enforcement, or others, she may withdraw to an earlier stage.

Feel Ambivalent—This is the stage in which 80-90 percent of women leave the battering situation, but they are not certain it is the right step and may return to the batterer.

Live Without Fear—This can take years to achieve and flashbacks can occur.

Victims in battering situations often experience strong feelings of desperation as they try one strategy after another to avoid the pain and psychological torture. It is very difficult for the general public and even social service and criminal justice personnel to empathize with these victims or comprehend why they stay in such dysfunctional and dangerous relationships.

Why Does She Stay?

There are as many reasons why women stay in abusive relationships as there are victims. As Jones (1994) noted, "There is no typical battered woman . . . Any girl or woman might be battered" (p. 163). One thing is clear, she does not stay for masochistic reasons or because she provokes and then enjoys being battered (Okum, 1986).

The question, "Why does she stay?" implies the woman, in fact, can leave. In reality, she actually may be physically restrained. She may be emotionally bound to the relationship, including having overwhelming feelings of power-lessness and fear combined with a belief that she has no alternatives. She may have tried to escape and been hunted down and forced to return. Studies indicate from 67 percent to 88 percent of battered women do leave their abusers for at least a day (Okum, 1986; Dobash and Dobash, 1979). Numerous victims leave and return repeatedly. One shelter reported women left an average of seven times before making the final break (Fact Sheet on Domestic Violence, 1995). Women stay in abusive relationships for many reasons including the following:

> The batterer's threats against the victim, children, and family members (which may include the abuse or killing of pets or destroying of keepsakes to reinforce the threat.)
>
> Lack of alternative living arrangements
>
> Lack of financial resources including the skills or opportunity to earn a living wage
>
> Love or feelings of hope for the batterer
>
> Self-doubt or fear of the unknown

Another reason women stay or return is the batterer's agreement to participate in counseling (Dobash and Dobash, 1979). This includes counseling by friends, family, religious groups, social service agencies, and courts to make the relationship work (Attorney General's Family Violence Task Force, 1989).

Probably the most important reason victims do not leave their batterer is because they believe their batter's threats and, in reality, attempting to leave or actually leaving, places the victim in the most danger. Between 20-40 percent of all women who seek divorce do so because their husbands are abusive, and almost one-half of all domestic assaults occur after separation or a divorce has been obtained (Brygger, 1990). Some 75 percent of the women who were murdered by their husbands were killed in the process of leaving them (Sonkin and Durphy, 1997).

In the end, it is ironic that the victim in a domestic battering situation is expected to leave her home, possessions, job, and all the familiar surroundings she has established because of a criminal act committed by an intimate acquaintance. Where else in society does such a double standard exist?

Community Response

Since the media is so influential in the development of public opinion, Jones (1994) and others have been particularly critical of the descriptions and analyses of domestic violence provided by print and television journalists. A quick review of almost any local or national news indicates a strong tendency to underestimate the damage done to the woman and either blame her for the violence or cloak it in a "love" relationship.

Incredible acts of violence and abuse are ascribed to the man's love of his partner, when, in fact, they are motivated by a need to control and dominate (Gosselin, 2003). Incidents are also attributed to the man "losing control," implying diminished capacity and responsibility on his part and/or that he was somehow goaded by his partner into committing acts he otherwise would not have done. If this theory were true, one must look at the number of victims who are struck where the bruises will not show so they can still go to work or the cases during pregnancy where women are only hit in the abdomen.

The medical community also has been cited as contributing to the problems faced by battered women through a failure to recognize the physical and psychological symptoms of battering, ineffective responses to the victims, and lack of communication and coordination with other social service agencies and the criminal justice system. While legislation requires reporting of child abuse and gunshot wounds, few requirements are made relative to reporting battering of women. Even when procedures require reporting, there is no certainty it will take place. In one study of women who had been deliberately and seriously injured by another person, doctors in 90 percent of the cases failed to follow required procedures and police reports were filed in only 50 percent of the cases. Even among those cases that were reported, many lacked the required information (Randall, 1990a).

Many times signs and symptoms of abuse are overlooked because of lack of information or education. Candib (1989) found 58 percent of medical schools required no training in domestic violence and in schools that did require training, an average of only three hours of the curriculum were devoted to any type of violence.

When hospital emergency room personnel are trained and a specific protocol is instituted to identify battered women, the impact is dramatic. In one study, the number of battered women identified after training and changes in procedures rose from 5.6 percent to almost 30 percent and then dropped again to 7.7 percent when the protocol was abandoned (McLeer, Anwar, and Herman, 1989).

Other social service agencies also have been cited as having problems dealing with the complexities of domestic violence. It was found in one study that service providers were knowledgeable of their own areas but were not informed about other services or resources available in the community (Davis, 1984). This was verified by other studies including one focused on domestic violence and alcohol use. It found women abusing alcohol may receive the wrong treatment or have their battering problems overlooked or minimized by staff who are untrained in domestic violence signs and symptoms or who are not knowledgeable about community resources and referral procedures (Lehmann and Krupp, 1983-84).

Criminal Justice System's Response

Criticism of the criminal justice system's response to domestic violence has been widespread both within the system and among outside observers. As Miller (1989) summarized from the various reports and studies that have been conducted:

> *For years the criminal justice system's inefficiency has impeded assistance for all battered women: the police have failed to respond appropriately to their needs, prosecutors have demonstrated deliberate impotence in their prosecutorial effort and judges have exacerbated these injuries by dismissing cases or failing to mete out meaningful punishments (p. 301).*

There continues to be considerable debate about the appropriate criminal justice policies relative to arrest and punishment. Law enforcement agencies, being the first to respond, have had policies that varied among inaction, mediation, separation, arrest of the perpetrator, and arrest of both the victim and the abuser (Gosselin, 2003). While more research is needed, arresting both the parties creates a chilling effect on the victim seeking further help, and mandatory arrest and incarceration policies are not effective in isolation.

The court system historically has underemphasized family violence situations and is increasingly overloaded with a growing number of domestic violence cases. As Hofford (1990), in a report published by the National Council of Juvenile and Family Court Judges, summarized:

> *The whole area of family violence has long been a troublesome one for the courts. Frankly, the courts have not handled these cases well. There is in recent years a heightened public awareness of this issue and the severe physical and emotional damage done to families caught in the generational cycle of violence. Yet the response of the criminal justice system, the juvenile and family court, and the service delivery systems has not kept pace (p. 2).*

In many systems, although assault cases are normally handled in criminal court, domestic violence cases either are screened out entirely or routed to family courts. This practice reflects the more than one-hundred year old belief that battering is a private family matter rather than a crime (Goolkasian,

195

1986). In many cases, being found guilty of spouse battering invokes lighter penalties than those for driving under the influence.

Impact of Violence on Children

One of the most devastating impacts of domestic violence is the harm done to children. Physical abuse in the home is the most common cause of death in children (Gosselin, 2003). Delinquency and significant emotional disability are far more prevalent among children from violent homes than among children from nonviolent ones. Windom and Maxfield (2001) found that a childhood marked by "abuse and neglect increased the odds of future delinquency and adult criminality by 29 percent" (p. 1). More specifically, abuse and neglect increases "the likelihood of arrest as a juvenile by 59 percent...and for a violent crime by 30 percent" (p. 2).

In 1996, nearly three million children were reported abused or neglected (National Committee to Prevent Child Abuse, 1997). While boys and girls are victimized at approximately the same rates, boys frequently sustain more serious physical injuries and emotional neglect than do girls (Gosselin, 2003). However, girls are three times more likely than boys to be sexually abused with rates as high as one in every five girls who reported being sexually abused by age eighteen (Gosselin, 2003).

Girls frequently run away to escape from an abusive home. This can result in them fending for themselves on the street any way they can. Given that girls are expected to have a higher standard of behavior than boys, running away can lead to contact with the criminal justice system where girls are twice as likely to be institutionalized for minor offenses as are boys (Office of Juvenile Justice, 1996). One study found that girls who were abused or neglected were "73 percent more likely than control group females to be arrested for property, alcohol, drug and such misdemeanor offenses as disorderly conduct, curfew violations or loitering" (Windom and Maxfield, 2001, p. 6). They also were at increased risk of arrest for violent crimes.

Witnessing their mothers being battered is very damaging to young girls who may begin to see women as second-class citizens who deserve to be treated poorly. Also, when they are in the developmental process of adopting female sex-roles, they may come to identify with their mothers and believe that being a victim of aggression is a normal role for women (Fleming, 1979). Boys who witness men battering their mothers are three times more likely to beat their spouses when they mature than are boys from nonviolent homes (Straus, Gelles, and Steinmetz, 1980).

The presence of spouse abuse in the home dramatically increases the probability that the children will be abused (McKibben, DeVos, and Newberger, 1989). Children were victims of abuse in at least 40 percent of the homes where spouse abuse took place (Gosselin, 2003) and mothers in 73 percent of the incestuous families were also victims of physical abuse (Truesdell, McNeil, and Deschner, 1986). Findings indicated mothers were normally not in collusion with the batterers, but were victims themselves.

Battered Women's Syndrome

There has been a great deal of misunderstanding regarding Battered Women's Syndrome and how it evolved. Some claim there is a Battered Women's Syndrome defense that can be evoked in any trial of a woman who kills her spouse or boyfriend. This is not the case. The syndrome is not an excuse or justification for harming someone. It, however, does go to the state of mind of the defendant, and just as in other criminal proceedings, may be introduced to support claims of self-defense. A history of abuse and duress does not replace existing claims of self-defense; it only supports them (National Clearinghouse for the Defense of Battered Women, 1999).

Much of the early research and program development focused on prevention and intervention for domestic violence. Little attention was given to what happened to the victims when there was no intervention or what was done when all else failed and they fought back. Increasingly, women are being arrested not only for homicide but also for criminal domestic violence or assault of their spouse or boyfriend when they defend themselves.

According to the National Clearinghouse for the Defense of Battered Women (1999), women are arrested when their abusers force their victims into criminal activity and also women are being charged with failure to protect their children from the batterer's abuse. The media has given a great deal of attention to cases such as *The Burning Bed*, the trial of Joel Steinberg and testimony of Hedda Nussbaum, and popular books such as Ann Jones' *Women Who Kill*. Publication of these cases and books generated interest in the victims who enter the criminal justice system charged with assault or murder of their partners.

Until the U.S. Supreme Court in the mid 1980s ruled expert witness testimony could be used to help establish a woman's frame of mind when the act took place, women faced great difficulty in proving that they had acted in self-defense. They were judged by the doctrine that the specified killing of another human being was justified only if one was in imminent danger of death and there were no other alternatives that a reasonable man would take. Women did not meet the traditional masculine view of self-defense, since women often struck after their partners had finished battering them and had gone to sleep, passed out, or in some other way were no longer an imminent threat or they acted in anticipation of or to prevent future injury. Combined with the basic bias against battered women, prosecutors and juries had little difficulty finding women guilty of murder.

Some have begun to view the concept of Battered Woman's Syndrome, which is the condition resulting from repetitive acts of physical and psychological harm, as a key to ensuring victimized women will have a case for fighting back and protecting themselves and often their children. Unfortunately, this is not always the case because the woman has to have an attorney who is knowledgeable about the various aspects of preparing a self-defense case in these circumstances (National Clearinghouse for the Defense of Battered Women, 1999). A high percentage, between 75-80 percent of battered women charged with killing their abuser are found guilty or enter a guilty plea (Bloom and Covington, 1998).

Many women, particularly in nonfatal cases, enter a guilty plea to the charges against them without understanding the ramifications of doing so. This occurs because they may be subject to additional battering if the batterer is still in the picture. Also, they fear losing their jobs, and/or fear losing custody of their children, or just want the problem to be resolved. However, legislation to punish batters by denying them employment options, welfare benefits for their children, public housing, immigration status, and child custody can apply to women as well as men if they plead guilty to a crime of criminal domestic violence (National Clearinghouse for the Defense of Battered Women, 1999).

Defense attorneys should explain the options and consequences to the woman and if she goes to trial—particularly when there has been a fatality—to ensure she is fully prepared. As one successful attorney put it:

> *Her presence and demeanor are critical. She must convey her fears and her apprehensions at the time of the fatal incident, tying together her present fear and apprehension with her past experiences* (Swerling, 1990, p. 29).

The defense attorney must obtain permission to have the testimony of expert witnesses introduced and then know how to use it along with the other facts gathered to prove self-defense. Certainly, the prosecutor will not be interested in showing the deceased person was a batterer. The attitude of the judge toward the defense, including his or her charge to the jury, is also important and is another area in which the defense attorney has an opportunity to influence the case.

The National Clearinghouse for Defense of Battered Women (1999) recommends:

> All battered women have access to representation in court and be provided support services, if necessary

Defense attorneys should be trained to understand battering and the long-term consequences of conviction for criminal domestic violence or other crimes involving domestic violence

Courts should provide resources for expert witnesses in the case of indigent clients to assist in trial, appeals, and parole or clemency

Implications of Offenders' Trauma/Abuse Histories for Corrections

In the past, little attention was given to the impact of domestic violence on women coming into the corrections system. Since women's institutions deal with abused women and those who have abused others in such high numbers, any program or intervention strategy must incorporate an understanding of domestic violence, its impact, and what treatments will be effective (Morton, 1994).

Since without intervention, children of men and women offenders have a greater chance of getting into trouble with the law, the first area to consider is the juvenile justice system. Here, the line between victim and perpetrator becomes particularly blurred. As noted earlier, it has been known for some time that many of the girls coming into the system have a background of trauma/abuse, regardless of their juvenile offense. Crawford's (1990) study of juvenile female offenders, for example, found that the average girl had been the victim of sexual abuse a minimum of three to sixteen times, between five and fourteen years of age. A family member most often perpetrated the crime and reporting it made no change or made it worse.

These and other studies point to the need to include screening for backgrounds of trauma/abuse among those coming into juvenile justice system. In many cases of children who have been abused, it may be necessary to deprogram their learned responses to threat and abuse before they can focus on successfully participating in other programs or activities. It seems clear that treatments that inflict more physical or psychological pain should be questioned (Morton, 1994). Taking an abused young girl or boy and heaping more pain and guilt on them will not produce an effective, law-abiding citizen. This issue must be addressed given the current emphasis on punishment in our society.

Some juvenile programs reflect sensitivity to girls' and boys' past experiences. Over a number of years, the California Youth Authority developed an extensive program that addresses victimization. A manual, *Impact of Crime on Victims*, includes sections on domestic violence and elder-abuse examining both issues in depth. Led by skilled counselors, these types of programs should help young people deal with their anger and other outcomes of abuse. Unfortunately, there are no instant solutions for girls and boys who have faced long-term abusive situations. Therefore, any services provided in residential facilities will need to be followed up in the community on release.

Women coming into the adult system have similar needs to those exhibited by juvenile girls, only their responses to and participation in violence often have had more time to evolve. As noted earlier, studies of women in prison have shown that as high as 94 percent were battered as children or adults (Browne, Miller and Maguin, 1999) with more than half (59 percent) having experienced some form of sexual abuse as children. Crawford's (1990) study of female offenders found that a family member most often committed the abuse and reporting it made no change or made it worse. Overall abuse rates among children were even higher in a 1996 National Council on Crime and Delinquency study of women in prison in which it was reported that more than 92 percent had experienced some from of abuse before eighteen years of age (Acoca and Austin, 1996). How helpless and angry these traumatized girls must have felt when they reported their abuse and were ignored or punished for talking about it.

The bottom line is that according to Windom and Maxfield (2001) experiencing violence as a child increases the risk of the following problems in adult women:

mental health concerns such as suicide attempts and posttraumatic stress disorder,

educational problems such as extremely low IQ scores and low reading ability,

occupational difficulties such as lack of work, high rates of unemployment, and employment in low-level service jobs and,

public health and safety issues including prostitution in males and females and alcohol problems in females (p. 7)

Based on their findings, Windom and Maxfield (2001) recommend early intervention at the first signs of abuse and neglect, particularly among those children who exhibit early behavioral problems. They encourage recognition of the high risk that neglect has on future violent criminal behavior and a reexamination of out-of-home placements since, in their study, removal from the home did not appear to increase children's risk of neglect and abuse. These findings are important for corrections in that they support the concepts of early intervention and parenting programs to help both female and male offenders avoid continuing the pattern of abuse and neglect in their children that will put them at risk.

What Staff Can Do

Twenty state correctional administrators, women's facilities program mangers, and others involved with female offenders stressed in a national survey that there was a need to develop programs for women in institutions that focused on victimization issues (Morash, Bynum, Koons, 1998). Several women's facilities reported having developed treatment programs to deal with the outcomes of domestic violence and ten offered programs for survivors of sexual abuse (National Institute of Corrections, 1998). These were usually based on the theory that women must come to grips with their background of trauma/abuse before they can successfully participate in other programs within the facility.

Both physical needs and emotional scars need to be addressed. There is usually not one single program that will be successful with all women given the heterogeneous nature of the problem, so a variety of programs should be available. Staff can assist by encouraging women to participate in programs in the institution and the community.

Supervision of women who have been abused can be complex. On the one hand, some may exhibit inappropriate physical behavior or verbally aggressive behavior. On the other hand, some women who have been abused may be passive and fearful in confrontational situations. They also may deny that the abuse occurred. Whatever their response, they need help to deal with their fears, guilt, and anger. Both security and treatment staff should work as a team in the facility to provide a supportive environment for women to learn new responses to enable women inmates to better cope with their situations.

Since many communities have developed community-based programs to work with survivors of domestic abuse and batterers, correctional personnel may find liaison with staff from these programs helpful. Working with the state or local agencies that aid victims of domestic violence has been a profitable experience for many correctional personnel developing programming for women offenders. A number of state correctional systems have developed relationships with community groups to provide staff training, specialized programs for offenders, and group home placement for offenders who are victims of domestic violence upon release.

The Bedford Hills Correctional Facility in New York, for example, with involvement from the community developed an extensive program on family victimization that included an institutional inmate survey, group counseling, and the development of videotapes to educate others about the problem (Browne, Miller, and Maguin, 1999). Sistercare, a community-based nonprofit agency, in Columbia, South Carolina has a long-standing relationship with the South Carolina Department of Corrections. Counselors provide group treatment for survivors of abuse in the institution and assistance to battered women during pretrial status, while on probation or parole, and on release. This includes temporary group home placement in the community for women and their children if they are in danger (Fact Sheet, 1993).

The growing interest in battered women fueled by the O. J. Simpson case may help staff in institutions and in the community expand domestic violence programs in corrections. In addition to the references listed at the end of this book, the following organizations offer information packages to provide staff with additional information and programmatic recommendations for abused women and delinquent girls:

> National Institute of Corrections (asknicic@nicic.org)
>
> National Criminal of Justice Reference Center (askncjrs@ncjrs.org)
>
> National Clearinghouse for the Defense of Battered Women http://dpa.state.ky.us, 125 S. 9th St., Ste. 302, Philadelphia, Pennsylvania 19107; 215-351-0010.

Summary

Many women and girls in the United States have survived sexual, physical, emotional, and other traumas/abuses, much of which occurred in the home. While having been abused is not an excuse for criminal activity, it does place one at risk for self-destructive behavior. Women who have been victimized are also at risk for being victimized again. Correctional personnel must recognize the impact that abuse has on female offenders and should provide counseling and support to help them learn to cope with what has happened to them so they will be able to move on with their lives.

7

Mothers in Prison

Introduction

The importance of bonding among men has become a common issue in the last few years as various groups have encouraged men to meet and form common ties. Also, some attention has been given to the importance of the bond that should develop between fathers and their children. In 1996, almost 40 percent of children in the United States were not living with their biological fathers (Davenport, 1996). As the number of fathers who are separated from their children has grown, religious, educational, and civic groups have stressed the need for children, particularly boys, to have a strong positive father figure in their lives. Sometimes overlooked in this debate is the powerful role a mother plays in the development of the future physical and emotional health of her children. Bonding is a two-way proposition, in addition to helping children it also can be beneficial to the mother's emotional health and feelings of self-worth.

In this chapter, the importance of bonding between children and their mothers will be explored. Also, programs to help maintain and strengthen relationships among incarcerated women and their children will be discussed. Finally, we will review steps to help women maintain positive relationships with their children.

Some question why anyone should be concerned about mother/child relationships. They argue that since institutions rarely have programs for male inmates to bond with their children why should anything be done for women inmates. Consider the following facts from state facilities and the need for women offenders to maintain and strengthen ties with their children becomes more obvious:

> 25 percent of women admitted to prison are pregnant or have recently delivered a child (Fogel, 1995)

> 64 percent of women in prison had minor children living with them prior to incarceration compared to 44 percent of men (Greenfeld and Snell, 1999)

incarceration of a woman disrupts the family considerably more than incarceration of a father (Bloom, 1993; Morton, 1998)

women are almost half as likely to be married as are male inmates (Johnston, 1997)

women inmates are three time more likely to have lived with their children prior to incarceration than are male prisoners (Johnston, 1997)

28 percent of incarcerated women's children live with their fathers compared to 90 percent of incarcerated men's children who live with the children's mothers (Mumola, 2000)

65 percent of incarcerated women's children live with grandparents and 10 percent are in foster care (Snell, 1992)

88 percent of incarcerated women have some contact by phone, mail, or visit with their children while in prison compared to 79 percent of incarcerated men (Mumola, 2000)

more than 54 percent of incarcerated women with children under eighteen never have a personal visit from their children (Mumola, 2000)

6 percent of women in prison who have children were convicted of a violent offense compared to 45 percent of men who committed a violent offense (Mumola, 2000)

38 percent of women with children compared to 18 percent of men with children have less than twenty-four months to serve in prison (Mumola, 2000)

50 percent of women with children made less than $599 per month prior to arrest compared to 37 percent of men who made less than $599 per month (Mumola, 2000)

the majority of women believe they will have responsibility for their children upon release (Crawford, 1990)

Bonding and Its Implications for Children

There is not uniform agreement on exactly what happens when mothers and children are separated. Young children in the community removed from their mothers for hospitalization or other reasons displayed immediate distress followed by misery and apathy (Rutter, 1995; Dunn, 1993). Another, much more serious effect of maternal deprivation is developmental retardation and general impairment of developmental progress. The longer the period of separation between the child and its mother, the greater the disturbance (Rutter, 1995).

In recent years, most researchers and child development specialists have rejected the idea of a mystical relationship between a mother and a young child. Rather than a golden period in which mother/child relationships must be fostered, researchers stress the quality of the relationships a child has with its mother and other significant caregivers throughout all stages of childhood and adolescent development.

The quality of the mother/father/child relationship sets the stage for all other relationships. Positive interaction is critical to the development of healthy social relationships and personality growth (Rutter, 1995). Young children internalize values and social norms based on positive interactions with their parents (Bretherton, Golby, and Cho, 1997).

The bond between mother/father/child becomes even more important as the child reaches adolescence. A great deal of a teenager's time is spent in testing the ideologies and roles of adult life. While the prospect of becoming an adult is exciting to a teenager, it is also very confusing and frightening. A strong bond with a parent provides a safe and healthy outlet for teenage expression (Watkins, 1987; Stafford and Bayer, 1993). Children separated from their mothers and fathers at this crucial juncture have a very difficult time establishing a healthy sense of their own identity (McGowan and Blumenthal, 1978). The interactions between children and their parents form mutually shared expectations and norms (Stafford and Bayer, 1993). Also, the shared intimacy, conversation, and humor involved in normal parent-child interactions establish the framework for children to be able to maintain intimate relationships of their own when they reach adulthood (Dunn, 1993).

Since the children of incarcerated women often do not have fathers present in their lives, their mother's role in their ongoing healthy social and emotional development can be very important. A lack of this bond may account for the problems many children of incarcerated women have in school and the high correlation between incarcerated mothers and delinquency among their children.

Impact of Incarceration on Children

Comprehensive studies of children whose parents are incarcerated are limited but those that are available indicate that the children experience a number of problems. The negative consequences include "poor emotional health and well-being, and lack of physical care and custody" (Seymour, 1998, p 472). The extent and depth of the problems are influenced by several factors:

the age of the child at separation

the length of the parent's incarceration

family cohesiveness and the strength of the bond with the mother

the type of crime

family and community support

the child's relationship with the custodian (Seymour, 1998)

A final factor not noted by Seymour is the degree of disruption in the child's life such as moving to a new neighborhood or changing schools.

Children with incarcerated parents may experience fear, anxiety, loneliness, anger, sadness, and guilt (Osborne Association, 1993). They may act out and become disruptive in school to the point that their academic and social skills deteriorate (Gabel, 1992).

When their mothers are incarcerated, few children stay with their fathers so they are uprooted and placed in the custody of grandparents, other family members, or foster parents. Some studies have indicated only about one-quarter of children live with their fathers. A more recent study found that the level of custody by fathers varied by state with lows of 3 percent of children in Indiana and Mississippi living with their fathers to highs of 21 percent in Pennsylvania (Pollock, 2001).

Inmates' children who do not live with their fathers are often a burden to grandmothers or other family members who lack the energy and resources to meet their needs (Henriques, 1982). Many children are likely to have contact with the child welfare system and most live in poverty (Seymour, 1998). In spite of increasing numbers of children with incarcerated parents being referred to child welfare agencies, a 1994 study reported that 97 percent of the 500 agencies surveyed did not have policies to guide their work with these children (Smith and Elstein, 1994).

Mother/daughter crime patterns are beginning to receive attention. Surveys of girls in juvenile facilities indicated that from 44 to 64 percent had mothers who had been arrested or incarcerated (Locy, 1999). Many of the programs linking mothers with their children hope to break this cycle (Bartley, 2000).

Corrections and Motherhood

One of the most serious pains of imprisonment for a mother is to be separated from her children (Kruttschnitt, Gartner, and Miller, 2000). Even if her relationships with her children have been less than ideal when she was in the community, she may develop unrealistic memories of that time and miss her children even more. She may want to be the "perfect mother" but may not have the skills to meet the emotional and physical needs of her children on release. It does not help if the children become hostile toward her and blame her for their discomfort while she was gone. Indeed, children often resent and fail to obey mothers who have been incarcerated. Mothers also often feel guilty about their period of separation and can overcompensate when trying to discipline or instruct their children.

Correctional administrators do not make the decision to incarcerate mothers, nor do they determine when they can be released. Many, particularly those working in women's institutions, are sensitive to the need for meaningful and positive contacts between mothers and their children. They support the development and maintenance of helpful programs despite naïve political and public outcries to make prison miserable and frightening.

Barriers to Maintaining Relationships

Most state correctional agencies reported they had some policies for visiting and using the telephone in male and female institutions (National Institute of Corrections, 1998). However, there are a number of challenges to maintaining positive ties between incarcerated mothers and their children. In many instances, the prison environment is not welcoming to children and their guardians. Long distances to facilities, lack of public transportation, invasive search procedures, strict rules regarding touching, limitations on having food, and crowding in visiting areas are among some of the problems that have to be overcome in establishing programs for women and their children (Bloom, 1995). In some short-term facilities, children under certain ages are not allowed to visit, and in others, no physical contact is permitted between children and their mothers.

In other situations, mothers may not want their children to visit them at the institution. They may be ashamed of their incarceration, or they may have told their children they were going to a hospital or some other story to cover their absence. Others cannot bear the pain of telling their children goodbye when the visit is over and watch their children cry at being taken away (Pollock, 2002).

Agency visiting and other policies are usually designed for male facilities. They often place limits on a warden's ability to modify practices to meet the needs of incarcerated women and their children. Agency liability if something goes wrong and regulations of other agencies and organizations also may pose problems.

Attitudes about motherhood and criminal activity are strong in the United States. Motherhood is considered a hallowed institution and many believe that if a mother commits a crime she automatically is an unfit mother. Reflecting these attitudes, legislative bodies in some states have placed limits on women maintaining custody of their children. Decisions may be made by courts and social services agencies that the mother is unfit. Women are often not consulted on the placement of their children, dissatisfied with where they are, fearful for their safety, and yet powerless to do anything about it.

Unfortunately, some correctional agency personnel can be influenced by the misconception that commission of a crime eliminates the woman's right to be concerned and involved with her children's lives. Attitudes of many including some correctional personnel are that being an inmate is mutually exclusive of being a good mother. Some research on women addicts indicates that they may have difficulty meeting the needs of their children while involved with drugs or alcohol (Morash and Schram, 2002). However, a study of female inmates by LeFore and Holston (1989) found that women in prison, including addicts, had the same understanding of how to raise their children as did women in the community who had similar backgrounds.

Legal Issues

Child welfare agencies are required by law to make "reasonable efforts to reunify families separated by incarceration—and courts may hold agencies legally accountable for maintaining ongoing communication with parents in prison and exploring fully the extent to which services might be provided to incarcerated parents" (Seymour, 1998, p. 3). This mandate could be useful in furthering a positive working relationship between correctional and child welfare agencies. While such collaboration is made more difficult by funding limitations and lack of resources for both corrections and child welfare, children and their mothers can benefit by increasing interagency cooperation.

Another legal issue is the matter of parental rights and custody of children whose mothers are in prison. Federal legislation, The Adoption and Safe Families Act of 1997, Public Law 105-89, mandates that children must have a plan for permanent placement within twelve months of removal from their parents. Research by the National Council on Crime and Delinquency found that 54 percent of women in the study were serving a sentence of a year or more with 15 percent reporting that one or more of their children had become wards of the state (Acoca and Austin, 1996). This means many female offenders may not be able to resume custody of their children within a year (Belknap, 2001).

Additionally, according to Genty (1995), twenty-five states have statutes covering termination of parental rights and the adoption of children of incarcerated parents. This is an example of legislation that has a disparate impact on women inmates more than it does on male inmates whose children normally stay with their mothers. These statutes make it even more important that welfare agencies, the courts, and correctional facilities housing women work together.

Women who are concerned about their children's safety and well being can be more difficult to manage. Knowing what is happening to their children and participating to the degree possible in decisions regarding them can improve women's outlook and help ease their eventual return to the community. Maintaining contact with her children and participating in planning for them also can have a positive impact on the children during their mother's incarceration and when she returns to the community.

Types of Programs

Prison Nurseries

In spite of the many barriers to be overcome, a number of creative programs have evolved over time. Among the first to be implemented were formal nurseries in prisons to house the infants of women inmates.

It was a common practice, in both England and the American Colonies, to have babies and young children in prison with their mothers. The conditions were horrendous and many of the children and their mothers did not survive. With the coming of the Progressive Movement in American corrections in the late 1800s, an emphasis on improving conditions for women in prisons grew. Since reinforcing women's traditional roles as wives and mothers was considered essential to their reformation, early programs focused on bonding between women and their young children.

The New York Reformatory for Women at Bedford Hills, under the progressive leadership of Dr. Katherine B. Davis, established a nursery for inmate's children in 1901. Other states followed suit and in the 1920s and 1930s, prison nurseries were fairly common in women's institutions around the country (Morton, 1996). By the late 1960s and early 1970s, the popularity of nurseries began to wane, and some states passed laws against having children live in prison (Boudouris, 1996).

Interest in prison nurseries began to increase in the late 1990s and by 2000, California, Washington State, South Dakota, and Florida had joined New York in operating nurseries for children whose mothers were in prison. All the programs emphasize nurturing behavior by the mother and provide parenting classes for women so they can learn and practice positive child rearing skills. The South Dakota program is limited to thirty days following delivery and the California program is community based (Pollock, 2001). The Nebraska program also includes overnight visits for older children (Dowling, 1997). Correctional administrators indicate that few if any security problems have occurred as a result of having young children with their mothers in prison (Pollock, 2001).

Other countries also struggle with questions of mothers and their babies in prisons. According to Morash and Schram (2002) "In all but a few countries correctional authorities allow incarcerated women to return to their homes to give birth, and then to keep their children with them in prison until they are one or two year of age" (p. 94). This author has observed children in prison in England and Scotland in the late 1980s. She also noted that when in China in 1982, prison officials reported that women were sent home to have their babies and could stay with them one year before leaving them at home and returning to prison to serve the rest of their sentence.

Short-term Community-based Options

Some advocate that expectant mothers be transferred from prison to a community residential setting to have their babies and keep them in a normal environment. The Federal Bureau of Prisons established one such program called MINT, Mothers and Infants in Transition. In this program, selected minimum-security women could be moved to community programs approximately two months prior to delivery and remain there for a specified period of time following birth. This program enabled women to be in a supportive environment during the latter stages of their pregnancy and stay approximately three months following the delivery of their child. They had to make arrangements for placement of their children and were encouraged to maintain contact with them until release (Gaseau, 2000).

Group Home Options

Given that a large number of women offenders can be classified as minimum security, many advocate that these women be allowed to remain in the community following their convictions. In 1996, Boudouris identified seventeen states that had community group homes for women and their children as an alternative to prison for females who had committed minor crimes or as transition centers for those leaving prison. Pollock in 2001 found that fourteen of the forty states responding to her survey indicated they had community-based facilities and that others had centers that served women sentenced directly from the court. These programs are more positive for mother/child relationships than is prison, more cost effective than institutionalization, provide for the development and practice of child care skills, and can accommodate children older than two years of age.

California has implemented such a program for women convicted of a nonviolent crime who are serving a sentence of less than three years and who receive a written evaluation that they and their babies would benefit from being together. The placement is reviewed by the court and the women and their children are placed in small, community-based institutions (Gaseau, 2000).

Extended Visiting Options

A number of facilities have short-term programs that allow babies and children to remain with their incarcerated mothers for short periods of time. Some provide for an overnight stay in the facility and others provide for children to be housed in the community at night and be at the facility during the day. These programs include camps for children and their mothers to increase bonding. The Pocatello Women's Correctional Center in Idaho, for example, sponsored a camp in the summer of 1998 for women who had gone through the facility's parenting program. The camp, which became an annual event, provides an excellent example of cooperation and collaboration between the facility and a variety of other agencies and groups including the local hospital, churches, and the university (Personal Communication with Bona Miller, former Warden, Pocatello Women's Correctional Center, September 2001).

Nonresidential Programs

Other programs target nonresidential activities for both younger and older children. An important part of the Nebraska mother/child program was the Mother Offspring Life Development (MOLD) component designed in 1976 to foster positive relationships between incarcerated mothers and their children when the children were at home (Blinn, 1997; Dowling, 1997). The Mothers and Their Children (MATCH) program started by the National

Council on Crime and Delinquency in 1978 was replicated in eleven states (Weilerstein, 1995). It focused on improving visiting, developing children's centers where women and children could play and learn together, and implementing a variety of supportive and educational services.

The Pennsylvania Department of Corrections' State Correctional Institution—Muncy developed an innovative program called "I Love You This Much." It consisted of a workbook developed by staff and inmates at the facility. The book was designed to help mothers communicate effectively with their children. It provides samples of letters that mothers could write and activities that could be done by the child at home to enable incarcerated mothers to "take an active role in the child's development, guidance, and daily life. It is a way for the parent to demonstrate genuine concern about the child's future" (Pennsylvania, 1998). According to Mary Leftridge-Byrd, deputy secretary, Pennsylvania Department of Corrections, a second edition, published in 1998, is available by contacting Muncy State Correctional Institution, Box 180, Route 405, Muncy, Pennsylvania 17756.

In February 1999, the Florida Department of Corrections received a $300,000 grant and implemented Reading Family Ties: Face to Face. This program enables mothers who are incarcerated in two rural institutions to have weekly family visits by videoconferencing with their families in Miami. Classes are held weekly with mothers to help them communicate more effectively with their children. Rini Bartlett, administrator of Female Offender Programs for the Florida Department of Corrections, describes one case where a four-year old boy hugged the computer screen after an hour of listening to his mother read to him (Bartlett, 2000).

Perhaps one of the most innovative and successful programs established to encourage visitation between mothers and their children is the Girl Scouts Beyond Bars program. The pilot for this program was implemented in 1992 by Marilyn C. Moses of the National Institute of Justice in cooperation with the Girl Scouts of America and the Maryland Correctional Institution for Women in Jessup (Moses, 1995). With the support of the local Girl Scout Council, a

Girl Scout troop was formed for the daughters of female inmates. The girls had regular scout meetings in the community where they participated in normal Girl Scout activities. Twice a month, the scout meeting was held at the women's facility. During these meetings, the mothers and their daughters participated in a variety of activities and troop projects from puppet shows and structured play to more serious discussions of self-esteem, drug abuse, relationships, pregnancy prevention, and coping with family crisis. After its initial success in Maryland, Girl Scouts Beyond Bars has been replicated in a number of locations (Moses, 1997).

According to reports on the program, Girl Scouts Beyond Bars has increased visitation and interaction between mothers and daughters since its inception. Mothers who never heard from their daughters began receiving numerous phone calls and letters. The classes taught in the program opened lines of communication between mothers and their daughters. They also taught mothers how to respond to difficult parental issues in spite of their inability to be with their children on a full-time basis.

The program increased morale among women inmates and decreased disciplinary problems. As one inmate said, "If anything goes wrong, they will shut this program down" (Moses, 1995, p. 5). The facility and the Girl Scout organization share the costs of the program. In most cases, grants from various organizations or donations from the community provide funding. The program requires ongoing support and commitment from both the Girl Scout organization and the facility staff to resolve the various logistical and operational issues involved in making it a success.

Components of Good Programming

Good programming for women and their children requires comprehensive planning, implementation, and evaluation or monitoring. Johnston (1997), in *Maternal Ties: A Selection of Programs for Female Offenders*, lists ten ingredients for developing successful programs. They are summarized as follows:

Understand the Population. Today's women prisoners have many of the same problems as those of previous generations; it is essential to understand the specific needs of the target population.

Identify Staff Resources. This involves identifying the skills staff may have in this area and building on them.

Solicit Community Involvement. Many organizations have expertise and resources that can be tapped in planning and implementing programs.

Solicit Input from Inmates. Inmates have the most to lose and the most to gain in having successful programming. They should be involved in planning.

Take a Team Approach. Many correctional facilities for women have a history of starting and stopping programs. This often results from not having a multidisciplinary approach to the development and implementation of services. The team should involve personnel from all major components of the facility including treatment and security staff.

Be Child Focused. Programs should be developed with the emotional, physical, and behavioral needs of children in mind.

Do Homework. As noted earlier, a number of programs have been developed around the country. They provide a basis of information that can be helpful in the planning process. Even if they have been phased out, they can provide guidance on why and how programs succeed and how to avoid making the mistakes that others have made.

Have Clear Goals and Objectives. As the cat said in *Alice in Wonderland*—"If you do not know where you want to go then it does not matter which way you go." Successful programs have clear goals and strategies to measure success.

Start Small. Starting with a selected population in a pilot program can help work out any difficulties in implementing the program.

Work with Staff. Staff, particularly line staff, in the facility can make or break a program. If they do not understand it or believe it is not necessary, they may be reluctant to do the work necessary to make it work.

What Staff Can Do

Regardless of whether a facility has a well-developed program or not, staff are going to be faced with the problems of women who are concerned about their children on a daily basis. Failure to address their concerns can result in severe management problems in the facility and make staff's job more difficult. To help relieve some of the problems, correctional personnel should work to create a supportive environment for inmates who are mothers.

One of the first things to be addressed is the need to keep women informed about the status of their children and their rights regarding them. For those who will be facing court hearings involving their children or whose children may be having difficulty in the community, not knowing what is happening can be extremely frustrating for the inmate. Staff should encourage women to communicate with their caseworkers or others involved with their children in a systematic fashion. Assisting inmates in making a written list of questions they have when dealing with social service agencies and others can help them have some feeling of control over their situation and become better organized in dealing with issues involving their children.

Coordination with community agencies is essential. Those outside corrections may have many misconceptions about female offenders and the criminal justice system. They may need help in understanding the system and overcoming their negative stereotypes about women prisoners.

Institution policy and procedures should facilitate mothers' access to services and programs (Acoca and Austin 1996). If the facility provides legal assistance or counselors related to women's children, inmates should be encouraged to seek help. If such help is not available in the facility, community volunteers can provide it.

Women should be encouraged to participate in visitation programs and staff should do whatever is consistent with the facility's policies to support children's positive visitation with their mothers. Staff need to understand these visits are often highly emotional experiences for both mothers and children (Acoca and Austin, 1996). Empathy and compassion in helping women work thorough their depression following visits is important.

Visits should be handled in a professional, humane manner. Caregivers should be assisted in understanding prison rules and the reasons for them. Staff members involved in visitation should try to imagine how they would react if they were approaching the institution for the first time. What questions would they have and what would they want to know? Providing adequate information and assistance can make the experience more pleasant and may help caregivers be more willing to bring children for visits.

Staff may need to examine their own feelings about mothers and their children. The 1996 National Council on Crime and Delinquency study found staff often had negative feelings about the women's ability to be mothers and their parenting skills (Acoca and Austin, 1996). While many women inmates have had limited mothering themselves and do need positive role models and help in being mothers, others were excellent mothers on the street. Those who need help should be provided the opportunity to improve their parenting skills and encouraged to do the best they can within the framework of their situation.

There remains wide variation in the quantity and quality of programs and services in women's institutions geared toward maintaining and strengthening ties between mothers and their children (Morton and Williams, 1998; Pollock 2001). There were disturbing trends in a 1995 survey of fifty states, the District of Columbia, and three Canadian Provinces. Fewer women's institutions offered parenting classes, furloughs, overnight visits with children, and children's centers in 1996 than they did 1985 (Boudouris, 1996). Massive budget cuts in states across the nation probably will result in even more reductions in programs for women and their children. On a positive note, there were considerably more facilities responding that they had access to community facilities for mothers and children. Still, even here, only twenty-three women's facilities out of eighty-six institutions responding to the survey had such programs (Boudouris, 1996).

Support of inmates and their children should not end when the women are released. AIM, Inc., a group based in Montgomery, Alabama that provides help and support for inmate mothers and their children, points out:

> *After the mother's release, the family situation may be worse than before her arrest. Often, inmates are released with no job, no housing, and little if any money. For women, these stressors are compounded with the difficulties of regaining custody and finding childcare. Clearly, without family, and social support, inmate families are unlikely to succeed* (AIM, 2001, p. 3).

With the goal of helping mothers upon their release, the Children's Center in Bedford Hill Correctional Facility in New York created a Sponsor a Baby Program. Community groups including religious organizations donate items the baby will need when an inmate mother leaves prison with her baby. If the baby's mother cannot leave prison following birth and is denied access to the prison nursery, family members who take the baby are provided assistance through the Sponsor A Baby program. This program annually serves some fifty families and babies (Conly, 1998; Bedford Hills, 1999).

Extensive programming for women offenders and their children is available in New York City through the efforts of the Women's Prison Association. This agency provides a wide variety of institutional and community-based services to women offenders. The programs include education and support of HIV or at-risk women, emergency and transitional housing, skill building workshops, child care, counseling, and other support to released women their children and families (Morash and Schram, 2002).

Summary

As Dowling (1997) so eloquently states "A mother may be guilty, but a child is always innocent" (p 83). With the dramatic increase in the number of incarcerated women in America's prisons, society cannot afford to expand the "Get Tough" philosophy to offenders' children. Pollock (2001) found "most women in prison are unable to access comprehensive, enriched programs to help with their parenting role" (p. 63). Even in the states that had more extensive programming, only a few women were able to use the services and some states "had virtually no parenting programs available" (Pollock, 2001, p. 63).

Correctional agency and facility administrators and staff need to be actively involved at all levels to develop and to maintain meaningful programs for incarcerated mothers and their children. The best programs will include a variety of options such as comprehensive parenting classes, several types of visiting, community residential programs, and postrelease community coordination of services for women who have been released from prison.

Failure to act will only contribute to the growing cycle of crime in our society. Conversely, a willingness to address the issues of female offenders and their children has the potential not only to reduce the recidivism rate of the offenders (Martin, 1997), but to decrease the future incarceration rates of their children.

Physical Health Issues
of Women Offenders

Objectives

❖ Describe some of the problems women can have when seeking medical care in the community.

❖ List the problems women can have with prison medical care.

❖ Discuss the issues in provision of medical care through contract-medical personnel.

❖ Identify issues related to access to medical care in women's facilities.

❖ Discuss the standard components in a comprehensive health care program in a women's facility.

❖ List the major physical health problems that can affect women offenders.

❖ For each of the illnesses discussed in this chapter, be able to describe the ailment, list the symptoms, and discuss the implications these illnesses have for staff working in a women's institution.

Introduction

Have you ever been ill and could not get a doctor's appointment? Or have you ever gone to a doctor or hospital emergency room and had your complaints and concerns ignored or ridiculed? Have you ever been given medicine or a test and not known what it was for or even questioned whether it was the correct one or the most effective one for your situation? If your answer is yes, then you have some idea of what it is like to feel that your pain or illness is not being taken seriously.

Are you always satisfied with the treatment and care you receive from the medical personnel you choose to provide your treatment? Do you resent having an insurance company tell you who you can consult for a medical problem or what treatment you may receive? Imagine if you were confined and had someone else in charge of every aspect of your contact with the medical system including being in control of every medicine or treatment you received. Then, you can begin to understand some of the problems of providing health services to women in prison.

In this chapter, issues related to incarcerated women's physical health will be reviewed. In the next chapter, mental health issues will be discussed. Since these matters usually involve more than just medical personnel, all staff should have a basic understanding of the problems involved in providing health care services to incarcerated women. These services should meet community standards and treatment should be the equivalent to what one could receive in society at large.

The American Correctional Association (ACA) has adopted three volumes of standards: *Standards for Adult Correctional Institutions* 4th Edition (2003c), *Performance-Based Standards for Correctional Health Care in Adult Correctional Institutions*, First Edition (2002b) and *Performance-Based Standards for Adult Local Detention Facilities*, 4th Edition (2004a) that can provide overall guidance in the development of a performance-based health care system. Under the American Correctional Association standards and the accreditation process, correctional agencies can accredit an entire institution or only a medical component of that institution.

Other professional associations including the American Public Health Association (APHA) and the National Commission of Correctional Health Care (NCCHC) have standards and/or policies that can provide information on issues related to health services for offenders. The National Institute of Corrections has developed guidelines called *Correctional Health Care: Guidelines for the Management of an Adequate Delivery System*, 2001 Edition, which provide a comprehensive discussion of health care in correctional institutions including a chapter on medical care for incarcerated women. Written by Jaye Anno, it is available on CD by contacting www.nicic.org.

Correctional staff always must resist the urge to diagnose women's medical problems or second-guess the advice of a trained medical service worker. Anyone giving medical advice without a license may be charged with a crime. It goes without saying staff that should never give an inmate medicine not specifically prescribed for her. Nor should staff deny access to medical services or any other medically related activity to women under correctional supervision.

Women and Health Care Problems

Some correctional personnel including medical staff express surprise that incarcerated women use medical services more frequently than do male inmates. When this author asked a director of nursing in a southern women's institution what was the most common medical problem women in that facility presented, without a moment's hesitation, she said "whining." Unfortunately, this attitude is all too common among some staff in women's institutions who do not understand that women in prison are not much different from women in the community in their use of medical care. Even health professionals, as noted in the example above, can take a negative view of women offenders' medical problems (Berry, 1996).

Women, in general, are much more likely to indicate they have a medical problem and to seek treatment for their illness than are men. They also are more likely to discuss health-related matters and their treatment or the lack of it. For example, most women are very willing to relive their pregnancy and delivery stories with each other, and old wives tales about the horrors of child-birth have terrorized generations of young women expecting their first babies.

Women in the community are treated differently by medical personnel than are men. The differences increase, particularly, if a woman has an unspecified pain or problem that defies initial diagnosis. Then, she is likely to be thought of as hysterical or told that her problem is all in her mind (Sandelowski, 1981). This may be the reason women are given more prescription medication, including tranquilizers and other mind-altering drugs, than are men (Addiction Research Foundation, 1996).

Some of the cavalier treatment women receive may be a result of medical training focused on what is normal for men. It also may be a result of the sex bias and gender values discussed earlier. For whatever reasons, women in general often are unsatisfied with medical personnel in the community and may even be suspicious of the care they receive.

Women and Prison Medical Care

Women enter prison with the same medical issues as men plus those related to the fact that they are biologically female. However, the medical problems they have in common with men may vary in number and severity. For example, women have higher rates of HIV than do men (Hammett, Widom, Epstein, Gross, Sifre, and Enos, 1995). Hammett, Harman, and Rhodes (2000) found women entering jail had three to four times higher rates for syphilis than did men. In the mental health area, Teplin, Abrams, and McClelland (1997) found that women in the Cook County, Illinois Jail suffered from depression at four times the rate of men and were twice as likely to have bipolar disorder as were men. As evidence of the trauma that women offenders suffered in the community, Teplin, et al. (1997) found 22 percent of the women in her sample from Cook County Jail suffered from Post Traumatic Stress Disorder and DeCou (1998) found 50 percent of the women in the county jail population had Post Traumatic Stress Disorder.

Several factors influence incarcerated women's greater need for health care. Some incarcerated women's health issues are exacerbated by neglect of health maintenance along with lifestyle problems of abuse of alcohol and drugs. Also, women in prison use more health care services because of their more complicated reproductive systems, sexually transmitted diseases, and pregnancies (*National Commission on Correctional Health Care*, 1994). Additionally, the unique health care needs of incarcerated "women are strongly impacted by social factors (education, poverty, family, support systems)" (Malesh, 2000, p. 52). Finally, incarcerated women's health is negatively influenced by long histories of physical and/or sexual abuse that the majority of them encountered as children and which continued when they were adults (Browne, Miller, and Maguin, 1999).

While in prison, women develop many of the same problems with medical services that women in the community have. As noted, they typically have more physical and mental health problems to begin with than do incarcerated men and use more of medical practitioners' time and consume more resources than do men. Unfortunately, in some instances, correctional and medical staffs have less empathy for illnesses that may result from the unhealthy lifestyles and behaviors of many female offenders. Medical personnel and other institutional staff also may see them as "fallen women" who deserve any problems they have.

Their situation is magnified by the fact that many of them may have received little or no medical services prior to being incarcerated (Berry, 2001). Those who did receive services may have gone to overburdened clinics for people with limited or no income where they may have had to fight for services and where staff had little time to educate them about their illnesses or other problems.

Women of color face additional problems beyond sex, gender bias, and poverty that include racial bias and stereotyping. This is a critical factor in their treatment since they tend to be incarcerated with more severe and intractable medical problems than their male counterparts. In most large correctional systems, women offenders, particularly women of color, have the highest rates of HIV infection and associated tuberculosis—far exceeding rates for male offenders (Ross and Lawrence 1998, p. 177).

Women of color also may be unable or unwilling to seek medical care for fear of being incarcerated because of drug use or other lifestyle behaviors that might result in prosecution and incarceration. The arrests of new mothers in South Carolina, most of whom were women of color, for using illegal drugs including marijuana, while pregnant received national attention. Their subsequent prosecution and incarceration for child endangerment sets a precedent that could have a far-ranging impact on the government's involvement in pregnancies.

In October 2003, the U.S. Supreme Court upheld the conviction of a South Carolina woman of color who had been sentenced to twelve years in prison for homicide by child abuse. She had used cocaine during her pregnancy and when her child was stillborn at eight and a half months, she was charged with death by child abuse since in South Carolina a viable fetus is considered a child. Attorneys for the homeless woman with an IQ of 79 argued that she had two other medical conditions that could have caused the stillbirth. South Carolina prosecutors said the law under which women face twenty years to life sentences if they engage in any behavior that might harm a fetus will be a deterrent to such actions (Richey, 2003). It remains to be seen if prosecutors will being charges against women who smoke, drink alcohol, or take other actions that could harm a fetus. However, it can have a chilling effect on women with substance abuse problems who might seek prenatal medical care.

All of these factors combined result in women who:

> have little knowledge about their bodies
>
> have limited medical care prior to incarceration
>
> perhaps have had negative experiences with medical personnel
>
> often have serious medical problems

have no choice or control over their situation

are encountering a prison medical system that may or may not be responsive to their needs

Pollock (2002) noted, "While the reality may be that most women receive better health care in prison than they would have on the outside, there is no doubt that some egregious situations have existed in the past and probably still exist in some institutions" (p. 77). Historically, correctional systems in the United States have had a poor track record of providing sex and gender specific services for incarcerated women. It was noted in the American Correctional Association's Public Policy on Correctional Health Care that:

Correctional facilities are generally designed for male detainees and so do not reflect women's stronger need for physical privacy and sustained group interactions. Little or no attention has been paid to the physical reproductive issues and special needs for services and treatment of mental disorders. Some of the gender specific needs of women that require special and differential focus revolve around pre- and postpartum problems and complications of pregnancy, primary responsibility for minor children, a history of domestic violence, early childhood physical and sexual abuse, adult rape, and a high probability of dual diagnosis of mental disorder and substance abuse. In addition, the prescription of psychotropic medications that may be necessary to treat these disorders may carry untold side effects that, in turn, further affect physical and emotional functioning (American Correctional Association, 1996, p. 15).

Faiver and Rieger (1998), in their discussion of medical services, point out correctional systems often have not recognized women's greater need for more medical services than males. Agencies have limited resources per capita for women or the same amounts as those given to male prisoners, or even have provided fewer resources, which results in a less-than-adequate response to women's medical needs.

Women have a right to access to care, the right to care that is ordered, and the right to a professional medical judgment . . . they must be free from deliberate indifference to their serious medical needs (Faiver and Rieger, 1989, p. 134).

Medical problems of incarcerated women are quite serious. A number of women enter the facility pregnant and these pregnancies are often high risk for the mother and her baby. Rates of HIV positive and accompanying AIDS-related illnesses are higher for incarcerated women than for men. One study of incarcerated women in New York found that women in prison were more than twice as likely to die as were women of the same age in the community (Ross and Lawrence, 1998).

Regardless of the facts, some among the correctional profession will always say "So what, they are criminals so why should we care?" Quoting Dr. Alvin J. Thomas, past president of the Washington State Medical Association, Anno (2001) noted that correctional personnel have ethical, moral, and legal responsibilities to provide the necessities of life and that:

> no jail or prison administrator has the right to impose the death sentence and failure to provide for the medical needs of those in custody is equivalent to pronouncing a death sentence (p. 3).

Contract Medical Care

There are two main ways correctional agencies work with the private sector. The first way is "privatization," which involves having a private sector company or organization contract with a correctional agency to build a facility, build and operate one, or just operate an existing facility. The organization can either be for-profit or not-for-profit. One of the largest for-profit companies in corrections is Corrections Corporation of America headquartered in Tennessee. An example of a not-for-profit organization is the Salvation Army that has a long history of working with corrections' clients.

The second way the private sector is involved in corrections is through contracting for services. In the health services area, correctional agencies contract with medical specialists individually or contract with a firm to provide all or part of the medical services in a facility. Contracting for medical services is the most common type of contracting used by corrections (National Institute of Corrections, 1996) and is the type that is the focus of this section.

Contractual medical care adds another wrinkle in the complicated matter of providing proper care to incarcerated women. In an attempt to provide cheaper or better care, a number of correctional agencies have contracted for a private company to deliver all or most of the health care in a system. This may work well in some instances; yet, if all parties are not knowledgeable about women's health needs, serious problems can occur.

A 1988 study of health care in New York's largest women's institution found inmates were treated by five different contract physicians who did not consult with each other and who did not maintain adequate records. There was inconsistent follow-up of those with diagnosed medical problems. Women in jails received no better care. One woman in "the most sophisticated contracted jail health service in the United States" died of complications of undiagnosed and untreated sepsis with sickle cell anemia several days after childbirth" (Ross and Lawrence 1998, p. 189). She had received no prenatal care in jail and no postpartum evaluation.

In other jurisdictions, incarcerated women and correctional facility administrators worry about medical staff turnover and whether the contract medical personnel, particularly the doctors, can speak English (Belknap, 2001) or be able to communicate with staff and offenders. One warden reported her institution had had six different doctors in four months and others are concerned about whether contract medical personnel will take the time and effort to understand security and other concerns involved with managing a women's prison health care system.

While similar problems might occur with in-house medical care, initiating contract medical care in a women's institution does not absolve correctional administrators of their responsibility to ensure services are provided. The correctional agency and its administrators are still liable for damages if the proper services are not provided in a timely fashion. Nor is contract medical care necessarily cheaper. Some contractors use what are called "loss leaders" at the beginning of a contract. That is, the services will be provided to the correctional agency at a price under the actual costs. Then, the price will increase as time passes and the agency is dependent on the contractor for all health care. Or, a contractor will bid in good faith and find that costs are higher than projected. Either way, the correctional agency must pay the higher costs or go through the expensive process of renegotiating a new contract or providing services another way.

A one-size fits all approach does not apply in contracting for women's health care. Agency health service administrators should make certain that contracts are tailored to be gender responsive to the system's women prisoners and ensure unrestricted access for women inmates to the full range of services they need. It also should incorporate a system to ensure the quality of care meets community standards and that continuity of care is provided during and following incarceration. Contracts should be developed with input from the administrators of women's facilities and carefully monitored by agency staff sensitive to the needs of female offenders who have expertise in medical matters to ensure that quality services are maintained.

Standard of Care

As noted earlier, the American Correctional Association and a number of other organizations that have concerns about women's health have developed health care standards and guidelines. The provision of adequate health care for incarcerated women also was addressed in a position statement issued by the National Commission on Correctional Health Care (See Appendix B for the statement). If correctional agencies providing health care or contracting for medical services would comply with the policy statements and standards of the American Correctional Association, the National Commission on Correctional Health Care, and other professional and governmental organizations concerned with women's health, many of the health problems of women in institutions would be resolved. While such action might require additional resources in the short term, over time it should save money as prevention and timely care improve women inmates' overall health.

Another issue which is addressed for all correctional staff in Chapter 10 but which needs to be reinforced here is the problem of medical staff misconduct. Women in prison are particularly vulnerable to abuse and Berry (2001) notes an alarming trend of sexual misconduct by medical personnel in women's facilities. She reports several cases in the California prison system that were not addressed until after Ted Koppel of ABC aired a segment on *Nightline* about the problem. According to Berry, two doctors at a women's facility were accused of sexually molesting and fondling women, requiring them to submit to unnecessary pelvic and breast examinations over a four-year period. After the newscast, one doctor was dismissed but the second was not removed for six months. "Both doctors had been criminally indicted" by 2001 (Berry, 2001, p. 42). This and other accounts reinforces the need to ensure that both male or female staff members who conduct examinations of incarcerated women are always accompanied by a female staff member.

Access to Care

In an attempt to cut down on what is seen as nuisance visits, some systems require inmates to pay for sick call visits. Given that women generally have medical problems requiring that they seek medical attention more often than do males in similar age groups, a pay-as-you-go sick call system will have a differential negative impact on incarcerated women and should be approached with care if at all. It discriminates against women because they have to pay for more sick calls than do males and it may discourage women from seeking medical care in time to prevent a more serious problem. This can end up costing agencies more to deal with advanced ill-nesses than it would have to catch these problems in their early stages. Experiments with having more open access to medical care have demonstrated that, while initially inmates may use the system more, in the long run, they will become comfortable with help being available when they need it and use the system responsibly.

Having access to medical care—including emergency service—is a critically important requirement in the correctional health care system. Even in the community at large, the wait to see a doctor or other medical personnel may be long, and staff may try to screen out or put off people they believe are not seriously ill. This is a dangerous and sometimes a life-threatening situation on the outside and it becomes even more critical in a prison where inmates do not have the choice to call another doctor or go to a different hospital. While the American Correctional Association standards require unimpeded access to medical care, in some facilities, correctional officers or other nonmedical personnel may be the ones who make the initial decision of whether the woman can see medical staff. If the woman is seen as a problem person or a chronic complainer, then staff may be reluctant to grant her permission to see medical personnel.

It is important to remember that nonmedical staff should be very cautious when dealing with medical problems and not make decisions about when and how a woman has access to medical services. Sometimes those who appear simply to be complaining have serious medical problems and will die without proper treatment. Medical staff may complain that they are seeing women who do not need treatment, but it is always better to have the medical staff see someone if there is any question that she may have a medical problem.

Comprehensive Health Care Program

Intake

Normally, correctional facilities begin addressing physical and mental health issues immediately upon admission. The first component of a comprehensive health care program in any women's institution is an intake screening, followed by a complete physical and mental health appraisal (American Correctional Association, 2003c, 4-4362). Of particular concern in the intake screening process is the determination of whether the woman has any immediate health problems requiring treatment or whether she has a communicable disease that might put others in the facility at risk. In New York, for example, 28 percent of women coming into the system in 1993 had medical problems that required immediate treatment and ongoing care (Ross and Lawrence, 1998). In addition to the items mentioned in the standard, to meet the needs of female offenders the following should be ascertained:

any problems with menstrual cycle

number of pregnancies and outcomes

history of breast disease and gynecological problems

family history of breast or ovarian cancer and osteoporosis

history of domestic violence and history of sexual abuse (Anno, 2001)

care and safety of children (Faiver and Rieger, 1998)

The screening is followed by a complete physical that, in addition to the regular intake physical given to all new inmates, should include the following items for women at a minimum:

pelvic examination,

breast examination,

Pap test,

a baseline mammogram (for those thirty-five years of age and older)

Additional testing during intake and throughout the woman's stay in the facility should be based on standards of the American Cancer Society, the American College of Obstetricians and Gynecologists, and other standard-setting bodies, as well as on age and risk (Anno, 2001). Then, given the data on heart attacks among women, family history, and other factors making the inmate at risk for this disease should be reviewed, as recommended by the American Heart Association.

Women who test positive for pregnancy and/or sexually transmitted diseases may have serious problems if not treated and should have follow-up services, as required (Anno, 2001). In some instances, women may be pregnant or have a serious sexually transmitted disease or other illness and not be aware of it. Women should be offered a HIV-test if pregnant (Fink, Goodman, Hight,

Miller-Mack, and DeGroot, 1998). This test is important because the women will need treatment to prevent "pre-natal HIV transmission" (Fink et al., p. 208).

Also, of particular concern are communicable diseases such as tuberculosis and hepatitis that can spread to staff and other inmates. Until results of such tests are known, women in intake should be separated from the general population. Counseling women about their medical problems should begin at intake.

Sick-Call Services

American Correctional Association standards specify that there be a process for inmates to request health services on a daily basis with clinical services available at least five days a week (ACA, 2003c, 4-4346). Unfortunately, not all correctional agencies participate in the accreditation program. Some inmate sick-call systems in women's institutions work like the old military sick call in which solders lined up for hours to consult medical personnel. This process maximizes limited health resources but does not necessarily coincide with when inmates become ill or feel sick.

Lacking control over her life, including her medical care, is a very frightening thing for any woman, but staff are often afraid women will abuse a system if it is more client oriented. Some abuse of medical services is probably inevitable. However, if health education is offered and the institutional climate is supportive and encourages positive decision-making, many abuse problems can be minimized.

Another unfortunate practice occurs when women have to see medical personnel in a male institution. Usually, a few women are seated on benches or placed in a holding cell near the officer's station. Dozens of male offenders hang off the bars of the other holding cells or march by the women. They make suggestive comments and gestures and speculate about what the women's medical problems are. This is humiliating to most of the women involved and creates a situation that can get out of hand and be a threat to security. Also, officers probably will be required to strip search the women going to and coming from clinics in male facilities.

Inpatient Services

Most health care service systems in women's institutions have an inpatient unit or infirmary. This area normally will be staffed with a variety of medical personnel on a twenty-four hour basis and will provide professional care for those too sick to be in the general population. The number of beds in this area is usually limited. While infirmary care is the most expensive way to provide treatment in the facility, it may cost less than a bed in a community hospital. Having infirmary care can prevent women recuperating from surgery or other medical conditions returning to the general population before it is safe to place them in that environment.

Health Maintenance

Correctional health service systems in women's institutions should have a component for coordinating treatment for chronic ailments and for providing preventive care and tests necessary for the long-term health of the inmate population. Some women's health problems will extend to the community so systems should be in place to provide continuity of care. Referrals to community service providers and a supply of medications are part of a system that helps to ensure the women continue necessary treatment on release.

Health Education/Prevention

Health education is a very important component of any health services program in a women's institution. Some staff might question why education programs are needed for women inmates. They may need to be reminded that keeping women healthy and knowledgeable about their physical and emotional health will make them easier to manage and make their care less costly to taxpayers. Health education can help alleviate women's concerns over minor problems they can handle themselves and make them aware of things they should bring to the attention of medical personnel. It also can help relieve much of the hostility and suspicion surrounding medical personnel. It is cost effective because when women get out of prison/jail and return home to their families, they will be more knowledgeable and be able to help their family members live healthier lives.

At a minimum, the health education program in a women's institution should include information on the following:

breast self examination

contraception

pregnancy prevention and self-care when pregnant

cessation of tobacco, alcohol, and substance abuse

HIV-harm reduction classes

parenting classes (Anno, 2001)

The old saying, "An ounce of prevention is worth a pound of cure" is certainly applicable in women's institutions. Eating right, exercising, practicing positive stress reduction techniques, and implementing other components of a healthy lifestyle may be foreign to many inmates. Basically, an emphasis on a wellness model or a healthy lifestyle approach to physical and emotional health can have both short- and long-term benefits for all in the institution—staff and inmates alike.

Involving incarcerated women in planning the programs and using peer-led groups can be very effective (Morrill, Mastroieni, and Leibel, 1998). Stressing a collaborative partnership between inmates, correctional staff, and medical personnel is a sound strategy in successful management of women's health education issues.

Supporting healthy lifestyles through gender-responsive diets for women and appropriate exercise programs will assist in the long-term health of female inmates. Diet is of particular concern since a 1998 study by the National Institute of Corrections found that almost 80 percent of the agencies responding to the survey reported that they offered "the same diets for men and women"

(p. 4). Differences in the remaining 20 percent typically were accounted for by special diets for pregnant women (National Institute of Corrections, 1998). *See* the section on "Weight Issues" on page 267.

Hospice

Given the types of illnesses women contract and the length of many sentences implemented in the "get tough" era, some women will come to the end of their life in prison. No inmate, male or female, wants to die in prison. Many placed on compassionate leave will live only a short time after release. They have in fact "held on" until they were out of prison.

If state law permits, the woman should receive compassionate release to the community. This works well if there is family or others who will be responsible for her care. Berry (2001) recommends correctional agencies develop policies and practices that include community-based alternatives for women who are dying. For those who have no other alternatives, a number of correctional systems have developed hospice programs involving the inmate's family, where possible, community volunteers, and other women inmates. The programs work much like those in the community and will help the woman die with dignity. Medical staff should include pain specialists, where needed, to ensure the woman is receiving the proper pain medication. Chaplains and other correctional staff will need to be involved to help the program go smoothly. This multidisciplinary team also should be prepared to help staff and inmates who have become close to the woman who is dying deal with their grief.

When no family or others are available to take the body, correctional systems should arrange a proper funeral even if it is in an inmate cemetery. Allowing inmates and staff to participate in the funeral or have a memorial service will help them reach closure with their loss and will help other women inmates understand that they will be treated with dignity if they die in prison. According to Junior, (2003) "Grieving is a different experience for each person . . . Individuals grieve for different lengths of time and express a wide range of emotions" (p. 77).

Common Medical Problems

While women may have most of the diseases and medical problems that men have, some are either unique in their manifestation in women or effect only women. Some of the more common ones are reviewed below.

Cancer

The word "cancer" strikes terror in the heart of anyone who is told she has it. Most people have family or friends who were incapacitated and eventually died of cancer. It is often difficult to understand that there are more than 100 types of cancer in which the cells become abnormal and grow uncontrollably (Richland, 1998).

Women who receive a diagnosis of cancer or who think they might have cancer may become withdrawn and depressed or they may act out, refuse treatment, or blame those around them—particularly correctional officers for their situation. Being a supportive listener and reinforcing the need for a positive attitude toward living with cancer can help alleviate some of the problems that may occur. Inmate support groups involving volunteers from the community can help women understand and cope with cancer more successfully.

Breast Cancer

One woman will be diagnosed with breast cancer every three minutes, and one woman will die of breast cancer every twelve minutes in the United States (Richland, 1998). Breast cancer is the second leading type of cancer death among women in the United States, following lung cancer. While the mortality rates among Caucasian women are falling, perhaps because of early detection, education, and screening, the death rate for African-American women is not decreasing (Governors' Spouses Program, 1996). With this prevalence in the community, it is to be expected that some women might enter the facility with breast cancer or develop it once incarcerated.

Health care personnel constantly stress the need for early diagnosis and treatment to reduce the morbidity from cancer. Early detection of breast

cancer is a three-step process involving breast self-examination, clinical examination of the breasts by a health care professional, and regular mammogram
tests. It is one of the few illnesses requiring the active participation of the individual woman in its diagnosis. Even taking all of the steps necessary for early
detection will not ensure that all cases are diagnosed when the cancer is small.

There has been much discussion concerning the age when women should
be treated, the frequency of tests necessary to protect them, and even the type
of treatment to be offered. The American Cancer Association guidelines
appear to be the most comprehensive (Governors' Spouses Program, 1996).
They indicate that women twenty years of age and older should be taught by
medical personnel to do monthly breast self-examinations and to note when
changes in their breasts indicate that they should seek medical attention.
Women between the ages of twenty and thirty-nine should have clinical breast
examinations conducted by a health care professional every three years. If
there are any problems, the exams may need to be done more often. Women
forty years of age to forty-nine years of age, who have no symptoms or high-
risk factors, should receive a clinical examination annually and have a
mammogram every one to two years. If there are high-risk factors or other
problems indicated, then the examinations and mammograms may need to be
done more frequently. The guidelines recommend that women fifty years of
age and older have annual mammograms and annual clinical breast examinations, in addition to their own monthly self-examination (Governors' Spouses
Program, 1996).

In many instances, it is possible to have a mobile mammogram unit from a
local hospital provide mammograms onsite. Whatever the source, the testing
program should be accredited by the American College of Radiology which
evaluates the equipment, the staff qualifications, the quality of images, and the
amount of patient radiation (Richland, 1998).

Treatments for breast cancer range from a lumpectomy in which only the
tumor is removed, to a radical mastectomy in which the breast, lymph nodes,
and chest muscles are removed. Following surgery, radiation, chemotherapy,

hormone therapy, and/or other treatments may be given. The type of treatment depends on the size of the tumor, how much it has spread, test results, the patient's age and medical history, and what she and her doctor decide is best.

Women who have had breast surgery should have access to reconstructive surgery, if needed, and properly fitted prosthesis, as necessary. Peer counseling groups can help incarcerated women share experiences, information, and support to help them in dealing with the emotional stress of having cancer.

Cervical Cancer

A second cancer in which the cure is closely impacted by early detection and treatment is cervical cancer. Early detection using Pap smear tests and aggressive treatment, including the removal of cervical tissue before it becomes cancerous, has drastically reduced deaths from this disease (*Harvard*, 1997a).

Abnormalities in cervical tissue are more common in incarcerated women than in women in the general population (Shuter, 2000; Hammett et al., 2000). While in the community, some incarcerated women will have had multiple sex partners, which leads to them being more likely to be infected with the human papilloma virus (HPV) (Faiver and Rieger, 1998) which has been linked to the progression of cervical cancer (*Harvard*, 1997a). Providing Pap tests and ensuring all inmates are tested on a regular basis are very important.

Pap tests normally are done annually unless positive results require additional testing. According to Faiver and Rieger (1998), the National Commission on Correctional Health Care standards require a pelvic examination and Pap smear within seven days of admission into a correctional facility and further require a gynecological assessment of young women within seven days of admission at a juvenile facility. Medical personnel also should be sensitive to the feelings of the women they are examining, particularly young women who may not have been sexually active or those women who may have been sexually assaulted as a child or as an adult.

Abnormal cells identified in Pap tests are divided into three classifications. Women with the most serious type should have the lesion or pre-cancerous cells removed. There is not yet agreement in the medical community on what the standard treatment should be in the lesser classifications. In some cases, the doctor will perform a test in which a lighted instrument is inserted in the cervix and biopsies are taken from abnormal areas. A second approach is to repeat the Pap test every six months to see if the abnormality persists. This issue may be resolved in the future as the National Cancer Institute began a multiyear study in 1997 to help determine the best course of action for minor abnormal Pap tests (*Harvard*, 1997a).

Obviously, a woman who has been told she has a positive or bad mammogram or Pap smear is going to be very distressed. In many instances, these tests are initially positive and subsequent testing proves that the earlier tests were incorrect. The woman, during this period, however, is likely to be anxious and may be difficult to manage. Staff members need to understand the fear and uncertainty accompanying these and other traumatic medical situations and take appropriate action to help relieve her anxiety and resolve her problems.

Cardiovascular Disease

Cardiovascular disease is the leading cause of death among women in the United States. One in nine women between the ages of forty-five and sixty-four has some form of cardiovascular disease and after age sixty-five the ratio is one in three (Governors' Spouses Program, 1996). Cardiovascular disease includes coronary artery disease (some may call it "hardening of the arteries") that causes heart attacks, hypertension (high blood pressure), strokes, and angina or chest pain.

It has long been assumed that women were at lower risk of having cardiovascular diseases than were men because female hormones helped protect them. However, some young women with high risk factors and all women after menopause are subject to these diseases. Some groups of women are at higher risk than are others. African-American women between the ages of thirty-five and seventy-four are one and one half times more likely to die of a heart attack than are Caucasian women (Governors' Spouses Program, 1996). They are three times more likely to die than women of the same age among races other than Caucasian. African-American women are 24 percent more likely to die of coronary artery disease, and their death rate for strokes is 83 percent higher than it is for Caucasian women (Governors' Spouses Program, 1996). African-American women who live to be more than seventy-five years of age, however, have a lower risk of dying from these diseases than do their counterparts in other racial groups (Governors' Spouses Program, 1996).

Heart Attack

A heart attack occurs when a clot or other blockage interferes with the flow of blood to the heart. If not treated immediately, part of the heart becomes traumatized and in severe cases, the heart stops and the woman can die.

One of the reasons women die of heart attacks at such a high rate is that they fail to recognize the symptoms. While some warning signals of a heart attack apply to both men and women, others, as indicated in the following chart from the American Heart Association, are more common in women than in men.

Heart Attack Symptoms

Women and Men

a heavy feeling in the chest, pressure, squeezing, or pain in the center of the chest that may last more than a few minutes or goes away and comes back

chest pain that spreads to the shoulders, neck, or arms

chest discomfort with lightheadedness, fainting , sweating, nausea, or dizziness

More Common in Women

stomach, abdominal pain, or unusual chest pain

nausea or dizziness

shortness of breath and difficulty breathing

unexplained anxiety, weakness, or fatigue

palpitations, cold sweat, or paleness (American Heart Association, 1997a).

Unfortunately, another cause of high mortality among women who have heart conditions is that medical personnel are sometimes unaware that women are at risk of developing heart conditions; thus, treatment is delayed. Any severe back pains, heaviness in the chest, shortness of breath or difficulty in breathing, blueness around the mouth, or any of the other symptoms described above should be considered serious and staff should seek medical care immediately for anyone exhibiting them.

Stroke

Another cardiovascular disease that must be identified and treated immediately is a stroke or "brain attack." Similar to a heart attack, a brain attack occurs when a blood vessel in the brain bursts or becomes clogged. The brain cells deprived of oxygen die. If it is extensive, a stroke can cause paralysis or death. Strokes also can contribute to the development of dementia and cause the person to have trouble speaking and walking. They also can make a person appear confused and forgetful.

Symptoms of a stroke include the following:

sudden weakness or numbness of the face, arm, or leg on one side of the body

sudden dimness or loss of vision, particularly in one eye

loss of speech, or trouble talking or understanding speech

sudden severe headaches with no known cause

unexplained dizziness, unsteadiness or sudden falls, especially along with any of the previous symptoms (American Heart Association, 1997)

High Blood Pressure

High blood pressure or having a systolic pressure (upper number) of more than 140 with a diastolic pressure (lower number) over 90 for an extended period of time contributes to the possibility of heart attacks and strokes (American Heart Association, 1995). Little is known about why women develop high blood pressure, but because it has very few outward symptoms, it is referred to as the "silent stalker." Without regular checks, it can damage one's body before it is identified. High blood pressure is dangerous because it makes the heart work harder to pump blood though constricted vessels contributing to congestive heart failure, strokes, and heart attacks.

Women with a history of close family members having high blood pressure or stokes are at high risk to have one or the other themselves. So, it is important for institutional staff to record the family history of incarcerated women to the extent possible. Race is also tied to the occurrences of these problems. High blood pressure tends to develop earlier in life among African-Americans and is usually more severe. African-Americans, therefore, are almost twice as likely to have a fatal stroke than are Caucasians (American Heart Association, 1995). Hispanics have a lower risk of heart attacks than whites but have a higher risk of strokes (American Heart Association, 1997a).

Women who have any combination of high blood pressure, diabetes, a history of heart attacks, chest pains, narrowed coronary blood vessels, narrowed arteries in the legs, congestive heart failure, or any type of rapid, irregular heartbeat are at risk of having a stroke. All women can improve their chances of preventing a stroke by having their blood pressure checked regularly. This means having their blood pressure taken at their annual physical unless they are at risk and then it will be up to their doctor to decide how often it should be checked. Taking blood pressure medicine if prescribed; stopping smoking; recognizing and treating diabetes; limiting alcohol; and eating a healthy diet that is low in fat, cholesterol, and sodium will also contribute to prevention and treatment of high blood pressure (American Heart Association, 1997a).

Many women in prison have multiple hereditary and lifestyle issues making them at risk for high blood pressure. Programs geared toward improved lifestyle, eating habits, and exercise should have a beneficial effect on preventing expensive and debilitating cardiovascular disease among the prison population.

Menopause

Menopause is the cessation of menstrual periods. While the average age of menopause is fifty-one, this natural process begins a number of years earlier when the body begins to produce less estrogen. Women who have their ovaries surgically removed also will experience menopause symptoms unless they are given hormone replacement therapy (*Harvard*, 1996).

While there are a number of symptoms that may accompany menopause, not all women experience the same symptoms, nor do they have symptoms at the same level of severity. According to *Harvard Women's Health Watch* (1996) some of the symptoms are as follows:

> Hot flashes, a sudden feeling of heat that spreads over the body, are among the most common symptom of menopause. Hot flashes occur at random and can be accompanied by sweating and flushed skin. While annoying in and of themselves, they are most annoying when they disrupt sleep.

> Vaginal tissues may be come drier and thinner. This can cause less flexibility, painful intercourse, urinary track problems, or sagging of the pelvic organs.

> Excessive menstrual flow, less menstrual flow, or irregular periods may occur during menopause. If the menstrual flow is excessive, the woman may become anemic and fatigued. Less menstrual flow or irregular periods may worry some women who are afraid they are developing cancer or some other disease.

Osteoporosis, which often is associated with menopause, is a disease that causes the bones to become more porous and gradually thin out. Bones then become fragile making them more likely to break. Osteoporosis is a major health threat in the United States affecting from 7 to 8 million people, 80 percent of whom are women.

Until they are in their mid-thirties, women gain more bone than they lose. From then until menopause, they usually balance out and gain about as much as they lose. The decreasing level of estrogen occurring in menopause causes an increase in bone loss. In its early stages, there are no outward signs. As the disease progresses, bone fractures especially in the spine, wrists, and hips occur. Eventually, the disease can lead to loss of height and curved backbone commonly referred to as "dowager's hump."

Those at risk of developing osteoporosis include those who:

smoke

use alcohol to excess

get little exercise

receive too little calcium (as an adult or child)

have had a bone break in a minor injury

use certain medicines such as steroids (commonly used to treat asthma and arthritis) and thyroid hormone (if the dose is too high)

go through menopause before age forty-five

have a close relative who had it (*Harvard*, 1996).

Those with severe osteoporosis can break a bone simply by picking up something heavy or putting the slightest pressure on their bones. Staff should be cautious in handcuffing, restraining, or taking other actions that might cause broken bones among those women with osteoporosis.

Women inmates should be provided screening for osteoporosis and given treatment, if tests indicate they have a problem. Prevention is important and includes education on how to prevent the disease, weight-bearing exercise, and diets to meet the needs of both younger and older incarcerated women.

Pre-menopausal women need 1,200 milligrams of calcium daily and post-menopausal women need 1,500 milligrams daily (Keamy, 1998).

Cardiovascular disease becomes more of a risk for women after menopause because of the lack of estrogen. Hormone replacement therapy (HRT) was strongly recommended for a number of years in the hope that it would reduce the symptoms of menopause and cardiovascular disease. However, recent research indicates that HRT can increase a woman's risk of developing cancer. Given the possible side effects of hormone replacement therapy, women receiving it should have close medical supervision. Other drugs to treat bone loss have been introduced and should be available to women, if needed.

Other treatments to help alleviate the symptoms of menopause include encouraging a healthy lifestyle. This, according to *Harvard Women's Health Watch* (1996), includes the following:

eating a healthy diet that is rich in fruit and vegetables with no more than 30 percent of calories daily coming from fat

increasing calcium

participating in moderate, weight-bearing physical exercise for about thirty minutes most days

Respiratory Diseases

Respiratory disease is a common health problem of women in prison, particularly among those who come into prison undernourished or in poor physical condition. They also may have used drugs or inhaled substances damaging to their lungs. Prison life, if a number of women are confined in small, poorly ventilated spaces, can cause respiratory infections to spread rapidly.

Women with respiratory problems should be encouraged to stop smoking and should not be around others who smoke. Making prisons smoke-free zones has become increasingly popular in the last few years. It reduces the risk of a number of illnesses and improves the quality of life for all in the facility.

Smoking-cessation classes and other support should be provided for staff and inmates before making the facility totally smoke free.

Most respiratory problems, if left untreated, can develop into serious illnesses. Some of the more serious respiratory diseases seen in prison are discussed below:

Asthma

Asthma is a serious respiratory disease in which the cells in the lung's air tubes make more mucus than normal. This clogs up the tubes and they swell. The muscles in the air tubes tighten making it difficult to breathe. The lungs close up and the person ceases to take in oxygen. As the woman is deprived of oxygen, her body begins to fight for air. Being deprived of air is frightening and if it continues, panic sets in. This, in turn, causes the asthma attack to worsen.

In severe attacks, the woman may have difficulty talking and following orders or instructions. Her neck muscles may bulge, and her lips and fingernails may have a blue or grayish color. In the case of severe attacks, the woman must take her medicine right away and be seen by medical personnel immediately. Failure to get medical care quickly can cause death (American Lung Association, 1997).

Attacks can be triggered by a number of things including an allergic reaction to food, other illnesses, cigarette smoke, and mold or other airborne contaminants, paint, cleaners, and other sprays. Infections and exercise can cause an attack in some people. They also can be triggered by emotional stress and, since incarceration is very stressful, women who are prone to having asthma attacks may have more while in prison.

The number of persons suffering from asthma has been increasing since the 1970s and since the 1980s, death rates among women from this disease have increased 50 percent compared to a 23 percent increase in men (Ross and Lawrence, 1998). The death rate among African-American women is higher than for other racial groups. While rates for women were higher than for men in all age groups, young women represented the largest group of newly diagnosed cases with an increase of 69 percent (Ross and Lawrence, 1998).

Pneumonia

Pneumonia is an infection in the lungs. If left untreated, it can cause death. Pneumonia is most likely to occur in women whose immune system is under attack from another disease or who have had a history of respiratory infections.

Someone can have pneumonia without knowing it, but she eventually will become so ill and suffer such severe shortness of breath that she will seek medical attention. Other symptoms of pneumonia are fever, chest pains, and a general feeling of malaise. It takes an average of six weeks for a person to regain her strength even after only a mild case of pneumonia. There is an immunization to help prevent pneumonia and anyone who has had pneumonia in the past should be reviewed to determine if she should receive the immunization.

Tuberculosis

Tuberculosis is a serious, highly contagious respiratory disease. It strikes hardest among young children, people more than fifty years of age, or those in a weakened condition. Tuberculosis, or TB as it is commonly known, was one of the leading causes of death in the world among all age groups, prior to the development of antibiotics. Most communities had at least one tuberculosis hospital where those with the disease could be treated. Since the disease is highly contagious and can be spread through the air, public health laws enable doctors to confine or quarantine people who have the disease. Ironically, in some jurisdictions, old TB sanitariums have been converted to correctional facilities.

Those at risk of contracting tuberculosis include:

people who work or live in the same space with someone who has TB

poor people

homeless people

immigrants from countries where the disease is common

nursing home patients

prisoners

alcoholics and intravenous drug users

people with medical conditions such as diabetes, certain types of cancers, and those who are underweight

especially people with HIV (Centers for Disease Control and Prevention, 1998).

The Centers for Disease Control and Prevention recommend all correctional facilities designate an individual staff person or team with experience in infection control to be responsible for developing, implementing, and monitoring comprehensive TB infection control policies. In addition to conducting a facility risk assessment and developing close relationships with community health departments, the Centers for Disease Control outline the following activities as essential to controlling this serious disease.

Screening

All correctional facility employees and inmates who have the disease should be identified promptly and reported to the health department. Staff and inmates who have positive skin tests should be evaluated for preventive therapy.

Containment

Persons suspected of having infectious TB should be promptly placed in a TB isolation room and further diagnostic work should be conducted on them. If they do have an active case of TB, they should be provided treatment. Staff should ensure the treatments are completed as directed and should closely supervise the taking of medicines and other required treatments. Persons who test positive for exposure to TB, but who do not have an active case, should have a thorough medical evaluation and be given preventive care, as needed.

Risk Assessment

This involves collection and analysis of the following:

the cases of active TB detected

the number of persons who have latent TB infection, their evaluation, and treatment

whether cases of TB are promptly reported and proper records are maintained

whether those with active cases are treated and their progress monitored

whether referrals to other correctional facilities and health departments are made and participation in treatment confirmed (Gayle and Castro, 1996).

Since correctional populations are at risk, staff and inmates should be tested on a regular basis to determine if they have contracted TB. With early diagnosis, proper treatment, and rest, most TB patients can be cured. However, it is very important for anyone taking antibiotics for TB, or any other disease to complete the full course of the medication prescribed. Several diseases, including TB, have developed strains that are immune to most antibiotics because people did not take all their prescription.

Other Contagious Diseases

Women inmates, like their male counterparts, should be tested for a number of communicable diseases. They often have higher rates of these diseases than do women in the community or than do male inmates. In some instances, these contagious diseases may have gone untreated for years and can jeopardize women's long-term health.

HIV/AIDS

Women in the United States are becoming infected with HIV and developing AIDS at a higher rate than males. This is also the case among incarcerated women. Studies of several states have revealed the rates of HIV infection are consistently higher among incarcerated women than among incarcerated men. According to Ross and Lawrence (1998), in Texas 7 percent of the state's incarcerated women were HIV-positive compared to 3 percent of the male population. In Maryland 15.5 percent of women inmates tested positive compared to 8.7 percent of male inmates (Ross and Lawrence, 1998). In some states, the number of HIV cases among male inmates has dropped while the cases among women have continued to rise (Ross and Lawrence, 1998).

Obviously, these data have serious implications for health care and other social service needs among the female population. HIV treatment, for example, increasingly relies on taking several medications on a complex schedule. If the individual misses a dose or the dose is incorrectly administered, serious consequences can occur.

Sexually Transmitted Diseases (STDs)

Women coming into correctional facilities have a higher incidence of sexually transmitted disease than do women in the community (Anno, 2001). Sexually transmitted diseases include

Chlamydia (especially among teenage women and those under twenty-five)

HPV Human Papilloma virus (genital warts)

Hepatitis B

Genital Herpes

Syphilis

Gonorrhea

HIV

Women may exhibit few signs of having sexually transmitted diseases, and in some women, the disease can go into recession but then return. If not diagnosed and treated, sexually transmitted diseases can cause infertility, arthritis, heart disease, and even death. In some cases, these diseases can be transmitted to the unborn fetus.

Studies of jail populations found high rates of sexually transmitted diseases. Trichomoniasis, a type of vaginal infection, was found in as high as 43 percent of female detainees in Rhode Island and in up to 47 percent of the women detained in New York (Shuter, 2000).

Hepatitis

Hepatitis A, B, C, D, and E are viral infections that can result in inflammation of the liver. The American Liver Foundation's website identifies hepatitis as the most common blood-borne infection in the United States with more than 5.5 million Americans infected in the general population.

Hepatitis causes a variety of symptoms including abdominal pain, fever, fatigue, loss of appetite, and nausea, followed by jaundice or yellowing of the skin and eyes. It often mimics the flu and may be overlooked unless medical staff are familiar with it and conduct the appropriate tests.

Hepatitis can be spread from person to person by hands contaminated with feces, food contaminated with feces, raw or undercooked shellfish taken from contaminated water, and food not cooked enough at the right temperature. Contact with blood products and unprotected sex with an infected person also can spread hepatitis. Infected mothers can pass it to their children at birth. Using intravenous drugs or having had a blood transfusion or organ transplant before 1992 are other ways the disease has been spread (Oakland, 1998).

All types of hepatitis are serious. If the person contracting hepatitis has other complicating conditions such as cirrhosis of the liver, death can result. In some cases, persons survive the acute phase of the disease and become carriers who can infect others without knowing it.

Treatment includes bed rest, extra fluids, and medications that are effective in 50 to 60 percent of the cases. However, most infected people carry the virus for the rest of their lives (Oakland, 1998).

Hepatitis can be prevented by proper sanitation, including vigorous hand washing and proper food preparation. Staff in correctional facilities including medical personnel should take universal precautions when coming in contact with any blood, blood products, or body fluids. Personal grooming items such as razors and toothbrushes should not be shared (Oakland, 1998).

Given the risk factors in the lifestyles of many women offenders, including unprotected sex with multiple partners and intravenous drug use, the prevalence of hepatitis is probably higher in prison than in the community. Testing programs to identify and treat those infected should be provided for institutionalized women. Prevention programs should include education to help staff and offenders know how to prevent the disease and what specific practices to follow to minimize its spread.

Diabetes and Other Insulin Diseases

Diabetes, sometimes referred to by inmates as "having sugar," occurs when the body does not produce enough insulin to process the sugar in the body. It is a very serious disease and if not treated can lead to loss of hearing, sight, and limbs, and cause strokes or even death.

Symptoms of diabetes depend on the type of diabetes. According to the American Diabetes Association (1998), Type 1 diabetes symptoms usually occur suddenly and include:

> frequent urination
>
> excessive thirst
>
> extreme hunger
>
> dramatic weight loss
>
> irritability
>
> weakness and fatigue
>
> nausea and vomiting

Those with Type 2 diabetes usually develop symptoms gradually. Their symptoms include:

any of the symptoms of Type 1 diabetes

recurring or hard-to-heal skin, gum, or bladder infections

drowsiness

blurred vision

tingling or numbness in the hands or feet

itching

Staff members need to be aware of three major complications, which according to the American Diabetes Association (1997), can occur with diabetics.

Hypoglycemia

Hypoglycemia, sometimes referred to as an insulin reaction, means the patient has low blood-glucose levels. It can occur if the women who use insulin eat too little or their meals are delayed. Extra exercise also can bring on a reaction. Typical symptoms of hypoglycemia include feeling cold, clammy, shaky, weak, or very hungry. Some people will become pale, develop a headache, act strangely, or behave erratically. They may slur their speech and appear intoxicated. They may become unconscious and if left untreated can die. Hypoglycemia must be treated immediately with juice or food.

Women in the institution who might be subject to insulin reactions should have quick access to such things as orange juice or candy. If they do not improve after eating or drinking something sweet, medical attention should be provided right away.

Hyperglycemia

Hyperglycemia or too much sugar in the blood occurs when too much food is eaten or the person has not taken enough insulin. Emotional stress, pregnancy, or illness also can cause high blood-sugar levels. Symptoms include excessive thirst, frequent urination, and nausea. Anyone exhibiting these symptoms should be referred for medical attention in a timely manner.

Ketoacidosis

Ketoacidosis or diabetic coma may occur when the level of sugar in the blood is too high. It is caused by a severe imbalance in the level of sugar and insulin. It usually develops gradually and can be detected through testing the blood or urine. Symptoms include dry mouth, thirst that cannot be quenched, excessive urination, dry, flushed skin, loss of appetite, labored breathing, and fruity-smelling breath. There also may be vomiting, abdominal pain, and unconsciousness. At the first sign of a severe imbalance in the blood sugar levels, the woman should be referred immediately to medical staff for treatment.

The American Diabetes Association (1997) recommends those with diabetes wear a medical alert ID necklace or bracelet. In case of the emergencies, the medical alert bracelet indicates the type of treatment needed. Institutional policies, which spell out the type and amount of jewelry women can have, should include the provision for medical alert bracelets or necklaces for those who need them. For women with diabetes and other serious medical conditions such as severe allergies, warning devices can mean the difference between life and death.

Currently there is no sure way to prevent diabetes. Those at risk include those

with close family members (sister, brother, parent) who have the disease

who are overweight. The American Diabetes Association (1997) has issued guidelines for height and weight that are included in Table 1, page 274.

who are under sixty-five and get little or no exercise daily

who are between forty-five and sixty-five. American Diabetes Association (1998) guidelines recommend that everyone forty-five years of age and over should consider being tested every three years. Those at risk should be tested at a younger age.

who had a baby weighing more than nine pounds at birth (American Diabetes Association, 1997)

If normal blood sugar levels can be maintained with proper diet, exercise and, if needed, medication, many of the side effects from diabetes can be controlled. However, as with all serious ailments, learning that she has diabetes can be very upsetting to an incarcerated woman. Controlling and managing diabetes requires the active participation of the woman, medical personnel, and other staff in the institution. It can be very difficult for the woman to stay on her diet and understand the medications she must take. Failure to do either can have serious consequences. In some instances, insulin shots one or more times a day may be needed and the woman also may have to have a finger stick for a blood glucose test up to four times a day (Faiver and Rieger, 1998). Women with diabetes generally will have to have meals at set times and may require healthy snacks between meals to maintain a stable blood-glucose level.

Counseling and staff support will be important to the long-term health of inmates with diabetes. Security and other operational procedures need to be reviewed to ensure the woman with diabetes can receive the necessary care.

Reproductive Issues

Pregnancy

According to a survey conducted by Fogel (1995), approximately 25 percent of women in prison were pregnant or had recently delivered a child. This percentage includes the almost 4,000 women who will give birth while they are in prison (Markovic, 1995). Studies have shown that many of these pregnancies are high risk for the mother and particularly the baby. Lack of adequate prenatal health care; inadequate diet; drug use; and sexually transmitted diseases, including HIV, contribute to the chance that the woman may abort or have a child with severe medical problems (Ross and Lawrence, 1998; Faiver and Rieger, 1998). Unfortunately, many women coming to prison have limited basic knowledge about pregnancy, the delivery process, proper diet, nutritional needs, and exercise. All of these are essential for a successful pregnancy. In addition to a lack of knowledge, the Michigan Department of Corrections found that all of the forty pregnant women incarcerated there in one year were considered high risk and most had a history of drug abuse, had no prenatal care before their incarceration, and had poor diets (Epp, 1996).

Prenatal Care

Pregnant women who test positive for drug use or who come to the facility on methadone treatment should be maintained on the drug to prevent fetal distress (Richardson, 1998). Alcohol withdrawal should be done in a hospital as delirium tremens (DTs) "is an obstetric emergency" (Richardson, 1998, p. 185).

All pregnant women should receive relevant prenatal tests to identify any risk factors such diabetes, sexually transmitted disease, or other impediments to a successful pregnancy. Counseling and education should be available to help the woman make the positive lifestyle choices that are best for her and the fetus. Segregation of pregnant women is not necessary unless justified for specific medical reasons.

It is important for prenatal vitamins, particularly folic acid, to be available for women who think they might be pregnant or who are pregnant. Folic acid plays a key role in the development of the central nervous system particularly in the first eighteen to thirty days of gestation. The Centers for Disease Control and Prevention estimates that an intake of 400 micrograms of folic acid per day lowers the incidences of spine and brain defects by about two-thirds (*Harvard*, 1998). While some folic acid is available in a normal diet, it is not enough, and it is recommended that women of childbearing years take a multivitamin containing 400 micrograms of folic acid during pregnancy and afterwards, if nursing (*Harvard*, 1998).

A series of steps recommended by the American College of Obstetrics and Gynecology can increase the chance of a healthy pregnancy. These include, upon approval of an obstetrician, an exercise program consisting of regular exercise three times per week. The College also recommends pregnant women should avoid hot, humid environments, drink plenty of water, and eat small, but nutritious meals, and snacks (Anno, 2001). The American Public Health Association standards encourage special diets including milk and extra food, vitamin supplements, and proper exercise as prescribed by medical personnel (McHugh, 1980).

Obviously, these recommendations cannot be met in correctional settings unless the staff members are willing to help pregnant women have a more successful pregnancy by adjusting the environment to accommodate the women's needs. Diets based on men's nutritional needs, for example, should be modified. Air-conditioning or fans may be needed in warm weather. Again, staff members need to realize these changes are not coddling inmates, but are made in the best interests of all concerned.

Delivery

Babies should take born in a licensed hospital that has the facilities to manage high-risk births (Anno, 2001). The birth should take place under the supervision of a certified midwife or obstetrician.

There has been considerable discussion about the use of restraints on pregnant women. According to Raeder (2003)

> *Amnesty International, Human Rights Watch, and the United Nations Special Rapporteur on Violence Against Women have all questioned this practice. In particular, Amnesty International has recommended legislation, regulation, policies, policies and practices to reflect a commitment to protect inmates against such abuse (p. 124).*

After six months of debate, the American Correctional Association in August 2003 passed a revision of the *Public Correctional Policy on Use of Force* that states:

> *Electronic devices, chemical agents and other types of restraints should not be used on females known to be pregnant or individuals having respiratory and other debilitating conditions until medical staff have been consulted or there is no other reasonable alternative* (American Correctional Association, 2003a).

The use of restraints on pregnant inmates is exacerbated in the United States by the practice of holding pregnant women in women's maximum-medium security facilities. In some instances, it may be the only facility for women in the state or it may be where medical care for women is available. While most incarcerated women are classified as minimum-custody inmates, central office's policies designed for male facilities require all inmates in higher security level facilities to be handcuffed, or placed in other restraining devices including belly chains and leg irons upon leaving a facility. These policies should be modified to ensure minimum-custody women who need to be transported from the institution to the community for prenatal care or tests are not shackled as though they were in maximum-custody.

Even those women who are classified as needing maximum-custody supervision, in later stages of pregnancy, should not be shackled. Women in the later stages of pregnancy may have problems with balance and restraining devices may cause them to fall. A woman in advanced stages of pregnancy or who is in labor poses a limited security risk. Berry (2001) recommends "there should be a nationwide ban on the use of shackles on women prisoners in labor" (p. 43). Certainly, placing women in restraints while in labor or in the delivery room is security overkill and as documented in Chapter 2 can cause death or injury of women and/or their babies.

Postpartum Care

The postpartum period is particularly difficult for most incarcerated women. Some systems return women to the prison as soon as six hours after delivery. Even with twenty-four to forty-eight hours in the hospital, there is little time for bonding between the woman and her child. Berry (2001) recommends that mothers be able to stay with their newborn infants for a minimum of seventy-two hours. Such bonding is important for the long-term health of the baby and the emotional health of the mother (Morton and Williams, 1998; Anno, 2001). Programs, such as those administered by the Federal Bureau of Prisons and the New York Department of Correctional Services, in which babies are kept with their mothers for various lengths of time, are being implemented once again in other states and should be considered by all correctional systems.

In any case, the new mother is likely to be depressed upon separation from her child and screening for postpartum depression should occur. Counseling services and medical intervention, as needed, should be provided for depression in postpartum mothers as well as for other issues including adoption of her children. Other programs that should be available are discussed in the chapter on mothers in prison.

Termination of Pregnancy

Anno (2001) notes that the American Public Health Association's standards call for women offenders to have access to contraceptives upon request. She recommends that this should apply to women in co-correctional institutions, those who are eligible for furloughs or are on work release, or women who need contraceptives for a medical condition.

Female offenders may have their pregnancy terminated through miscarriage or abortion (Malesh, 2000). A miscarriage is a spontaneous abortion in which the fetus is expelled prematurely and does not live. Therapeutic abortion is another way that a pregnancy can be terminated.

Most women who miscarry will suffer the same grief cycle as those who loose a full-term baby or child. Berry (2001) recommends that facility administrators should encourage programs staffed by specialists from the community to help a woman who has had a miscarriage or the death of a child. Staff should provide support for a woman who has had a miscarriage and refer her to the appropriate staff for counseling.

Abortion is a very controversial issue that must be considered in medical case planning for incarcerated women. While abortion is a very emotional issue, it is a procedure that is legally available to women in the community. Correctional officials should not "hinder a women's right to obtain an abortion and should not require a court order before allowing a woman to obtain one" (Raeder, 2003, Appendix A, p. 132).

Women inmates should not be forced or coerced into having an abortion, but it should be an available option for those who chose it or for those whose medical condition make it advisable. As discussed in Chapter 2, the question of who pays for the procedure is not clear even though the Federal Court in Washington State ruled that:

> *The termination of an unwanted pregnancy is also considered a serious medical need and denial of an abortion constitutes a deliberate medical indifference regardless of the prisoner's ability to pay,* Monmouth County Correctional Institution Inmates v. Lanzaro, *1987 (p 54).*

Raeder (2003) notes that whether or not correctional agencies are required "to pay for the abortion, policies that require inmates to pay for transport and security may be suspect" (Appendix A, p. 134).

Weight Issues

Eating disorders such as Anorexia Nervosa and Bulimia Nervosa are discussed in Chapter 9 as mental health disorders. However, many women are overweight when they enter the facility or become so after admission.

Many women inmates are accustomed to eating high fat, high carbohydrate diets. Once in the institution, the food they receive is frequently high in fat and carbohydrates and thus, high in calories. This situation is exacerbated when agency administrators require women's institutions to serve the same diet that is served to male inmates—which occurs in some 80 percent of the agencies reporting in a 1998 survey by National Institute of Corrections. They often do not allow any deviation from the planned menu unless ordered by a physician. One study, of incarcerated women in California, found about 30 percent of women were clinically obese when admitted. By the end of three months in prison, 89 percent had gained an average of fourteen pounds and 49 percent were clinically obese (Rasche, 1993). Women's institutions should provide meals based on the caloric needs of women—not the calories needed by men.

Weight guidelines are expressed in the relationship of body weight to height and the definition of what constitutes being overweight varies. Faiver and Rieger (1998) observed that, in their opinion, while being overweight is a significant issue when related to other medical conditions, it is not by itself a serious problem unless the person is 50 percent or more above her ideal weight. Other experts define obesity as being more than 20 percent over normal weight guidelines (*Harvard*, 1995b). The most common gauge is to use Body Mass Index (BMI), which is a measure that determines the ratio of height to weight. Using this scale, individuals with a BMI of 40 or more are classified as obese. Those with a BMI of 50 or over are classified as extremely obese (Tanner, 2003). New, more stringent guidelines of women's ideal weight compared to their height are based on a growing body of evidence that gaining weight increases the risk of premature death from heart disease, diabetes, and certain cancers (*Harvard*, 1995b).

The U.S. Department of Agriculture and the Department of Health and Human Services weight guidelines are listed in Table 1 at the end of this chapter. In certain cultures, being heavy is considered a sign of contentment and having a good life. Other segments of the population become obsessed with weight and make their situations worse by using crash diets.

The only safe way to lose weight and keep it off is by changing one's lifestyle—particularly increasing exercise and decreasing the intake of fat calories. Even losing ten to fifteen pounds and keeping it off can significantly reduce blood pressure, dangerous cholesterol, and the chance of developing diabetes (*Harvard*, 1995b). Inmates should be encouraged to control their weight and maintain an active lifestyle for their long-term health and to help minimize costly medical care that must be provided by the corrections system and taxpayers.

Dental Care

One area that has received little attention over the years is dental care for women offenders. Given that most of the women have multiple medical needs and generally have had limited routine medical care in the community, it could be assumed that their dental needs also would be a problem. In a 1994 study of women admitted to Rikers Island in New York by Badner and Margolin, only 41 percent had received dental care in the previous year and one-third reported they had tooth pain upon admission to the jail. The treatment they received in the community usually consisted of having a tooth removed. Dentists participating in the research study gave the women an oral examination. They found the women had an average of 2.3 decayed teeth, 3.5 missing teeth, and 4.5 filled teeth each. Their conclusion was that the women had serious dental problems and needed substantial dental care. Many of the women also need prosthetic devices. Given that the women averaged between twenty and thirty years of age, the number of dental problems was a strong indication of limited dental care in the community (Badner and Margolin, 1994).

Unfortunately, few systems particularly at the local level, provide dental examinations or preventive care (Anno, 2001). Since untreated dental problems often progress to serious infections, correctional agencies should provide needed dental care to include education and preventive cleaning to incarcerated women on a regular basis. Pregnant women are also susceptible to serious dental problems that need treatment.

Substance Abuse

The final medical problem to be addressed is substance abuse. Some may question why it is included here and not in the chapter on mental illness. It could fall in either but is really an overarching problem that incorporates issues from both disciplines and requires a multidisciplinary approach and commitment from a wide variety of staff to ensure programs are successful.

The National Center on Addiction and Substance Abuse (CASA) noted in the Introduction to its 1996 report:

In the worst way, American women are closing the gap with men: women are increasingly likely to abuse substances at the same rate as men and women are starting to smoke, drink, and use drugs at an earlier age than ever before. Women

*get drunk faster than men, become addicted quicker, and develop substance re-
lated diseases sooner. At least one of every five pregnant women uses drugs,
drinks, or smokes, putting herself and her newborn in great and avoidable danger . . . Today some 40 percent of crack addicts are women. The percentage of
women (3.7 %) and men (3.9%) who abuse prescription drugs is already equal.
Women receive 2/3 of the prescriptions for tranquilizers and antidepressants
written.*

According to CASA (1996) there are 4.5 million women who abuse alcohol,
3.5 million women who abuse prescription drugs, and 3.1 million who abuse
illegal drugs in the United States. This description is of women in the community and one does not have to work with female offenders very long to realize that substance abuse is a major issue in women's prisons. Studies of the
prevalence of substance abuse reinforce this observation. Nationally, Snell
(1992) found that 50 percent of women in prison reported using drugs the
month before they were incarcerated. Greenfeld and Snell (1999) found that
25 percent of incarcerated women reported they committed crimes to get
money for drugs. State and local figures can be even more compelling. For
example, 84 percent of incarcerated women in Hawaii abused drugs while
on the street (Goldkuhle, 1999) and 82 percent of women in the Hampton
County Correctional Center were arrested for drug offenses (DeCou, 1998).

In spite of the high levels of abuse, treatment options while in prison and in
the community once released are limited. Greenfeld and Snell (1999) found
that only 20 percent of women with substance abuse problems received treatment in prison. Of even more concern, Pendergast, Wellisch, and Falkin
(1995) after reviewing substance abuse programs for women in prison and in
community corrections reported that many of them excluded pregnant
women and those with co-occurring disorders who were the very populations
who needed treatment the most.

Alcohol and drug addictions are diseases that without treatment become
worse over time and cause increasingly severe biological, psychological, and
social problems (Center for Substance Abuse and Treatment, 1994). Bloom,

Owen, and Covington (2003) recommend a holistic multidimensional approach to the treatment of women with substance abuse problems because it:

> *allows clinicians to treat addiction as the primary problem while also addressing the complexity of issues that women bring to treatment: genetic predisposition, health consequences, shame, isolation, and a history of abuse, or a combination of these. For example, while some women may have a genetic predisposition to addiction, it is important in treatment to acknowledge that many have grown up in environments in which drug dealing, substance abuse and addiction are ways of life (p. 74).*

Substance abuse treatment should be available in all facilities housing women. Since the effects of drugs and alcohol are different for women compared to men (*see* Bloom et al., 2003, p. 52 for discussion of differences), programs should be designed from the ground up to meet the needs of women not just added on to a program designed for men. Unfortunately, some believe that gender-responsive drug treatment means putting women offenders through a program designed for men and then tacking on a few hours of treatment designed for women. Effective gender-responsive treatment should deal with the whole woman and her physical, emotional, and social situation including any history of abuse and trauma.

Correctional staff should be supportive of women participating in treatment programs. Those working with women need to understand that substance abuse, trauma (sexual, physical, and psychological abuse), and mental health status are interrelated. Incarcerated women with substance abuse problems should be monitored closely to ensure their emotional and physical safety needs are met (Bloom et al., 2003). Staff training should include identification of symptoms of drug and alcohol abuse (ACA, 2003c, 4-4305), and correctional employees should understand and support the facility's treatment program including components to address relapse prevention and aftercare services (ACA, 2003c, 4-4377).

Summary

Access to adequate and appropriate medical care and continuity of care is not only in the best interest of the ongoing health of those in the facility and the communities the inmates will return to, it is also a legal necessity. Most correctional personnel will argue that it is better to make the necessary changes in internal practices voluntarily, rather than have them mandated by the court.

Studies have found women's institutions frequently lack the medical services that are routinely available for men. These include such things as skilled psychiatric care, programs for those with retardation, geriatric units, physical therapy and access for those with physical disabilities, and diagnostic services and other treatments that are needed on a regular basis (National Commission on Correctional Health Care, 1994). Add to this general neglect, the additional health care issues related to women's reproductive systems and other gender-related needs and it is clear that providing women with access to adequate medical care that meets community standards will continue to be a serious problem for correctional personnel for the foreseeable future.

Many women enter the institution with serious medical problems and may have engaged in lifestyles in the community that place them at risk. They typically will have more health-related problems than do male inmates. Medical and correctional personnel will need specialized training in gender-related medical concerns of female offenders to help them understand the needs of this population and the time and care that will be required to meet those needs.

Wellness and stress-reduction programs, proper diet and regular weight-bearing exercise, and programs dealing with trauma and substance abuse help provide both for the long-term health of the inmates and represent potential savings to taxpayers. Positive working relationships among medical staff, correctional personnel, and inmates will result in more meaningful health services and treatment programs. Correctional personnel must follow through to ensure women receive the treatment needed and are referred to medical attention promptly if any problems occur. This includes the development of a continuum of treatment plans that will carry over to the community upon release.

As Malesh (2000) noted:

> *preventative health care and related education are now considered the corner-stones of good health . . . Critical to meeting the particular health needs of the female offender is a focus on health promotion, involvement in her own health care, access to health related information, and a comprehensive, holistic, and multi-disciplinary approach . . . comparable in quality to those available to the general public (p. 52-53).*

Recently the U.S. Department of Health and Human Services through the Office on Women's Health in Region V began developing a regional consortium to improve the health of women in prisons in the states of Illinois, Indiana, Michigan, Minnesota, Ohio, and Wisconsin. The project involved profiling incarcerated women in the region, identifying innovative programs in the facilities, providing funding and assistance in building a regional consortium, and facilitating linkage and follow up activities (Horersch and Deppisch, 2003). Activities such as this are an encouraging development in the implementation and evaluation of new, comprehensive, gender-responsive, collaborative approaches to the treatment of women offenders' health needs.

Table 1 Height/Weight* and At-Risk Weight†‡ for Women

Height	Weight	At-Risk Weight
4'10"	91-119	129
4'11"	94-124	133
5'0"	101-132	138
5'1"	104-137	143
5'2"	104-137	147
5'3"	107-141	152
5'4"	111-146	157
5'5"	114-150	162
5'6"	118-155	167
5'7"	121-160	172
5'8'	125-164	177
5'9"	129-169	182
5'10"	132-174	188
5'11"	136-179	193
6'0"	140-184	199

*No shoes   *No clothes

Source: U.S. Department of Agriculture and Department of Health and Human Services, 1995.
†The chart shows unhealthy weights for men and women thirty-five years of age or older. At-risk weights are lower for those younger than this. (Source: American Diabetes Association, 1997).

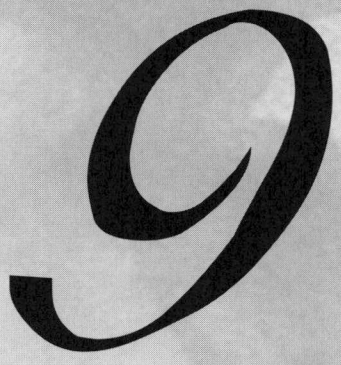

Mental Health Issues
of Women Offenders

❖ Define what is meant by an offender with mental illness.

❖ List four misconceptions or myths about people with mental illness.

❖ Discuss the prevalence of mental illness among female offenders.

❖ Describe why appropriate mental health treatment of women with mental illness is important in correctional institutions.

❖ List the components of a comprehensive mental health program in a woman's correctional institution.

❖ Describe problems those with mental illness may face in prison.

❖ List three steps that should be taken to improve the institutional environment for women with mental illness.

❖ Define the major mental illnesses that may affect women in prison, their causes, symptoms, treatments, and what correctional staff can do to better manage them.

Introduction

An offender with mental illness is an individual whose thought processes and reasoning power are diminished or otherwise impaired by psychological or neurological disorder (Ashford, Sales and Reid, 2001). Mental illness in both the community and in correctional institutions frequently is untreated because of a general lack of understanding about it, limited resources available for treatment, and the social stigma and negative consequences associated with having a mental illness. In spite of limitations, prison administrators are responsible for providing programs and treatment to often seriously ill offenders.

Offenders with mental illness can suffer from one or more disorders that may or may not be related to the crime they committed. This heterogeneity necessitates a wide variety of treatments and intervention strategies to help ensure the safe management of the facility and the release of offenders who have an enhanced ability to succeed in the community (Peters and Hills, 1997).

The four primary myths about people who have mental illness are summarized below (American Correctional Association, 1997).

Mentally ill persons are faking illness or could get well if they just tried harder. Mental illness is a real sickness and, while some people may try to fake a mental illness, an evaluation by a mental health specialist almost always can identify someone who is not mentally ill. True mental illness is not a personal weakness and cannot be cured through will power. It is a disruption in the way the brain works and must be treated just like a disruption in any other part of the body. Proper mental health treatment, sometimes over a long period of time, is needed to cure or alleviate the problems of mental illness.

Once you have a mental illness, you will always have it. Mental illness comes in many forms and degrees of severity. Proper medication and other treatments, including counseling, can alleviate the symptoms of many mental illnesses. Many people who receive medical care and remain in treatment can lead normal, productive lives. Often a mental illness is transitory and with the right treatment will not reoccur.

You can tell people are mentally ill by looking at them and observing their behavior. Most mentally ill people do not exhibit bizarre behavior. Only those with severe mental illness or with a disorder in an acute or active stage may act out or engage in strange behavior.

Mentally ill people are often violent. Only a few mentally ill people become violent. Their cases are usually widely publicized leading the public to think violence among the mentally ill is common. In fact, many people with mental illness are frightened, confused, passive, and victimized by others. There are indications, however, that certain types of disorders such as antisocial personality disorder and psychopathy increase "the risk that an individual will engage in violent behavior" (Coid, 1998, p. 57). This emphasizes the need for careful screening/assessment, diagnosis, and treatment of those with mental illness.

Women in the community are diagnosed as mentally ill more often than are men. This often results from women's willingness to seek help and discuss their problems more readily than do men (Pollock, 2002). Also, society expects women to behave in culturally appropriate ways and when they fail to do so, they are thought of as abnormal, crazy, or mad (Belknap, 2001). If their behavior seriously violates community expectations, they may be classified as "bad" and confined in a prison instead of a mental hospital.

Women offenders tend to suffer from mental illness in greater numbers than do women in the general population (Robins and Regier, 1991; Link, Cullen, and Andrews, 1992). With de-institutionalization or closing of many mental hospitals, some women with mental illness who would have been treated in that setting are being sent to correctional institutions where they become prisoners instead of patients (Ross and Lawrence, 1998).

The stress of incarceration can contribute to the development of mental health problems. Prison life is stressful for a person whose brain is working properly and as Torrey (1997) noted, "Being in jail or prison when your brain is playing tricks on you is often brutal" (p. 31). He goes on to explain that prisons are designed to house people who have broken the law. Facilities have strict rules and procedures and inmates are expected to understand and obey regulations without questioning them. Mentally ill people, however, are often unable to understand or comply with institutional procedures because of their delusions, hallucinations, or other brain abnormalities. This can result in restrictions on their movements and other punishments that are inappropriate for mentally ill offenders (Torrey, 1997).

Women offenders can experience emotional and mental health problems when incarcerated that increase levels of stress and that can make it difficult for them to cope in institutions. This stress can lead to depression, low levels of self-esteem, posttraumatic stress symptoms, high levels of anxiety, and difficulty in communicating, problem solving, decision making, and goal setting (Pomeroy, Kiam, and Abel, 1998).

Estimates of the prevalence of mental health problems among incarcerated women vary from 25 to 60 percent (Acoca, 1998). In one study 20 percent of incarcerated women reported that they had attempted suicide at some time in their lives (Holley and Brewster, 1996). In general, an average of 45 percent of women in prison are considered to have a mental illness or disorder (Acoca, 1998). Some people have a tendency to think that any woman who commits a crime must be unstable or mentally ill. It is important "to avoid the stereotype that women (offenders) automatically need (mental health) services more than male inmates" (Pollock, 2002, p. 80).

The many women who are mentally ill and are sent to prison instead of being placed in a mental health facility obviously put a tremendous strain on correctional staff to provide adequate diagnostic and treatment services. Researchers cite a variety of problems with treating women offenders with mental illness in prison. These include limited appropriate housing and programs to meet female offenders' needs, failure to provide gender-responsive treatment programs designed for women, lack of standardized identification and screening procedures for women's mental health disorders, and limited qualified and trained staff to provide diagnosis and treatment (Acoca, 1998).

The failure of correctional systems to provide adequate screening, assessment, and treatment for women with mental illnesses in institutions is a serious problem (Bloom, 2003). It can result in women with mental illness not receiving the treatment they need and without adequate treatment programs and effective training, correctional staff may find it difficult to distinguish between behavior that is related to mental health problems and behavior that results from disciplinary problems (Acoca, 1998).

Components of a Comprehensive Mental Health Program

It is essential that correctional facilities housing women have diagnostic and treatment programs available to meet the needs of the population. According to Faiver and Ort (1998), a comprehensive mental health program should contain the following elements that are listed below along with a description of how they apply in a woman's facility. Additionally, a final component that should be available with any treatment program — evaluation — is discussed.

Mental Health Screening

Conducted at intake, the initial mental health screening consists of determining whether the woman has any mental problems, has had previous suicide attempts, is on any medication, or has other problems that might require immediate referral for mental health treatment. While both the American Correctional Association and the National Commission on Correctional Health Care standards call for staff to do the screening, the American Correctional Association standards appear to provide more latitude in who can do the screening. The American Correctional Association's Standards for Adult Correctional Institutions (4-4370) and Performance-Based Standards for Correctional Health Care in Adult Institutions (1-HC-1A-27) specify that the screening must be done by a "mental health trained or qualified mental health professional" (American Correctional Association, 2003c, p. 108 and 2002, p. 14). The National Commission on Correctional Health Care standards for mental health care specify that screening should be done by a qualified mental health professional (Anno, 2000).

Intake Mental Health Assessment

Following the screening, a mental health professional should conduct an intake mental health assessment within two weeks of the woman's arrival at the facility (American Correctional Association, 2003c, 4-4371). The components recommended by American Correctional Association to be included in the initial mental health assessment for intersystem transfers is on page 321 (American Correctional Association. 2003c, 4-4371, p. 109). The items must be modified to be gender responsive and include elements relevant to women. For example, the standard specifies a "review of history of sexual abuse-victimization and predatory behavior" (p. 109). While this question may be appropriate for some women who have a history of abusing others, a more common mental-health issue for women would be the collection of data relative to trauma or assault both physical and sexual that they may have suffered as children or adults.

Also, the location and status of the woman's children should be addressed as this is the source of much of the anxiety woman experience during incarceration. It is, however, an area that often is overlooked in the assessment and evaluation of incarcerated women. As Van Voorhis, Peiler, Presser, Spiropoulis, and Sutherland (2002) noted in an analysis of classification systems used in women's institutions, "we were especially struck with the absence of records pertaining to parenting" (p.49).

While it is not specified in the standard, the assessment should contain an interview with the woman and she should be involved in the development of her treatment plan to the degree possible. It is important to note that some women inmates may not wish to reveal problems they may be experiencing or may minimize their mental health histories. This is particularly true of women who have experienced sexual abuse. Interviewers should be sensitive to this issue and trained to work with traumatized women. Other women may overemphasize their problems as a cry for help.

It is imperative that the personnel conducting the screening/assessment of incoming inmates and other staff working with new or unknown inmates be particularly observant and cautious even if initial interview and records indicated a lack of a significant mental health history. Resources should be available to provide professional mental health evaluations and follow-up services for women identified in the initial and intake assessments as having mental health needs. These services also should be available for women who manifest mental health problems during incarceration.

Professional Mental Health Referral Resources

Some correctional systems will have women whose mental health problems are too severe to be treated by mental health professionals in the facility. All facilities must have "provision(s) for referral and admission to licensed mental health facilities for those offenders whose psychiatric needs exceed the treatment capacity of the facility" (American Correctional Association, 2003c, 4-4336, p. 108). Relationships with mental health treatment facilities are often difficult for correctional personnel to develop and maintain. Many state mental hospitals are trying to reduce their long-term residential programs and treat patients in the community. They also are facing budget cuts similar to those correctional systems across the country are experiencing. Women with mental illness who have a committed a crime too often are seen as criminals who should be punished and not as patients in need of mental health care. Correctional staff may have to advocate internally and externally to ensure that treatment outside the facility is available.

Right to Refuse Treatment

According to Haney and Specter (2001), "legal doctrines (for treatment of the mentally ill in prison) are often contradictory and operate at cross purposes with one another" (p. 51). However, the principle of deliberate indifference to serious medical needs discussed in the legal-issues chapter also applies to mental health issues.

Just as questions have been raised about the availability and adequacy of mental health care, some issues have been raised about too much or harmful therapeutic interventions. Grana (2002) notes that some women's "prisons find it much easier to hand out medication than to treat the real causes "of women inmates' mental health problems" (p. 169). Acoca (1998) in a study of health care in women's prisons also identified the over use of psychotropic drugs. On the one hand, the courts have granted inmates with mental illness some rights to refuse treatment. On the other hand, in *Washington v. Harper* (1990), the U.S. Supreme Court ruled that given the requirements of the prison environment, the due process clause permits the state to treat a prison inmate who has a serious mental illness with antipsychotic drugs against his will, if the inmate is dangerous to himself or others and the treatment is in the inmate's medical interest (p. 227).

The National Commission on Correctional Health Care standards indicate that medications should be forced only in an emergency situation when the person represents a threat to herself or others and then "only after all least restrictive measures have been used" (Anno, 2000, p. 92). Obviously, clear facility policies and procedures are needed in this sensitive area.

Outpatient Follow-up Services by Mental Health Specialist

Outpatient follow-up services by a mental health specialist should include short-term intervention and long-term treatment for women who have been identified as having a mental illness. The mental health specialist also should coordinate the development of a multidisciplinary treatment plan for chronically mentally ill women. This plan should include the appropriate approaches for staff to take in working with the mentally ill woman and signs or problems that should be reported to the mental health personnel.

Case Management

Case management consists of ongoing monitoring on a regular basis of the stability of those women who have exhibited or are at risk of developing a mental illness. Given the number of women in prison who suffer from serious mental illness, the smooth management of correctional facilities depends on ongoing monitoring and provision of early intervention for those who have problems. Mental health staff should be available twenty-four hours a day seven days a week to ensure that crises can be handled in an expedient manner.

Crisis Intervention

Crisis intervention includes the provision of an immediate response by a mental health professional to a severe episode of mental stress. It can include initial intervention to help the woman regain control and referral for follow-up, if necessary. As with physical problems, if women know they have someone to turn to in a crisis situation, they will be less anxious and be less likely to act out by hurting themselves or others.

Psychiatric Services

Facilities should have a psychiatrist on staff or on call. This is particularly critical for women offenders who come to the institution with a higher likelihood of having a mental illness than do men and are more likely to experience mental health problems once incarcerated (Acoca, 1998).

Access to a Psychiatric Inpatient Unit

A small percentage of women will require more intensive treatment than can be obtained in an outpatient setting. An inpatient unit should provide the supportive environment needed to stabilize the woman who is in an acute state. If these units are administered by agencies other than the departments of correction, memorandum of agreements should be in place to ensure that women inmates will be accepted in the program and the program will be monitored by both agencies regularly. Regardless of where these units are located or who operates them, they should be licensed by the state mental health agency.

Transition or Intermediate Care Unit

There also should be access to a transition unit or intermediate-level residential setting to aid in transitioning women back to the general institutional population. It also can serve as a halfway house for those experiencing a mental health crisis not severe enough for inpatient care.

Evaluation

Finally, mental health services should be evaluated to ensure that they are reaching the outcomes established for them. Veysey (1998) notes:

> Attention must be given to outcomes that acknowledge the wide variation in women's life experiences, adaptive styles, and modes of recovery. Measures should be developed through a joint effort by mental health professionals, researchers, and the women using services. While this is a generic issue, it is equally valid in the assessment and evaluation of mental health programs in correctional settings (p. 387).

It should be added that in the correctional setting, staff from throughout the facility should be involved in the development of outcome measures. The American Correctional Association's *Performance-Based Standards for Correctional Health Care in Adult Correctional Institutions* (2002b) can provide assistance in developing such measures.

Providing Mental Health Treatment

While mental health specialists provide much of the treatment, other staff in the facility play a critical role in identifying problems at an early stage. Staff should refer women to the appropriate mental health service and provide a supportive environment for the woman with mental illness both during and after treatment.

The *National Commission on Correctional Health Care* standards (*see* Appendix) require that mental health staff notify correctional personnel of any inmates with special needs who have mental illness so that their illness can be considered prior to making housing, program, work, disciplinary, or other supervision decisions (Anno, 2000). While mental health staff may not be able because of confidentiality policy considerations to reveal the inmate's diagnosis, they should explain why certain precautions or other actions should be taken.

Mental health services should be built on a wellness model as was recommended for physical health programs (Morton, 1998). The model should emphasize prevention and early intervention. Since prison is an extremely stressful environment, anything to reduce the stress or improve the overall conditions of confinement will go a long way toward helping prevent costly mental illness from occurring and will speed recovery for those who do develop such illnesses.

In addition to developing and maintaining a healthy facility environment, four other steps should be taken to help ensure proper treatment is provided and these are summarized below.

1. **Housing**- Care must be taken in making housing placements for women who have a mental illness. In some instances, it will be necessary to house them in individual (one-person) rooms or cells. In other cases, it may be advantageous to have them housed with another woman who can provide stability and reassurance for the disturbed or anxious inmate with mental illness. Obviously, such assignments should be made in consultation with the mental health staff and the proposed roommate. Inmates without mental illness should not be placed in a caretaker role, made to feel responsible for another inmate, or given authority over a woman with mental illness (American Correctional Association, 2003c, 4-4393). The National Commission on Correctional Health Care standards provide that inmate workers who are trained and carefully supervised can assist as adjuncts to mental

health workers (Anno, 2000). But it is critical that even in these situations, one inmate is not allowed to control another inmate.

2. **Heat**- Administrators and all staff should understand that a woman who is taking psychotropic medications should not be exposed to excessive heat because the medication impairs her ability to adjust to higher temperatures and she can suffer serious medical complications (Faiver and Ort, 1998). This means that women who are taking such medication may require specially designed work assignments and living arrangements so their lives are not jeopardized. Again, it should be noted, this is not coddling the woman but is perhaps saving her life and reducing the chance of a wrongful death suit against the facility and its staff.

3. **Policies and Procedures**- All correctional facilities are required by both the American Correctional Association and National Commission on Correctional Health Care standards to have policies and procedures covering psychiatric emergencies and suicide attempts (American Correctional Association, 2003c, 4-4405; Anno, 2000). Correctional staff must receive training in these and other issues related to the treatment of those with mental illness. Policies also should be in place to cover the use of therapeutic restraints. These policies should cover what types can be used and for how long, and under what circumstances. Careful adherence to institutional policies and procedures related to therapeutic restraints is essential for all correctional staff and such restraints should not be used as punishment (American Correctional Association, 2003c, 4-4190).

4. **Cooperative Relationships**- Mental health professionals should work with staff, particularly correctional officers, and others who are involved with the day-to-day management of women with mental illness. Strategies for working with the mentally ill woman need to be developed based on the individual woman's situation so that disciplinary procedures and other supervision techniques reinforce her treatment program.

Correctional staff are a key ingredient in the successful treatment of women with mental illness (Hafemeister, Hall, and Dvoskin, 2000). They are with the inmate on an ongoing basis and have more opportunity to interact and observe behavior more than do mental health specialists. This makes their role invaluable to the inmates' well being and eventual successful transition to the community upon release. Correctional officers' success in working with inmate's with mental illness is predicated on their receiving specialized training, supervision, and reinforcement for positive, appropriate relationships toward those under their care (Ellis, 1993).

As noted by Hafemeister, Hall and Dvoskin (2000),

An important and often overlooked aspect of responding to the needs of inmates with mental illness is to simply talk and listen to them. Line staff simply talking to troubled inmates can have a dramatically beneficial impact. They can resolve a crisis by saying things that will help the inmates to calm down or provide instruction on ways to avoid similar crisis in the future. For inmates who are confused and anxious frequent and surprisingly brief visits by staff can provide reassurance that the inmate has not been psychologically abandoned. . . . During periods of extreme psychological stress, an important part of therapy is to provide a non-threatening source of company—it can be comforting simply to have someone who will listen to you (p. 431-432).

Equally important is the problem of negative reinforcement. Negative or threatening behavior by correctional staff can damage progress the inmate might be making. Hafemeister, Hall, and Dvoskin (2000) recommended seven ways to improve cooperative relationships between correctional and mental health staff that are summarized below.

Enhance communication between the two groups. Being responsive to requests for assistance in crisis or day-to-day management situations is important and depends on positive communication.

Use treatment teams. Treatment teams can enhance communication between correctional and mental health staff. This approach combined with unit management has been successfully used by some states and the Federal Bureau of Prisons (Jurick and Winn, 1987). In addition to improving the prison environment for those inmates with mental illness, unit management also reduced staff turnover (Jurick and Winn, 1987).

Incorporate mental health staff in agency and institutional orientation and basic correctional officer training and also ensure their involvement in ongoing in-service training. Training for correctional staff should include:

> *learning how to recognize the early signs and symptoms of serious mental illness and suicide; the nature and effects of various psychotropic medications, how to access mental health service at the facility. . . . and how to inform clinicians in behaviorally specific manner of what led the officer to suspect mental illness* (Hafemeister, Hall, and Dvoskin, 2000, p. 424).

Ensure that referrals are promptly transmitted to mental health staff and that they are quickly evaluated and responded to appropriately by mental health staff.

Have a good recordkeeping system and monitor the recordkeeping process. Good documentation provides assistance to correctional and mental health personnel and also can protect them from charges of failure to respond to serious mental health needs.

Ensure that officers' time in observation and working with offenders is maximized. For example, clustering inmates who need close observation in adjoining cells can improve supervision and save the officer's time in walking from one area to another.

Select who supervises those with mental illness with care. Not everyone is willing or has the basic skills and patience required for working with this group of offenders.

Mental Illnesses and Incarcerated Women

A number of mental illnesses can affect incarcerated women. Some of the more common ones are discussed below. While correctional staff are not expected to be experts in diagnosing mental illnesses, they need to become familiar with some of the signs and symptoms of typical mental illnesses they may encounter. They also should know what they can do to help ensure those suffering from mental illness receive the treatment they require.

Many women in prison suffer from more than one disorder or problem. For example, in Alaska some 79 percent of the women with mental illness in the Department of Corrections' Women's Psychiatric Unit had a co-occurring substance abuse disorder in addition to their other mental health problems (Patrick-Riley, Worrall, and Sage, 2003).

The concept of co-occurring disorders has evolved over the last twenty years and initially focused on male offenders (Alexander, 1996). Recently more attention has been given to women with co-occurring disorders. The National GAINS Center for People with Co-Occurring Disorders in the Justice System, established in 1995, can provide information and technical assistance in the planning and implementation of cost-effective programs for female offenders. For additional information, contact the GAINS Center, 262 Delaware Avenue, Delmar, New York. Phone: (800) 311-GAIN, E-mail: gains@prainc.com.

General guidelines are provided below to assist correctional staff in working effectively with offenders who have a particular illness. These suggestions do not substitute for specific instructions that staff might receive from agency or institutional mental health professionals. As with other issues discussed in this text, correctional personal always must follow agency and facility policies and procedures when working with women inmates who have mental illness.

Clinical Depression

Everyone occasionally has a bad day, has the blues, or feels sad. Individuals even may be preoccupied and sad about some catastrophic thing that is happening in their life such as serious illness or death of a loved one. These feelings are quite normal and are a temporary reaction to the problems of daily life. Under normal circumstances, this temporary depression often can be relieved with a change of scenery, a thoughtful response from someone else, or some other distraction in their life.

If feelings of gloom do not dissipate over time, then clinical depression may develop. In its most severe form, clinical depression can disrupt all of life's activities. Clinical depression, like heart disease and cancer, is a major public health problem affecting more than "17 million Americans per year, two-thirds of whom are women" (*Harvard*, 1997b, p.1). While depressive disorders are the most prevalent mental illness, one in four people will become depressed at some time during his or her life. People with depression are also the most responsive to treatment. Modern drug therapy is successful in 80-90 percent of the cases (*Harvard*, 1997b).

Depression encompasses several illnesses including dysthymia (more chronic symptoms), bipolar disorder (cycles of terrible lows and inappropriate highs), and depressive disorders not otherwise specified (*Harvard*, 1997b). Some women may have one episode in their life while others may suffer from depression from childhood on. Responses also vary, with some women having mild cases during which they can continue to function while others have severe cases that disrupt their whole lives.

Causes

The exact causes of depression are not known. However, the factors listed below can make a person more vulnerable to the disease (*Harvard*, 1997b). Many female offenders have one or more of these symptoms:

a family history of depression, particularly among close relatives

a close family member, particularly a parent, who has committed suicide

a personal history of substance abuse, eating disorders, or a family history of these problems

unresolved grief over the loss of a loved one, divorce, or other major loss. Just being in prison represents a significant loss of everything in one's life and is a serious potential cause of depression.

A woman's unresolved anger, unresolved self-reproach or low self-esteem might be a result of a miscarriage, the end of a relationship, or in the case of incarcerated women feeling guilt over having committed a crime.

Why Women?

There are three major explanations for why women are twice as likely to suffer from depression as are men.

Gender Conditioning

Women are taught from childhood to be sensitive to the feelings of others and "good women" subjugate themselves to what others want them to do (Belknap, 2001). They learn to bottle up their aggression or turn it inward (Urquhart and Cullen, 2003). Traditionally, girls are taught to be modest and defer to others. As these young women grow to adulthood, the commitment to staying in the background and the pressures to be a "good girl" contribute to a loss of self-esteem and confidence that is common among those with depression (*Harvard*, 1997b).

Life Experiences

About 15 percent of new mothers suffer depression following the birth of their babies, and this depression may last several months (*Harvard*, 1997b). The depression may result from a physical separation from their baby, the stress of childbirth, the demands of caring for the infant, and/or the hormonal changes following cessation of pregnancy. Losing a baby to a miscarriage can be as depressing as losing a full-term child. Women too often are urged to "forget it" and that it "was for the best" and are not given an opportunity to grieve for their baby.

Traditionally, women were taught to believe they would suffer depression when they experienced menopause. This has not proven to be the case. While some women may mourn the loss of the ability to have children, many more see it as a liberating experience in their life. Again, hormones may play a part in how different women react to this stage.

Having been a victim of abuse or having witnessed abuse also can contribute to feelings of helplessness and anger. If not resolved, these feelings can attack a woman's self-esteem and contribute to the development of depression. Abuse may cause a woman to use drugs or alcohol to self-medicate to ease the physical and emotional pain of the abuse, which also can contribute to depression (Morash and Schram, 2002).

Incarcerated women fifty years of age or older are more likely to become depressed than their male counterparts. This is thought to be because, as women outlive their husbands, friends, and in some cases their children, they experience more social isolation and loss of important relationships. Also, older women are often portrayed more negatively by the media than are older men. They sometimes are ignored entirely by society. These negative reactions can result in some older women feeling they are not valued and can contribute to their depression (Morton, 1992).

Medical Conditions

Certain illnesses such as strokes, heart attacks, or cancer can trigger depression. Medications used to treat these and other diseases also can contribute to the onset of depression. Since depression can cause confusion and memory loss, it can be mistaken for dementia or Alzheimer's disease. It also can underlie or be caused by another mental illness such as substance abuse or anxiety disorders (*Harvard*, 1997b).

Symptoms of Depression

According to the National Institute of Mental Health (*Harvard*, 1997b), professional help should be sought when a woman experiences four or more of the following symptoms for more than two weeks.

a persistent empty or anxious mood

loss of interest or pleasure in ordinary activities

decreased energy, fatigue

sleep disturbances (insomnia, early morning waking, or sleeping to much)

eating disturbances (loss of appetite and weight, or severe weight gain)

difficulty concentrating, remembering, or making decisions

feelings of hopelessness or extreme pessimism

feelings of guilt, worthlessness, hopelessness

thoughts of death or suicide; suicide attempts

irritability

excessive crying

chronic aches and pains that do not respond to treatment

Treatment

First, depression must be diagnosed. Studies indicate that primary physicians in the community failed to diagnose it 50 percent of the time (*Harvard*, 1997b). Since women in institutions are so vulnerable to having depression, medical personnel should be particularly vigilant in assessing them. Depression is a mental illness that has an impact on the whole body, which means both physical and psychological examinations are recommended.

The treatment will vary with the severity of the disease. Two of the most common treatments are antidepressant medication and psychotherapy (*Harvard*, 1997b). As with any drug, the individual's reaction to a particular antidepressant will depend on her body chemistry; therefore, one drug may be more effective with some women than with others. This means it may be necessary to try more than one before finding the one with the best results and the fewest side effects.

Psychotherapy can be effective if there is a good match between a skilled professional and the patient. It can provide insight into the factors that are contributing to the depression and give guidance toward a better understanding of the things that may trigger the disorder. A skilled therapist can help the woman cope with the side effects of the medication and the frustration of trying several medications to identify the most effective one.

Treatment for depression can be very effective. As noted earlier, 80 to 90 percent of those treated for depression experienced some benefits and were able to return to a normal productive life (*Harvard*, 1997b).

What Correctional Staff Can Do

Anyone having the symptoms noted above should be referred to the facility's medical or mental health staff. Staff should try to maintain as normal a relationship as possible with women under their supervision who are being treated for depression. It may take several weeks for the treatments to produce a noticeable effect. Staff can encourage the woman to keep taking her medicine or attending therapy sessions. They can be alert for behavioral changes or atypical behavior that may signal that an adjustment in her treatment regimen may be necessary. Such changes should be reported to the appropriate officials. Staff also can acknowledge that the woman is in pain and is suffering and encourage positive feelings of self-worth by a kind word or by complimenting her work.

Post-traumatic Stress Disorder (PTSD)

Approximately 2 percent of the general population in America suffers from a psychological condition known as Post-Traumatic Stress Disorder (*Harvard*, 1995a). According to Bloom, Owen, and Covington (2003), it is the second most prevalent mental illness found among female inmates. Although women and men appear to suffer from it in equal numbers, they usually have different experiences that trigger the disorder. PTSD is most commonly associated in men with wartime experiences. In women, it is most often associated with rape or other physical or psychological abuse or having observed such abuse as children or adults (*Harvard*, 1995a).

Women with PTSD will relive the trauma they had, again and again. This can occur in their dreams as well as in their conscious thoughts and is accompanied by attempts to avoid any experience that ignites the event.

Causes

Post Tramatic Stress Disorder is one of the few mental illnesses that can be linked with a specific set of events; yet, everyone who is exposed to a traumatic event will not develop PTSD. According to *Harvard Women's Health Watch* (1995a), when researchers compared people who had traumatic events in their lives and those who did not develop PTSD with those who had similar events and did develop the disease, they found the following:

> The reaction depended on the woman's interpretation of the event. What might be troubling to one person may be catastrophic to another. Exposure to abuse early in life, seeing someone else being abused, or being a victim yourself, and/or experiencing trauma over a long period of time will cause women to be at high risk for developing the disease.
>
> Women who suffer from depression, anxiety, or have family members with these diseases are also at risk for PTSD. Apparently some people's chemical and neurological makeup inclines them to be more likely to develop PTSD.
>
> Women who experience trauma without the opportunity to receive professional counseling, whose family and friends fail to acknowledge the problem—or as often happens in cases of rape, are blamed for the event—will be more likely to develop PTSD than women with a strong support system. Women who are single, poor, and with few community ties are also more vulnerable than those who have close family ties and are on a financially sound footing.
>
> If a woman is under stress when a traumatic event takes place, she will be more likely to develop PTSD than a woman who is not experiencing chronic stress when the abuse occurs.
>
> Women who believe they have little control over their lives or what happens to them have developed what is referred to as "learned helplessness." Those who believe they cannot influence what happens to them have more difficulty dealing with traumatic events and thus are more likely to develop PTSD.

Symptoms

First, a person has a traumatic experience or a series of events in which she fears for her life, sustains a serious injury, or saw someone else receive a life-treating injury or die. If she feels helpless and is horrified by the event(s), she may experience some or all the following:

Reliving the experience

She will relive the event over and over again, in spite of attempts to repress the memory. This may include having recurring images, thoughts, and perceptions, nightmares, flashbacks, or unrealistic reactions to something that triggers the memory of the event

Avoidance

She will try to forget the event by avoiding thinking about it, not remembering what happened, ignoring what is going on around her, displaying feelings of helplessness and hopelessness, and having no thoughts for the future, her family, or herself

Intensity of feelings

This may manifest itself in insomnia, outbursts of rage and anger, inability to concentrate, being unusually alert, or being easily frightened (*Harvard*, 1995a).

Treatment

Treatment may include both medication and counseling geared towards helping the woman understand the traumatic event or series of events. The treatment usually progresses through three stages (Herman, 1992). The first stage is to establish an environment where the woman feels safe. The second stage is to process reliving the event and the feelings of sadness that accompanies it. The final stage is to help the woman move beyond the trauma and reconnect with ordinary life around her.

It is important for people who have experienced a traumatic event to seek counseling as soon as possible after the incident. Debriefings in which the survivor is encouraged to talk about her experience and her feelings about it help the individual know she is not alone, understand what happened, and develop strategies for dealing with the event (*Harvard*, 1995a). Early treatment often can avoid the development of the disorder. This is why progressive correctional agencies have crisis intervention counseling for staff members who have been involved in a serious incident such as when there has been a riot, serious injury, or death. Counseling should be available to women inmates in the case of a serious incident and available to those who already have developed the illness as a result of their experiences in the community.

What Correctional Staff Can Do

Staff can encourage women who exhibit the symptoms noted above to seek professional help to aid in alleviating the disorder. They also can observe what types of situations appear to trigger outbursts or recurrences of the painful memories and pass this information along to the appropriate correctional and mental health staff member.

For example, a female staff member normally can pat down male inmates without difficulty. But when a male staff member pats down a female inmate who has been sexually abused and suffers PTSD, he may inadvertently trigger intense feelings of anger or fear. This, in turn, can result in an altercation or confrontation that can be avoided by having female officers conduct pat-down searches. Also, male staff should not be present when women inmates are being strip searched as this action often can be associated with rape and abuse (Morash and Schram, 2002). Having a woman staff member place restraints on a female inmate and conduct the pat-down searches and strip searches is the best practice to avoid problems with female inmates who have been abused. Male staff should not be placed in a position of strip searching, removing women's clothing, or taking other actions that would simulate rape.

Panic Disorder

A panic attack is a "sudden inexplicable feeling of terror accompanied by a barrage of distressing physical symptoms and a fear of dying or going crazy" (*Harvard*, 2000b, p. 4). Mental health specialists may diagnose recurring panic attacks as panic disorder. It is a serious disorder that makes it difficult for those suffering from it to function. Individuals with panic disorder attempt suicide at rates twenty times higher than those who do not have the disorder

(*Harvard*, 2000b). Panic attacks tend to come on suddenly, like a spasm, can be chronic and, if left untreated, the disorder tends to worsen.

Panic disorder is widespread, with more than 2-3 million Americans, the majority of them women, suffering from panic disorder at some time in their lives (*Harvard*, 2000b). During an attack, the woman can become totally unable to function and there is little way to predict when one will occur. Fear of experiencing another attack can become such an obsession that the woman begins to withdraw and tries to avoid any stimulus that she thinks might trigger an episode.

Causes

Research indicates there may be both neurobiological and psychological factors in the development of panic disorder. It tends to run in families and half of those who suffer from panic disorder have at least one relative who suffers from it. However, it is unclear whether the relationship is environmental (learned) or genetic (inherited) (*Harvard*, 2000b).

People with panic disorder may have an exaggerated neurobiological system that causes the flight-or-fight response to a danger signal when none exists. Most people with panic disorder suffered anxiety or panic even as children. Studies of brain functioning "suggest that people with panic disorder may have faulty brain receptors that block the availability of the body's own anxiety-reducing neurochemicals" (*Harvard*, 2000b, p. 5). Investigators are examining the part of the brain that involves the sense of fear to determine if there is a relationship between this part of brain functioning and panic disorder.

Symptoms

According to the American Psychiatric Association's *Diagnostic and Statistical Manual of Mental Disorders*, Forth Edition (1994), symptoms of panic attacks include four or more of the following that occur within a ten-minute time frame:

racing or pounding heart beat

sweating

feeling chest pain or discomfort

trembling or shaking

feeling dizziness, lightheaded, fainting

sensation of shortness of breath or smothering

tingling or numbness sensations

feelings of choking

experiencing hot flushes or chills

having nausea or abdominal distress

having feelings of unreality or depersonalization

feeling terror—a sense that something catastrophic is going to happen and they are completely unable to stop it

fearing loosing control or losing one's mind

fearing dying.

Women with panic disorder also may experience other mental problems. Women who are depressed or who have been abusing alcohol and drugs are more susceptible to having panic attacks. Also, women who attempt suicide are more likely to suffer from panic disorder than are those in the general population (Reprinted with permission from the *Diagnostic and Statistical Manual of Mental Disorders*, Fourth Edition, Text Revision [copyright 2000.] American Psychatric Association).

Treatment

Since panic disorder mimics other serious diseases such as heart attacks, to assess the problem, the presence of other physical and emotional disorders has to be eliminated. Once this is done, treatment consists of combinations of psychotherapy and medications (American Psychiatric Association, 1994). In a study reported in the *Harvard Women's Health Watch* (2000b), 312 patients were randomly assigned to (1) antidepressant medication alone, (2) cognitive-behavioral therapy alone, (3) a placebo, (4) cognitive-behavioral therapy with medication, and (5) cognitive-behavioral therapy with a placebo. Those treated with a combination of cognitive-behavioral therapy and antidepressants were more successful than the others in controlling their attacks. Those who received cognitive-behavioral therapy alone or with a placebo were better able to maintain their improvement once treatment was discontinued.

Cognitive-behavioral therapy helps individuals learn how to deal with anxiety-producing thoughts and manage their feelings through deep breathing and other stress-reducing techniques. The treatment period is usually from six to eight weeks and has a 70 to 90 percent success rate of relieving the most serious symptoms or curing the disorder (*Harvard*, 2000b).

What Correctional Staff Can Do

Treat panic like any serious disorder. Refer the woman to medical services and do not attempt to diagnose the problem as a panic attack even if the woman has had them before. Let the medical personnel decide if the illness is a panic attack or other problem.

Understand the woman's reluctance to participate in activities that she thinks may trigger an attack. Provide a supportive environment and remind her that no matter how frightened she is, the feelings will pass. This can help her control thoughts of dying or losing control. She also should be encouraged to take deep breaths rather than short ones (*Harvard*, 2000b). She should be encouraged to stick with the treatment program designed by the facility mental health personnel.

Schizophrenia

Schizophrenia is a serious debilitating neurobiological disorder. It is the most common, chronic, debilitating, and least understood of all the major mental illnesses. It is estimated that some two million people will suffer from schizophrenia during their lifetime (Karaylorgau, 1997).

Causes

While there is no agreement on what the specific causes of schizophrenia are, the following factors are thought to contribute to its development:

Biochemical imbalance

Like diabetes and cancer, there may be some genetic or chemical imbalance in the body that causes the disease.

Heredity

Schizophrenia runs in families. Among families with no history of the disease, only 1 percent of the children will develop the disease. When one parent has the illness, the child has a 10 percent risk of developing the disease. When both parents have schizophrenia, the child has a 40 percent chance of contracting the disease (Karaylorgau, 1997).

Environment

A chemical imbalance may predispose a person to develop the disease, but the environment may trigger it. While parents do not cause schizophrenia, some families are so dysfunctional that the children do not develop the skills to cope with stressful situations.

Birth Defects

Some complications during pregnancy or birth may increase the risk that the child will become schizophrenic (American Psychiatric Association, 1994).

Symptoms

Persons suffering from schizophrenia often will exhibit bizarre behavior that may include the following symptoms summarized from the American Psychiatric Association's Manual (1994):

Distorted reality

They may view the world differently and become anxious or afraid of real or imagined stimulus. They may engage in strange or ritualistic behaviors that make sense in their delusion but are bizarre to a normal observer.

Hallucinations

Someone suffering from schizophrenia may see and hear things that are not there. They may hear voices that tell them what to do. They also may see threatening animals or insects attacking their body.

Delusions

They may believe someone is trying to hurt them, poison them, or gang up on them. They even may believe the medicine they are taking for the disease is hurting them.

Disordered Thinking

Here the individual cannot think logically or concentrate on what is going on around her. She may jump from subject to subject in an inappropriate manner.

Bizarre Expressions of Emotions

A woman with schizophrenia may exhibit strong inappropriate emotions or no emotions at all. She laughs when something is sad or cries when she is happy. She may exhibit emotions similar to someone with bipolar disorder. This means she will experience highs and lows for no reason.

Fear

She may exhibit unreasonable fear and be unable to control her negative or threatening thoughts.

Isolation

Those with schizophrenia may withdraw from others, neglect to bathe or groom themselves, dress inappropriately, and/ or hoard items.

Treatment

No specific cure for schizophrenia is available, but with the right applica-tion of medications and follow-up mental health care, many women with the disease can lead independent lives. Antipsychotic drugs do not cure the dis-ease, but they do relieve the symptoms and can have a positive effect on the individual (American Psychiatric Association, 1994). Counseling can provide a supportive environment to enable the inmate to discuss her experiences with the disorder and explain her feelings about it.

Treatment is often a mix of inpatient hospitalization, residential care, partial hospitalization, and outpatient therapy. A mix may be necessary to relieve the stress caused by the disease, adjust the medicine, stabilize the patient, and pro-vide the training and support necessary to help her adjust to life in the com-munity. Some women may never be free of symptoms or be able to handle the tasks of everyday living. For these women, long-term assistance will be needed in the prison and in the community (American Psychiatric Association, 1994).

What Correctional Staff Can Do

As with all inmates with mental illness, staff can begin by treating the woman with respect. Developing an understanding of the disease and how it can manifest itself will help staff dispel many of the myths and false informa-tion about schizophrenia.

If a woman begins to manifest the symptoms described above, she should be referred to a mental health specialist for an assessment. Those managing women who have been diagnosed with the disease should remember that the inmate's hallucinations and bizarre perceptions are very real to them.

Staff needs to be aware of the women's delusions and fears and try to avoid triggering them. Inmates with schizophrenia will need a supportive, calm envi-ronment, and some time alone. Obviously, these conditions are difficult to achieve in many correctional settings, but they will contribute to more suc-cessful management of this population.

If a crisis should occur, staff should get back-up assistance because the woman may exhibit violent or self-destructive behavior. The woman should be separated from the rest of the population. This will help control her violent outburst and protect the staff, other inmates, and the woman herself.

Female offenders with schizophrenia can be difficult to manage and require staff to understand that they are working with individuals who are not thinking clearly. Since the illness can interfere with the woman's decision-making ability, she may refuse treatment or medications and engage in disruptive behaviors. She even may start treatment, seem to be making good progress and then without warning stop participating in the program. She may exhibit this pattern over and over.

Such behavior can be particularly frustrating for staff who may become angry, disillusioned, or even frightened. It is important for correctional staff to maintain a positive attitude, create a supportive environment, and encourage the woman to continue her treatment program. This persistence can pay dividends, as many of the women will continue treatment and their conditions will improve. Staff should be vigilant when working with this population.

Borderline Personality Disorder

Borderline Personality Disorder (BPD) is a "severe, chronic, disabling, and potentially lethal psychotic condition" (Borderline, 2000, p.1). Women make-up about 75 percent of those diagnosed with Borderline Personality Disorder (American Psychiatric Association, 1994).

Borderline Personality Disorder is common among women inmates and is "characterized by a person's emotions overwhelming her thinking ability" (Morash and Schram, 2002, p. 143). In one study, women diagnosed with Borderline Personality Disorder were also more likely than men to have been charged or convicted of arson (Coid, Kahtan, Gault, et al., 2000).

Borderline Personality Disorder affects approximately 2 percent of the civilian population but its prevalence in prison is higher. Some 11 percent of psychiatric outpatients and 19 percent of inpatients meet the diagnostic criteria for Borderline Personality Disorder (Kass, Skodol, Charles, Spitzer and Williams, 1985).

Those with Borderline Personality Disorder have conflicting and unstable emotions, behavior problems, self-image defects, and marked impulsivity that begins in early adulthood (American Psychiatric Association, 1994). Some 69-75 percent of those with Borderline Personality Disorder resort to self-destructive behaviors such as self-mutilation, alcohol and drug abuse, serious over or under eating, and suicide attempts (Clarkin, Widiger, Frances, Hunt, and Gilmore, 1983). The completed suicide rate for those with Borderline Personality Disorder is 3 to 9.5 percent, which is comparable to other serious psychiatric disorders such as depression and schizophrenia (McGlashan, 1986).

According to the Borderline Personality Disorder Research Foundation (2000), the disorder is hard to treat because of the nature of the illness. Such things as unstable relationships and intense anger make establishing the therapeutic setting necessary for the effective treatment of Borderline Personality Disorder very difficult. Mental health staff may be reluctant to treat those with Borderline Personality Disorder because of the inmates' hostility toward the clinician. Also, their persistent suicidal thoughts and feelings can cause clinician burnout (Borderline, 2000).

According to the American Psychiatric Association (1994), women with pervasive patterns of instability in interpersonal relationships, self-image deficits, and marked impulsively beginning by early adulthood, and who also exhibit five or more of the following behaviors may be diagnosed by mental health staff as having Borderline Personality Disorder.

frantic efforts to avoid real or imagined abandonment

a pattern of unstable and intense interpersonal relationships characterized by alternating between extremes of idealization and devaluation identity disturbance: markedly and persistently unstable self-image or sense of self

impulsivity in at least two areas that are potentially self-damaging (for example, spending, sex, substance abuse, reckless driving, binge eating)

recurrent suicidal behavior, gestures, or threats, or self-mutilating behavior

affective instability due to marked reactivity of mood (for example, episodic dysphoria, instability or anxiety usually lasting a few hours and only rarely more than a few days

chronic feelings of emptiness

inappropriate, intense anger or difficulty controlling anger (for example frequent displays of temper, constant anger, recurrent physical fights)

transient, stress-related paranoid ideation or severe dissociative symptoms (American Psychiatric Association, 1994, p. 654)

Researchers found that adolescent girls with diagnosed Borderline Personality Disorder compared with those with other mental disorders were more likely to have a history of physical abuse — especially sexual abuse. Those girls with Borderline Personality Disorder tended to have a history of abuse from multiple perpetrators and to have been physically as well as sexually abused. The abuse typically occurred in conjunction with neglect and rejection by the primary caregivers (American Psychiatric Association, 1994).

Co-occurring disorders may be present and include Mood Disorders, Substance-Related Disorder, Eating Disorders (particularly Bulimia), Post-traumatic Stress Disorder, and Attention-Deficit/Hyperactivity Disorder. Borderline Personality Disorder also frequently co-occurs with other Personality Disorders (Reprinted with permission from the *Diagnostic and Statistical Manual of Mental Disorders*, Fourth Edition, Text Revision [copyright 2000.] American Psychatric Association).

On a positive note,

> *impairment from the disorder and risk of suicide are greatest in the young-adult years and gradually wean with advancing age. During their thirties and forties, the majority of individuals with this disorder attain greater stability in their relationships and vocational functioning* (Reprinted with permission from the *Diagnostic and Statistical Manual of Mental Disorders*, Fourth Edition, Text Revision [copyright 2000.] American Psychatric Association).

Causes

Limited research has been conducted on this disorder (Borderline, 2000); however, "physical and sexual abuse, neglect, hostile conflict, and early parental loss or separation are more common in the childhood histories of those with Borderline Personality Disorder" (American Psychiatric Association, 1994, p. 652). The disorder is about five-times more common among first-degree relatives who have the disorder than it is in the general population (American Psychiatric Association, 1994).

Treatment

The Correctional Service of Canada (CSC) implemented one of the most comprehensive programs for women who "exhibited a combination of all or most of the following behaviors: persistent and severe self-destructive behavior, identity disturbance, depression, difficulty controlling anger, severe dissociation, problems in intimate relationships, suicidality, severe anxiety, low self-esteem, and severe substance abuse" (Laishes, 1997, p. 8).

According to Laishes (1997), the Intensive Healing Program was implemented by the Regional Psychiatric Centre in the Prairies in 1996. It consisted of cognitive-behavioral therapy and acquisition of new skills and coping strategies. Positive behaviors were reinforced by correctional staff in a therapeutic community setting with the emphasis placed on the here and now rather than the past. Also included were individual counseling, group programs, and medication, as necessary. A comprehensive evaluation component was built into the program that involved both inmates and staff.

What Correctional Can Staff Do

Correctional staff play a pivotal role in the treatment and supervision of women who have Borderline Personality Disorder. Since this population is very sensitive to the environment and become fearful of even the most minor changes, correctional staff should stay calm, keep to a set schedule as much as possible, be particularly observant of signs of potential self-destructive behavior, and be vigilant and careful when outbreaks of anger or aggressive behavior occur. Correctional staff should refer inmates to the appropriate mental health personnel and work with mental health staff in carrying out treatment plans.

This is a taxing group to work with, so staff should remind themselves that these individuals are suffering from a mental disorder that requires a high level of patience and professionalism. Not all staff can work with them and those who are experiencing difficulties or symptoms of burnout should consult with their supervisor.

Suicide

Suicide and self-destructive acts are very real problems in correctional settings. They have a very negative impact on the staff, offenders, and their families (Rowan, 1998). The prison environment influences suicidal behavior in a number of ways. Rowan (1998) lists these factors as including:

the authoritarian environment of prison

lack of control over one's future

isolation

shame/guilt

the dehumanizing aspects of incarceration

fear

the lack of understanding from some correctional staff

Prison is a depressing place and if the inmates cannot cope with it, killing themselves may seem like a rational solution to their problems.

Suicide attempts and other self-destructive behavior also may be related to serious mental illness. Women may commit suicide or attempt suicide in response to bad news or other traumatic events in their lives. Juveniles placed in an adult facility commit suicide eight times more frequently than they do if placed in juvenile facilities (Rowan, 1998).

Self-destructive behavior including mutilating can spread from one inmate to another. That is, if one woman commits suicide or engages in other self-destructive behavior, the others may react and copy her behavior.

Symptoms

According to the American Psychiatric Association (1994), symptoms of a suicide attempt include the following:

change in eating and/or sleeping habits

withdrawing from other inmates and activities

violent, rebellious behavior

uncharacteristic neglect of personal hygiene and appearance

radical personality change

frequent complaints of physical aches and pains

difficulty concentrating

loss of interest in what is going on around her

persistently saying she is worthless, indicating nothing matters anymore, or there is no use in trying

putting her affairs in order by, for example, giving away her favorite things

suddenly becoming cheerful and happy after a period of depression (American Psychiatric Association, 1994).

Others symptoms include:

verbalization of self-harm, making threats

strong guilt or shame over the offense

prior suicidal attempts or self-harm gestures such as cutting her wrists or neck

current or prior mental illness particularly if accompanied by irrational thoughts or hallucinations

history of alcohol/drug abuse (Rowan, 1998)

Treatment

Treatment of suicide and other self-destructive behavior is complex. It involves both medication and counseling by mental health professionals and usually lasts for some period of time. Treatment normally requires monitoring of both medication and behavior.

Problems occur when inmates who engaged in self-destructive behavior are labeled "manipulative" (Haycock, 1989). This label is particularly dangerous when working with female offenders because they often are stereotyped as being manipulative. Correctional staff and mental health workers often conclude that the women who have engaged in self-destructive behavior are not in danger and are simply attempting to manipulate their environment. This leads to suggestions that the behavior should be ignored and not reinforced through intervention or attention (Ashford, Sales and Reid, 2001, p. 314).

According to Haycock (1992), labeling some inmates as "manipulative" or "attention seeking" and others as truly suicidal is a dangerous practice. While others argue that labeling is a legitimate component of a treatment approach, Ashford et al. (2001) caution that labeling self-harm as manipulative behavior in correctional facilities is highly charged:

> *No staff wants an inmate 'getting by with something' and response to such actions is often severe . . . and may unwittingly prevent inmates from receiving appropriate attention and care . . . All acts of self-injury reflect personal break-downs resulting from crisis of self-doubt, poor coping and problem-solving skills, hopelessness, and fear of abandonment, (and are) the ingredients of potentially suicidal behavior* (p. 315).

What Correctional Staff Can Do

Any inmate talk of suicide or wanting to die, threats to injure herself, nonfatal attempts at suicide, or mutilation must be taken very seriously. Rowan (1998) recommends that correctional staff take an active role in preventing suicide and working with those who have attempted suicide. He stresses the need for having good interpersonal communication skills, documenting offenders' behavior, referring offenders to mental health service providers, and encouraging offenders to participate in treatment (Rowan, 1998). Staff should report physical plant problems that could contribute to making living areas suicide-resistant and comply with national and state standards (Rowan, 1998; Ashford et al., 2001). Some women will attempt self-destructive behavior many times before they are successful. Incidents of this nature should be documented and reported to facility medical personnel as specified in the institution's policies and procedures.

Anxiety and Phobias

Anxiety is an uncontrollable or unrealistic fear of the future. Everyone is anxious at sometime in her life; however, inmates with anxiety disorders exhibit fear and other behaviors over a prolonged period of time.

Anxiety is a generalized fear, while a phobia is an uncontrollable or unrealistic fear of things or situations when there is no real danger. In correctional settings, one of the most familiar phobias is claustrophobia—a fear of small confined or enclosed places. Without a clear way to get out of the situation, the person feels trapped and her fear can grow out of control very quickly. When the person is exposed to the triggering item over a significant period of time without some sort of intervention, her fears build and her control over her behavior weakens (American Psychiatric Association, 1994).

Symptoms

The symptoms of anxiety and phobias are as follows:

unusual display of nervousness

sweating

dizziness

muscles become tense

heart begins racing or beating rapidly

breathing becomes rapid, sometimes accompanied by complaints of feelings suffocated (American Psychiatric Association, 1994)

Treatment

Almost everyone has had some symptoms of anxiety or phobia at some time in her life. Sometimes certain conditions such as being pregnant may trigger a phobia-like claustrophobia. Most individuals can think through the situation rationally and control their fears. The problem comes when the mind refuses to think rationally and fear takes control. Just as in panic disorder, as the anxiety or phobia progresses, the individual becomes obsessed with avoiding the object of her fear. Suffering severe symptoms may interfere with the woman's ability to cope with the problems of daily living, and she will need professional help. Treatment can include both medications to relieve the symptoms and counseling to help the individual understand the causes of her fears (American Psychiatric Association, 1994).

What Correctional Staff Can Do

Being in prison is in and of itself very stressful. This combined with other problems can trigger anxiety or a phobia. Staff should remain calm and let the inmate know her problem is being taken seriously. Staff should never make fun of or threaten a woman who has one of these disorders. If the symptoms persist or the person appears to be in distress, staff should contact the institution's medical or mental health personnel for an assessment of the problem and treatment.

Memory Loss and Confusion Disorders

Everyone experiences memory lapses from time to time. Trying to remember a name, find a misplaced item, or remember to stop at the store can be upsetting because of the fear of Alzheimer's disease or other brain disorders. It is often said that it is normal to forget where you put your keys, it is not normal to forget what a key is used for. However, significant memory loss results when disease or injury destroys cells and nerve endings in the brain. This resulting loss interferes with the ability to remember, reason, think, and understand others. A woman with this disorder can appear confused about time and place, not recognize people, and not know what to do with common objects. In its advanced stages, dementia or mental deterioration can result in a loss of the ability to control bodily functions.

Memory loss and confusion are not a part of normal aging (*Harvard*, 2000a). Acute confusion in anyone, including older women, means that something is wrong and immediate medical attention is needed.

In some cases, memory loss may be a reversible condition. There may be an imbalance in something as simple as one's thyroid that can cause confusion and memory loss. Or, it can result from a reaction to medication or a build up of certain drugs. When the thyroid is treated or the person stops taking the drugs, the confusion and memory loss goes away.

However, there are two common incurable types of dementia, Alzheimer's disease and multi-infarct disease. The causes of Alzheimer's disease are unknown, but multi-infarct disease is caused by damage to the brain from strokes, often small and undiagnosed. The strokes cause small amounts of blood to seep into the brain and kill brain tissue. It is more common in men than in women and risk factors include arteriosclerosis, previous strokes, heart attacks, angina, high blood pressure, and diabetes (Rob and Reynolds, 1991).

Both diseases are more common in older people than in younger ones. Alzheimer's disease can begin as young as forty years of age. It affects only 2 percent of those who are sixty-five years of age and up to 50 percent of those over eighty-five years of age (*Harvard*, 1999). As Americans are aging as a society, the incidences of these diseases are becoming more common. Women in institutions probably will contract these diseases in similar numbers to their free-world counterparts.

Symptoms

Memory loss and confusion disorders are hard to distinguish from normal forgetfulness and absentmindedness in their early stages. As they grow worse, however, the symptoms noted below from the *Harvard Women's Health Watch* (1999) become more severe.

Phase I

problems remembering common things

problems concentrating on something

the woman may become more withdrawn, anxious, and irritable

Phase II

difficulty recounting current events and her own past

poor judgment and trouble with tasks such as cooking

difficulty finding words to express thoughts

may deny there is a problem or be depressed

Phase III

clearly requires assistance with basic tasks such as dressing

conversation disjointed at times

mood swings are common

Phase IV

severe disorientation, no longer remembers where she lives or how to find her cell

severe memory loss, may forget she is in prison

severe problems in communicating; some may scream uncontrollably

wandering, may pace about in an agitated state, or may need assistance walking

severe anxiety, delusions, hallucinations, and sleep disturbances are common

inability to care for herself. She is unable to feed, bathe, or dress herself

Phase V

the brain shuts down

becomes bed ridden

unable to speak or eat

may lapse into a coma

Treatment

The treatment for multi-infarct dementia consists of trying to control the causative factors. The damage done to the brain in most cases cannot be reversed (*Harvard*, 2000a).

There is no cure or known way to prevent Alzheimer's disease; however, there are a number of treatments being explored that will improve functioning or delay the progression of the disease. Those with these diseases can sometimes take medications that will help relieve the anxiety, anger, or depression that accompanies the illness. Counseling to help the woman understand and cope with the disease and encouragement to use her abilities as long as possible are recommended (South Carolina Department of Mental Health, 1996). "Alleviating their emotional distress is as important as tending to their physical needs" (*Harvard*, 1999, p. 4). Helping women maintain their functioning and independence for as long as possible is the primary goal of any treatment program.

What Correctional Staff Can Do

Refer anyone exhibiting symptoms of memory loss or confusion to the proper medical personnel immediately. According to Rob and Reynolds (1991), strategies for managing those with incurable dementia diseases are as follows:

Behavior—Agitated/Upset

Try to determine why the woman is agitated.

Establish eye contact and approach slowly from the front.

Maintain a calm demeanor and tone of voice. Try to distract the woman with a simple chore or activity.

Play soothing music and keep other noise to a minimum.

Behavior—Overreacting, Aggressive, Hostile

Get back-up, if needed.

Keep instructions simple.

Keep noise and other activity in the unit low.

Understand that the woman actually may be frightened and the hostility is a fight-or-flight response.

If possible, remove the confused woman from the situation that is bothering her.

Avoid arguments and explanations as they are usually beyond her understanding.

If possible, avoid restraining her as she may calm down without having to endanger her or staff.

Behavior—Suspicious

Keep to a daily routine.

Explain any deviation from that routine slowly and calmly.

When possible, explain what you are doing and do not whisper or appear to be talking about her behind her back.

Behavior—Wandering

Try to find out why she is trying to leave the housing unit. Someone may be threatening her or she may be afraid of something.

Ensure she gets frequent exercise. Supervised walks, sweeping the dorm or other activities that will lessen the tension should be encouraged.

Attach a bracelet that will activate a signal if she goes outside a prescribed area.

Behavior—Disoriented at Meal Times

Stick to an established routine.

Cut food into bite-sized pieces.

Provide one eating utensil.

Use bendable straws for drinks.

Serve soup in a mug with a handle.

Be certain the food is not too hot or too cold.

Behavior—Choking While Eating

Be certain individuals are in an upright position before they begin to eat.

Diet should consist of moist foods—applesauce, cottage cheese, scrambled eggs, and pureed vegetables and fruit.

Serve thick liquids, as they are easier to swallow.

Serve clear liquids only through a clear straw.

Be certain you know how to do the Heimlich maneuver properly.

Summary

This description does not include all the types of mental illnesses incarcerated women can manifest. Correctional staff should review their particular institutional population to identify other conditions and how to manage them. Good sources of information include the facility's medical and mental health personnel and national and local organizations focusing on mental health issues. Also, almost every area of the country has public or private mental health clinics. Personnel in these programs are an excellent source of additional information and might be willing to assist in the facility's staff training activities.

Working with inmates who have mental illness is difficult. However, consistent, constructive supervision in conjunction with comprehensive treatment can go a long way toward resolving many mental health problems. All staff—medical and other correctional personnel—have to work together to make mental health treatment in correctional facilities successful. Effective treatment of mental illness also often involves coordination and cooperation with agencies and personnel outside the facility. Helping facilitate the work of outside consultants in the institution is an important part of maintaining good relationships. Consultants may need assistance in understanding facility rules and operating procedures. At the same time, they may be a source of new ideas for better management of this population.

It is important to remember that women with mental illness are sick. They may act inappropriately, but many times this is related to their disease rather than an inherent character flaw. Their behavior can be bizarre, aggravating, tragically funny, dangerous, and/or provoking. While it is easy to get tired of their problems and the management difficulties they cause, they are ill and in most cases their illness dictates their behavior and even their awareness that something is wrong.

Staff must maintain a supportive professional manner in working with individuals who have a mental illness. Just as with those who develop physical illness, the types, duration, and severity of the mental illnesses varies from individual to individual. Staff observations and actions may be a significant factor in positive outcome of the treatment. Staff are often the first to observe out-of-the-ordinary behavior. It is important that they know, understand, and follow their facility's policies and procedures in this area.

Staff may be asked by the counselor treating a particular person to approach her in a special way. They even may be requested to take a specific type of attitude toward an inmate. These types of instructions are a very important part of the treatment program and should be followed to the letter.

Working with inmates who have mental illness can be time consuming, aggravating, frustrating, and depressing. Correctional employees need to keep track of their own mental health and not take the inmate's problem home with them. Staff may find it useful to practice stress reduction strategies (*see* Cornelius, 1994). These will help them when inmates with mental illness refuse treatment, act out, or engage in otherwise disruptive behavior. It also helps to keep a sense of humor and maintain compassion.

Correctional staff are a key ingredient in maintaining the safety and security of those with mental illness as well as the others in the facility. This only can be accomplished by being vigilant and maintaining a positive supportive attitude because with staff encouragement many women with mental illness will improve.

AMERICAN CORRECTIONAL ASSOCIATION MENTAL HEALTH APPRAISAL COMPONENTS (MANDATORY) STANDARD

Assessment of current mental status and condition

Assessment of current suicide; potential and person-specific circumstances that increase suicide potential

Assessment of violence potential and person-specific circumstances that increase violence potential

Review of available historical records of inpatient and outpatient psychiatric treatment

Review of history of treatment with psychotropic medication

Review of history of psychotherapy, psychoeductional groups, and classes or support groups

Review of history of drug and alcohol treatment

Review of educational history

Review of history of sexual abuse-victimization and predatory behavior*

Assessment of drug and alcohol abuse and/or addiction

Use of additional assessment tools, as indicated

Referral to treatment as indicated

Development and implementation of a treatment plan, including recommendations concerning housing, job assignment, and program participation

(American Correctional Association, 2003c, 4-4371, p. 109)

*Note: The assessment components include the requirement to "specify history of sexual abuse-victimization and predatory behavior." While this question may be appropriate for some women, the standard does not include questions concerning physical, sexual, and psychological abuse most women encounter as children or adults. This information should be solicited because it is critical in the treatment of women and probably would apply in a number of cases to men as well.

Also, note that the standard does not include any query about the women's children. To make the standard gender responsive, this information should be added because the status of their children is the source of much of the anxiety experienced by incarcerated women.

Security and Supervision for Women Offenders

❖ Describe the similarities between security and supervision in men's and women's facilities.

❖ Discuss security and supervision specific to women's institutions.

❖ Identify behaviors that should be avoided in working with women inmates.

❖ Discuss appropriate behaviors that will strengthen women's ability to successfully adjust to the facility and the community on release.

❖ Identify what staff can do to successfully supervise women in prison.

Introduction

In this section, we will explore the similarities and differences in security and supervision of male and female inmates. We will review some of the pitfalls staff should avoid in working with women and suggest behaviors that can have a positive impact on the operation of the facility and on women inmates. The chapter includes strategies staff can use to manage women more successfully in institutions.

This chapter builds on the information about how women are socialized, the different expectations we have of them, and how they differ from men, topics which were explored in earlier chapters. Therefore, it is important to remember the research and the issues that were highlighted in each chapter. For example, women become involved in crime in different ways than do men.

Much of the recent research on female offenders has focused on what is called the "pathways" theory. Steffensmeier and Allan (1998) explain that women's lives are typically quite different from men's. Different life experiences can put women at risk of committing crime and can determine their patterns of offending. Security and safety in a women's facility will be more efficient and effective if these differences are understood and if they are reflected in the institution's policies, procedures, programs, and practices.

Common themes that have been highlighted in previous chapters include:

gender roles and expectations

impact of race, class, and economic status

importance of relationships in women's lives, particularly with family members

history of sexual and physical abuse

involvement in substance abuse

physical and mental health issues

Understanding how these forces have an impact on women's lives will make working with female offenders easier. It also will improve the security and safety of the facility.

Security Similarities and Differences

Goals of Good Security

The primary concern of staff in any correctional facility is to maintain a safe and secure environment for both themselves and the inmate population (Clear and Cole, 2000; Seiter, 2002). The primary goals of good security and supervision are the same in both women's and men's facilities. The first, and most important, goal is that staff, inmates, and visitors must feel and be safe (Seiter, 2002). Neither staff nor inmates will feel secure in an environment where conflict, violence, or abuse is tolerated.

From time to time, all correctional facilities will experience escalating tensions. All staff members in both male and female facilities are responsible for reporting problems they encounter to the appropriate supervisor and supporting security procedures in the facility. Criminal activity, harassment, discrimination, misconduct, and other threats to the maintenance of order in the facility cannot be permitted.

The second goal of good security in a facility is maintaining order. This is achieved through the development and implementation of sound policies and procedures (Seiter, 2002). All facilities have policies and regulations, which staff and inmates must follow. These include rules on:

contraband, or what inmates can and cannot have in prison

searches

counts, or ways of accounting for prisoners' whereabouts

internal and external security supervision

procedures for emergencies including riots, medical concerns, fire, and weather

control of tools

transportation of inmates

inmate movement

visiting

other aspects of inmate life in the institution

Facility policy and procedures also govern staff activities and behavior on the job. Staff compliance with these rules is as much a necessity as it is for inmates. Staff cannot expect inmates to respect and obey rules and regulations if they see employees flagrantly ignoring policies and practices or complaining about them.

The third goal of security in both male and female correctional facilities is the prevention of escapes. Old corrections hands used to say; "You can't treat them, if you can't keep them." Prevention of escapes is accomplished in part through the development and implementation of an objective classification system that enables staff to assess inmates' backgrounds and behavior and adjust security and supervision to meet risks that are identified (Seiter, 2002). Remember, all correctional personnel—not just correctional officers—have a legal obligation to prevent escapes (Collins, 2004).

The fourth goal in maintaining a safe and secure environment in either a male or female facility is to ensure that all staff (including contract personnel and volunteers) regardless of where they are in the facility take a team approach and work together. It also means all people working in the institution must be knowledgeable about security procedures, programs, and services available in the facility and actively practice good security in the workplace at all times.

While women's and men's correctional facilities have a number of things in common, sometimes the way that staff members in each accomplish their tasks in each type of institution may be different. For example, control of contraband often involves staff conducting pat-down searches or observing offenders partially clothed. Using cross-gender supervision to carry out these functions is normally not a problem in male facilities, but in women's facilities it can quickly lead to complaints of sexual harassment or sexual misconduct.

Components of Security

Seiter (2002) identifies seven components that are essential to maintaining a safe and secure institutional environment. We will examine each of these and explore some of the differences between implementation of the component in male and female facilities. As staff members review these issues, they may be able to think of other ways that security policies and practices should be modified to ensure that facilities are gender responsive.

(1) Inmate Classification

Comprehensive classification systems enable officials to predict security and escape risks. These classification systems also provide information regarding program or treatment needs that the offender might have and can identify the types of future bed spaces needed.

Both male and female facilities will have classification systems. Unfortunately, some forty states use the same classification system for males and females and they typically base their systems on the National Institute of Corrections' model, which was designed for use in male facilities (Morash, Bynum, and Koons, 1998).

A number of questions have been raised about the validity and reliability of using the same classification system for men and women. Some believe that women have become more dangerous over the last few years so using a system based on the dangerousness of males is appropriate. Others think that it is an equity issue; if you use a system for males, you must use the same one with females. Neither of these rationales is accurate. First, the increase in the number of women in prison is based more on public policies toward drug enforcement than on a more violent woman. In fact, the percentage of women incarcerated for violent offenses has dropped in the last twenty years. Second, equity does not mean things must be the same, and it does not mean using something that is not effective with women just because it is used with men.

Van Voorhis et al. (2002) noted research that indicates, in addition to males being more dangerous, there are differences between men and women in at least three other areas. First, with males, criminal history, age, and education are important classification variables; for women, experience with sexual and physical abuse as children and/or adults, dysfunctional relationships, number of children, and single parenting seem to be more relevant to their classification.

Second, since most existing classifications systems were validated based on their application to the male population, it is "unethical to apply any assessment to a population other than the one used for its construction and validation" (Van Voorhis et al., 2002, p. 4).

Third, research has demonstrated many correctional classification systems either do not use data from populations of women or underuse information from female inmates in the development of classification criteria. This results in women being placed in higher level security than is warranted, which costs the correctional system more. For example, if the criteria require a certain score for the number of offenses an offender has committed and a woman has written ten bad checks (a common offense committed by women) and each is counted as a separate crime, she will be classified as needing a higher level of supervision than is warranted based on the number of crimes. Counting a woman who is on welfare or who is a full-time homemaker the same as a man who is unemployed is another example of overclassification. Ignoring the impact of victimization and trauma on women means that supervision and safety needs based on these experiences are overlooked.

(2) Physical Security

The physical design of the facility should be based on the types of inmates housed in the facility and the potential security and supervision needs they have. Given the cost of constructing high-security facilities, building large medium-maximum institutions for women should be questioned. Data indicate that up to two-thirds of women can be classified as needing minimum security. Housing them in a higher-level facility costs more than keeping them in the appropriate-level facility. Larger facilities run on the male "get-tough model" can result in negative responses by women and result in more anger and hostility against staff (Kruttschnitt, Gartner, and Miller, 2000). Funds spent to put multiple rows of razor ribbon and other hardware common in male facilities into women's prisons could be better spent in developing small women-centered community-based facilities that would be more effective and cheaper in the long run for taxpayers.

(3) Policies and Procedures

Written policies and procedure must be current, implemented, and monitored for compliance. Systemwide policies and procedures designed to meet the needs of male offenders should be applied only to men.

Gender-responsive policies and procedures should be developed to apply to women offenders. Morton (1998) called for a new model for working with female offenders that included:

the use of incarceration as a last resort and only for those who represented a danger to themselves and others

programs and services including security that were humane, women-centered, and individualized based on the needs of women

policies and practices that reflected the biological characteristics of women and the impact of gender and acculturation in their lives carefully selected staff who were given training to help them understand gender differences and how to work with women

ongoing monitoring and periodic evaluation of supervision, programs, and management of female offenders to ensure they were accomplishing the goals they were designed to address

Bloom, Owen, and Covington (2003) developed guiding principles for gender-responsive policies based on the latest research, which should be of assistance to anyone seeking to better understand and manage women offenders. These principles are as follows:

Gender: Acknowledge that gender makes a difference.

Environment: Create an environment based on safety, respect and dignity.

Relationships: Develop policies, practices, and programs that are relational and promote healthy connections to children, family, significant others, and the community.

Services and Supervision: Address substance abuse, trauma, and mental health issues through comprehensive, integrated, and culturally relevant services, and appropriate supervision.

Socioeconomic Status: Provide women with opportunities to improve their socioeconomic conditions.

Community: Establish a system of community supervision and reentry with comprehensive, collaborative services (p. 76).

Many of these principles are also included in the American Correctional Association's policy on women offenders (*see* Appendix A).

(4) Inmate Accountability

There must be a system in place that enables staff to know that inmates are where they are supposed to be at all times. Inmate counts are certainly necessary, but they are time consuming for staff and can be disruptive to programming, work, and inmate sleep. Since women are generally less of an escape risk than are men, count procedures should reflect this difference. With proper analysis, it may be found that fewer counts are needed in a women's facility to ensure accountability.

(5) Control of Contraband

There must be procedures which prevent contraband from entering the facility as well as detecting, confiscating, and disposing of any unauthorized items that are obtained by inmates in the facility.

Contraband is a problem in any correctional facility; however, it is usually not as much of an issue in women's facilities as it is in male facilities (Pollock, 2002). Women, for example, rarely make shanks as offensive or defensive weapons. The problem comes when what is allowed in a men's institution is applied to a women's facility. It is exacerbated when systems limit what an inmate can have by what fits into a duffel bag or similar receptacle.

Limits on possessions are certainly need, but women need more and different kinds of things than do men. For example, cosmetics and other personal care items needed by women are typically not included in general lists of items inmates can have because men do not need them. If women have items that are not on the list of approved items, they can be punished. Such problems can be resolved by allowing women's institutional administrators to develop their lists of contraband items based on the needs of the women in their facilities.

Searching women's facilities for contraband can take more time than it does in a men's facility. In addition to having more things, personnel conducting searches have to take particular care that they are not exposed to blood-borne pathogens. Specially marked containers for used tampons and sanitary pads are needed in all women's bathrooms, and the contents should be disposed of as provided for in agency or facility policy.

Women are very protective of their things, particularly any items associated with their children. Staff members can help ease tensions and acrimony by handling inmate's possessions during searches as they would like their own things to be treated.

(6) Professional Staff

Knowledgeable, competent staff who can effectively implement security procedures are a major component of institutional safety and security. Until Title VII of the Civil Rights Act was extended to cover state and local government in the early 1970s, women were not allowed to work in men's facilities so employment in a women's prison was seen as a dead end by both women and men in the system. The perception of lesser status of those working in a women's facility and a dislike for working with women offenders are still problems today. Many men who work in women's facilities are teased by their male counterparts who work in men's facilities. They often are asked, "Why don't you work in a 'real' correctional facility" (Personal Communication, Warden Richard Bazzle, February, 2003).

Women also face criticism. A woman working in a male facility who was applying for a senior position in a women's facility was told by her male supervisor, "I would take out my gun and shoot myself before I would work in a female facility" (Personal Communication, Major Small, March, 2004).

Not all women working in a women's institution are comfortable there. They may have adopted the attitude of many in the community and some staff working in male facilities that women offenders are inherently bad people and are too much trouble to supervise. This can happen, for example, when women employees transfer from a male to female facility and have not received the training they need to understand women offenders. This also can occur when staff have lived in the same neighborhood or have had similar life experiences as the women they are supervising and believe that if they "made it" so could these women. Carefully selecting, training, and supervising of staff can help resolve many of these problems.

(7) Basics of Prison Operations

This all encompassing component includes all aspects of prison management and the provision of programs and services that will encourage staff and inmate compliance with institutional rules. It also includes sanctions for those who violate them. As noted earlier, staff in women's facilities tend to hold women to a higher standard of conduct and issue more disciplinary charges than is true in male facilities. This practice should be eliminated because it wastes valuable staff time and facility resources and trivializes those rules that are truly related to institutional safety and security.

Seiter (2002) concludes his discussion of the components of a good security program by noting that "creating and maintaining a safe and secure environment is one of the most difficult tasks for staff and administrators, and it is one that requires constant effort and diligence" (p. 207).

Gender-responsive Supervision and Security Issues

In addition to the goals of all correctional facilities to provide a safe and secure facility, which men and women's institutions have in common, several areas must be addressed specifically at women's facilities. In some instances, such as sexual misconduct, the issue may be a problem in male facilities but manifests itself differently in a women's facility.

Inappropriate Relationships/ Sexual Misconduct

While inappropriate relationships can and do occur in male facilities, they have become a primary concern of administrators of women's facilities because of their prevalence and the disastrous consequences they have for both staff and inmates. They are also a serious threat to the safety and security of everyone in the facility (Human Rights Watch, 1996; National Institute of Corrections/American University, 2000).

Inappropriate relationships can be defined as actions or behaviors that can be interpreted as overfamiliarity between staff and inmates, unprofessional or unbecoming behavior by a staff person, volunteer, visitor, contract employee, or anyone serving in or as an agent of a correctional agency (McCampbell and Layman, 2000). This type of behavior usually begins with small things such as an inmate asking a staff person to mail a letter for her, exchanging bits of personal information, calling each other by first names, or engaging in gossip about other inmates or staff. McCampbell and Layman (2000) note that such behavior "often leads to sexual misconduct if allowed to progress" (Section IX p. 7).

Sexual misconduct is defined as:

> *any behavior or act of a sexual nature directed toward an inmate by an employee, volunteer, visitor, or agency representative. This includes acts or attempts to commit such acts including but not limited to sexual assault, sexual abuse, sexual harassment, sexual contact, conduct of a sexual nature or by implication, obscenity, and unreasonable invasion of privacy. Sexual misconduct also includes but is not limited to conversations or correspondence, which suggests a romantic or sexual relationship between an inmate and any party mentioned above* (McCampbell and Layman, 2000, Section III, p. 1).

Historically, sexual abuse and sexual harassment of women inmates has been a way of life in some correctional facilities (Human Rights Watch, 1996). In a recent study by the National Institute of Corrections, thirty-six states reported "substantial misconduct between staff and inmates" in 1998 (National Institute of Corrections, 2000, p. 10). Kathleen Hawk Sawyer, former director of the Federal Bureau of Prisons, has stated "that sexual misconduct has been the single most frustrating issue" for her to deal with during her term as director (McCampbell and Layman, 2000, p.1).

As with most problems, reasons for the ongoing, inappropriate relationships between women inmates and staff are complex. Some staff, both male and female, are predators, taking out their sexual aggression on women who have little recourse but to submit. In other instances, staff are lonely or have difficulties relating to family or friends in the community. They seek comfort and affection from a captive population. In other situations, women inmates may manipulate staff with sex.

McCampbell and Layman (2000) point out that institutional culture evolves through the complex interaction of inmate and staff characteristics and behaviors, institutional management (or lack thereof), agency and institutional policies, and community values. This culture can encourage healthy professional relationships between staff and inmates or evolve into a "sexualized work environment" in which boundaries between inmate and staff become blurred and unprofessional conduct becomes the norm (Section IX, p. 4).

Sexual or other inappropriate relationships with women inmates should never occur. Staff are the keepers. As such, they are responsible for maintaining order and ensuring that all in the facility are kept safe. Even in cases where a staff person appears to have been manipulated, he or she is still considered responsible for controlling the situation. Inappropriate relationships with inmates are not a joke. They jeopardize the safety and security of all in the institution and must be eliminated when dealing with incarcerated women.

Consequences of Sexual Misconduct

Engaging in inappropriate relationships or sexual misconduct has a number of potentially negative impacts on staff. Some of these identified by McCambell and Layman (2000) are listed below:

losing their job and jeopardizing future employment opportunities

having their name/picture in the paper/humiliating their family/losing their good name and self-respect

facing criminal prosecution and possible imprisonment

registering as a sex offender for life under Megan's Law

destroying personal life including spouse/boyfriend, girlfriend, children, and other family members

being subject to possible blackmail and coercion by inmates

jeopardizing the safety and security of other staff members by failing to carry out duties while engaging in the misconduct

risking the introduction of contraband into the institution

encouraging additional manipulation of staff by inmates

having a negative impact on the culture of the facility

placing other staff members in danger

contracting sexually transmitted diseases

Everybody loses when sexual misconduct occurs. It is, however, a very powerful vice and easy to drift into. One agency investigator who interviewed staff members who had been terminated for misconduct reported all understood that their actions were wrong, but engaged in them anyway (Personal Communication, Betsy Stewart, April 2001).

Prevention Strategies

The Women's Rights Project of Human Rights Watch investigated a number of allegations of sexual abuse in women's institutions. The group's report, *All Too Familiar: Sexual Abuse of Women in U.S. State Prisons*, should be reviewed by anyone having responsibility for managing women inmates. While much of the information comes from inmate interviews, it paints a chilling picture of problems in this area and contains several recommendations for actions that can be taken to improve safety and security in women's institutions (Human Rights Watch, 1996).

Another source of information about sexual misconduct and how to best prevent or manage it is the National Institute of Corrections. Since the mid 1990s, the National Institute of Corrections has conducted a number of studies, provided technical assistance and training, and developed several publications to help agencies deal effectively with this problem.

Managers and staff in correctional agencies and institutions must take steps to help ensure inappropriate relationships do not occur. In the event that misconduct does happen, swift and certain action must be taken to identify the problems and take corrective action.

Some of the strategies that can be taken to help avoid misconduct include the following which have been summarized from the *National Institute of Corrections/American University Training Manual* (2000) and the Human Rights Watch report (1996) unless otherwise noted:

> If a state does not have a statute making sexual relationships between inmates and staff illegal, agency administrators should recommend enactment of such a law by the state legislature.

> In those states where laws exist, they should be strictly enforced and those violating the law must be held fully accountable for their actions.

> The correctional agency and the institution should have a clear policy specifically banning inappropriate relationships and sexual misconduct between staff and inmates. Policies should be developed in compliance with national standards, be in writing, and be communicated to staff and where appropriate to inmates (Seiter, 2002).

> The number of agencies having policies covering sexual misconduct has grown from three with separate policies in 1996 to twenty in 2000 with additional agencies reporting they were developing policies in this area (National Institute of Corrections, 2000). The Federal Bureau of Prisons and a number of states have taken the position that inmates are not able to give consent to having sex with staff; therefore, any activity of a sexual nature is forbidden even if it looks as if there had been no coercion.

> Procedures should be in place to monitor all policies and procedures through security and policy audits to ensure compliance is maintained (Seiter, 2002). Having policies and procedures on paper is not sufficient. They must be current, understood by all, used, monitored, and consistently enforced.

> A system should be in place to enable staff or inmates to file complaints directly with the warden or outside investigators. The system should

provide for protection from retaliation for complainants and witnesses. Comprehensive procedures should be in place for a complete investigation of complaints. There should be provisions for the involvement of outside agencies, as needed.

Policies and procedures should specify consequences for staff and inmates who engage in inappropriate relationships or sexual misconduct. Care must be taken in dealing with allegations to ensure that the staff and inmates will feel free to report misconduct (Human Rights Watch, 1996). If an inmate or staff person intentionally lies about a relationship for vengeful purposes, then he or she should be held accountable.

Provisions should be made to safeguard individuals from retaliation by their alleged abusers or others in the facility.

In the event a woman becomes pregnant by a staff member, she should be provided all the necessary medical care. Mental health counseling should be available to help her cope with the aftermath of rape or sexual assault. Abortion counseling also should be provided if requested, but the decision to continue or terminate the pregnancy must be the woman's.

Derogatory, vulgar, or sexist language should be clearly prohibited and staff and inmates who violate this policy should be disciplined.

Except in legitimate emergencies, staff members should take appropriate actions to provide the maximum amount of privacy consistent with security needs. This may include, when possible, allowing the inmate to have some control over the door to her room so she feels safe at night. If the door is solid, having a window in place will allow security checks without opening the door. Policy should cover:

(a) requiring male staff to announce their presence in housing areas

(b) allowing women to cover their cell windows for a short time to dress and undress

(c) providing privacy screens or curtains in showers and stalls in bathrooms

(d) ensuring that male staff are not placed in a compromising position by being out of sight and sound of another staff member. Also, staff members should ensure that their office windows remain uncovered at all times.

Searches should be conducted when there is a reasonable belief that contraband is present. Women staff members should conduct pat-down searches, when at all possible. Strip searches of female inmates always should be conducted by women employees with the procedure done out of sight of other inmates and male staff. Body cavity searches should be conducted by qualified medical personnel, only if there is reasonable cause to suspect the woman is concealing contraband, and then only with female staff members present. American Correctional Association standards permit search by "correctional personnel trained by a health care personnel" (American Correctional Association, 2003c, p. 53). This probably was done because medical personnel feel that doing body-cavity searches interferes with their ethical doctor-patient relationship (Anno, 2001). It also might reflect correctional administrators' concerns about resources and could represent a short-term savings by using correctional staff rather than higher paid medical personnel to conduct body-cavity searches. However, it is the view of this author that this could result in anyone, male or female, with a modicum of training doing vaginal searches of girls and women. This would not be a good practice as improperly trained correctional staff could hurt the girl or woman, cause her to relive past sexual abuse, or result in her having future medical problems.

Staff found to be involved in serious, inappropriate activities or sexual misconduct should be removed from the facility, disciplined, fired, and referred for prosecution, as appropriate.

All staff working with women inmates should receive comprehensive pre-employment screening and subsequent training in gender-responsive supervision and other issues related to women.

Women inmates should be provided an orientation to the facility's policies prohibiting inappropriate behavior and sexual misconduct and taught how to report any alleged violations.

Having outside monitors and an independent review board also strengthens the maintenance of a safe environment for women inmates (Morton, 1996).

Red Flags for Staff Misconduct

The National Institute of Corrections at the conclusion of its workshop "Staff Sexual Misconduct with Inmates" asked participants to list behavior they considered hot buttons or red-flag events. The items listed were actions that correctional personnel identified as potentially indicating inappropriate relationships between staff and inmates. The list is as follows:

over-identifying with the inmate ("my inmate") or their issues (in other words, being blind to inmate's actions)

horseplay, sexual interaction between staff and inmates

inmates knowing personal information about staff

isolation from other staff

inmate has a letter from or photos of staff

staff granting special requests or showing favoritism

inmates in an unauthorized area or repeatedly out of their assigned place

staff spending an unexplainable amount of time with an inmate

telephone calls to and from staff/inmates

inmate grapevine, inmate snitches, inmate/staff rumors

staff in the facility during "off hours"

pregnancy or diagnosis of sexually transmitted disease

staff overly concerned about an inmate

drastic behavior change on the part of an inmate or staff

341

staff having sole involvement with a particular inmate

indispensable inmate: "Only one who can do this job"

high/low number of inmate grievances

inmate wanting to go to work early or volunteering to stay late

staff member confronting another staff person over an inmate

staff intercepting inmate disciplinary infractions or editing infractions

staff tracking outside inmate calls (number and content of call)

inmate improving his/her appearance, dress, make-up, hair

isolated posts/positions/work assignments

staff cannot account for time

staff's family being involved with an inmate's family

increase in contraband in an area

staff working in a secluded area with inmate(s)

staff taking inmates out of cell at unusual times

staff in personal crisis (divorce, ill health, bankruptcy, death in family)

unusual balance, or activity, in an inmate's commissary account

staff having excessive knowledge about an inmate and his/her family

staff intervening, or helping with the inmate's personal life and/or legal affairs

staff sharing food or snacks with inmates

staff testifying for an inmate, requesting special treatment for an inmate

staff delegating their duties to inmates (supervisor of cleaning, assignments)

staff bringing in large amounts of food, soda, snacks

overheard conversations between staff and inmates, which is sexualized in nature, or refers to the physical attributes of staff or inmates inmate sexual activity (National Institute of Corrections/American University, 2000, Appendix 4).

Dealing with Inappropriate Behavior

Anyone observing any inappropriate relationships between staff and inmates should report them to his/her supervisor. Behavior that could be misunderstood by inmates or other staff should be avoided. Staff members should not discuss their personal lives with women inmates or with other staff when they can be overheard. For example, discussions of a pending divorce can be taken as a sign of vulnerability (*see* Cornelius, 2002).

Inmates should not be taken to any areas in the institution where they cannot be observed by other staff. In cases where such actions cannot be avoided, staff should ensure that their supervisors know about the situation and that there are no other alternatives.

Professional behavior must be maintained and staff must not compromise their principles. Staff must ensure they are firm and fair in all their interactions with inmates and other staff. Some women inmates may remind staff of their mother, sister, or even themselves. This may make supervision difficult, but staff must not play favorites, under any circumstances, with those under their supervision. Inmates, like all people, sometimes misinterpret other's actions. Kindness may be taken for affection, which may equate in the inmate's mind to sex. This does not mean that staff should not be kind to inmates, it means that they should treat all inmates with the same concern and compassion.

Even the strongest person sometimes can be tempted by a situation. Staff having difficulty objectively supervising those in their care, should consult with their supervisor.

Since outsiders frequently do not understand the institutional environment or the stress involved in the job, some correctional staff find themselves associating almost exclusively with coworkers. While it may be difficult, given the long hours and rotating shifts (particularly where there are twelve-hour shifts) for staff to make the effort, it is critically important that they develop a life outside their job and away from the people with whom they work. They must maintain strong healthy relationships with family and friends outside the correctional community so the prison and the inmates do not become the total focus of their lives.

As McCampbell and Layman (2000) point out:

> *The staff inmate relationship is not an equal one. It must remain a superior/subordinate relationship the integrity of which must be protected by the staff with respect and the utmost ethical behavior (Section IX p. 21).*

Communication

Another area of difference between safety and security in men and women's facilities focuses on issues of communication. As has been discussed, women usually are acculturated differently in American society. In general, they have stronger verbal skills than most men and learn to talk more about issues affecting them than do men. While men limit information, women share almost everything, talk about their feelings, and use words to think through their problems and how to solve them (McCampbell and Layman, 2000). Often, they will ask for suggestions, when what they really want is someone to listen while they talk through a problem and find their own solution.

Working with women inmates requires using several communication tools including listening attentively. Sometimes, what women are saying can get lost in the verbiage. It is often necessary to listen carefully to get the message.

Owen (1998) quoted a California prison administrator as saying,

> *The men take answers at face value. When you tell them 'no,' they go away, but women want to discuss their particular problem in great detail. . . . Women take more time and some staff are not prepared for that.*

Since one of the characteristics of an institution is that the inmates are totally dependent on staff for most of their activities, possessions, and other aspects of everyday life, one should expect inmates to be demanding.

Working with women inmates requires that staff have infinite patience, both in listening to what the women are saying and in coping with questions the women pose about almost everything in the institution. They, like many people, do not respond well to "do it, just because I said to" or "it's the rule." Most women inmates in the institution have not been exposed to military discipline or team sports where they would have been taught to work together. Responding with understanding and explaining things within reason usually will result in women inmates being easier to manage.

Women in prison are more willing to express their emotions than are men. They will cry, scream, make verbal threats, and practice other self-defeating behavior. It is important for staff to help them talk through what is bothering them and to assist them in learning how to express themselves more effectively. Learning to respond assertively rather than aggressively in conflict situations and to think through actions before leaping into something may help incarcerated women function more effectively in the institution and when they return to the community (Urquhart and Cullen, 2003).

Because of the relational way women work and their tendency to share everything, one person's "business" quickly can become everyone's "business." Anyone who has ever played the children's game of Gossip understands how incorrect information abounds in a women's institution. In Gossip, one person whispers a message in another person's ear and that person passes it on around a circle of people. What comes out at the end is usually a quite different message than the original one. Gossip can relieve boredom or make the bearer feel important. It also can be used maliciously to cause trouble or get back at staff or other inmates who have made the person angry.

Tracy (1991) notes that women tend to have more close female friends than do men and they understand the difference between good and bad gossip. As she puts it "when women tell stories about other women who are not their friends, whom they envy, with whom they cannot identify, they seek to destroy. As all women know, gossip can be destructive and terrible" (cited in Chesler, 2003, p. 155)

Maintaining clear, ongoing messages about what is happening in the facility can help avoid some gossip and keep inmates calm in times of stress. It is also important that staff in women's facilities learn to respect each other and to be fair, consistent, and honest in their relationships with other employees and inmates. A level of trust can help defuse inaccurate information and help maintain order. Certainly, staff should not participate in the gossip in a women's facility and should discourage women inmates from doing so.

Women normally will want to make and receive more telephone calls than do male inmates. This is primarily based on the fact that female offenders have more children under eighteen than men have (National Institute of Corrections, 1998). Telephone calls are very important because they enable women to talk directly to their children who may not be able to visit. This contact reassures them about their children's safety and reminds them they still have a place in their children's lives. Allowing women access to the phone and providing other ways for them to communicate with their children and the children's caregivers, within the regulations of the facility, will help the overall management of the population. Ensuring fair access to the phone and providing that everyone has her share of time is also important.

All phone calls will not go well. A woman may learn something bad has happened to her family. She may find out that her child is sick or her boyfriend has another lover. Staff should be prepared for anger or emotional outbursts following a phone call. Pulling the woman aside and simply listening to her and letting her vent her frustrations and fears may resolve the problem. If this does not solve the problem and the woman seems depressed or too upset to function, she may need to be referred to the appropriate counselor for assistance as was described in a previous chapter.

Different Rules and Regulations

Since women's facilities normally have multiple security levels, they typically have more complex rules and regulations than men's facilities. The rules and regulations should be gender responsive and permit items such as cosmetics, personal hygiene supplies, adequate, gender-appropriate clothing, and other amenities to help women keep clean, healthy, and improve their self-image.

Sometimes gender-responsive modifications in agency policies on possessions and other changes to meet women's different needs are made at the institutional level and are not included in general agency policy (National Institute of Corrections, 1998). This probably will mean that they are not covered in agencywide staff training and new employee orientation. This can make it difficult for new staff and those individuals transferring from a male facility to a women's institution to understand the differences. Therefore, differences in policy and practice in the women's institution must be covered in the institutional orientation for new staff including those moving from male facilities.

The rules normally have to accommodate women on several security levels, since the number of institutions for women is limited in most jurisdictions. Therefore, minimum, medium, and maximum-security women can be working, eating, and interacting together. Some facilities even may have women who are on work release in the general population. It is sometimes difficult for staff to understand why separate groups have different rules. Women inmates also have difficulty understanding why they are not all treated the same. It is important for staff to be knowledgeable about the differing regulations and be patient with inmate complaints. Staff should provide thorough explanations that will help resolve alleged unequal treatment issues.

Women inmates often take the language that staff use very literally. Therefore, when a staff member asks an inmate to do her a "favor" and clean a certain area that inmate may think the staff member is indebted to her for doing a favor. Since bartering favors was a way of survival for many women prior to their incarceration, they may feel they can trade favors with staff. Such misunderstanding in communication can have a negative impact on facility safety and should be avoided (McCampbell and Layman, 2000).

Often, women will question the need for certain rules and will be unsatisfied with how they are applied. Within reason, staff's willingness to work with them to help them understand the reasons for the rules should contribute to compliance (Acoca, 1998).

Possessions

Women tend to accumulate more possessions than do men. Look at advertisements in a women's magazine and count all the things society teaches women are essential for them to maintain their femininity. Think of all the items women in the free world use just to get ready for work.

While women may have many of their belongings removed because they are in prison, it is still typical in most institutions for women to have more possessions than the average male inmate has. For example, most women's institutions allow inmates to use cosmetics as they are important for incarcerated women's mental health (Faiver, 1998). Also, in some male facilities, inmates are not expected to change clothes, even underwear, every day. Most women change clothes including underwear, every day. Women having menstrual periods may change underwear several times a day and may even need to change clothes more than once a day. Allowances for additional clothing should be included in institutional policy and practice.

If women are provided uniforms, they should be designed for women's bodies. Women inmates should not forced to wear men's clothing that does not fit and which demeans them. For example, jumpsuits mean that women have to undress to use the bathroom. To get a male uniform that will fit across the woman's bust usually means the shirt is long enough to be almost a dress and if it is a jumpsuit, the crotch will be at the woman's knees. This is certainly not the way to help women feel good about themselves and their abilities to overcome their problems.

Adding insult to injury, some agencies make it a rule violation to alter state-issued uniforms. While these policies are generally designed to keep inmates from acknowledging gang affiliation, there is limited rationale for sanctioning women who alter uniforms to keep from tripping over pants legs that are too long or who take in waist bands to keep their pants from falling off.

It goes without saying that women's shoes should be made for a woman's foot size. Putting women in male boots can have long-term consequences for their feet by rubbing and damaging them.

Some have raised questions about giving women access to tampons and panty liners using security as a reason for banning them. According to Anno (2001):

> The usual explanation is that tampons can be used to hide drugs or for purposes of masturbation or homosexual behavior. This is nonsense. Prohibiting tampons will not deter any of these activities because the tampon is not a necessary component of any of them (p. 244).

Panty liners are used for days when a woman's period is light or to absorb leaks or other drainage. Correctional agencies should make both liners and tampons available to women as a part of the issue of sanitary supplies. Women should not have to ask male staff for sanitary napkins, tampons, or panty liners. Nor should they be limited to so many a month. Women's periods vary with some needing only a few sanitary supplies while others will need more.

Women should be provided their own panties and bras. To save money, the agency can allow women to receive them from home if they wish. Having your own underwear may not be a problem in male facilities so some administrators overlook that it is a real problem for women to have to wear someone else's panties or bras. It is best if women have access to laundry facilities and can do their own laundry. However, if a common laundry is used, a system should be in place to ensure women get back their own underwear.

Some agencies mandate that women can only wear sports bras. While this may be adequate for small-busted women, regular sports bras may not give larger busted women enough support, particularly, if they are doing any heavy exercise. In all cases, women should be provided the type of bra that will provide the proper support.

As noted earlier, women inmates also can be very possessive about their things. For many, their room or space in the facility becomes their home, and they are very protective of it. Clothing, pictures of their children, correspondence, books, religious items, Mother's Day and birthday cards, and other possessions can have an emotional attachment for many women. The fact that women have more things and those things should be treated with respect during searches means routine searches, moving women to other facilities or within the institution, or other actions involving women's possessions will take more time. Staff should plan for this extra-time requirement so they will not be rushed and the women will be easier to manage.

Visiting

Women inmates receiving visits from their children usually will take more interest in them than do male inmates whose families visit. In most situations, women visit their husbands, boyfriends, or male family members in prison and children come along because they are living with their mothers. Visits in women's institutions usually involve female family members, guardians, or in some cases social workers bringing children to visit their mothers. While security procedures must be followed, care should be exercised in searching children or exposing them to the many harsh realities of the prison environment. Adults accompanying the children can be permitted to assist in the search— making a game of changing clothes if a strip search is warranted or if there is a suspicion of contraband contained in diapers.

If contraband is found on a young child, consistent with institution policies, the adult bringing the child should be held accountable and restricted from the institution as prescribed by policy. The child should be permitted to visit his or her mother if brought by another person.

Contact visiting between mothers and their children is very important. There will be few high-risk inmates in a women's facility so the majority of visits should allow direct contact between the woman and her children. Very high-risk inmates can be allowed contact visits through the use of separate rooms that are glass fronted for good visibility. This space also can be used for attorney visits or other visitation that requires a degree of privacy. Allowing high-risk inmates visitation can be an incentive for good behavior.

Staff should expect mothers and children to be reluctant to part. Both children and the women may cry and try to delay leaving the visiting area. Again, patience will be necessary. Institutions that have programs for women to maintain long-distance contact with their children or that provide for "summer camps" or regular times that women can spend all day and even visit overnight with their children will minimize the pain of separation. The Indiana Women's Prison in Indianapolis, Indiana has a very comprehensive family preservation program. It involves an extensive range of programs including parent education, parenting teenagers, parent support groups, grandmother support groups, responsible mother/health baby program for expectant mothers, parental bonding through a children's visitation center, summer day camp five days for mothers and grandmothers, and a parent teen day twice a year, special holiday parties at Mother's Day, Easter, Valentine's Day, Halloween, and Christmas, and an outreach program to link the mother with home, children, and caregivers (Family Preservation Program, 2003).

Supervision of Work Details

The majority of women will work willingly on prison details and other institutional assignments. Some staff report women are more willing to please than are men (Federal Bureau of Prisons, 1993). It is important to remember when managing women inmates that they often have few vocational skills in nontraditional work. Women working on institutional maintenance usually will need to be taught how to use hammers, pliers, and other tools. They also typically will not be as strong nor have the endurance most male inmates have. This is particularly true of upper body strength. With careful conditioning and training to use the required equipment, women can master most of the work assignments available in the facility. However, staff should anticipate having to teach women how to work with unfamiliar tools and how to perform tasks in nontraditional work assignments. This will require time and patience but should result in the work getting done effectively while the women can learn marketable skills to help them when they leave the institution.

For a variety of reasons discussed earlier, women inmates, attend sick call more than do men of the same age. Women also may have more medical restrictions placed on them than do men. This is particularly true of pregnant women or those who recently have had a baby or miscarriage. While some women may abuse sick call, correctional staff should not prohibit access to medical care nor should they punish a woman based on their opinion of whether they think the inmate is malingering.

Positive behavior should be reinforced by explaining what a woman did right on the job and how it contributed to getting the job done. Women often do not know how to accept praise. They attribute their success to luck or others rather than to their own efforts (Maniglia, 1998). Helping them accept ownership for their successes will contribute to their sense of self-worth and the likelihood they will do well in the future.

When it is necessary to correct the way a woman is doing a job, staff should explain in nonjudgmental language what she did incorrectly. This should be done out of hearing of other inmates if at all possible. Care should be taken not to use derogatory words such as "stupid" or "clumsy." If the performance was related to lack of knowledge or skill, taking time to explain the appropriate information will enable her to do it right. Staff should make certain the inmate has an opportunity to practice the skill if needed. If the problem is in her attitude or she is unwilling to do the job, staff should explain the importance of completing the task in a satisfactory manner and help the inmate stick with it until the job is completed. Some women inmates have rarely successfully completed a job in their lives and do not think they can start now. Reinforcing their efforts and helping them complete tasks will reinforce positive outcomes in the future (Federal Bureau of Prisons, 1993).

Relationships

According to Hawkins (1995), women do not subscribe to the inmate code that is common in male facilities. While some female offenders "do their own time" and want little to do with other women or with staff, most women are more than willing to interact with both staff and other inmates. Female offenders generally use words more than they use violence in conflict situations.

Women inmates traditionally are more socially oriented than male inmates are (McCampbell and Layman, 2000). Their relationships with other inmates can become intense. Where male inmates avoid interaction with others, women frequently form pseudo families when in prison (Clear and Cole, 2000). Older women may be referred to as "mother." Women of similar ages frequently will call each other sisters. These relationships develop because of women's need for social and personal closeness with other people (Heffernan, 1972).

Women naturally hug each other, put their arms around each other, cry with each other, comfort each other when they are distressed, and they become excited with others upon receiving good news. They also will argue and fight with other "family" members, modeling some of the same behavior they experienced on the street. While much of the gossiping, bickering, and displaying of other dysfunctional behavior may seem petty to staff, it can be very real to the inmate. Maintaining a professional demeanor, helping people work through their problems, and defusing disruptive behavior will help the women cope more effectively with the institutional environment.

On occasion, women will form strong homosexual ties (Leger, 1987). In male facilities, dominance and power will result in homosexual relationships developing between a strong inmate and a weak one for protection against violence. Relationships in a women's facility are usually not coercive and form out of a need to be loved and cared for by another human being. Women may refer to each other as "husband and wife" and want to demonstrate their affection for each other.

Chaddock (1996) found nonviolent sexual offenses more common in women's facilities than in male ones. She also notes that these types of offenses do not necessarily mean the women will engage in "other types of disruptive behavior" (p. 77).

Homosexual behavior may be very upsetting to some staff who see it as an abomination in direct conflict with their religion or other beliefs. Most facilities have rules against sexual relationships between inmates even those that might be consensual and these should be enforced in a nonprejudicial manner. Staff having difficulty addressing this matter objectively should talk to their supervisor or a counselor (Acoca, 1998).

Staff Attitudes

Not everyone can work well with women inmates. How correctional personnel view women, in general, and women inmates, in particular, will go a long way in determining how effective they will be when working with women. Society builds strong negative stereotypes of women as inferior and as individuals who create problems for themselves and others. Research indicates that, in general, even women tend to blame other women who are in trouble for the difficulty they are in (Chesler, 2003). For example, experienced prosecutors often do not want women to serve on juries in rape cases because they have seen women not be able to identify with the female victim. They want to believe that the woman did something to cause the assault or that she deserved to be raped. This is done in part as a way of convincing themselves that they could never be raped (Chesler, 2003).

It is important for both male and female staff to examine their feelings and preconceived notions about women. Staff who do not like women, have no respect for them, and cannot have some empathy for their situation should not work in a women's facility.

Working in a women's facility requires patience and skills not everyone possesses. Supervisors should be vigilant in identifying staff who are not comfortable with women and find they do not have, or cannot acquire the skills to work with them. If they do not request a transfer to another facility, then they may have to be involuntarily assigned or terminated. Women inmates must not be subjected to damaging attitudes and treatment from staff or others.

Sometimes staff can develop a paternal attitude towards inmates, particularly if they see their behavior as childish or do not see the women as responsible adults. One example of this is when staff call inmates "girls." This sends a not–so–subtle message that women are supposed to be childlike, helpless, and unable to act as adults. There will be inmates, particularly the younger ones, whose behavior is immature; however, all women in the facility must be treated as adults and helped to assume responsibility for their actions.

Addressing "isms"

While the United States used to be known as a "melting pot" in which immigrants and others adopted the culture and values of the white majority, this changed as the population of the country became more diverse. Increasingly policymakers and others realized while people from different racial and cultural groups might be not have the same values and beliefs as the dominant American culture, there was value in heterogeneity. Also, minorities and immigrants began to resist loosing their cultural identity (Cross, Bazron, Dennis, and Isaacs, 1989).

A lot of attention was given to managing diversity and understanding the multicultural work force in the 1980s and 90s (Geber, 1990.) A number of correctional agencies have continued to provide training in this area because nowhere is the need to understand a multicultural, multiracial environment more needed than in the correctional arena. Whether it is staff from the rural areas where institutions are located working with inmates from urban areas or predominately white staff working with a mostly minority inmate population, understanding how to work with racially and culturally diverse populations is critical to the safety and security of the facility.

As Mondragon (1991) points out:

Cultural ties are particularly important to the incarcerated because of their separation from the outside world. An offender population made up of many backgrounds and cultures creates a serious potential for problems. A correctional environment that allows various ethnic groups to preserve their identities, and at the same time promotes their peaceful co-existence, can reduce tensions (p. 6)

In addition to understanding issues in working with women offenders, all staff must address their stereotypes about others who may have another skin color, religious belief, socio-economic background, ethnic association, or are different in some way (*see* Smalls, 2004). This includes those women who may have a handicap, mental problem, or other disability. It is vital to the safety and security of the institution that decisions and actions should not be made based on stereotypes. The more staff members and inmates learn about people who have a different skin color, who worship in a different church, who have a different educational background, or who have come from a different culture or part of the country, the more smoothly the institution can operate and the better relationships in it will be.

In many parts of the country, racism impacts everyone's life, male or female, nonwhite or white. Both staff and inmates tend to carry their beliefs and prejudices about race from the community to the institution. Since the majority of incarcerated women are minorities, usually African-Americans or Latinas, understanding that women from these minority groups can have different outlooks and beliefs is important. For example, according to Guy-Sheftall (2003) many African-American women believe they have "experienced a special kind of oppression in this country, one that is both racist and sexist, because of their dual racial and gender identities" (p 178). Guy-Sheftall (2003) goes on to explain that struggles with poverty and minority status can influence how black women view the world and that the reality of their lives should not be ignored in making public policy decisions.

There is a tendency to see all people from the same racial or cultural background as being the same. This is particularly true of the Latino or Hispanic population. The federal government, for example, places twenty different nationalities under one Hispanic label. Acosta-Belen and Bose (2003) note that "this practice (of lumping all Latinos together) tends to eclipse the many different national origins, races, social and cultural experiences, and histories of the various individual Latino groups" (p. 198). This reinforces the point that just as all women are not alike, nor are all people of one race or cultural background alike.

It is possible to offend someone simply by not understanding her culture or background. Assuming anyone who is been on welfare is lazy, does not want to work, or is cheating taxpayers, for example, is grossly unfair. Praeger (1995) notes that even governmental agencies charged with assisting those receiving Aid to Families with Dependent Children treat clients "with rudeness, impatience, mistrust, and scorn … which makes the recipient feel stupid, guilty, and worthless" (p. 525).

Newspaper columnist, Leonard Pitts (2004) notes that African–Americans tend to "circle the wagons when one of our own is in trouble" (p. A 11). Coming together to support your own can happen with any minority group when one or more members are seen as being attacked by the dominant group. This phenomenon plays itself out in correctional institutions between staff and inmates, administrators and line officers, or with other groups that can be seen as being of a higher rank or different from the dominant group. Prison gangs, for example, developed in men's institutions along racial lines to "protect" members from other groups and to use their strength in numbers to wield power over others.

While women tend to cluster and socialize along racial lines, they have not developed the gang mentality so common in men's facilities. However, staff must be aware that women inmates will identify and support other female inmates if they feel they are being treated unfairly. This is why it is always better to correct a woman inmate out of the presence of other inmates, if possible. Mutual support also can carry over to situations when an inmate is injured or dies in the institution. Her pain becomes other inmates' pain, so staff should be prepared when such events occur to work not only with the inmate who has a problem but also with those close to her as well.

Anyone who jumps to support his or her "brothers" or "sisters" just because they are of the same race, sex, religion, or because they have other traits in common, should take Pitts' (2004) advice when he says:

> *We—blacks—ought to be more thoughtful about who we choose to rally around, ought to be less automatic in leaping to the defense. Yes, we are a forgiving people in a forgiving nation. But we need to grow beyond the notion that someone deserves our support because he is black and in trouble.*
>
> *After all, we've spent 400 years trying to get white people to understand that black is not a flaw. Sometimes, though, we ourselves forget: It is not a character reference, either (p. A 11).*

"Isms" have no place in corrections, period. It is important to find common ground with those who are different and learn how to work effectively with people of all types. If staff members or inmates discriminate against others, they should be counseled out of the presence of others. If the behavior does not stop and it is damaging to staff, inmates, or the facility, it should be reported to a supervisor.

Staff should take advantage of opportunities to learn as much about other cultures, races, religions, and backgrounds as they can. Inmates also should be given racial and cultural diversity training. Everyone in the facility must be sensitive even to such differences as where a person has lived. A woman from a rural area, for example, may not understand the language or behavior of a woman who comes from an urban area and is used to fighting for survival on the streets. The ability to understand others and function effectively in a culturally diverse environment is essential for the success of a women's facility.

Correctional staff should not reinforce stereotypes if they want female offenders to succeed in the institution or when they are released. Knowledge and understanding can overcome prejudices if everyone works together.

Winfeld and Spielman (1995) recommend the following things staff can do to eliminate "isms":

Insist on inclusive language in all verbal and written communication

Refuse to tolerate jokes about race, sexual orientation, religion, and so forth

Encourage others to be tolerant and accepting

Actively support people who are being singled out because they are different (p. 51)

Additionally, staff should ensure nondiscrimination policies are practiced when working with both inmates and other staff members.

To learn about cultures, religions, minority groups, and others who are different, Hanamura (1989) recommends:

Talk with someone who can help you understand the barriers you are up against when working with an individual who is "different."

Read about the group of people you would like to learn about.

Get help from community resources or agencies versed in the area that you want to learn about.

Simulate an experience outside the realm of what you typically do, and record how you feel in the simulation. (For example Morton (1993) as one part of a training program on elderly offenders asks participants to use walkers, wheelchairs, crutches, and fogged or scratched glasses to simulate a disability. After everyone has gone though a series of activities, they are asked to reflect on how it felt and what they learned from their temporary aging experience.)

Consider yourself both a teacher and a learner; be clear about what you do not know.

Do not allow the person or group who is "different" to intimidate you. Get advice from others if you are not sure what to do.

Examine a previous situation in which you were successful in working with someone who was "different."

Develop an action plan and make it happen. Be aware of timing and the political climate in striving for effectiveness in working with people who are different (pp. 112-114).

Remember that we usually have more in common than we realize and that everyone has some unique qualities.

Other Security Concerns

Generally, women do not make the types of violent attacks on other inmates or staff that men do. Nor are they as likely to commit infractions at the same rate as men (Chaddock, 1996). In fact, many women inmates report feeling safer in prison than they did on the streets (Personal Communication, Major Small, June 2001). However, staff must be observant at all times and not be complacent because they are working with women. A few women in the facility will be very dangerous in certain situations and others may be quite volatile. While it is impossible to predict with 100 percent accuracy which women will be problems, some research suggests that young women early in their sentence, repeat offenders, and those with substance abuse problems have the potential to be security and behavioral risks (Chaddock, 1996).

One custody issue unique to women's institutions is the control and transport of pregnant women. In 1998, some twenty-one states had specific policies and procedures concerning this area with some varying the types of restraints based on the trimester of the woman's pregnancy (National Institute of Corrections, 1998). Missouri's policy, for example, specified standard restraints based on the inmate's security level be used during the first trimester and then only handcuffs thereafter. The policy also provided that pregnant women could be strip-searched but could not be required to squat. Women in labor were to be transported to the hospital without restraints but a staff member with restraints was to accompany her (National Institute of Corrections, 1998).

According to National Institute of Corrections (1998), other states provided that leg restraints for pregnant women should not be used without medical approval (New York), security personnel would assist pregnant women in negotiating steps, and entering and exiting vehicles (Louisiana), and "electronic control devices" such as stun guns and stun belts were prohibited (Kansas). All states should have comprehensive policies to protect the health of the mother and child while meeting only those security procedures necessary for the safety of the facility and the public.

As noted in Chapter 8, care must be taken when applying restraints to women, particularly those who are pregnant or who have other medical problems. At least thirty-nine states have "women in labor" policies requiring medical personnel to evaluate individual cases prior to placing pregnant women in restraints (National Institute of Corrections, 1998). Chaining a woman to the delivery table while she is giving birth unfortunately is still done in some jurisdictions. This is security overkill as a woman who is having a baby is in no condition to run. The practice is barbaric and should be abolished.

Every effort should be made not to have male officers on a women's housing unit alone or have men transport women inmates without the presence of a woman staff member. This procedure will help protect male staff members from charges of inappropriate behavior.

Women should be transported separately from male inmates. In spite of staff's best efforts to keep them separate, the women can be subjected to inappropriate comments and attention if confined in transport with men. To avoid women being harassed or enduring unwanted behavior, they should be kept entirely separate from male offenders.

On long trips, women may need to use the restroom more often than the typical male. They should be transported in two-piece sets of clothing rather than coveralls or jumpsuits to facilitate their using the restroom. They usually will take longer to use the restroom than do men and they may need access to hygiene products and should not be placed in a position to have to ask for supplies publicly.

Impact of Family Violence on Staff

Correctional agencies not only need to be concerned about inmates' exposure to family violence but also need to be concerned about the experiences of staff in regard to family violence. Given the widespread nature of family violence, it is reasonable to assume a number of staff in any correctional facility have been either abusers or victims of abuse. It is important for staff to know that they are not permitted to take out their aggressive tendencies on incarcerated women or other staff who might be vulnerable to abuse. Reports of such behavior should be investigated thoroughly and action taken to ensure it will not continue.

If staff members have an abusive background, they should be encouraged to seek counseling. Violence can be cyclical and can pass from generation to generation if there is not intervention to learn different ways of dealing with stress, sharing decision making, and getting along with others in the family. Getting assistance and counseling can help staff members ensure their spouse and children will not suffer the same pain they did as a child. It also may improve the way they deal with their coworkers and the inmate population.

Correctional employees are not immune to becoming victims of domestic violence themselves. In some instances, correctional personnel have been killed by their abusers. If another staff person is observed to be in an abusive situation, he or she should be encouraged to get help and be supported in his or her efforts to resolve the problem.

Emphasizing the Positive

Many of the women in correctional institutions have had very difficult lives and many have committed serious crimes or taken other actions that cannot be undone. Unfortunately, they cannot go back and undo the bad things in their lives. They have survived and it is important for staff to help them identify their strengths and focus on the positive things they can control. Assisting them in strengthening their self-image, improving their self-confidence, and learning new skills will help them resolve many of the problems that occur when women do not feel good about themselves or know how to cope with life.

Advocacy

Female offenders, in spite of growing numbers, are still to a large extent the "forgotten offenders." Many correctional agencies are so involved with keeping control over massive numbers of male offenders and dealing with increasingly fewer resources that women offenders get lost in planning and policy deliberations. As one warden of a women's facility was told by a director of corrections a number of years ago when she came to a wardens' meeting, "You don't need to come to these meetings, we are dealing with real inmate issues here." It is encouraging to note that this warden still worked for the agency long after the director had moved on.

As Hawkes (1991) notes, "Female offenders have no base of power from which to operate." The progress that has occurred in the treatment of women offenders has come about because someone in the community or in the system advocated for better services. Usually the ones who did this were the correctional staff who worked with women every day.

It is up to those working with women offenders and other concerned individuals to join with the American Correctional Association, the Association on Programs for Female Offenders, and other professional associations to advocate for gender-responsive programming and services for women and girls in the system. Together with those in both the private and public sectors, we must all lead the way in developing new and creative programs for this population. More and better interventions, particularly in the areas of violence against women and girls, are desperately needed and may prevent women and girls from turning to crime. A variety of community alternatives to traditional prisons will address crime committed by women and girls more effectively than does institutionalization. For those who do need to be confined for their own safety or for that of the community, gender-responsive programming will help them be easier to manage and will enable them return to the community as more responsible citizens. Change is needed but will not come about unless men and women who work in corrections act together for a better, safer future for women and girls

Summary

Pollock (2002) notes women adapt to prison in different ways than do men. In men's facilities, the social structure and relationships among inmates tends to be based on power and control. Men's facilities have more problems with gangs and contraband, particularly drugs and violence than do female facilities. Yet, in most systems, the same security policies and practices are applied to both women and men. One example of this that was noted earlier is to require minimum-custody women to be treated the same as maximum-security men just because they have a medical condition that requires them to be housed in a max unit. Sending two armed officers to accompany a minimum-security woman to a doctor's visit outside the facility is only one example of the waste that occurs because of this practice. This example is reinforced even more by recent research which indicates that even maximum-security men "may be quite different from" maximum security women (Van Voorhis and Presser, 2001, p. 5).

Ensuring security procedures are gender responsive is not only a more fiscally responsible way of managing women, it also can make their incarceration less traumatic and help ensure they do not offend again. As has been noted, just because women are different does not make them difficult if you understand the differences and how to respond and manage them.

Successful supervision and security in a women's institution requires staff to have confidence in their own feelings and be in control of their own behavior at all times. It requires staff to explore their own biases and stereotypes and to be knowledgeable about cultures different from their own. Staff never should have inappropriate relationships with inmates or other staff and should maintain a professional demeanor at all times. They must confront inappropriate behavior while respecting the backgrounds of women inmates and their need for love and affection.

It is important for staff to follow institutional rules and regulations and help women in the facility understand and abide by them as well. Staff must exercise good judgment while being flexible, firm, professional, and fair. When in doubt about the appropriateness of any action, or if they encounter problems, staff should contact their supervisor.

Working in a women's facility is not for everyone, and it presents daily challenges. Treating incarcerated women as human beings and learning as much about the facility and the women incarcerated there as possible will go a long way toward ensuring success.

A note of caution that may sound elementary but which often causes people to make snap and incorrect judgments about women, is the fact that all women are not alike. We tend to talk a lot about the characteristics of women offenders, but these are only part of the picture. Women have many things in common with each other, they have many things in common with men, and yet they are all individuals. It is important to remember—even if it is one person at a time and even though there are some women who will not change, staff can and do have a very positive impact on women's lives.

Appendices

APPENDIX A

PUBLIC CORRECTIONAL POLICY ON FEMALE OFFENDER SERVICES

Introduction:

Correctional systems must develop service delivery systems for accused and adjudicated female offenders that are equivalent to those provided to males. Additional services must also be provided to meet the unique needs of the female offender population.

Policy Statement:

Correctional systems must be guided by the principle of parity. Female offenders must receive the equivalent range of services available to other offenders, including opportunities for individualized programming and services that recognize the unique needs of this population. The services should:

A. Ensure access to a range of alternatives to incarceration, including pre-trial and post-trial diversion, probation, restitution, treatment for substance abuse, halfway houses, and parole services;

B. Provide acceptable conditions of confinement, including appropriately trained staff and sound operating procedures that address this population's needs in such areas as clothing, personal property, hygiene, exercise, recreation, and visitations with children and family;

C. Provide access to a full range of work and other programs designed to expand economic and social roles of women, with emphasis on education, career counseling and exploration of non-traditional vocational training, relevant life skills, including parenting and social and economic assertiveness, and pre-release and work/education release programs;

D. Facilitate the maintenance and strengthening of family ties, particularly those between parent and child;

E. Deliver appropriate programs, including those that address medical, dental, mental health, prenatal, substance abuse, child and family, family violence awareness, and legal needs; and

F. Provide access to release programs that include aid in achieving economic stability and the development of supportive family relationships.

This Public Correctional Policy was unanimously ratified by the American Correctional Association Delegate Assembly at the Congress of Correction in San Antonio, TX, Aug. 23, 1984. It was reviewed at the Winter Conference in Nashville, TN., on Jan. 17, 1990, with no change. It was reviewed and amended Aug. 9, 1995, at the Congress of Correction in Cincinnati, OH. It was reviewed and amended Aug. 16, 2000, at the Congress of Correction in San Antonio, TX.

APPENDIX B

WOMEN'S HEALTH CARE IN CORRECTIONAL SETTINGS

Position Statement

The National Commission on Correctional Health Care recognizes that the number of female inmates is large and is growing annually, and present unique and increasing health problems for correctional facilities. Therefore, the Commission recommends the following:

1. All correctional institutions should be required to meet recognized community standards for women's services as promoted by standards set by the National Commission on Correctional Health Care.

2. Correctional health services and women's advocacy groups should collaborate to provide leadership for the development [of] policies and procedures that address women's special health care needs in corrections.

3. Correctional institutions should provide intake procedures that include histories on menstrual cycle, pregnancies, gynecologic problems, and nutritional intake (by conducting a nutritional assessment) (Anno, 1991).

4. Correctional institutions should provide intake examinations that include a breast exam and, depending on the patient's age, sexual history, and past medical history, a pelvic exam, Pap smear, and baseline mammogram (Anno, 1991).

5. Correctional institutions should provide laboratory tests to detect sexually transmitted diseases (STDs) including gonorrhea, syphilis, and chlamydia for all females, especially since many are asymptomatic for STDs. Additionally, females should receive a pregnancy test on admission to correctional facilities (Anno, 1991). Further, since new research has indicated that pregnant women who are infected with HIV are less likely to transmit the virus to their newborn if they are treated with AZT during their pregnancy, women should be educated about this new finding and encouraged to be tested for HIV if they are pregnant.

6. Comprehensive services for women's unique health problems should be provided in prisons, jails, and juvenile detention and confinement facilities:

   A. Considering the special reproductive health needs of women, the frequency of repeating certain tests, exams, and procedures (e.g., Pap smears, mammograms, etc.) should be based on guidelines established by professional groups such as the American Cancer Society, and the American College of Obstetricians and Gynecologists, and should take into account age and risk factors of the female correctional population (Anno, 1991).

   B. Considering the high levels of victimization (sexual and physical) within the female inmate population, and considering the circumstances of incarceration of violent female offenders (i.e., they have frequently committed interpersonal altercation violence against a family member or intimate), counseling to resolve issues of victimization and perpetration of violence against intimates (such as conflict resolution skills or parenting skills) should be available.

   C. Considering the large number of women who are incarcerated who have dependent children, counseling on issues of parenting and child custody issues should be available to women in correctional institutions.

   D. Considering the high rates of depression women report upon incarceration, counseling should be available to women in correctional facilities to address this issue.

   E. Considering the high rates of alcohol and/or drug problems women report on incarceration, counseling should be available to women in correctional facilities to address this issue.

   F. Considering the unique developmental needs of female adolescents, special attention should be given to these needs in the provision of the aforementioned services.

G.   Considering that many female adolescents who enter the juvenile justice system have unique educational needs, special attention needs to be given to counseling and habilitation in this area.

Adopted by the National Commission on Correctional Health Care Board of Directors: September 25, 1994. Reprinted with permission of NCCHC.

References

References

Acoca, L. 1990. Defusing the Time Bomb: Understanding and Meeting the Growing Health Care Needs of Incarcerated Women. *Crime and Delinquency*, 44 (1). 40-69.

_____. 1998. *Understanding and Working Effectively with Women Offenders: A Training Curriculum Developed for the Idaho Department of Corrections.* Pocatello, Idaho: Idaho Department of Corrections.

Acoca, Leslie and James Austin. 1996. *The Hidden Crisis: Women in Prison.* San Francisco: The National Council on Crime and Delinquency.

Acosta-Belen, Edna and Christine E. Bose. 2003. U.S. Latinas: Active at the Intersections of Gender, Nationality, Race, and Class. In Robin Morgan, ed. *Sisterhood is Forever: The Women's Anthology for a New Millennium.* New York: Washington Square Press.

Adams, Elizabeth Kemper. 1930. *Women Professional Workers: A Study for the Women's Educational and Industrial Union.* New York: Macmillan.

Addiction Research Foundation. 1996. *The Hidden Majority.* Toronto, Ontario, Canada: Addiction Research Foundation.

Adler, Freda. 1975. *Sisters in Crime: The Rise of the New Female Criminal.* New York: McGraw-Hill.

AIM, Inc. June, 2001. *Aid to Inmate Mothers: Facts about Mothers in Prison.* Available: http://www.inmatemoms.org

Alexander, Mary Jane. 1996. Women with Co-Occurring Addictive and Mental Disorders: An Emerging Profile of Vulnerability. *American Journal of Orthopsychiatric Association.* 61-70.

Alpert, G. P. and J. J. Wiorkowski. 1979. Female Prisoners and Legal Services. *Quarterly Journal of Corrections.* 1: 28-33.

American Association of University Women. 1992. *How Schools Short Change Girls: A Study of Major Finding on Girls and Education.* Washington DC: American Association of University Women.

_____. 1993. *Hostile Hallways.* Washington DC: American Association of University Women.

American Correctional Association. 1954. *Manual of Correctional Standards.* New York: American Correctional Association.

_____. 1959. *Manual of Correctional Standards.* New York: American Correctional Association.

_____. 1966. *Manual of Correctional Standards.* Washington, DC: American Correctional Association.

_____. 1975. *Proceedings of the One Hundred and Fifth Annual Congress of Correction of the American Correctional Association.* Laurel, Maryland: American Correctional Association.

_____. June, 1996. *Public Correctional Policy on Correctional Health Care.* Lanham, Maryland: American Correctional Association.

_____. 1997. *Correctional Officer Correspondence Course Book IV: Managing Special Needs Offenders,* 3rd Edition. Lanham, Maryland: American Correctional Association.

American Correctional Association. 2002a. 2002 *Directory of Adult and Juvenile Correctional Departments, Institutions, Agencies, and Probation and Parole Authorities.* Lanham, Maryland: American Correctional Association.

_____. 2002b. *Performance-Based Standards for Correctional Health Care in Adult Correctional Institutions, First Edition.* Lanham, Maryland: American Correctional Association.

_____. 2003a. 2003 *Directory of Adult and Juvenile Correctional Departments, Institutions, Agencies, and Probation and Parole Authorities.* Lanham, Maryland: American Correctional Association.

_____. 2003b. *Public Correctional Policy on Use of Force.* Lanham Maryland: American Correctional Association.

_____. 2003c. *Standards for Adult Correctional Institutions,* 4th Edition. Lanham, Maryland: American Correctional Association.

_____. 2004a. Female Offenders. *Corrections Compendium.* 29 (3).

_____. 2004 *Performance-Based Standards for Adult Local Dentention Facilities,* 4th Edition Lanham, Maryland: American Correctional Association.

American Diabetes Association. 1997. *What You Need to Know About Diabetes.* Mount Morris, Illinois: American Diabetes Association.

_____. 1998. *ADA Alert.* Mount Morris, Illinois: American Diabetes Association.

American Heart Association. 1995. *High Blood Pressure.* Dallas, Texas: American Heart Association.

_____. 1997. *What's Your Risk of Brain Attack?* Dallas, Texas: American Heart Association.

_____. 1997a. *Silent Epidemic: The Truth About Women, Heart Disease and Stroke.* Dallas, Texas: American Heart Association.

American Lung Association. 1997. *Facts about Asthma.* New York: American Lung Association.

American Psychiatric Association. 1994. *Diagnostic and Statistical Manual of Mental Disorders* 4th Edition. Washington, DC: American Psychiatric Association.

_____. 2000. *Diagnosic and Statistical Manual of Mental Disorders,* 4th Edition, Text Revision Washington, DC: American Psychiatric Association.

Anno, Jaye. 2000. National Correctional Health Care Standards. In Jose B. Ashford, Bruce D. Sales, and William H. Reid, eds. *Treating Adult and Juvenile Offenders with Special Needs.* Washington, DC: American Psychological Association.

_____. 2001. *Correctional Health Care: Guidelines for the Management of an Adequate Delivery System, 2001 Edition.* Washington, DC: U.S. Department of Justice, National Institute of Corrections. Also online at www.nicic.org.

Ashford, Jose B., Bruce D. Sales, and William H. Reid, eds. 2001. *Treating Adult and Juvenile Offenders with Special Needs.* Washington, DC: American Psychological Association.

Attorney General's Family Task Force. 1989. *Domestic Violence: A Model Practical for Police Response.* Philadelphia: Office of the Attorney General.

Aylward, A. and J. Thomas.1984. Quiescence in Women's Prison Litigation: Some Exploratory Issues. *Justice Quarterly.* 1/2: 253-276.

Bacon, Janice. 1966. Pregnant and Battered. Turning Point: Columbia, South Carolina. *Sistercare Newsletter.*

Badner, Victor and Robert Margolin. 1994. Oral Health Status among Women at Rikers Island Correctional Facility. *Journal of Correctional Health Care.* 1: 55-72.

Bartlett, Rini. 1999. *Status Report on Female Offenders.* Tallahassee, Florida: Florida Department of Corrections.

_____. 2000. Helping Inmate Moms Keep in Touch: Prison Program Encourages Ties with Children. *Corrections Today.* 62(7): 102-104.

Bartley, Nancy. 2000. State hopes residential parenting program will help halt crime cycle. The Seattle Times–South Bureau. April 4. Available: http://www.seattletimes.com/news/local/htm198/baby03-2000403.html

Beck, A. and J. Karberg. 2001. *Prisoners and Jail Inmates at Mid-Year 2000.* Washington DC: U.S. Department of Justice, Bureau of Justice Statistics.

Beck, A. and C. Mumola. August, 1999. *Prisoners in 1998.* Washington, DC: U. S. Department of Justice, Bureau of Justice Statistics.

Bedford Hills Correctional Facility. 1999. *Children's Center Fact Sheet.* Bedford Hills, New York: The Children's Center.

Belknap, Joanne. 1996. *The Invisible Woman: Gender, Crime, and Justice.* Belmont, California: Wadsworth.

_____. 2001. *The Invisible Woman: Gender, Crime and Justice,* 2nd Edition. Belmont, California: Wadsworth.

Berger, M. 1994. *Women Beyond Freud: New Concepts of Feminine Psychology.* New York: Brunner/Mazel.

Bernards, Neal, and Terry O'Neill, eds. 1989. *Male/ Female Roles.* San Diego, California: Greenhaven Press.

Berry, E. 1996. Women Prisoners and Health Care. In K. Moss. *Man-Made Medicine.* Durham, North Carolina: Duke University Press.

_____. 2001. Bad Medicine: Health Care Inadequacies in Women's Prisons. *Criminal Justice.* 16(1): 38-43.

Blanchette, Kelly. 2002. Classifying Female Offenders for Effective Intervention: Applications of the Case-Based Principle of Risk and Need. *Forum on Correctional Research.* 14(1): 31-35.

Blinn, Cynthia. 1997. *Maternal Ties: A Selection of Programs for Female Offenders.* Lanham, Maryland: American Correctional Association.

Bloom, Barbara. 1993. Incarcerated Mothers and Their Children: Maintaining Family Ties. In American Correctional Association ed. *Female Offenders: Meeting the Needs of a Neglected Population.* Laurel, Maryland: American Correctional Association.

Bloom, Barbara. 1995. Imprisoned Mothers. In K. Gabel and D. Johnston, eds. *Children of Incarcerated Parents.* New York: Lexington Books.

_____. 2003. A New Vision: Gender-Responsive Principles, Policy, and Practices. In Barbara E. Bloom, ed. *Gendered Justice: Addressing Female Offenders.* Durham, North Carolina: Carolina Academic Press.

Bloom, Barbara and Meda Chesney-Lind. 2000. Women in Prison: Vengeful Equity. In Roslyn Muraskin. *It's a Crime: Women and Justice,* 2nd Edition. Upper Saddle River, New Jersey: Prentice Hall.

Bloom, Barbara and Stephanie Covington. 1988. *Gender-Specific Programming for Female Offenders: What is it and Why is it Important?* Paper presented at the 50th Annual Meeting of the American Society of Criminology, Washington, D.C.

_____. 1999. Gender-Responsibility: An Essential Element in Women's Programming. National Symposium on Women Offenders. December13-15. Washington, DC: Office of Justice Programs, 67-92.

Bloom, Barbara, Barbara Owen, and Stephanie Covington. 2003. Gender Responsive Strategies: Research, Practice, and Guiding Principles for Women Offenders. Washington, DC.: U.S.: Department of Justice, National Institute of Corrections. Also on line at www.nicic.org

Borderline Personality Disorder Research Foundation. 2000. Borderline Personality Disorder. Available: On-line http://www.borderlineresearch.org/about_disorder/index.html.

Boudouris, James. 1996. *Parents in Prison: Addressing the Needs of Families.* Lanham, Maryland: American Correctional Association.

Bretherton, Inge, Barbara Golby, and Eunyoung Cho. 1997. Attachment and the Transmission of Values. In Joan E. Grusec and Leon Kuczynski, eds. *Parenting and Children's Internalization of Values.* New York: John Wiley and Sons.

Brettell, Caroline B. and Carolyn F. Sargent , eds. 2001. *Gender in Cross-Cultural Perspective*, 3rd Edition. Upper Saddle River, New Jersey: Prentice Hall.

Brown, Dorothy M. 1984. *Mabel Walker Willebrandt: A Study of Power, Loyalty, and Law.* Knoxville: The University of Tennessee Press.

_____. 1987. *Setting a Course: American Women in the 1920s.* Boston: Twayne.

Browne, Angela. 1987. *When Battered Women Kill.* New York: The Free Press.

Browne, Angela, Brenda Miller, and Eugene Maguin. 1999. Prevalence and Severity of Lifetime Physical and Sexual Victimization among Incarcerated Women. *International Journal of Law and Psychiatry.* 22 (3-4): 301-322.

Brygger, M. P. 1990. Domestic Violence: The Dark Side of Divorce. *Family Advocate.* Summer. 48-51.

Bureau of Justice Statistics. 1999. *Selected Findings: Prior Abuse Reported by Inmates and Probationers.* Washington, D.C.: U.S. Department of Justice.

Burke, P. and L. Adams. 1991. *Classification of Women Offenders in State Correctional Facilities: A Handbook for Practitioners.* Washington DC: National Institute of Corrections.

Calder, Isabel, ed. 1935. *Colonial Captivities, Marches and Journeys.* New York: Macmillan.

Camp, C. and G. Camp. 1996. *Corrections Yearbook 1996.* South Salem, New York: Criminal Justice Institute.

_____. 1998. *Corrections Yearbook 1998.* Middletown, Connecticut: Criminal Justice Institute.

_____. 2000. *The Corrections Yearbook 2000: Adult Corrections.* Middletown, Connecticut: Criminal Justice Institute.

Campbell, J., M. Poland, J. Waller, and J. Ager. 1992. Correlates to Battering During Pregnancy. *Research in Nursing and Health*, 15.

Candib, L. M. 1989. Violence Against Women: No More Excuses. *Family Medicine.* 21(5): 339-342.

Canestrini, K. 1994. Follow up study of the Bedford Hills Family Violence Program. In Angela Browne, Brenda Miller, and Eugene Maguin. 1999. Prevalence and Severity of Lifetime Physical and Sexual Victimization among Incarcerated Women. *International Journal of Law and Psychiatry.* 22(3-4): 301-302.

Carlen, Pat. 2001. Questions of Survival in Gender-Specific Projects for Women in the Criminal Justice System. *Women, Girls, & Criminal Justice.* 2 (4): 51, 52, and 64.

Caroselli, Marlene. 1990. *The Language of Leadership.* Amherst, Massachusetts: Human Resource Development Press.

Casenave, N. 1979. Middle-income Black Fathers: An Analysis of the Provider Role. *Family Coordinator.* 27: 583-592.

Center for Substance Abuse and Treatment. 1994. *Practical Approaches in the Treatment of Women Who Abuse Alcohol and Other Drugs.* Rockville, Maryland: Department of Health and Human Services.

Centers for Disease Control and Prevention. 1990. Family and Other Intimate Assaults—Atlanta 1984. *Morbidity and Mortality Weekly Report.* 39(31): 525-529.

_____. 1998. *Tuberculosis: Get the Facts.* Atlanta, Georgia: Centers for Disease Control and Prevention.

Chaddock, Amy. 1996. A Comparative Study of Male and Female Prison Misconduct Careers. *The Prison Journal.* 76(1): 60-80.

Chesler, Phyllis. 2003. *Woman's Inhumanity to Woman.* New York: Plume.

Chesney-Lind, Meda. 2000. Women in the Justice System: Gender Matters. *In Topics in Community Corrections—Annual Issue.* Washington, DC: National Institute of Corrections, U.S. Department of Justice.

Chesney-Lind, Meda and Randall G. Shelden. 1994. *Girls, Delinquency, and Juvenile Justice,* 2nd Edition. Belmont, California: West/Wadsworth.

Clarkin, J. F., T. Widiger, A. Frances, S. W. Hunt, and M. Gilmore. 1983. Prototypic Typology and Borderline Personality Disorder. *Journal of Abnormal Psychology*. 92: 263-275.

Clear, Todd and George F. Cole. 1990. *American Corrections*, 2nd Edition. Pacific Grove, California: Brooks and Cole.

_____. 2000. *American Corrections*, 5th Edition. Belmont, California: West/Wadsworth.

Cobble, Dorothy Sue, ed. 1993. *Women and Unions: Forging a Partnership*. Ithaca, New York: ILR Press.

Coid, J. W. 1998. Axis II Disorders and Motivation for Serious Criminal Behavior. In A. E. Skodol, ed. *Psychology and Violent Crime*. Washington, DC: American Psychiatric Press. 53-97.

Coid, J. W., Nadji Kahtan, Simon Gault, et al. 2000. Women Admitted to Secure Forensic Services: Comparison of Women and Men. *Journal of Forensic Psychiatry*. 1(2): 275-295.

Coley, Sorya M. and Joyce O. Beckett. 1988. Black Battered Women: A Review of the Empirical Literature. *Journal of Counseling and Development*. February. 66: 266-269.

Collins, William C. 1993. Pat Searches of Females by Male Officers Banned by Ninth Circuit as Cruel and Unusual Punishment. *Correctional Law Reporter*. 4(6).

_____. 1998. Equal Protection and Women's Prisons: Is the Parity Era Over? In Joann B. Morton, ed. *Complex Challenges, Collaborative Solutions: Programming for Adult and Juvenile Female Offenders*. Lanham, Maryland: American Correctional Association.

_____. 2001. *Correctional Law for the Correctional Officer*. Lanham, Maryland: American Correctional Association.

_____. 2001a. Sexual Abuse of Female Inmates Leads to $350,000 in Damages. *Correctional Law Reporter*. 12(5):1.

Collins, William. 2004. *Correctional Law for the Correctional Officer*, 4th Edition. Lanham, Maryland: American Correctional Assocaition.

Collins, William C and Andrew Collins. 1996. *Women in Jail: Legal Issues*. Washington DC: U.S. Department of Justice, National Institute of Corrections.

Conly, Catherine. 1998. *The Women's Prison Association: Supporting Women Offenders and Their Families*. Washington, DC: U.S. Department of Justice, National Institute of Justice

Cooper, H. H. A. 1979. Women as Terrorists. In Freda Adler and Rita J. Simon, eds. *The Criminology of Deviant Women*. Dallas: Houghton Mifflin.

Cornelius, G. 1994. *Stressed Out! Strategies for Living and Working with Stress in Corrections*. Lanham, Maryland: American Correctional Association.

_____. 2002. *The Art of the Con: Avoiding Offender Manipulation*. Lanham, Maryland: American Correctional Association.

Crawford, Jackie. 1990. *The Female Offender: What Does the Future Hold?* Laurel Maryland: American Correctional Association.

Creidon, Pamela, ed. 1993. *Women in Mass Communication,* 2nd Edition. New Park, California: Sage.

Cripe, Clair. 1997. *Legal Aspects of Correctional Management.* Gaithersburg, Maryland: Aspen Publishers.

Cross, Terry, Barbara J. Bazron, Karl W. Dennis, and Mareasa R. Isaacs. 1989. *Toward a Culturally Competent System of Care: A Monograph on Effective Services for Minority Children who are Severely Emotionally Disturbed.* Washington, DC: Child and Adolescent Services Program, Georgetown University Child Development Center.

Davenport, Dan. 1996. Why We Need Fathers. *Better Homes and Gardens.* June: 46-51.

Davis, L. V. 1984. Beliefs of Service Providers about Abused Women and Abusing Men. *Social Works.* 29(3): 243-250.

DeCou, Kate. 1998. Responding to the Comprehensive Needs of Incarcerated Women: Management and Treatment Challenges. *Journal of Correctional Health Care.* 5(2): 129-137.

DiIulio, John. 1987. Prison Discipline and Prison Reform. *The Public Interest.* Fall: 71-90.

Ditton, Paula. 1999. *Mental Health and Treatment of Inmates and Probationers.* Washington, DC: U.S. Department of Justice. Bureau of Justice Statistics.

Dobash, R. P. and R. E. Dobash. 1979. *Violence Against Wives.* New York: Free Press.

Dowden, C. and D. A. Andrews. 1999. What Works for Female Offenders: A Meta-Analytic Review. *Crime and Delinquency.* 45: 438-452.

Dowling, Claudia G. 1997. When Mom Can't Come Home. *Life.* September: 84-90.

Doyle, James. 1985. *Sex and Gender.* Dubuque, Iowa: William C. Brown.

Dunn, J. 1993. *Young Children's Close Relationships: Beyond Attachment.* Newbury Park, California: Sage Publications.

Edwards, Todd A. 2000. *Female Offenders: Special Needs and Southern State Challenges.* Atlanta, Georgia: Southern Legislative Conference of The Council of State Governments.

Ehrenreich, Barbara. 2001. *Nickel and Dimed: On (not) Getting by in America.* New York: Metropolitan Books/ Henry Holt and Company.

Ellis, J. 1993. Security Officer's Role in Reducing Inmate Problem Behavior: A Program Based on Contingency Management. *Journal of Offender Rehabilitation.* 20 (1-2): 61-72.

Epp, Jan. 1996. Exploring Health Care Needs of Adult Female Offenders. *Corrections Today.* 58(6): 96-97, 105, 121.

Facella, Carol. 2000. Madonna/Whore Dichotomy. In Nicole Rafter, ed. *Encyclopedia of Women and Crime.* Phoenix, Arizona: The Onyx Press.

Fact Sheet on Domestic Violence. 1993. Columbia, South Carolina: Sistercare, Inc.

Faith, Karlene. 1993. An Interview with Freda Adler. *Critical Criminologist.* 5(1): 3-4 and 6-10.

Faith, Karlene. 1993. *Unruly Women: The Politics of Confinement and Resistance*. Vancouver, British Columbia, Canada: Press Gang Publishers.

Faiver, K., ed. 1998. *Health Care Management Issues in Corrections*. Lanham, Maryland: American Correctional Association.

Faiver, Kenneth L, and Robert S. Ort. 1998. Special Mental Health Issues. In Faiver, K. ed. *Health Care Management Issues in Corrections*. Lanham, Maryland: American Correctional Association.

Faiver, Kenneth L. and Dean P. Rieger. 1998. Women's Health Issues. In K. Faiver. *Health Care Management Issues in Corrections*. Lanham, Maryland: American Correctional Association.

Family Preservation Program. 2003. Contact Person, Janet Schadee, Program Director, 317-639-2671, Ext. 306. Indiana Women's Prison, 401 North Randolph Street, Indianapolis, Indiana 46201.

Farkas, Mary Ann, and Kathryn R. L. Rand. 1999. Sex Matters: A Gender-Specific Standard for Cross-Gender Searches of Inmates. *Women & Criminal Justice*. 10(3): 31-56.

Farr, Katherine Ann. 2000. Classification for Female Inmates: Moving Forward. *Crime and Delinquency*. 46(1): 3-17.

Federal Bureau of Prisons. 1993. *Working Successfully with Female Offenders: Participant's Guide*. Washington DC: U.S. Department of Justice, Federal Bureau of Prisons.

Feinman, Clarice. 1980. *Women and the Criminal Justice System*. New York. Praeger.

_____. 1983. An Historical Overview of the Treatment of the Incarcerated. *Prison Journal*. 63: 12-26.

Figgie International. 1988. *The Figgie Report Part VI: The Business of Crime, the Criminal Perspective*. Richmond, Virginia: Figgie International.

Fink, Mary Jo, Anne Kathryn Goodman, Ellen Hight, Ellen Miller-Mack, and Anne DeGroot. 1998. Critical Prevention, Critical Care: Gynecological and Obstetrical Aspects of Comprehensive HIV Prevention and Treatment among Incarcerated Women. *Journal of Correctional Health Care*. 5(2): 201-223.

Fleming, J. B. 1979. *Stopping Wife Abuse*. Garden City, New Jersey: Anchor Books.

Flowers, R. B. 1995. *Female Crime, Criminals, and Cellmates: An Exploration of Female Criminality and Delinquency*. Jefferson, North Carolina: McFarland and Company.

Flynn, Edith E. 1998. Freda Adler: A Portrait of a Pioneer. *Women & Criminal Justice*, 10(1): 1-26.

Fogel, Catherine I. 1991. Health Problems and Needs of Incarcerated Women. *Journal of Prison and Jail Health*. 10 (1): 43-45.

_____. 1995. Pregnant Prisoners: Impact of Incarceration on Health and Health Care. *Journal of Correctional Health Care*. 2: 169-190.

Foner, Philip S. and Sally M. Miller. 1982. *Kate Richards O'Hare: Selected Writings and Speeches*. Baton Rouge, Louisiana: Louisiana State University Press.

Forbes, Malcolm. 1990. *Women Who Made a Difference*. New York: Simon and Schuster.

Freedman, Estelle B. 1981. *Their Sisters' Keepers: Women's Prison Reform in America, 1830-1930*. Ann Arbor: The University of Michigan Press.

Gabel, K. 1982 *The Legal Issues of Female Inmates*. Washington DC: U.S. Department of Justice, National Institute of Corrections.

Gabel, S. 1992. Children of Incarcerated and Criminal Parents: Adjustments, Behaviors, and Prognosis. *Bulletin of the American Academy of Psychiatry Law*. 20: 35-45.

Gaseau, Michelle, ed. 2000. Mother and Child Bonding Behind Bars. The Corrections Connection News Center - Feature Story. Available: http://www.corrections.com/news/feature/index.html

Gayle, Helene and Kenneth Castro. 1996. *Prevention and Control of Tuberculosis in Correctional Facilities*. Atlanta, Georgia: Centers for Disease Control.

Gelles, T. R. 1997. *Intimate Violence in Families*. Thousand Oaks, California: Sage Publications.

Genty, P. M. 1995. Termination of Parental Rights among Prisoners: A National Perspective. In K. Gabel and D. Johnston, eds. *Children of Incarcerated Parents*. New York: Lexington Books.

Geber, Beverly. 1990. Managing Diversity. *Training*. 27(7): 23-30.

Gilliard, D. K. and A. J. Beck. 1996. *Prison and Jail Inmates, 1995*. Washington, DC: U.S. Department of Justice, Bureau of Justice Statistics.

_____. 1982. *Prison and Jail Inmates at Midyear 1997*. Washington DC: U.S. Department of Justice, Bureau of Justice Statistics.

Gilligan, Carol. 1982. *In a Different Voice: Psychological Theory and Women's Development*. Cambridge, Massachusetts: Harvard University Press.

Giordano, Pegay C., Iani Millhollin, Stephen Cernkovich, M.D. Pugh, Jennifer Randolph. 1999. Delinquency, Identity and Women's Involvement in Relationship Violence. *Criminology*. 37(1): 17-40.

Glick, Ruth and Virginia Neto. 1977. *National Study of Women's Correctional Programs*. Washington DC: U.S. Department of Justice.

Goffman, Irving. 1961. *Asylums*. Garden City, New Jersey: Anchor Books.

Goldin, Claudia. 1990. *Understanding the Gender Gap: An Economic History of American Women*. New York: Oxford University Press.

Goldkuhle, Ute. 1999. Health Service Utilization by Women in Prison: Health Needs Indicators and Response Effects. *Journal of Correctional Health Care*. 6 (1): 63-83.

Goodwin, Marjorie H. 1992. *He Said—She Said: Talk as Social Organization Among Black Children*. Bloomington: Indiana University Press.

Goolkasian, Gail A. 1986. *Confronting Domestic Violence: The Role of Criminal Court Judges*. Washington, D. C.: Department of Justice, National Institute of Justice.

Gosselin, Denise K. 2003. *Heavy Hands: An Introduction to the Crimes of Domestic Violence*, 2nd Edition. Upper Saddle River, New Jersey: Prentice Hall.

Governors' Spouses Program. 1996. *Women's Health Campaign,* 2nd Edition. Washington, DC: National Governors' Association.

Gowdy, Voncile. 1998. *Women in the Criminal Justice System—A Twenty Year Update.* Washington DC: U.S. Department of Justice, National Institute of Justice.

Graham, J. and B. Bowling. 1995. *Young People and Crime.* Home Office Research Study, No. 145. London: Her Majesty's Stationary Office.

Grana, Sheryl J. 2002. *Women and (In)Justice: The Criminal and Civil Effects of the Common Law on Women's Lives.* Boston: Allyn and Bacon.

Gray, John. 1992. *Men are from Mars, Women are from Venus: A Practical Guide for Improving Communications and Getting What You Want from a Relationship.* New York: HarperCollins.

Greenfeld, L. A. and T. Snell. 1999. *Women Offenders.* Washington, DC: U.S. Department of Justice, National Institute of Justice, Bureau of Justice Statistics.

Guy-Sheftall, Beverly. 2003. African American Women: The Legacy of Black Feminism. In Robin Morgan, ed. *Sisterhood is Forever: The Women's Anthology for a New Millennium.* New York: Washington Square Press.

Hafemeister, Thomas, L., Susan R. Hall, and Joel A. Dvoskin. 2000. Administrative Concerns Associated with the Treatment of Offenders with Mental Illness. In Jose B. Ashford, Bruce D. Sales, and William H. Reid. eds. *Treating Adult and Juvenile Offenders with Special Needs.* Washington, DC: American Psychological Association.

Hales, Dianne. 1999. *Just Like a Woman: How Gender Science is Redefining What Makes a Woman.* New York: Bantam.

Hammett, Theodore M., Patricia Harmon, and William Rhodes. 2000. The Burden of Infectious Disease among Inmates and Releases from Correctional Facilities. In Vol. II. of The *National Commission on Correctional Health Care/National Institute of Justice's Report to Congress on the Status of Soon-to be-Released Inmates.* Washington, DC: U.S. Department of Justice.

Hammett, Theodore M., Rebecca Widom, Joal Epstein, Michael Gross, Santiago Sifre, and Tammy Enos. 1995. *1994 Update: HIV/AIDS and STD's in Correctional Facilities.* Washington, DC: U.S. Department of Justice, National Institute of Justice.

Hanamura, Steve. 1989. Working with People who are Different. *Training and Development Journal.* June: 110-114.

Haney, Craig and Donald Specter. 2001. Treatment Rights in Uncertain Legal Times. In Jose B. Ashford, Bruce D. Sales, and William H. Reid, eds. *Treating Adult and Juvenile Offenders with Special Needs.* Washington, DC: American Psychological Association.

Hanson, R. A. and H. W. Daley. 1995. *Challenging the Conditions of Prisons and Jails: A Report on Section 1983 Litigation Discussion Paper.* Washington, DC: U.S. Department of Justice, Bureau of Justice Statistics.

Harlow, Caroline. 1999. *Selected Findings: Prior Abuse Reported by Inmates and Probationers.* Washington, D.C.: U.S. Department of Justice.

Harris, Jean. 1988. *They Always Call Us Ladies: Stories from Prison*. New York: Charles Scribner's Sons.

Harris, M. and Dudley P. Spiller Jr. 1977. *After Decisions: Implementation of Judicial Decrees in Correctional Settings*. Washington D.C.: National Institute of Law Enforcement and Criminal Justice.

Harris, Mary B. 1936. *I Knew Them in Prison*. New York: Viking.

Harrison, Paige M. and Allen J. Beck. 2003. *Prisoners in 2002*. Washington, DC: U.S. Department of Justice, Bureau of Justice Statistics.

Harrison, Paige M. and Jennifer C. Karberg. 2003. *Prison and Jail Inmates at Mid-Year 2002*. Washington, DC: U.S. Department of Justice, Bureau of Justice Statistics.

Harvard Women's Health Watch. 1995a. Post Traumatic Stress Disorder (PTSD). Boston, Massachusetts: Harvard Medical School. August: 1-3

_____. 1995b The New Weight Guidelines. Boston, Massachusetts: Harvard Medical School. November: 1.

_____. 1996. Planning for Menopause. Boston, Massachusetts: Harvard Medical School. July: 1.

_____. 1997a. Pursuing the Pap Smear Question. Boston, Massachusetts: Harvard Medical School. April: 1.

_____. 1997b Depression. Boston, Massachusetts: Harvard Medical School. November. 1-3.

_____. 1997c. Gender Research and Recommendations. Boston, Massachusetts: Harvard Medical School. March: 7.

_____. 1998. Folic Acid Fortification: Is It Enough? Boston, Massachusetts: Harvard Medical School. February 1.

_____. 1999. Alzheimer's Disease. Boston, Massachusetts: Harvard Medical School. March: 2-4.

_____. 2000a. Aging, Memory, and the Brain. Boston, Massachusetts: Harvard Medical School. July: 1-3.

_____. 2000b. Panic: Worry in the Extreme. Boston, Massachusetts: Harvard Medical School. August: 4-8.

Hawkes, Mary Q. 1991. Women's Changing Role in Corrections. In Joann B. Morton, ed. *Change, Challenge and Choices: Women's Role in Modern Corrections*. Laurel, Maryland. American Correctional Association.

_____. 1994. *Excellent Effect: The Edna Mahan Story*. Laurel, Maryland: American Correctional Association.

Hawkins, R. 1995. Inmate's Adjustments in Women's Prisons. In K. Hass and G. Alpert, eds. *The Dilemmas of Corrections: Contemporary Readings*. Prospect Heights, Illinois: Waveland.

Haycock, J. 1989. Manipulation and Suicide Attempts in Jails and Prisons. *Psychiatric Quarterly*. 60: 85-98.

Haycock, Jay. 1992. Listening to "Attention Seekers" the Clinical Management of People Threatening Suicide. *Jail Suicide Update*. 4 (4): 8-11.

Haynes, Fred E. 1939. *The American Prison System*. New York: McGraw-Hill.

Hearst, Patricia C. 1982. *Every Secret Thing*. Garden City, New York: Doubleday & Company.

Heffernan, Esther. 1972. *Making It In Prison*. New York: Wiley.

_____. 1994. Banners, Brothels and a "Ladies' Seminary": Women and Federal Corrections. In John W. Roberts, ed. *Escaping Prison Myths: Selected Topics in the History of Federal Corrections*. Washington, DC: The American University Press.

Helton, A. 1986. Battering During Pregnancy. *American Journal of Nursing*. August: 910-913.

Henderson, J. D., Hardy Rauch, and Richard L. Phillips. 1997. *Guidelines for the Development of a Security Program*, 2nd Edition. Lanham, Maryland: American Correctional Association.

Henriques, Zelma. 1982. *Imprisoned Mothers and Their Children: A Descriptive and Analytical Study*. Lanham, Maryland: University Press of America.

Herman, J. 1992. *Trauma and Recovery*. New York: Harper Collins.

Hofford, Meredith. 1990. *Family Violence: Improving Court Practice*. Reno, Nevada: National Council of Juvenile and Family Court Judges.

_____. 1991. Family Violence: Challenging Cases for Probation Officers. *Federal Probation*. 9(4): 12-17.

Holley, Philip D. and Dennis Brewster. 1996. The Women at Eddie Warrior Correctional Center: A Description from a Data Set. *Journal of the Oklahoma Criminal Justice Research Consortium*. 3: 107-114.

Horesch, Michelle, and Jodine Deppisch. 2003. *Building a Regional Consortium to Improve the Health of Women in Prison: Region V Incarcerated Women's Project*. Presented September 8 at the Tenth National Workshop on Adult and Juvenile Female Offenders, Portland Maine.

Human Rights Watch, Women's Rights Project. 1996. *All Too Familiar: Sexual Abuse of Women in U. S. State Prisons*. New York: Human Rights Watch.

Isikoff, Michael. 2003. Hard Time for Corporate Perps. *Newsweek*. On-line: http://www.msnbs.com/news/850346.asp?0cv=Kb10&c01=1

Jacobs, Edward and Nina Spadaro. 2003. *Leading Groups in Corrections: Skills and Techniques*. Lanham, Maryland: American Correctional Association.

Jacobs, James B. 2001. The Prisoners' Rights Movement and Its Impact. In Edward J. Latessa, Alexander Holsinger, James W. Marquart, and Jonathan R. Sorensen, eds. *Correctional Contexts: Contemporary and Classical Readings, 2nd Edition*. Los Angeles: Roxbury.

James, Ann. 1994. *Next Time She'll be Dead: Battering and How to Stop It*. Boston: Beacon Press.

_____. 1999. Violence Against Women is a Serious Problem. In James Torr and Karen Swisher, eds. *Violence Against Women*. San Diego, California: Greenhaven Press.

Jarjoura, G. Roger 2000. Juvenile Delinquency and School Influences. In Nicole H. Rafter, ed. *Encyclopedia of Women and Crime*. Phoenix, Arizona: The Onyx Press.

Johnston, D. 1995. The Care and Placement of Prisoner's Children. In K. Gabel and D. Johnston, eds. *Children of Incarcerated Parents*. New York: Lexington Books.

_____. 1995a. Effects of Parental Incarceration. In K. Gabel and D. Johnston, eds. *Children of Incarcerated Parents*. New York: Lexington Books.

_____. 1997. Developing Services for Incarcerated Mothers. In Cynthia Blinn, ed. 1997. *Maternal Ties: A Selection of Programs for Female Offenders*. Lanham, Maryland: American Correctional Association.

Jones, Ann. 1994 *Next Time She'll be Dead: Battering and How to Stop It*. Boston: Beacon Press.

_____. 1999. Violence Against Women is a Serious Problem. In James Torr and Karin Swisher, eds. *Violence Against Women*. San Diego, California: Greenhaven Press.

Jordon, B. Katherine, John A. Fairbanks, and Juesta M. Caddell. 1996. Prevalence of Psychiatric Disorders among Incarcerated Women, II: Convicted Felons Entering Prison. *Archives of General Psychiatry*. 53: 513-519.

Junior, Victoria Young. 2003. Helping Female Inmates Cope with Grief and Loss. *Corrections Today*. 65 (3): 76-78 and 94.

Jurik, N. C. and R. Winn. 1987. Describing Correctional-Security Dropouts and Rejects: An Individual or Organizational Profile? *Criminal Justice and Behavior*. 14 (1): 5-25.

Kanowitz, Leo. 1969. *Women and the Law: The Unfinished Revolution*. Albuquerque: University of New Mexico Press.

Karaylorgau, Maira. 1997. *Genetic Studies in Schizophrenia*. New York: Laboratory of Human Neurogenetics, The Rockefeller University.

Karlsen, Carole. 1995. The Devil in the Shape of a Woman: The Economic Basis of Witchcraft. In Linda K. Kerber and Jane S. De Hart, eds. *Women's America: Refocusing the Past*. New York: Oxford Press.

Karsten, Margaret F. 1994. *Management and Gender: Issues and Attitudes*. Westport, Connecticut: Quorum.

Kass, F., A. E Skodol, E. Charles, R. L. Spitzer, and J. B. Williams. 1985. Scale Ratings of DSM-III Personality Disorders. *American Journal of Psychiatry*. 142: 478-483.

Kauffman, Kelsey. 2001. Mothers in Prison. *Corrections Today*. 63(1): 62-67.

Keamy, Lisa. 1998. Women's Health Care in the Incarcerated Setting. In Michael Puisis, ed. *Clinical Practice in Correctional Medicine*. St Louis: Mosby.

Kerber, Linda K. and Jane S. De Hart, eds. 1995. *Women's America: Refocusing on the Past,* 4th Edition. New York: Oxford University Press.

Keve, Paul W. 1986. *The History of Corrections in Virginia*. Charlottesville, Virginia: University of Virginia Press.

Kline, Sue. 1993. A Profile of Female Offenders in State and Federal Prisons. In *Female Offenders: Meeting the Needs of a Neglected Population*. Laurel, Maryland: American Correctional Association.

Krantz, Sheldon and Lynn S. Branham. 1991. *The Law of Sentencing, Corrections, and Prisoner's Rights: Cases and Materials,* 4th Edition. St. Paul, Minnesota: West.

Kreps, Gary L. 1993. *Sexual Harassment: Communication Implications.* Cresswell, New Jersey: Hampton Press.

Kruttschnitt, Candace, Rosemary Gartner, and Amy Miller. 2000. Doing Her Own Time? Women's Responses to Prison in the Context of the Old and the New Penology. *Criminology.* 38(3): 681-717.

Laishes, Jane. 1997. *Mental Health Strategy for Women Offenders.* Available: On-line http://www.csc-scc.gc.ca/text/prgrm/fws/mhealth/toc_e.shtml (6/22/2001).

Lamphere, Louise. 2001. The Domestic Sphere of Women and the Public World of Men: The Strengths and Limitations of an Anthropological Dichotomy. In Caroline B. Brettell and Carolyn F. Sargent, eds. *Gender in Cross-Cultural Perspective,* 3rd Edition. Upper Saddle River: New Jersey: Prentice Hall.

Landry, Bart. 2000. *Black Working Wives: Pioneers of the American Family Revolution.* Berkeley: University of California Press.

Langan, P. A. and J. M. Dawson. 1995. *Spouse Murder Defendants in Large Urban Counties.* Washington, D.C.: U.S. Department of Justice.

Latessa, Edward J., Alexander Holsinger, James W. Marquart, and Jonathan R. Sorensen. 2001. Prison Litigation and Inmates' Rights. In Edward Latessa et. al. *Correctional Contexts: Contemporary and Classical Readings,* 2nd Edition. Los Angeles: Roxbury.

LeFlore, Larry and Mary Ann Holston. 1989. Perceived Importance of Parenting Behaviors as Reported by Inmate Mothers: An Exploratory Study. *Journal of Offender Counseling, Services, and Rehabilitation.* (4): 5-21.

Leger, Robert. 1987. Lesbianism among Women Prisoners: Participants and Non Participants. *Criminal Justice and Behavior.* 14: 463-479.

Lehmann, N. and S. L. Krupp. 1983-84. Incidence of Alcohol-Related Domestic Violence: An Assessment. *Alcohol Health and Research World.* 8(2). 23-27.

Lerner, G. 1986. *The Creation of Patriarchy.* New York: Oxford University Press.

Lewis, W. David. 1965. *From Newgate to Dannemora: The Rise of the Penitentiary in New York, 1796-1848.* Ithaca, New York: Cornell University Press.

Link, B., G. F. Cullen, and H. Andrews. 1992. Violent and Illegal Behavior of Current and Former Mental Patients Compared to Community Controls. *American Sociological Review.* 57: 272-292.

Locy, Toni. 1999. Like Mother, Like Daughter: Why More Young Women Follow their Mom's into Lives of Crime. *U.S. News and World Report,* October 4: 18-21.

Lombroso, C. 1895. *The Female Offender.* London: Fisher Unwin.

Loving, Nancy and Lynn Olson. 1976. *Proceedings: National Conference on Women and Crime.* Washington, DC: National League of Cities and U.S. Conference of Mayors.

Lynd, Robert and Helen Lynd. 1956. *Middletown: A Study in American Culture*. New York: Harcourt Brace Jovanovich.

Maguire, K., A. L. Pastore, and T. J. Flanagan, eds. 1993. *Sourcebook of Criminal Justice Statistics: 1992*. Washington DC: Bureau of Justice Statistics.

Mahay, Jenna, Edward O. Laumann and Stewart Michaels. 2001. Race, Gender, and Class in Sexual Scripts. In *Sex, Love, and Health in America: Private Choices and Public Policies*. Chicago: University of Chicago Press.

Malesh, Wendy. 2000. Health Care Related Issues for the Female Offender. In Loretta Eley, ed. *Working Effectively With Women in Conflict with the Law*. Ontario, Canada: Correctional Services of Canada.

Maniglia, Rebecca. 1998. Female Development a Juvenile Justice Treatment. In Joann B. Morton, ed. *Complex Challenges, Collaborative Solutions: Programming for Adult and Juvenile Female Offenders*. Lanham, Maryland: American Correctional Association.

Markovic, Vesna.1995. Pregnant Women in Prison: A Correctional Dilemma? *The Keepers Voice*. 16(3): 1-7.

Martin, M. 1997 Connected Mothers: A Follow-up Study of Incarcerated Women and Their Children. *Women & Criminal Justice*. 4: 1-23.

Maunsell, Catherine. 2000. Institutional Program Needs of Women Offenders. In Loretta Elay, ed. *Working Effectively with Women in Conflict with the Law*. Ontario: Canada, Correctional Service of Canada.

McCampbell, Susan W. and Elizabeth P. Layman. 2000. *Training Curriculum for Investigating Allegations of Staff Sexual Misconduct with Inmates*. In National Institute of Corrections/ American University, Washington College of Law. December. *Staff Sexual Misconduct with Inmates Training Program*, Bethesda, Maryland.

McClellan, Dorothy S. 1994. Disparity in the Discipline of Male and Female Inmates in Texas Prisons. *Women & Criminal Justice*. 5(2): 71-97.

McFarlane, J. 1989. Battering During Pregnancy: Tip of the Iceberg Revealed. *Women and Health*. 15(3): 69-84.

McGaha, Glenda S. 1987. Health Care Issues of Incarcerated Women. *Journal of Offender Counseling, Services and Rehabilitation*. 12 (1).

McGlashan, T. H. 1986. The Chestnut Lodge Fellowship Study III: Long-Term Outcomes of Borderline Personality. *Archives of General Psychiatry*. 43: 20-30.

McGowan, B. G. and K. L. Blumenthal. 1978. *Why Punish the Children? A Study of Children of Women Prisoners*. Hackensack, New Jersey: National Council on Crime and Delinquency.

McHugh, Gerald Austin.1980. Protection of the Rights of Pregnant Women in Prison and Detention Facilities. *The New England Journal of Prison Law*. 6(2): 231-263.

McKelvey, Blake. 1936. *American Prison: A Study in American Social History Prior to 1915*. Chicago: University of Chicago Press.

McKibben, L., E. DeVos, and E. H. Newberger. 1989. Victimization of Mothers of Abused Children: A Controlled Study. *Pediatrics*. 84(3).

McLeer, S. V., R. A. H. Anwar, and S. Herman. 1989. Education is Not Enough: A Systems Failure in Protecting Battered Women. *Annals of Emergency Medicine*. 18(6): 651-653.

Merlo, Alida V. and Joycelyn M. Pollock, eds. 1995. *Women, Law, and Social Control*. Boston: Allyn and Bacon.

Michigan Department of Corrections. 2000. *Critical Issues in Managing Women Offenders: Trainer Manual*. Lansing, Michigan: Michigan Department of Corrections.

Miller, Larry S. and John T. Whitehead 1996. *Introduction to Criminal Justice Research and Statistics*. Cincinnati, Ohio: Anderson.

Miller, Susan L. 1989. Unintended Side Effects of Pro-Arrest Policies and Their Race and Class Implications for Battered Women: A Cautionary Note. *Criminal Justice Policy Review*. 3(3): 299-317.

Mondragon, Eloy L. 1991. Exploring Corrections' Link to Multiculturalism. *Corrections Today*. 53 (7): 6.

Morash, M. and T. Bynum. 1995. *Findings from the National Study of Innovative and Promising Programs for Women Offenders*. Washington, DC: National Institute of Justice.

Morash, Merry, T. Bynum, and B. Koons. 1996. *Findings from the National Study of Innovative and Promising Programs for Women Offenders*. East Lansing Michigan: Michigan State University.

_____. 1998. *Women Offenders: Programming Needs and Promising Approaches*. Washington, D.C.: U.S. Department of Justice, National Institute of Justice.

Morash Merry and Pamela C. Schram. 2002. *The Prison Experience: Special Issues of Women in Prison*. Prospect Heights, Illinois: Waveland Press.

Morgan, Philip. 1993. Bound Labor: The British and Dutch Colonies. In Jacob Ernest Cooke, ed. *Encyclopedia of the North American Colonies*. New York: Charles Scibner's Sons.

Morrill, Allison C., Elizabeth Mastroieni and Sarah R. Leibel. 1998. Behavioral HIV Harm Reduction Programs for Incarcerated Women: Theory and Practice. *Journal of Correctional Health Care*. 5: 225-237.

Morris, Allison. 1987. *Women, Crime, and Justice*. Oxford: Basil Blackwell.

Morton, Joann B. ed. 1991. *National Public Correctional Policy*, 2nd Edition. Laurel, Maryland: American Correctional Association.

_____. 1992. Older Female Offenders. In American Correctional Association, ed. *Female Offenders: Meeting the Needs of a Neglected Population*. Laurel, Maryland: American Correctional Association.

_____. 1993. Training Staff to Work with Elderly and Disabled Inmates. *Corrections Today*. 55(1): 42-47.

_____. 1994. Battered Women and Family Violence: Implications for Criminal Justice. *The State of Corrections*. Laurel, Maryland: American Correctional Association.

_____. 1994. Martha E. Wheeler: Redefining Women in Corrections. *Women & Criminal Justice*. 5(2): 1-20.

_____. 1996. Vision and Reality: Treatment of Women Offenders. *The State of Corrections*. Lanham, Maryland: American Correctional Association. 197-208.

_____. 1998. Programming for Women Offenders. In Joann B. Morton, ed. *Complex Challenges, Collaborative Solutions: Programming for Adult and Juvenile Female Offenders*. Lanham, Maryland: American Correctional Association.

Morton, Joann B. and Deborah Williams. 1998. Mother/Child Bonding: Incarcerated Women Struggle to Maintain Meaningful Relationships with Their Children. *Corrections Today*. 60(7): 98-105.

Moses, Marilyn C. 1995. *Keeping Incarcerated Mothers and Their Daughters Together: Girl Scouts Beyond Bars*. Washington DC: National Institute of Justice

_____. 1997. The Girl Scouts Beyond Bars Program: Keeping Incarcerated Mothers and Their Daughters Together. In C. Blinn, ed. *Maternal Ties: A Selection of Programs for Female Offenders*. Lanham, Maryland: American Correctional Association.

Moyer, Imogene, ed. 1992. *The Changing Roles of Women in the Criminal Justice System: Offenders, Victims, and Professionals*, 2nd Edition. Prospect Heights, Illinois: Waveland Press.

Mumola, C. J. 2000. *Incarcerated Parents and Their Children*. Washington, DC: U.S. Department of Justice, Bureau of Justice Statistics.

Muraskin, Roslyn. 1993. Abortion: Is it Abortion or Compulsory Child Bearing. In Roslyn Muraskin and Ted Alleman, eds. *It's a Crime: Women and Justice*. Englewood Cliffs, New Jersey: Regents/Prentice Hall.

_____. 2000. Disparate Treatment in Correctional Facilities, In Roslyn Muraskin, ed. *It's a Crime: Women and Justice*, 2nd Edition. Upper Saddle River, New Jersey: Prentice Hall.

Muraskin, Roslyn. 2000. *It's a Crime: Women and Justice*, 2nd Edition. Upper Saddle River, New Jersey: Prentice Hall.

National Center on Addiction and Substance Abuse (CASA). 1996. *Substance Abuse and the American Woman*. New York: Columbia University.

National Clearinghouse for the Defense of Battered Women. 1999. *When Battered Women are Charged with Crimes: Brief Overview and Recommendations*. Philadelphia: National Clearinghouse for Defense of Battered Women.

National Commission on Correctional Health Care. 1994. *Position Statement: Women's Health Care in Correctional Settings*. Chicago, Illinois: National Commission on Correctional Health Care. Available on line at www.ncchc.org/resources/statements/womenshealth.html

National Committee to Prevent Child Abuse. 1997. *1996 Annual Fifty State Survey*. Chicago: National Committee to Prevent Child Abuse.

National Institute of Corrections. 1996. *Privatization and Contracting in Corrections: Results of an NIC Survey–Special Issues in Corrections*. Washington, DC: U.S. Department of Justice, National Institute of Corrections.

_____. 1998. *Current Issues in the Operation of Women's Prisons: Special Issues in Corrections*. Longmont, Colorado: U.S. Department of Justice, National Institute of Corrections Information Center.

National Institute of Corrections. 2000. *Sexual Misconduct in Prisons: Law, Reminders and Incidence*. Longmont, Colorado: U.S. Department of Justice, National Institute of Corrections.

National Institute of Corrections/ American University, Washington School of Law. 2000. *Staff Sexual Misconduct with Inmates Training Manual*. December 3-8. Washington D.C.: National Institute of Corrections/ American University.

Newell, Roger. 2000. Working with Female Victims/Survivors of Partner Abuse. In Loretta May, ed. *Working Effectively with Women in Conflict with the Law*. Ontario, Canada: Corrections Service of Canada.

Novick, L. F., R. Della-Penna, M. Schwartz, E. Remlinger, and R. Lowenstein. 1977. Health Status of the New York City Prison Population. *Medical Care*. 15 (3).

Oakland County Health Division. 1998. *Public Health Fact Sheet : Hepatitis A and Hepatitis C*. Pontiac, Michigan: Oakland County Health Division.

Office of Women's Health. 1997. *Violence Against Women Fact Sheet*. Washington, D.C.: U.S. Public Health Service.

Okum, L. 1986. *Women Abuse: Facts Replacing Myths*. Albany, New York: State University of New York.

Oliver, William. 2000. Preventing Domestic Violence in the African American Community: The Rationale for Power Culture Interventions. *Violence Against Women*. 6(5). 533-549.

Osborne Association. 1993. How Can I Help? Working with Children of Incarcerated Parents. In *Serving Special Children*. Vol. 1. New York: The Osborne Association.

Owen, Barbara. 1998. *In the Mix: Struggle and Survival in a Women's Prison*. Albany, New York: State University of New York Press.

Owen, Barbara and Barbara Bloom. 1995. Profiling Women Prisoners: Findings from National Surveys and a California Sample. *The Prison Journal*. 75(2): 165-185.

Palmer, J. W. and S. E. Palmer. 1999. *Constitutional Rights of Prisoners*, 6th Edition. Cincinnati, Ohio: Anderson.

Parenti, Christian. 2000. *Lockdown America: Police and Prisons in the Age of Crisis*. London: Verso.

Patrick-Riley, Colleen, William Worrall, and David Sage. 2003. *Structuring An Adult Female Offender Mental Health Unit*. Presentation at the 8th National Workshop on Adult and Juvenile Female Offenders, Portland, Maine, September.

Pendergast, Michael L., Jean Wellisch, and Gregory P. Falkin. 1995. Assessment of and Services for Substance-Abusing Women Offenders in the Community and Corrections Setting. *The Prison Journal*. 75(2): 240-256.

Pennsylvania Department of Corrections State Correctional Institution-Muncy. 1998. *I Love You This Much*, 2nd Edition. Pamphlet from the Pennsylvania Department of Corrections' State Correctional Institution–Muncy.

Peters, Roger H. and Holly A. Hills. 1997. *Intervention Strategies for Offenders with Co-Occurring Disorders: What Works?* New York: The National GAINS Center for People with Co-Occuring Disorders in the Justice System.

Pitts, Leonard. 2004. When Black Community can be Wrong to Pull Together. *The State*. Columbia, South Carolina. April 3, A 11.

Pleck, Elizabeth. 1989. Criminal Approaches to Family Violence, 1640-1980. *Family Violence*. 11: 19-54.

Pollock-Byrne, Joycelyn. 1990. *Women, Prison, & Crime*. Pacific Grove, California: Brooks/Cole.

Pollock, Jocelyn. 1995. Gender, Justice, and Social Control: A Historical Perspective. In A. Merlo and J. Pollock, eds. *Women, Law and Social Control*. Needham Heights, Massachusetts: Allyn and Bacon.

_____. 2001. A National Survey of Parenting Programs in Women's Prisons in the U.S. *Women, Girls & Criminal Justice*. 2 (4): 49-50 and 60-63.

_____. 2002. *Women, Prisons & Crime*, 2nd Edition. Belmont, California: Wadsworth.

Pomeroy, Elizabeth C., Risa Kiam, and Eileen Abel. 1998. Meeting Mental Health Needs of Incarcerated Women. *Health and Social Work*. 71-75.

Praeger, Roberta. 1995. The World is Worth Living In. In Margaret L. Anderson and Patricia H. Collins, ed. *Race, Class, and Gender*, 2nd Edition. Belmont, California: Wadsworth.

Raeder, Myrna. 2003. Legal Considerations with Regard to Women Offenders. In Barbara Bloom, Barbara Owen, and Stephanie Covington. *Gender-Strategies: Research, Practice, Guiding Principles for Women Offenders*. National Institute of Corrections. Appendix A. 107-130.

Rafter, Nicole H. 1987. Even in Prison, Women are Second-Class Citizens. *Human Rights*. 14(2): 28-31.

_____. 1989 Gender and Justice: The Equal Protection Issue. In Lynne Goodstein and Doris MacKenzie, eds. *The American Prison: Issues in Research and Policy*. New York: Plenum.

_____. 1990. Partial Justice: *Women, Prisons, and Social Control*. 2nd Edition. New Brunswick, New Jersey: Transaction.

Randall, T. 1990. Domestic Violence Begets Other Problems of Which Physicians Must be Aware to be Effective. *Journal of the American Medical Association*. 264(8): 940-944.

_____. 1990a. Domestic Violence Intervention Calls for More than Treating Injuries. *Journal of the American Medical Association*. 264(8): 939-940.

Rasche, Christine. 1993. *Special Needs of Female Offenders*. Tallahassee Florida: Florida Department of Education.

Reichel, Philip L. 1997. *Corrections*. Minneapolis/St. Paul: West.

_____. 2001. *Corrections: Philosophies, Practices, and Procedures*. Needham Heights, Massachusetts: Allyn and Bacon.

Reid, P. 1979. Racial Stereotyping on Television: A Comparison of the Behavior of Both Black and White Television Characters. *Journal of Applied Psychology*. 465-471.

Reid, P and M. Paludi. 1993. Developmental Psychology of Women: Conception to Adolescence. In F. Denmark and M. Paludi, eds. *Psychology of Women: A Handbook of Issues and Theories*. Westport, Connecticut: Greenwood Press.

Reiss, Albert J., Jr. and Jeffrey Roth, eds. 1993. *Understanding and Preventing Violence*. Washington, D.C.: National Academy Press.

Renvoize, Jean. 1978. *Web of Violence: A Study of Family Violence*. London: Routledge and Kegan Paul, Ltd.

Renzetti, Claire M. and David J. Curran. 1989. *Women, Culture, and Society*. Stanford: Stanford University Press.

Rhode, Deborah L. 1997. *Speaking of Sex: The Denial of Gender Inequality*. Cambridge, Massachusetts: Harvard University Press.

Richardson, Anna Steese. 1909. *The Girl Who Earns Her Own Living*. New York: B. W. Dodge.

Richardson, Stamatia. 1998. Preferred Care of the Pregnant Inmate. In Michael Puisis, ed. *Clinical Practice in Correctional Medicine*. St. Louis: Mosby.

Richey, Warren. 2003. Court Upholds Murder Verdict in Stillbirth Care. *The Christian Science Monitor*. October 7: 2.

Richland Medical Center. 1998 *General Overview of Breast Cancer Handout*. Columbia, South Carolina: Richland Memorial Hospital.

Rob, Caroline and Janet Reynolds. 1991. *The Caregiver's Guide: Helping Elderly Relatives Cope with Health and Safety Problems*. Boston: Houghton Mifflin.

Robins, L.N. and D. A. Regier. 1991. *Psychiatric Disorders in America: The Epidemiologic Catchment Area Study*. New York: Free Press.

Romer, N. and P. Cherry. 1980. Ethnic and Social Class Differences in Children's Sex Role Concepts. *Sex Roles*. 6: 245-263.

Ross, Phyllis and James Lawrence. 1998. Health Care for Women Offenders. In T. Alleman and R. Gido, eds. *Turnstile Justice: Issues in American Corrections*. Upper Saddle River, New Jersey Prentice-Hall.

Ross, Robert R. and Elizabeth A. Fabiano. 1986. *Female Offenders: Correctional Afterthoughts*. Jefferson, North Carolina: McFarland.

Rowan, Joseph R. 1998. *Suicide Prevention in Custody*. Lanham, Maryland: American Correctional Association.

Rutter, M. 1995. Maternal Deprivation. In M. H. Bornstein, ed. *Handbook of Parenting*. Hillsdale, New Jersey: Erlbaum.

Samaha, J. 1994. *Criminal Justice*, 3rd Edition. Minneapolis/St. Paul: West.

Sandelowski, M. 1981. *Women, Health, and Choice*. Saddle River, New Jersey: Prentice-Hall.

Schechter, S. 1982. *Women and Male Violence*. Boston, Massachusetts: South End Press.

Seiter, Richard P. 2002. *Correctional Administration: Integrating Theory and Practice*. Upper Saddle River, New Jersey: Prentice Hall.

Seymour, Cynthia 1998. Children with Parents in Prison: Child Welfare Policy, Program, and Practice Issues. In Cynthia Seymour and Creasie Hairston. *Child Welfare Journal of Policy, Practice, and Program: Special Issue with Parents in Prison.* 67(5): 469-493.

Sharp, Susan, ed. 2003. *The Incarcerated Woman: Rehabilitative Programming in Women's Prisons.* Upper Saddle River, New Jersey: Prentice Hall.

Shaw, Margaret and Kelly Hannah-Moffat. 2001. Risk Assessment in Canadian Corrections: Some Diverse and Gendered Issues. *Women, Girls & Criminal Justice.* 2 (1): 1-2, 12-13.

Shuter, J. 2000. Public Health Opportunities for the Correctional Intervention on Inmates with Communicable Disease. In *Vol. II The National Commission on Correctional Health Care/National Institute of Justice's Report to Congress on the Health Status of Soon to be Released Inmates.* Washington, DC: U.S. Department of Justice, National Institute of Justice.

Simon, R. 1975. *The Contemporary Women and Crime.* Rockville, Maryland: National Institute of Mental Health.

Skinner, Pam. 2000. Self-Injury in Female Offenders. In Loretta Elay, ed. *Working Effectively with Women in Conflict with the Law.* Ontario, Canada: Correctional Service of Canada.

Smalls, Carla, ed. 2004. *The Full Spectrum: Essays on Staff Diversity in Corrections.* Lanham, Maryland: American Correctional Association.

Smillie, Eunice M. 1981. *Elizabeth Fry.* Maple, Ontario: Belsten

Smith, B. and S. G. Elstein. 1994. *Children on Hold: Improving the Response to Children whose Parents are Arrested and Incarcerated.* Washington, DC: U.S. Department of Health and Human Services, Children's Bureau.

Snell, Tracy L. 1992. *Women in Jail, 1989.* Washington, DC: U.S. Department of Justice, Bureau of Justice Statistics.

Snell, Tracy. L. and Danielle C. Morton. 1994. *Women in Prison, 1991.* Bureau of Justice Statistics Special Report. Washington, DC: U.S. Department of Justice, Bureau of Justice Statistics.

Sonkin, Daniel J. and Michael Durphy. 1997. *Learning to Live Without Violence: A Handbook for Men,* 5th edition. Volcano, California: Volcano Press.

South Carolina Department of Mental Health. July, 1996. Getting the Facts on Mental Illness—Alzheimer's Disease. Columbia, South Carolina: South Carolina Department of Mental Health.

Stafford, L. and C. L. Bayer. 1993. *Interaction Between Parent and Child.* Newbury Park, California: Sage Publications.

Steffensmeier, D. and E. Allan. 1991. Gender, Age, and Crime. In J. F. Sheley, ed. *Criminology: A Contemporary Handbook.* Belmont, California: Wadsworth.

_____. 1998. The Nature of Female Offending: Patterns and Explanations. In R. T. Zaplin, ed. *Female Offenders: Critical Perspectives and Effective Interventions.* Gaithersburg, Maryland: Aspen.

Stewart, William R. 1911. *The Philanthropic Work of Josephine Shaw Lowell.* New York: Macmillan.

Straus, M A., R. J. Gelles, and S. K. Steinmetz. 1980. *Behind Closed Doors: Violence in the American Family*. Garden City, New Jersey: Anchor/Doubleday.

Strickland, Katherine. 1976. *Correctional Institutions for Women in the U.S.* Lexington, Massachusetts: Lexington Books.

Swerling, Jack. 1990. Defending the Battered Woman. *South Carolina Lawyer*. November/December.

Tanner, Deborah. 1990. *You Just Don't Understand: Women and Men in Conversation*. New York: William Morrow and Company.

Tanner, Lindsey. 2003. Obesity Ballooning in U.S. Adults. *Bangor Daily News*. October 14: A6.

Task Force on Corrections. 1973. *Corrections*. Washington, D.C.: National Advisory Commission on Criminal Justice Standards and Goals.

Taylor, Ella. 1989. *Prime-Time Families, Television Culture in Post War America*. Berkeley, California: University of California Press.

Teeters, Negley K. 1955. *The Cradle of the Penitentiary: The Walnut Street Jail at Philadelphia 1773-1835*. Philadelphia, Pennsylvania: Pennsylvania Prison Society.

Temin, Carolyn E. 2001. Let Us Consider the Children. *Corrections Today*. 63(1): 66–68.

Teplin, Linda, Karen M. Abrams, and Gary M. McClelland. 1997. Mentally Disordered Women in Jail: Who Receives Services? *American Journal of Public Health* 4: 604-609.

Thomas, J. 1984. Law and Social Praxis: Prisoner Civil Rights Litigation and Structural Mediations. In S. Spitzer and A. T. Scull, eds. *Research in Law, Deviance and Social Control*, Vol. 6. Greenwich, Connecticut: JAI Press.

Tjaden, Patricia and Nancy Thoemmes. 2000. *Full Report of the Prevalence, Incidence, and Consequences of Violence Against Women: Findings from the National Violence Against Women Survey*. Washington, D.C.: National Institute of Justice and the Centers for Disease Control and Prevention.

Torrey, E. Fuller. 1997. *Out of the Shadows: Confronting America's Mental Illness Crisis*. New York: John Wiley & Sons.

Tracy, Laura. 1991. The Secret Between Us: Competition Among Women. Cited in Phyllis Chesler. 2003. *Woman's Inhumanity to Woman*. New York: Plume.

Tracy, P., M. Wolfgang, and R. Figlio. 1990. *Delinquency Careers in Two Birth Cohorts*. New York: Plenum Press.

Travis, C. 1992. *The Mismeasurement of Women*. New York: Simon and Schuster.

Truesdell, D. L., J. S. McNeil, and J. P. Deschner. 1986. Incidents of Wife Abuse in Incestuous Families. *Social Work*. 31(2): 138-140.

Unger, R. and M. Cranford.1992. *Women and Gender: A Feminist Psychology*. Philadelphia: Temple University Press

Urquhart, Judith and Murray Cullen. 2003. *Cage Your Rage for Women*. Lanham, Maryland: American Correctional Association.

U.S. Census Bureau. 1999. *Current Population Reports*. Washington DC: U.S. Census Bureau.

U.S. Comptroller General. 1980. Report to U.S. Congress of the United States. *Women in Prison: Inequitable Treatment Requires Action*. Gaithersburg, Maryland: U.S. General Accounting Office.

U.S. Department of Education. 2001. Table 248, Earned Degrees Conferred by Degree Granting Institutions by Level of Degree and Sex of Student. *Digest of Educational Statistics*, 2000. Washington DC: U.S. Department of Education.

U.S. Federal Bureau of Investigation. 2001. *Crime in the United States: Uniform Crime Reports, 2000*. Washington, DC: U.S. Department of Justice.

U.S. General Accounting Office. 1979. *Female Offenders: Who Are They and What are the Problems Confronting Them?* Washington, DC: U.S. General Accounting Office.

_____. 1980. Report to the Congress of the United States: *Women in Prison: Inequitable Treatment Requires Action*. Gaithersburg, Maryland: U.S. General Accounting Office.

_____. 1999. A Report to the Hon. Eleanor Holmes Norton, House of Representatives. *Women in Prison: Issues and Challenges Confronting U.S. Prison Systems*. Washington, D.C.: Government Printing Office.

Valian, V. 1998. *Why So Slow? The Advancement of Women*. Cambridge, Massachusetts: MIT Press.

Van Voorhis, Patricia and Lois Presser. 2001. *Classification of Women Offenders: A National Assessment of Current Practices*. Washington, DC: U.S. Justice Department, National Institute of Justice.

Van Voorhis, Patricia, Jennifer Peiler, Lois Presser, Georgia Spiropoulis, and Jennifer Sutherland. 2002. *Classification of Women Offenders: A National Assessment of Current Practices and the Experiences of Three States*. Cincinnati, Ohio: Center for Criminal Justice Research, University of Cincinnati.

Veysey, Bonita M. 1998. Specific Needs of Women Diagnosed with Mental Illness in U.S. Jails. In Bruce L. Levin, Andrea K. Blanch, and Ann Jennings, eds. *Women's Mental Health Services: A Public Health Perspective*. Thousand Oaks, California. Sage.

Vito, G. and R. Holmes.1994. *Criminology: Theory, Research, and Policy*. Belmont, California: Wadsworth.

Walker, L. 1979. *The Battered Women*. New York: Harper and Row.

_____. 1984. *The Battered Woman Syndrome*. New York: Springer.

_____. 1994. Battered Women Syndrome-Presentation at the American Correctional Association Winter Meeting. January. Orlando, Florida.

Wallace, Donald H. 2001. Prisoners' Rights: Historical Views. In Edward Latessa, et al. *Correctional Contexts: Contemporary and Classical Readings*. Los Angeles: Roxbury.

Ward, David A, and Gene G. Kassenbaum. 1965. *Women's Prison: Sex and Social Structure*. Chicago: Aldine.

Watkins, K. P. 1987. *Parent-Child Attachment*. New York: Garland.

Weilerstein, R. 1995. The Prison MATCH Program. In K. Gabel and D. Johnston, eds. *Children of Incarcerated Parents*. New York: Lexington Books.

Weitzman, I. J. 1979. *Sex Role Socialization: A Focus on Women*. Palo Alto, California: Mayfield.

Wheeler, P. A., R. Trammel, J. Thomas, and J. Findlay. 1989. Persephone Chained: Parity or Equality in Women's Prisons? *The Prison Journal*. 69 (1): 88-102.

Whitney, Janet. 1937. *Elizabeth Fry: Quaker Heroine*. London: George G. Harrap.

Widom, Cathy S. and Michael Maxfield. 2001. *Research in Brief: An Update of the Cycle of Violence*. Washington, D.C.: U.S. Department of Justice: National Institute of Justice.

Will, J. A., P. A. Self, and N. Datan. 1976. Maternal Behavior and Perceived Sex of Infants. *American Journal of Orthopsychiatry*. 46: 135-139.

Wines, W. C., ed. 1871. *Transactions of the National Congress on Penitentiary and Reformatory Discipline*. Albany, New York: Weed, Parsons and Company.

Winfeld, Liz and Susan Spielman. 1995. Making Sexual Orientation Part of Diversity. *Training and Development*. April: 50-51.

Wishart, Margaret D. 1984. *Meeting the Health Care Needs of Incarcerated Women*. Presented at the 114th Congress of Correction, American Correctional Association, San Antonio, Texas.

Women's Prison Association of New York. 1996. *Breaking the Cycle of Despair: Children of Incarcerated Mothers*. New York: Women's Prison Association of New York.

Young-Bruehl, E., ed. 1990. *Freud on Women: A Reader*. New York: Norton.

Zager, Mary Ann. 2000. Gender and Crime. In Nicole H. Rafter, ed. *Encyclopedia of Women and Crime*. Phoenix, Arizona: The Onyx Press.

Zapoleon, Marguerite W. 1961. *Occupational Planning for Women*. New York: Harper & Brothers.

Zatz, Marjorie. 2000. The Convergence of Race, Ethnicity, Gender and Class in Court Decision Making: Toward the 21st Century. In Juile Horney, ed. *Policies, Processes and Decisions of the Criminal Justice System*, Vol. 3 Washington, DC: U.S. Department of Justice, National Institute of Justice.

LEGAL CASES

Barefield v. Leach, Civ. Act. No. 10282 (D.N.M., 1974).

Bell v. Wolfish, 441 U.S. 520 (1979).

Berrois-Berrios v. Thornburg, 716 F. Supp. 987 (E.D. Ky. 1989).

Calloway v. City of New Orleans, et al., 534 So. 2d 182 (La. App. 4 Cir. 1988).

Canterino v. Wilson, 546 F. Supp. 174 (W.D. Ky., 1983).

Cason v Seckinger, 231 F. 3rd 777 (11th Cir. 2000).

Cooper v. Pate, 378 U.S. 536 (1964).

Daskalea v. District of Columbia, 227 F. 3rd 433 (DC Cir. 2000).

Estelle v. Gamble, 429 U. S. 97 (1976).

Farmer v. Brennan, 511 U.S. 825 (1994).

Galvan v. Carothers, 855 F. Supp. 285 (9th Cir. 1997).

Glover v. Johnson, 478 F. Supp. 1075 (E.D. Mich. 1979).

Harris v. McRae, 448 U.S. 297 (1980).

Holt v Sarver, 309 F. Supp. 362 (E.D. Ark., 1970).

Hudson v. McMillian, 503 U.S. 1 (1992).

Hudson v. Palmer, 468 U.S. 517 (1984).

Johnson v. Avery, 393 U.S. 483 (1969).

Johnson v. Phelan, 69 F. 3d 144 (7th Cir. 1995).

Jordan v. Gardner, 986 F.2d 1521 (9th Cir. 1993).

Klinger v. Department of Corrections, 31 F. 3d 727, 731 (8th Cir. 1994).

Lee v. Washington, 390 U.S. 333 (1968).

Lewis v. Casey, 561 U.S. 333 (1996).

Mary Beth G. v. City of Chicago, 723 F. 2d 1263 (1983).

Monmouth County Correctional Institutional Inmates v. Lanzaro, 834 F. 2d (3d Cir. 1987), cert denied, 486 U.S. 1006 (1987).

Nelson Consent Decree arising out of a U.S. District Court Case *Nelson v Leeke*, c/a No 82-876 (D.S.C.)

Pargo v. Elliot, 894 F. Supp. 1243 (W. D. Iowa, 1995) affirmed 69 F. 3d 280 (8th Cir., 1995).

Procunier v. Martinez, 46 U.S. 396 (1974).

Pugh v. Locke, 406 F. 2d 318 (1976).

Rhodes v. Chapman, 452 U.S. 337 (1981).

Roe v. Wade, 410 U.S. 113 (1972).

Ruffin v. Commonwealth, 62 Va. 790 (1871).

Southerland v. Thigpen, 784 F. 2d 713 (5th Cir. 1986).

State v. Oliver, 70 N.C. 60, 61-72(1874).

Turner v. Safley, 482 U.S. 78 (1987).

United States Ex Rel. Guy v. McCauley, 385 F. Supp. 193 (E. D. Wisc. 1974).

Washington v. Harper, 494 U.S. 210 (1990).

Webster v. Reproductive Health Services, 492 U.S. 490 (1989).

Wilson v. Seiter, 501 U.S. 294 (1991).

Wolff v. McDonnell, 418 U.S. 539 (1974).

Women Prisoners of the District of Columbia Department of Corrections v. District of Columbia, 93 F. 3d 910 (D.C. Cir. 1996).

Index of
Authorities Cited

Mastroieni, Elizabeth, 241
Maunsell, Catherine, 164
Maxfield, Michael G., 196, 201, 202
McCampbell, Susan W., 335, 336, 344, 347, 353
McClellan, Dorothy S., 177
McClelland, Gary M., 229
McFarlane, J., 191
McGaha, Glenda S., 132, 133, 134
McGlashan, T. H., 306
McGowan, B. G., 209
McHugh, Gerald Austin, 264
McKelvey, Blake, 9, 10
McKibben, L., 197
McLeer, S. V., 194
McNeil, J. S., 197
Merlo, Alida, 99, 100, 101, 131
Michaels, Stewart, 89
Michigan Department of Corrections, 107, 138, 146, 148, 171, 177
Miller, Amy, 3, 31, 52, 147, 177, 179, 211, 330
Miller, Brenda, 130, 183, 185, 186, 201, 203, 230
Miller, Larry S., 109
Miller, Sally M., 16, 17
Miller, Susan L., 195
Miller-Macke, Ellen, 239
Millhollin, T. J., 54
Mondragon, Eloy L., 356
Morash, Merry, 108, 153, 186, 202, 213, 216, 223, 293, 298, 328
Morgan, Philip, 7
Morrill, Allison C., 241
Morris, Allison, 55
Morton, Joann B., 20, 22, 29, 30, 32, 33, 55, 82, 94, 120, 126, 127, 128, 130, 131, 134, 200, 215, 222, 265, 286, 293, 330, 341, 359
Moses, Marilyn C., 175, 218, 219
Moyer, Imogene, 100
Mumola, C., 115, 208
Muraskin, Roslyn, 4, 57, 63, 67, 81, 96, 97

N

National Center on Addiction and Substance Abuse, 269-270
National Clearinghouse for the Defense of Battered Women, 197, 198, 199
National Commission on Correctional Health, 272, 368
National Committee to Prevent Child Abuse, 196
National Institute of Corrections, 233, 242, 334, 335, 338, 343, 346, 347, 360–361
    American University, 69, 202, 212, 334, 338, 343
National Institute of Justice, 183
Neto, Virginia, 123
Newberger, E. H., 197
Newell, R., 191
Novick, L. F., 132

O

Oakland County Health Division, 259
Office of Juvenile Justice, 196
Okum, L., 192
Oliver, William, 184, 185
Olson, Lynn, 28
O'Neil, Terry, 85
Ort, Robert S., 280
Osborne Association, 59, 210
Owen, Barbara, 33–34, 55, 102, 147, 271, 331, 344

P

Palmer, J. W., 49
Palmer, S. E., 49
Paludi, M., 87, 88, 89, 91
Parenti, Christian, 44, 51, 56, 70
Pastore, A. L., 131
Patrick-Riley, Colleen, 290
Peiler, Jennifer, 281
Pendergast, Michael L., 270

Index of
Subjects

E

education
  academic programs, 35,159-160
  college courses, 159-160
  General Equivalency Diploma (GED), 159
  illiteracy, 161
  of incarcerated women, 128-129
  job training, 161
  libraries, 162-163
  life-skills programs, 162
  percentage of educated offender, 128-129
  Personal Responsibility and Work Opportunity Reconciliation Act of 1996, 97-98
  program services, 129
  social, 22-23, 54
  staff attitude towards, 16
  vocational, 18, 19, 29, 35, 98, 129, 160
education of staff. *See* staff training
Eighth Amendment
  cruel and unusual punishment, 50
  Estelle v. Gamble, 1976, 50, 61
  Farmer v. Brennan, 50
  Hudson v. McMillian, 1992, 50
  Pugh v. Locke, 1976, 50
  Rhodes v. Chapman, 1981, 50
  Wilson v. Seiter, 1991, 50
Eighth Circuit Court of Appeals
  Klinger v. Department of Corrections, 1994, 68
  Pargo v. Elliot, 1995, 68
  Women Prisoners of the District of Columbia Department of Corrections v. District of Columbia, 1996, 68
emergency procedures, 327
employment
  Civil Rights Act of 1964, 94
  equal opportunities, 94-95
  Fair Labor Standards Act of 1938, 94
  gender discrimination, 94-95
  Industrial Revolution, 94
  protective legislation, 97
England, mothers in prison with children, 216
Equal Credit Act, 187
equal pay for women, 25
equal protection, 50-51. *See also* Fourteenth Amendment
  Barefield v. Leach, 1974, 67
  Butler v. Reno, 1995, 69
  Canterino v. Wilson, 1983, 68
  Glover v. Johnson, 1979, 68
  Klinger v. Department of Corrections, 1994, 68
  Pargo v. Elliot, 1995, 68
  parity issues, 67-68
  policy and program initiatives, 32
  women-centered, 33
  Women Prisoners of the District of Columbia Department of Corrections v. District of Columbia, 1996, 68
equal treatment, Federal Bureau of Prisons' provisions, 69
equity-parity, 67-69, 76
escape prevention, 327
Espionage Act, 16
Estelle v. Gamble, 50, 61-62
ethnic groups, 20. *See also* health care; racism
  abuse, 184
  African-Americans. *See* African-American women
  Asian-Americans, 88
  assertive communication, 92-93
  Civil Rights Act of 1871, 45
  civil rights movement, 25
  crime rate, 101-102, 114
  cultural issues, 34
  domestic violence, 184, 190
  facilities for, 20
  Fourteenth Amendment, 50
  gender roles, 88-89
  Hispanics. *See* Latina/Hispanics

National Congress on Penitentiary
and Reformatory Discipline.
See American Correctional
Association
National Council on Crime and
Delinquency, 201, 214, 217-
218
National Council of Juvenile and
Family Court Judges, 195
National Crime Victimization Survey
(NCVS), 109, 111
National Criminal Justice Reference
Center, 110, 204
National Federation of Business and
Professional Women, 17
National GAINS Center for People
with Co-Occurring Disorders
in the Justice System, 290
National Institute of Corrections
(NIC)
*Correctional Health Care:
Guidelines for the Management
of an Adequate Delivery System,*
2001 Edition, 228
data publications, 110
domestic violence information
publications, 204
gender-responsive programming,
33-34, 36, 241-242
grant opportunities, 32
Information Center
(www.nicic.org), data
resources, 110
National Institute of
Corrections/American
University Training Manual,
338-339
prison menu statistics, 267
sexual misconduct information,
69, 336-339
staff "Sexual Misconduct with
Inmates" workshop, 341-343
training opportunities, 75
National Institute of Justice (NIJ)
on abuse issues, 183

data publications, 110
gender-responsive programming
funding, 36
Girl Scouts Beyond Bars, 218
National Institute of Mental Health,
293
National Organization of Women's
Judicial Education Program,
96-97
National Public Policy for
Corrections, 31
Nebraska,
MOLD program, 217
prison nursery and older child
program, 215
neglect. *See* abuse
Nelson v. Leeke, 53
Neto, Virginia, 123
Newgate Prison (London), 11
New Jersey
State Reformatory for Women
(Clinton Farms), 18, 20
New Mexico State Penitentiary
Barefield v. Leach, 1974, 67
New York
Bedford Hills Correctional
Facility, 14, 17, 20, 185, 203,
223, 234
Children's Center, 223
Department of Correctional
Services, 186-187, 265
domestic violence programs, 203
Mt. Pleasant Female Prison, 10
New York City Correctional
Institution for Women, 132
prison nursery, 215, 266
Rikers Island, 269
Sponsor a Baby Program, 223
Women's Prison Association, 223
Women's Workhouse, 18
Nightline (TV show), 236
North Carolina Supreme Court, 188
North Dakota,
incarceration rates, 15, 115
nurseries in prison, 215-216

facility distance from families, 142, 167
family member counseling, 167
Girl Scouts Beyond Bars, 219
overnight visits with children, 215, 217
policies on, 167, 327
security, 350-351
vocational education. *See* education, vocational
volunteers, 19-20
sexual misconduct. *See* sexual misconduct
volunteer services, 174-175

W

Wade v. Roe, 1972, 63
Walker, Dr. Lenore, 189
Walnut Street Jail (Philadelphia), 9
Washington D.C.
Women's Detention Center, 28
Washington State,
prison nursery, 215
Washington State Medical Association, 233
Washington v. Harper, 1990, 283
Webster v. Reproductive Health Services, 1989, 63
weight problems of women offenders, 173-174, 267-268
welfare history of incarcerated women, 129
West Virginia
U.S. Industrial Reformatory for Women (Alderson), 17, 18
Willebrandt, Mabel Walker, 16, 17
Wilson v. Seiter, 50
Winfrey, Oprah, 90

witch trials, 6-7
Wolff v. McDonnell, 50
women, civilian and as staff
changing roles and criminality, 26
civil rights movement, 25
education of, 16
employment of, 19
equal pay, 25
"new female criminal," 26-27, 39
occupations, 24
as property, 187
rights of, 18
staffing of female facilities, 11-12
women of color, 20, 230; *See also* African-American women; Latina/Hispanic women
women offenders. *See* offenders
Women in Prison (Bureau of Justice Statistics), 108
Women Prisoners of the District of Columbia Department of Corrections v. District of Columbia, 1996, 68
Women's Christian Temperance Union, 17
women's facilities, 141-142
deficiencies in, 55-56
Women's Prison Association, 223
Women's Reformatory Model, 13-15
Women's Rights Movement, 188, 189
Women's Temperance Movement, 188
Women Who Kill (Jones), 198
work history of incarcerated women, 129, 157
work programs, 151, 155, 157-159
work release, 177-178
World War I, 15, 16
World War II, 21, 23, 84
wrap-around services, 35, 177

About the Author

About the Author

Dr. Joann Brown Morton has been a member of the American Correctional Association since 1970. She has served in numerous capacities including vice president and chair of several committees. She is president of the Association on Programs for Female Offenders. She has more than thirty-five years in corrections serving as director of Southeastern Management Training Council at the University of Georgia, division director with the South Carolina Department of Corrections and retired from teaching at the University of South Carolina in 2004. She remains active in state and national correctional organizations and serves as a consultant on issues related to women offenders, women employees, older offenders, and other management concerns. Dr. Morton has published widely including articles in *Corrections Today* and the *State of Corrections* and has edited three books for ACA. She has received ACA's highest awards: both the E. R. Cass Correctional Achievement Award and the Peter P. Lejins Research Award.